FORTRESS OF FINANCE:
THE UNITED STATES TREASURY BUILDING

PAMELA SCOTT

TREASURY HISTORICAL ASSOCIATION
WASHINGTON, DC

Library of Congress Control Number: 2010929897
ISBN: 978-0-615-36629-6

To Everyone Who Made This Book Possible.

Table of Contents

The United States Treasury Building is perhaps the most recognized government office building in the country. Every American and people around the world who have ever handled the U.S. ten-dollar bill have seen the Treasury Building on the reverse of the currency since 1929. The building in its massive scale symbolizes the strength of the United States government and the department that was the birthplace of dozens of departments, bureaus, and agencies, most still active in the executive branch. The Treasury Building is the oldest departmental office building in Washington, and the Department of the Treasury enjoys the unique distinction of being located on the same site since the seat of government transferred to Washington, D.C. in 1800.

The Treasury Historical Association, a nonprofit, all-volunteer organization created in 1973, has the mission of assisting the Department of the Treasury in education on the history of the agency and in the preservation and the restoration of Treasury's historic properties, particularly the Treasury Building. The association's initiative to sponsor the research and development of this book has contributed to the organization's fulfillment of its charter.

Enrolled in the U.S. Registry (National Register, no. 71001007) of Historic Places in 1972, the Treasury Building, as a National Historic Landmark, has in recent decades been protected by federal statutes, Treasury's policies, and the efforts of the Treasury Historical Association, to ensure that its architecture, furniture, and extensive fine arts collection remain preserved for generations to come. Through the Department of the Treasury's initiatives since the mid-1980s, many rooms and public spaces of the Treasury Building have undergone exten-

sive restoration, much accomplished with private contributions made through the Treasury Historical Association. These efforts have helped return many areas of the building to the elegance and grandeur of its original interior Victorian designs.

Pamela Scott's *Fortress of Finance* provides us a detailed account of the development of the Treasury Department's workplace in Washington from the beginning of the capital city in 1800 with the creation of the department's first facility, the Treasury Office, to the completion of the current Treasury Building. Each was the largest executive office building in Washington when it was built and housed the largest civilian agency of those times. The Treasury Office and the Treasury Building were products of architects who have earned great fame either before or after their work for the Treasury. These men—George Hadfield, James Hoban, Robert Mills, Thomas U. Walter, Ammi B. Young, Isaiah Rogers, and Alfred B. Mullett—were among the most influential, respected, and talented architects of their time and had the greatest impact on the development of the federal buildings in Washington, as well as of government field office facilities throughout the nation.

Ms. Scott's research, spanning more than eight years, has enabled her to reveal to us the trials and tribulations of each of these creative architects who were challenged with debates about building design, construction methods, material selection and delivery, employee and contractor work hours, and project scheduling. These debates and outright confrontations were with labor forces, suppliers, members of Congress individually as well as the entire legislative body, secretaries of the Treasury, and even one another as well as with outside architects and engineers. Despite these distractions and delays, the architects of today's Treasury Building succeeded in developing a cohesive and integrated plan for the building, and proceeded in successfully implementing their designs for their respective wings of the building in a construction effort that spanned thirty-three years.

Many of the architects' plans had to be modified as construction proceeded—sometimes at the last minute—to meet the ever-changing missions and requirements of the Treasury Department, as well as alterations caused by outside forces. For example, when construction was completed on the south wing of the building, exactly one hundred and fifty years ago, Young had not anticipated that, in addition to housing Treasury's clerical offices, "his building" would be used as barracks to encamp Union troops during the American Civil War years. Nor did he and his successor, Isaiah Rogers, anticipate that certain areas of the south wing and the new west wing would need to be significantly modified to serve as a factory. Resulting from legislation that created the predecessor of today's Bureau of Engraving and Printing, currency notes were produced in the Treasury Building from the Civil War years until 1880. Yet, Young and Rogers met the challenges, as did each of the other architects, in adjusting their plans to the department's evolving requirements.

Other unexpected uses of the Treasury Building included one of its rooms becoming President Andrew Johnson's temporary office for six weeks immediately following Abraham Lincoln's assassination. He wished to allow Mary Todd Lincoln the courtesy of remaining in the Executive Mansion to settle her personal affairs and have a private grieving period. Many years later, an underground vault area of the building was adapted for potential use of another president, Franklin D. Roosevelt, providing him safe haven during World War II, if needed. A bomb shelter was outfitted with residential and office furnishings to enable the Commander-in-Chief's work to continue if there were an enemy attack on the city.

The exterior of this magnificent Greek Revival Building, with its massive granite monolithic pilasters and imposing porticos, belies its intricate and delicate interior decorative elements. Artisans working in close concert with architects, engineers, and construction managers between 1836 and 1869 created architectural and emblematic sculpture and frescoes both to adorn the Treasury Building and to express the department's functions within the federal government. These interior elements with their extensive iconography, observed primarily by Treasury employees, visitors conducting official business in the building, and attendees at the department's Saturday public tours of the Treasury Building, are described in great detail by Ms. Scott. The most elegant interior is Mullett's Cash Room in the north wing, one of the most ornate spaces in the city of Washington at the time, if not in the nation. As Ms. Scott has described, it was selected as the venue for the inaugural ball and reception of President Ulysses S. Grant, prior to its being put into service and fulfilling its intended role as the "bankers' bank," where financial institutions would be able to draw their stock in trade—coin and currency—from the building's great underground vaults.

Ms. Scott's book has interwoven some of the most significant social history of the department with its design and construction histories. *Fortress of Finance* is the first comprehensive architectural history of the creation of the Treasury Building, a well-deserved tribute to its architects, the many hundreds of workers who constructed the magnificent edifice, and many thousands of Treasury employees who have served the American public from within this building.

Thomas P. O'Malley
Chairman, Board of Directors
Treasury Historical Association
Washington, DC

Preface

When I began this book in 2002 I knew that the Treasury Curator's Office had collected documents from many sources over several years, had sponsored Historic Structures Reports on each of its four wings, compiled on a DVD all of the building's known drawings, and collected originals and copies of a large number of photographs. I expected it would take two years to add to this knowledge base and write a book that was both scholarly and accessible to the general reader. One way of accomplishing this dual goal was to develop one subject within each chapter that would have wide appeal. Hence, the burning of the Treasury Office by arsonists in 1833; the construction and fate of the east wing's 1842–1909 colonnade; J. Goldsborough Bruff's quirky but meaningful decorations for the south wing; the department's response to and role in the Civil War while the west wing was under construction; and the design, construction, and use of the north wing's Cash Room were intended to explore in some depth a range of interesting episodes in the Treasury's evolution.

As soon as I combined what I knew with the curator's holdings about the Treasury Office (1798–1833) for the first chapter, I realized that I had a very incomplete and disjointed story. So, the paper chase began. I was astonished at the completeness of the documentation I found in the National Archives, albeit spread among several record groups. Within a few months I was able to reconstruct the motives, challenges, and rewards of a wide range of participants from presidents to suppliers of materials.

The greatly increased size of each section of the Treasury Building, erected wing by wing between 1836 and 1869, meant that the paper trail was much more voluminous. The incoming and outgoing letters received by the Commissioners of Public Buildings were intact, as were the letters received by the Bureau of Construction, and later by the Supervising Architect of the Treasury. One problem was that most of the outgoing letters beginning in 1852, preserved via press copy versions available on microfilm, were illegible. Retrieval of the originals meant a summer of copying most of the second half of the bureaucratic story. What remained was collecting outside perceptions of what was happening. Local newspapers were one untapped resource and I spent several weeks, all tolled, searching newspapers on microfilm from the 1830s to 1870; most of what I found is still unavailable in digital format. If the multiple bureaucratic sources provided the skeleton of each chapter's narratives, public and private accounts provided the flesh, particularly when descriptions of interiors provided entirely new information about how the building's artists responded to the historic events and aesthetic trends of their eras.

There is a general perception among many historians of Washington's architecture that there is nothing left of note to be said about our nation's founding public buildings. These histories of the Treasury Office and the Treasury Building, while not definitive, disprove that myth, as well as the belief by many that architectural, social, and political history are antithetical to one another. On the contrary, they support one another in many ways.

Pamela Scott
April 2010

Acknowledgements

ost of the debts I incurred during the eight years while researching and writing *Fortress of Finance* can be paid by thanking here the many scholars, archivists, and curators who were so generous in their professional help. My debts to Thomas P. O'Malley, chairman of the board of the Treasury Historical Association, and Dr. Paula A. Mohr, former curator of the Treasury Building, however, simply cannot be expressed by mere words. Their joint dedication to seeing this book through long hiatuses allowed me to explore in depth the building's history. Moreover, they both read each chapter, offering their valuable insights about the Department of the Treasury and the history of its building. Tom's commitment has been unfailing as he joined me in the final editing and proofreading of the manuscript and the preparation of the index.

I also thank all of the board members of the Treasury Historical Association whose support made this work possible. Miss Abby Gilbert, in particular, deserves special thanks for generously sharing her vast knowledge of sources about the department and the building as well as her assistance with the newspaper research.

Dr. Richard Cote, curator of the Treasury Building, and members of his staff, Guy Munsch, conservator/associate curator, Mary Edwards, tour program coordinator, Merrill Lavine, registrar, as well as Lynn Zaycosky, visual information specialist of Treasury's Printing and Graphics Division, were unfailingly helpful as I collected images for the book.

Two scholars of American architecture, Dr. Paula Mohr and Dr. Edward Zimmer, read the manuscript and made valuable suggestions on its improvement. Ed's keen editorial eye helped immensely, particularly in taming the once unwieldy footnotes. Dr. Michael Richman drew upon his comprehensive knowledge of the history of American sculpture to solve two mysteries concerning the Hamilton and Gallatin statues. Dr. Bruce Laverty and Michael Seneca at the Athenaeum of Philadelphia not only helped me mine the Thomas Ustick Walter Papers, but directed me to a previously unidentified Walter watercolor of the Treasury Building. Steven Haynes and Juanita Sprague, curators at the Maine Granite Industry Historical Society Museum, were extraordinarily generous with their expertise about Dix Island's history and hammering granite in the nineteenth century. Earle G. Shettleworth, Maine State Historic Preservation Officer, helped me understand Isaiah Rogers's early career. Dr. Carl Lounsbury, Colonial Williamsburg, clarified many aspects of early construction methods. William Allen, architectural historian in the Office of the Architect of the Capitol, helped me unravel Jefferson's design for the White House's east terrace. Architect Amelia Salmon contributed to my understanding of Indian-themed chandeliers. They are all exemplars of what scholarly fellowship should be. Andrew Zimmer's rapid solutions to software problems were also greatly appreciated.

Most of my archival research was done in the National Archives where one finds many dedicated custodians of American history. Archivists Wayne DeCesar and John Vandereedt, who specialized in the particularly voluminous and complex records of the Treasury Department, helped me navigate the several records groups that relate to the department's various functions. Gene Morris, Civil Records Reference, authorized access to original letterpress volumes of the letters sent by the Bureau of Construction and Supervising Architect of the Treasury kept in remote storage, a turning point in my research. Richard Smith and Raymond Cotton, Cartographic and Architectural Archives Branch, were particularly helpful as I examined drawings of the Treasury Building. Rod Ross and Bill Davis, Center for Legislative Archives, answered many requests for access to congressional records. I thank all of these archivists for their cheerful professionalism and thank as well all of NARA's other archival and reference staffs who assisted me over the years.

Photographer Franz Jantzen played a key role in preparing all the images for their best possible reproduction; their clarity and depth are largely due to his efforts. Staff members in the Geography and Map Division, the Photoduplication Service, and the Prints and Photographs Division of the Library of Congress; Richard Aldacushion, Washington Post Writers Group; Peter Easton, London; Wendy Jane Glavis, Hubert Schutter descendent; Jennifer King, Gelman Library, George Washington University; Alissa Lane, Maine Historical Society; Carol H. Nielson, International Society of Daughters of Utah Pioneers; Susan Raposa, Commission of Fine Arts; Mary Labate Rogstad, Vermont Historical Society; Teresa Romito, Image Library, Metropolitan Museum of Art; Stephan Saks, New York Public Library; Elizabeth Trautman, Maine Historic Preservation Commission; and Olga Tsapina, Huntington Library, provided illustrations for *Fortress of Finance*. Thank you all for your assistance.

At EEI Communications, Jayne Sutton, project director, and Cindy Peters, designer, both had an unerring sense of how the book's design would respond to its content and were a pleasure to work with.

"The Style of Accommodation Would Depend on Our Means:" The Treasury Office, 1798–1800

Chapter One

Introduction

The Treasury Office stood near the corner of 15th and F streets from 1800 until 1833. It was the federal government's third building erected in Washington, completed while both the President's House and Capitol were still unfinished. Its creation and evolution illuminates the early workings of the federal government, the city's growing bureaucratic and artisan populations, and the emerging profession of American architecture. That this short-lived building shines a bright light on so many important matters is remarkable. It is remarkable that enough federal records and private accounts survive to reveal the complex interactions between government officers, architects, workmen, and the public for a time period when most documentation concerning American architecture has been destroyed. It is remarkable because many of these documents explain public and private motivations and conflicts as well as the multiple processes involved in realizing public architecture under the country's still-developing political system. The Treasury Office was not a prelude to the Treasury Building (1842–present) but an independent expression of its time and the concerns of those involved in its making.

"Administrative Machinery:" The Founding and Functions of the Treasury Department

"Most of the important measures of every Government are connected with the Treasury," first Secretary of the Treasury Alexander Hamilton (1755–1804) wrote in May 1792, while he was still formulating how the department was to function within the federal government. (fig. I-1) The Treasury Department was the third executive department created by the First Federal Congress, established by an act on September 2, 1789, the Department of Foreign Affairs (now State) preceding it by six weeks and the Department of War by nearly a month. Its history actually began in 1775 when the Second Continental Congress approved the printing of bills of credit to finance the Revolutionary War. Moreover, the six Treasury Department

I-1 Caroline Ransom, *Alexander Hamilton*, 1880; purchased in 1881 for the Treasury Building.

divisions created in 1789 had earlier counterparts in the Continental and Confederation Congresses. In 1800 when the government moved to Washington from Philadelphia, Treasury was the only one of the four executive departments—State, Treasury, War, and the Post Office—to have its own building. More than two centuries later, the Treasury Department is the only executive department still located on the site it occupied within the President's grounds in 1800.[1]

Unlike the legislation establishing the other executive departments, Congress in 1789 stipulated that the Treasury have six divisions and defined the duties of each. The Secretary of the Treasury "developed tax, debt, financial, and economic policies; the management of the government's finances; and law enforcement." The secretary was to report directly to Congress on "all matters referred to him … or which shall appertain to his office." A broad slice of two centuries of American history could be written based on the Treasury Department reports alone, their scope so broad, inclusive, and detailed about the relationship between the nation's physical development and its financial management.[2]

The divisions supervised by the Secretary of the Treasury were devised to check the work of one another as protection for the government against fraud. The office of Assistant Secretary of the Treasury was changed to the Commissioner of Revenue in 1792, both charged with the collection of duties and other federal income until the office was abolished in 1802. In 1794 Hamilton summarized the sources of the government's revenue, how it was collected, and the methods the Treasury Department used to account for its expenditure. Public monies came from six sources: duties on imports; liquor distilled in the United States; patents; interest on foreign and domestic loans; and debts from individuals.

Aside from the secretary's office, the most powerful division within the Treasury Department bureaucracy was the Comptroller's Office, which supervised all government expenditures approved and appropriated by Congress. The Auditor's Office examined and verified each account submitted by those who worked directly for the government, under government contract, or provided goods and certified their balances. The Treasurer received, stored, and disbursed the public's monies, paid wages, and purchased supplies of every description for federal agents. The Register's Office kept the records of the settled accounts, the invoices already certified by clerks in the Comptroller's and Auditor's offices that had been sent in for payment. These were often accompanied by explanatory correspondence that now puts flesh on the bones of bare history recorded in the Register's ledgers of monies received and expended.

Hamilton formulated the nation's first monetary policy according to the principles of President George Washington's Federalist administration, which was dedicated to making the federal government the country's preeminent civic, legal, and military authority. Hamilton deftly wielded the financial power of the Treasury to make the Department the leading agent of the Federalist goal of "welding thirteen disparate states, each revolving in its own orbit, into one sovereign nation." The department's field agents initiated, monitored, and controlled federal expenditures in every substantial community in the country. All their activities were supervised by the Secretary of the Treasury and the officers and clerks of the six divisions, from New York's Federal Hall in 1789–90, then in Philadelphia where the government was located until it moved to Washington in 1800.[3]

The administration of the Treasury Department could thus directly affect Americans everywhere, and as directed by Hamilton, it did. Its fiscal operations involved government stockholders (state and federal), borrowers, bankers, and investors; its customs service reached merchants, ship-owners, and fishermen; its procurement policies concerned manufacturers and contractors; and its internal revenue service affected countless citizens.[4]

The Treasury Department's monetary policies remained essentially the same during the one-term presidency of John Adams, also a Federalist, whose Secretary of the Treasury Oliver Wolcott, Jr., (1760–1833) supervised the department's move to Washington in 1800. Because the next presidential election was to be held within a few months, Wolcott wisely did not move his entire household to Washington. Rather, he rented a room in John Coyle's boarding house, the westernmost of the Six Buildings on the north side of Pennsylvania Avenue between 21st and 22nd streets, one of the better addresses in Washington.

For political reasons, President Thomas Jefferson was unable to appoint immediately his choice of Secretary of the Treasury, Albert Gallatin (1761–1849), upon taking office in March 1801, but gave him an interim appointment in May until Congress confirmed him in February 1802. (fig. I-2) When Gallatin was first appointed, Jefferson wanted him to break up Hamilton's bureaucracy, believing Hamilton had initially created its size and complexity to accumulate undue personal and professional power.

Jefferson wished to consolidate the divisions to "a keeper of money, a keeper of accounts, and the head of the department," but Gallatin felt he needed a year to "thoroughly understand every detail of all those several offices ... Until I know them all I dare not touch the machine." In the end, Gallatin recognized the wisdom and efficiency of Hamilton's organization of the Treasury Department and declined to change it

I-2 Matthew Wilson, *Albert Gallatin*, 1879; purchased in 1879 for the Treasury Building.

materially. Gallatin and Jefferson worked closely with the country's leading architect, Benjamin Henry Latrobe, to provide fireproof storage rooms for the Treasury Department's records, the first national archive.[5]

A major policy change under Jefferson's Democratic-Republican Party concerned the country's $42.4 million debt, of which $11.8 million had been incurred during the Revolution. To Hamilton, "the debt of the United States ... was the price of Liberty," and his solution was to pay the debt with bonds issued by the federal government, essentially using borrowed money to pay bills. Jefferson and Gallatin were committed from the beginning to streamline the government's operating costs to pay off the national debt within twenty years. Through their joint efforts, even with the payment of $25 million for the Louisiana Purchase in 1802, the government was debt-free in six years. Jefferson and Gallatin expanded the country's system of internal improvements considerably, which in turn led to increased federal revenues from customs duties. Gallatin's oversight of the department was so successful he remained during James Madison's first term until he was sent to Paris to negotiate an end to the War of 1812. Upon his return, he declined Madison's invitation to take up his former post because the job was too demanding.[6]

Hamilton and Gallatin were giants who dominated the intellectual leadership and financial and managerial policies of the office of the Secretary of the Treasury. During the period before the Treasury Office was destroyed by fire in 1833, they were succeeded by six secretaries, only two of whom served longer than two years. William H. Crawford of Georgia oversaw the reconstruction of the Treasury Office after the War of 1812 under James Monroe. An important administrative change during Crawford's tenure was the transfer on March 6, 1817, of the auditing functions of the State, War, and Navy departments to the Treasury Department. These auditors had been located in the War Office on the west side of the President's House and they remained there because there was no room for them in the Treasury Office, but they were under the jurisdiction of the Secretary of the Treasury. An 1817 compilation of the number of rooms needed to carry out the Treasury's expanded functions convinced Crawford that the scale of the department's responsibilities required comparable quarters to function well. This accounting was a factor in the construction of two additional (and larger) executive offices within the President's House enclave between 1818 and 1820, those for the State and Navy departments.[7] (fig. I-3)

When the Treasury Department moved back into its rebuilt offices in 1817—having been burned out along with Washington's other public employees during the War of 1812—the Secretary of the Treasury had four rooms, both the First Comptroller and First Auditor each had five rooms, the Fifth Auditor, Treasurer, and the Office of Discount and Deposit had two rooms each, while the Register occupied seven rooms. Moreover, the Branch Bank of the United States, where the government's monies were on deposit, occupied two rooms. Offices for the eight employees of the General Land Office, created as part of Treasury in June 1812, were in a rented house. The department was so pressed for space that four small rooms had been carved out of the broad central corridors on the Treasury Office's two main floors.

Proposed staff increases in several offices, especially in the recently annexed auditors' offices, increased Crawford's calculation of rooms necessary to house the department in 1817 to seventy-three, considerably more than the thirty rooms (including two fireproof storage spaces) then in the Treasury Office. It took the destruction by fire of the Treasury Office in 1833 to consolidate the expanding Treasury bureaucracy into a building adequate for its needs. By 1836, when Andrew Jackson initiated construction of the Treasury Building, the department's original six divisions had expanded to eleven; in 1883 when all four of its wings were completed they were occupied by sixteen division chiefs and their clerks.[8]

Jefferson inherited entrenched civil servants who were all Federalists. After humorously noting that few died and none resigned, Jefferson set about replacing approximately half the clerks with his own supporters to establish political parity within the government bureaucracy. Shortly after Richard Rush's appointment as Secretary of the Treasury in 1825, he complained that he had inherited a department of octogenarians. In fact, many of them, including Register Joseph Nourse, John Woodside, a clerk in the Comptroller's Office, and Joseph

President's House, and State, Treasury, War, and Navy Departments.

TREASURY.

NAVY.

STATE.

WAR.

NORTH VIEW.

I-3 By 1820 the Treasury and State Offices were east of the President's House, War and Navy west.

Stretch, a clerk in the Register's Office, had been civil servants since the 1780s. Some, including Woodside and Stretch, were Revolutionary War veterans. Many of the clerks who survived Jefferson's reorganization of the department were dismissed during Andrew Jackson's famous purge of the government bureaucracy in 1829. Nourse's firing was a *cause célèbre* in Washington because he was accused of stealing $10,000. Although he eventually was cleared of all charges and it was found that the government actually owed him more than $23,000, Nourse was ruined after a half-century's loyal service to the government.

Louis McLane's two-year tenure, the second of Jackson's five secretaries of Treasury, was marred by the Treasury Office's destruction by fire on March 31, 1833, an event he witnessed. Shortly thereafter Jackson transferred McLane,

appointing him Secretary of State in May 1833, because the independent Delawarean refused to remove the government's deposits from the Bank of the United States. Jackson also replaced McLane's successor, William J. Duane, over the same issue after he had served for two years.

"Handsome Brick Buildings on the President's Square:" Planning the Treasury Office and the Move to Washington

Although the Capitol's vast cast of players vying for recognition makes its nearly forty-year design and construction history Washington's favorite early melodrama, creating the Treasury Office was hardly without intrigue. Both the location and character of the executive office buildings were

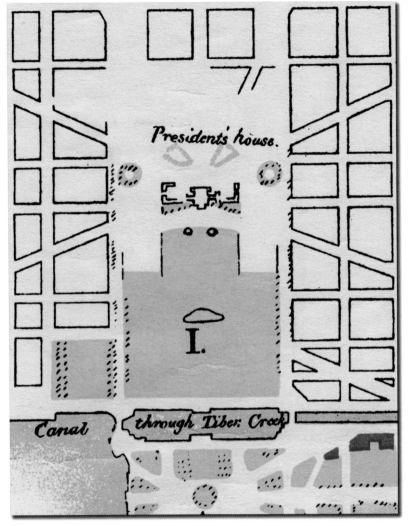

I-4 P.C. L'Enfant's 1791 manuscript map with the executive offices attached to the President's House.

George Washington recorded in his diary for June 29, 1791, that he,

called the Several Subscribers [owners of land] together and made known to them the Spots on which I meant to place the buildings for the P. & Executive departments of the government and for the Legislature of Do. [Ditto] A Plan was also laid before them of the city in order to convey to them general ideas of the City—but they were told that some deviations from it would take place—particularly in the diagonal Streets or avenues … and in the removal of the President's house more westerly for the advantage of higher ground.[9]

The earliest engraving of the city, published in Philadelphia in March 1792, depicted L'Enfant's alternate plan for the President's House—a long, rectangular residence with a recess in the center of its south facade rather than a projecting portico found on the manuscript. (fig. I-5) Both maps located the President's House south of where James Hoban built a smaller building beginning in 1792. In the engraving, two-thirds of L'Enfant's monumental complex was south of the intersections of New York and Pennsylvania avenues and the President's Grounds. Four distinct buildings are shown ranged in pairs flanking an open central court. These probable executive buildings faced what appear to be terraces overlooking the sloping south lawn, the west end of the Mall, the Potomac River's broad expanse, and the Virginia highlands in the distance.

Almost certainly Washington directed L'Enfant to place the executive departmental office buildings within the presidential precinct. By February 1796 the commissioners recognized that both the locations and designs of these buildings, and one for the Supreme

debated by presidents, congressmen, and the city's commissioners, as well as the architects and contractors who designed and built them. Surviving manuscript and early printed maps of P. Charles L'Enfant's 1791–92 plan of the federal city disagree in their depiction of the President's House complex that included plans for buildings to house the executive departments, Treasury, State, War, and the Postmaster General. The plans depicted on the 1791 manuscript have been largely scraped away, but a broken image of the sprawling President's House seems to have four L-shaped attached wings, likely for the executive departments. (fig. I-4) President

Fortress of Finance: The United States Treasury Building

Court, would be "a cause of much public discontent." They were willing to locate the Post Office Department and the Supreme Court near the Capitol to placate landowners in that neighborhood, but insisted that the executive departmental offices logically belonged near the President's House. In 1798, when Congress was ready to appropriate funds to erect them, President John Adams suggested that they be built near the Capitol, ostensibly to better facilitate the workings of Congress, but in reality to weaken the power of the executive branch, which he thought excessive.[10]

The Commissioners of the District of Columbia, and at least two of the original proprietors of land near the President's House who would have been most materially affected, quickly explained Washington's rationale: "the Business of the heads of Department was principally with the President." In the spring of 1798, the commissioners were already hard-pressed to get two offices erected in time for the federal government's planned move to Washington in the summer of 1800. By the time Adams relented three weeks later, the commissioners had already drafted the advertisement to be placed in newspapers seeking proposals to construct the Treasury Office, the first of the buildings they undertook.[11]

Planning for the Treasury Office had begun more than two years earlier. In November 1795 Washington sent Commissioner Alexander White (1738–1804) to Philadelphia to try to collect monies due on land sales in Washington, but particularly to monitor the mood of the restive Fourth Congress. In May 1795 Washington appointed White the sixth of the city's commissioners, a man especially qualified to lobby Congress because he had served as a Federalist member of the House of Representatives from Virginia from 1789 until 1793 and still had many friends serving in Congress. As a northern Virginian, he was well versed in the background and complex contemporary

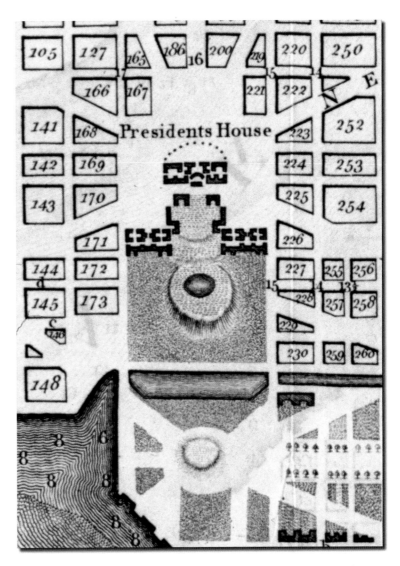

I-5 The 1792 printed map placed the range of offices south of Pennsylvania Avenue.

political situation, as well as the physical conditions, involved in creating the federal city out of sparsely settled farmland with little existing infrastructure to supply labor and building materials. White began his lobbying by meeting privately with House members and listening to their opinions, especially concerning the halting progress in constructing the President's House and the Capitol.

The initial scheme in 1791 for funding the construction of the public buildings depended in part on adequate revenues from the sale of lots within the city. After three disappointing auctions, in December 1793 the original three commissioners agreed to sell 6,000 lots for $480,000 to a real estate syndicate composed of financiers Robert Morris, John Nicholson, and James Greenleaf. When the syndicate was unable to meet their May 1, 1795, payment, the progress on the public buildings—indeed, the whole enterprise of a federal city on the Potomac River—was in doubt. White's "mission" (as he termed it) in Philadelphia was to instill confidence in the city's future and to promote the commissioners' memorial (or petition) submitted by President Washington to both houses of Congress on January 8, 1796. This memorial asked the legislators to agree to and guarantee a loan for the completion of the buildings already underway and included estimates for erecting the executive offices and a building for the Supreme Court.

White exercised his considerable political skills upon the members of a select House committee, appointed to consider the memorial. Some were enthusiastic about the architectural quality of the designs White showed the committee for both the President's House and the Capitol. Others "expressed great displeasure at the Style of the Buildings, but said as they had gone so far [they were] willing to finish them." The real issue the committee debated was whether Congress should borrow the money from private banks to complete the public buildings by 1800 or put off the move to Washington until enough lots had been sold to pay for the buildings.[12]

White impressed upon members of Congress that the public buildings in Washington would be finished, "but that the style of accommodations would depend on our means" at a time when many felt the experiment of a federal city was a failure. In January 1796 he compiled and had printed for the committee a detailed accounting of the monies spent and needed for the public buildings underway. "Two buildings may be erected on the President's square, at the expense of 100,000 dollars, sufficient to accommodate, in a handsome manner, the

departments of State, Treasury and War, and the General Post-Office; and 100,000 dollars, be conceived sufficient to erect a Judiciary." Two days later White wrote his fellow commissioners two letters, stating in the first that, when pressed by committee members to estimate the total costs for the public buildings, he answered that two "elegant [executive office] Buildings" would cost $200,000. In a short note written later in the day, White recanted his earlier estimate noting that $100,000 would be sufficient to erect both buildings.[13]

Late in January 1796 White wrote the department heads asking each to determine the amount of space they would need in Washington. When Secretary of the Treasury Oliver Wolcott replied verbally that his department would need forty rooms, White wrote fellow commissioners William Thornton and Gustavus Scott that "there is no doubt but the President must approve both of the Scites [sic] and Plans of these Offices. I never had an Idea of their being appendages to the President's House, but that they should be placed on the Square in lower corresponding situations and that they should be built of Brick much in the Style of the Hotel" recently built as a private venture. When Thornton and Scott learned that Wolcott wanted forty rooms, they concluded: "we must build much cheaper than has been customary here."[14]

Wolcott's written reply to White called for a minimum of twenty-nine large rooms not counting space for the department's several messengers nor storage areas for its voluminous records. Wolcott was not exaggerating the department's space needs; sixty-five of the government's one hundred twenty-seven permanent officers and clerks who moved to Washington from Philadelphia from May through July 1800 were employees in the Treasury Department's six divisions.[15]

Once the commissioners' memorial began to be debated, questions arose about the legality of mortgaging Washington lots under the deeds

CONGRESS HALL and NEW THEATRE, on Chesnut Street PHILADELPHIA.

I-6 Many favored Congress Hall in Philadelphia (left) as the architectural model for the Treasury Office.

of trust with the original proprietors who still retained a financial interest in them. (fig. I-6) But the main issue that concerned Congress was the feasibility of completing the Capitol and President's House for the sums projected by the commissioners. Congress had ample evidence that the administration of the city's affairs by the present and former commissioners, and the estimates of building costs by the architects and builders they directed, had not been reliable in the past. White and his fellow commissioners (with Washington's urging) were determined to reverse such negative views by committing more

of their time to the city's affairs and moving prudently in their deliberations.

"The plans of the buildings for the Executive Departments and their scites [sic] will be determined in time," White wrote his fellow commissioners in mid-February 1796, further noting "it would in my opinion be improper to commence these, or even contract for materials until we have a more certain command of money—or until the Capitol shall be considerably advanced, for though these Buildings may be necessary previous to the removal of the Government, yet the Capitol principally attracts the attention of the People, and it will be more encouraging to see the Buildings now in hand going on with spirit." In early May 1796 White met with Washington and one of the items on his agenda was the offices. "He thinks nothing should be done towards erecting Buildings for the Executive Departments until the President's House and Capitol are finished, or so far advanced that their reasonable completion may be relied on," White reported to his colleagues.[16]

It was not until October 1796 that the commissioners again turned their attention to the executive offices, asking Washington to determine their sites because they wished their locations to be established before he left office in March 1797. "We will then cause plans to be drawn—agreeable to the opinions of the executive Officers, expressed to Mr. White in Philadelphia, and submit them to your consideration, and, if approved the buildings will commence as soon as our funds admit of it. Our opinion is that they ought to consist of two handsome brick buildings on the president's square, so situated, as to give the most agreeable appearance to the whole."[17]

In November Washington stopped in the federal city en route from Mount Vernon to Philadelphia and chose their sites. He decided to align the two buildings with the south facade of the President's House, rather than place them southeast and southwest of the house as L'Enfant had planned. Nearly five years earlier, Washington had recognized that the President's House would appear isolated within the extensive grounds the French engineer had allotted for a larger building, noting that "this will necessarily occasion a Division of the Excess, on the two sides." Washington's decision to place the Treasury Office on the east side of the President's Square, and thus closer to the Capitol, was almost surely because the department's clerks frequently sent communications via its messengers to the Postmaster General, Congress, and the Supreme Court located to its east.[18]

"Sensible That Such Treatment:" Designing the Treasury Office, 1797

Thornton recalled eighteen months after the fact that the commissioners had held a limited invited competition. "The Board applied to Mr. Hadfield and Mr. Hoban to draw each a plan for the Executive offices."[19] On January 25, 1797, the commissioners sent George Hadfield's "plan of the proposed two buildings for the executive departments" to Washington in Philadelphia.

> It is proposed that they be built of the best stock brick, and slightly ornamented with free-stone to make them correspond with the President's house. These buildings, though intended to be finished in the interior in the plainest style, will, in the opinion of the Superintendents [Hoban and Hadfield], cost, from sixty to eighty thousand Dollars, each.[20]

The commissioners felt the foundations for both buildings should be laid during the 1797 building season, but on February 15 Washington wrote them that he was "decidedly of [the] Opinion that the edifices for the executive offices ought to be suspended" in favor of finishing the President's House. Hadfield's drawings, however, were in the hands of the cabinet officers ten days later and on his last day in office, March 3, 1797, Washington signed them, noting they were "much approved" by himself and the executive officers. In the same letter he authorized the commissioners to begin both buildings "when the funds and other circumstances will permit."[21]

George Hadfield (1763–1826), born of an English father and Italian mother near Florence but educated at the Royal Academy in London where he won its gold medal for excellence in design in 1784, was one of a handful of European-trained architects to work on the federal buildings. When his stellar career in England came to a halt in January 1795 after being blackballed for election to the Architects' Club, Hadfield was receptive to his friend John Trumbull's suggestion that he emigrate to America. Hadfield accepted the commissioners' invitation to superintend completion of the Capitol in the spring of 1795 and on September 15 took up his duties. Like his predecessor Stephen Hallet and his successor Benjamin Henry Latrobe, Hadfield was critical of Thornton's winning design for the Capitol. He gingerly tried to correct its perceived faults, but Thornton's sense of ownership of the design was combined with his powerful position as one of the three commissioners. Thornton, the amateur architect, and Hadfield, the superbly trained and talented professional, were soon at odds.[22]

In the middle of November 1797 the commissioners began preparations for beginning the executive offices the following spring by inviting expatriate London builder William Lovering to estimate its construction costs based on Hadfield's drawings. A week later they averaged Lovering's estimate of $96,792 per building along with Hoban's of $98,545, and included the figures in a draft petition to Congress seeking appropriations for building the Treasury and War Offices and for the Supreme Court. They did not consult with Hadfield and he complained that Lovering had "deviated" from his intentions because Lovering did not have in hand Hadfield's section drawings. On January 12, 1798, the commissioners asked Hadfield to make "such sections & explanations as may enable [Lovering] to make such corrections in his statements as may agree with your intentions in the execution of the buildings." Hadfield borrowed his original drawings to aid him in making the sections, but it is uncertain whether he actually made drawings showing interior walls because on February 23 the commissioners submitted to Congress the same

November estimates, having commissioned Lovering to make a section drawing to aid him in his calculations.[23]

Commissioner White was once again dispatched to Philadelphia to lobby on behalf of this new plea for funds, now based on a concrete design and a firm estimate from experienced builders for at least the Treasury Office. His long report to Thornton and Scott on March 8 contained alarming news. Some members of Congress were suggesting that a small house for the President, as well as executive offices, be erected near the Capitol, the President's House altered to serve as the Supreme Court. (fig. I-7) Others proposed that the President's House be finished for the use of Congress. Several members of both camps believed that either one or the other buildings underway should be finished by 1800, but not both. Exterior work on the President's House was nearly finished, but only the north, or Senate, wing of the Capitol had been raised above ground level and its interiors were still incomplete. During debates "the old clamour [sic] against the Style of the Buildings was revived" and, after a tumultuous session, a resolution passed "recommending the appropriation of $200,000, at three annual Installments, which it is expected will compleat [sic] the Capitol, the President's House and the Executive Office[s], the Judiciary not being considered as immediately necessary." This sum was totally unrealistic, but it was a step towards winning congressional support for buildings for the executive offices.[24]

Three days later White alerted his colleagues in Washington that Congress was unlikely to make a final decision until President John Adams's views were officially expressed. Adams's "dislike of the City of Washington" was well known to those in political circles, and James Madison alerted Jefferson that it "will cause strong emotions." White met with Adams who did not object to the distance of one-and-one-half miles separating the President's House

I-7 President John Adams wanted the executive offices to be built on Capitol Hill.

and Capitol, but did feel that the departmental office buildings should be near the Capitol for the convenience of Congress. If Adams's views prevailed, White recommended finishing the Capitol's south wing for the executive offices instead of for the House of Representatives.[25]

The commissioners wrote Adams a forceful letter in the middle of March arguing that President Washington had always intended the departmental offices be near the President's House to consolidate the functions of the executive branch. Moreover, they noted that to change their location would not only cause further delays at such a crucial juncture but would undermine local confidence in the federal city.

Before the original proprietors of land signed their agreements with the federal government, Washington explained L'Enfant's idea of dispersing federal facilities throughout the city's 6,111 acres. Each owner would benefit because "their" local government building would act as a magnet, attracting buyers and increasing the value of their lots. To deviate so markedly from the original intention would cause an uproar in the city. The commissioners had to send Adams three additional letters before he replied that he respected their opinions in the matter.[26]

As soon as Congress appropriated funds, the commissioners moved quickly to begin constructing the Treasury Office. Early in May 1798 they drafted the newspaper advertisement inviting contractors to submit bids.

Generally in America at this time, contractors, or "undertakers"—analogous to developers of later periods—included all materials and labor costs in their bids for substantial buildings. (fig. I-8) Washington, Jefferson, and the commissioners decided by 1792 to control quality and, they hoped, construction costs of the Capitol and President's House by hiring their own workforce as day laborers and by contracting directly with suppliers for materials. By 1798 the commissioners apparently decided that the spiraling costs of these buildings were in part attributable to their method of construction oversight. Moreover, disagreements with individuals and with classes of workmen, as well as difficulties obtaining adequate materials, were among the irksome problems they faced weekly.[27]

The commissioners' resolve to hire a contractor to build the Treasury Office was probably strengthened when in early April 1798 the stone cutters at the public buildings struck for higher wages. The officials acted decisively. On April 16 they wrote twenty-one stonecutters at the Capitol and nine at the President's House, declining to raise wages and gave them a month to vacate their government-owned houses. By hiring a general contractor to supply materials and workmen, the commissioners expected that the Treasury Office's construction costs would be predetermined and labor disputes would be the contractor's problem.[28]

The commissioners probably decided to rely on the highly competitive marketplace among Washington's skilled construction workers to determine the Treasury Office's cost before they began the War Office. They also waited until the first building was well underway and felt secure about its approximate final cost before contracting for the second. They drafted the newspaper announcement on May 7 for the Treasury Office for a brick building to contain fourteen rooms on each of the two main floors and eight in the attic.[29]

Washington,

Commissioners' office, May 7, 1798.

THE commissioners will receive proposals until the 10th of June next, for building in the city of Washington, one of the executive offices for the United States, of the following external dimensions:—148 feet in length, and 57 feet, 6 inches in breadth—cellar walls, 30 inches—first story 23 inches, and second story 18 inches—partition walls averaging 15 inches—to contain on the ground floor 14 rooms—same number on the second story, and in the roof, eight rooms, with a passage. The whole external of the building to be of stock brick; the inside walls of hard burnt brick; cellars of best foundation stone, to the height of the girders. The outside walls, as far as they shew above ground to the plinth, to be of plain ashlar free stone; soles of windows, fills of doors and string course, of free stone; the house to be covered with cypress shingles; the rooms in general to be 16 feet by 20, finished in a plain, neat manner, of the best materials; six small rooms to be groined.

A plan and elevation of said building and bill of particulars, are lodged in the office for the inspection of those who may wish to contract; also, a copy of said bill, at the office of Clement Biddle, esquire, at Philadelphia.

Proposals sealed up, will be received until the 20th of June next, on which day, the board will proceed to contract with such person, as shall appear, under all circumstances, to offer the best terms. Per order of the commissioners.

Thomas Munroe, clerk.

M10   2awt19thJe

I-8 The advertisement for bids to erect the Treasury Office appeared in only a few nearby newspapers.

The published announcement soliciting bids angered Hadfield who still had his drawings. At a May 10, 1798, meeting the commissioners asked for their return but Hadfield required clarification of his role in the Treasury Office's construction, including how he would be credited. "After such an explanation, I shall deliver all the Drawings necessary, for without such no estimate can be made, and no Building ought to be commenced." The commissioners could not understand his thinking. "We know not why a further explanation is necessary respecting the plan of the Executive Office. You were asked to draw the plan, and did so, and have all the honor flowing from a full approbation of it, by the Executive of the United States."[30]

When the commissioners sent a messenger to retrieve the drawings, Hadfield wrote a fuller explanation of his position that hinged on the question of professionalism from the point of view of a European-trained architect.

> It is true that I was asked to draw a Plan amongst others, which I did without hesitation, and I am not insensible of the high honour [sic] paid me by a full approbation—but there never has been those explanations between us, on this subject, so necessary on such occasions, although I have frequently endeavoured [sic] that there should. Therefore the Drawings are still my own property, and not the property of the United States.[31]

The commissioners disagreed, considering Hadfield a government architect on salary and expected to undertake such jobs. With no further discussion, on May 18 they gave Hadfield three months notice that his position as superintendent at the Capitol was terminated. Ten days later they notified Hadfield that Hoban would replace him immediately and that he would receive three months salary "as soon as you Shall deliver the public papers now in your possession." Hadfield informed the commissioners that he would continue to work at the Capitol in "strict adherence" to his contract and took his case to President Adams asking for an investigation. Adams referred the matter to Secretary of State Timothy Pickering, who urged the commissioners to either reinstate Hadfield or to find him another position both because Adams was "disposed to distrust the propriety

of your proceeding" and because he wished to avoid an investigation.[32]

Thornton wrote Pickering privately and the commissioners wrote him officially outlining their dealings with the English architect, their main criticism being that he lacked practical building knowledge. In fact, Hadfield had repeatedly challenged many aspects of Thornton's Capitol design while he was its superintending architect, much to that commissioner's pique. Hadfield continued to refuse to surrender his drawings and on June 18, 1798, two days before bids on the Treasury Office contract were due, the commissioners dismissed Hadfield outright. Like his predecessor L'Enfant, Hadfield was fired because he refused to submit to their authority when their ruling directly contradicted his professional standards and sense of justice.[33]

Hadfield apparently gave his drawings to Adams, for Pickering wrote the commissioners: "Mr. Hadfield has made a tender to the President of his drawings for the Executive Offices." On June 25, two days after the Treasury Office contract was signed, the commissioners wrote Pickering: "You will likewise please to submit to the consideration of the President, the propriety of forwarding to us the plan of the Executive Buildings on which the late President's [Washington's] approbation is endorsed, it being our warrant for erecting the Buildings. Hadfield claimed in 1801 that his drawings were obtained from him "surreptitiously"—although they are not again mentioned in the commissioners' records until 1819 when they were returned to him. Hadfield twice petitioned Congress for payment for his design but was unsuccessful. He was nominally considered the architect of the four buildings without receiving any payment for their design nor having any say whatsoever in their construction.[34]

When Jefferson became President in 1801, Hadfield wrote him about the episode's effect on getting work in Washington and blamed

Hoban and Thornton. Jefferson then saw to it that Hadfield received at least three government commissions, a design for the Marine Barracks (1801–05), for a jail (1802–03), and perhaps a design for the President's grounds (1808).[35]

Hadfield's drawings signed by Washington on March 3, 1797, have never been found. The surviving watercolor for the executive offices, an elevation preserved among Jefferson's papers, was one of several drawings the commissioners hired Lovering to make. (fig. I-9) Signed by the commissioners and the contractor, Leonard Harbaugh, it served as one of three contract drawings for the Treasury Office. It was signed the same day as the written contract, June 23, 1798. On July 10 Lovering submitted an invoice, a list of his four drawings, three estimates, and one bill of particulars, listed in the order in which he did the work. This detailed document reveals gradual changes in the Treasury Office's form, size, and architectural embellishment as his 1797 estimate to build Hadfield's design for $96,792 was reduced to $43,382.29 in four stages.[36]

Omitting Hadfield's portico with four expensive Greek Ionic columns nearly halved the building's projected costs, followed by "a Second Elevation to Lower the Stories" which replaced Hadfield's third story with a garret story covered by a hipped roof, its rooms lit by dormers. The penultimate alteration "to heighten the 2nd Story and to introduce Ground Rooms," or a raised basement, dates from about May 1798. Lovering's last entry corresponds with the surviving contract drawing dated June 23. The commissioners signed a contract based on drawings that were modifications of Hadfield's design because the latter was their official "warrant." When the English architect's drawings were temporarily lost to them, they were free to alter the prototype design for the executive offices to accord with their own tastes and the monies available to them.[37]

Like Hoban's original design for the President's House, Hadfield's executive offices were intended to be three-story buildings and they, like Hoban's mansion, were reduced to two-and-one-half stories. The horizontal dimensions

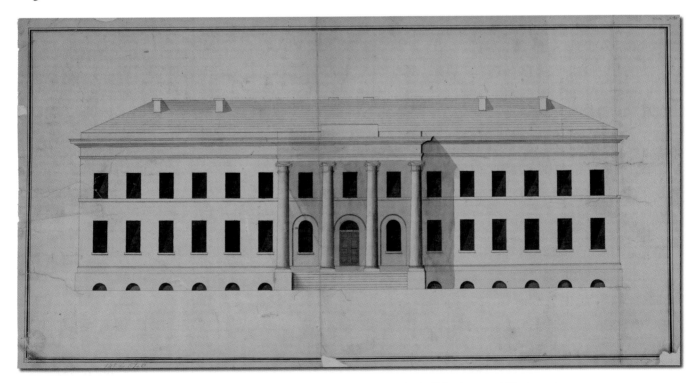

I-9 William Lovering's drawing for the Treasury Office was signed by its builder Leonard Harbaugh.

I-10 The brick Treasury Office and its additions were a notable part of Washington's skyline in 1826.

for the Treasury Office that appeared in the newspaper announcements were probably those specified by Hadfield, 148 feet by 57 feet, 6 inches; in comparison, the President's House measured 170 feet by 86 feet. The height of Hadfield's three-story design is unknown; certainly it would not have been as tall as the fifty-eight-foot height of the President's House. (fig. I-10)

Hadfield produced a sophisticated Neoclassical design that would have been at home in current English architectural situations. The executive offices were intended to complement the more traditional President's House, its modern American Federal style still retaining many characteristics of eighteenth-century Anglo-American buildings. On two earlier occasions before Hadfield was asked to design the executive offices, Commissioner White commented on the appropriateness of the "hotel" as the

architectural model for the executive offices. At the end of January 1796 he opined that they should be built of brick "much in the style of the Hotel" and two weeks later stated that "two handsome Buildings, somewhat inferiour [sic] to the hotel" would be sufficient to house the departments. In 1793 the Boston investor in the city, Samuel Blodgett, chose Hoban's design for a hotel that would be built from the proceeds of a lottery and owned by its winner. Sometime after signing the Treasury Office contract on June 20, 1798, the commissioners approved subtle alterations to Lovering's reduction of Hadfield's design that led to its close resemblance to Blodgett's Hotel.[38] (see fig. I-12)

Apparently the commissioners (perhaps in consultation with Hoban whom they hired to superintend the Treasury Office's construction) considered that a simple American Federal appearance for the executive offices would better harmonize with the President's House than Hadfield's Neoclassical design. The modified design included: red brick walls contrasting with the lighter colored stone basement, lintels, and belt course; pedimented gable windows set low on the high hip roofs; and Federal-style fan and side-lit entrances on the east and west ends (rather than Hadfield's probable simpler arched entries set within blind arches). Together these modifications changed the executive offices from a contemporary European Neoclassical design that was more avant-garde than the President's House to one that was slightly more old fashioned than Hoban's centerpiece.

The revised Treasury Office's design was also decidedly more in tune with current American tastes and ideas about political propriety, as congressmen repeatedly voiced to Commissioner White. Its appearance now resembled the Philadelphia buildings that had been the setting for much of America's founding political history. In fact, Congress met in 1798 in Congress Hall attached to the Pennsylvania State House, popularly known as "Independence Hall." (see fig. I-6) The commissioners and their architectural advisors may well have thought that changing Hadfield's design would influence the perception among congressmen, as well as Americans in general, about the proper relationship between the President's House and the executive offices—a mansion for the president but simple office buildings for the government's functionaries. White often recounted to his colleagues comments made by conservative members of Congress concerning the unnecessary splendor of the Capitol and President's House; such charges would not be made about the executive department's office buildings erected during their watch.

No image of Hoban's submission for the executive offices competition is known, but on the evidence of his designs for the South Carolina State House, the President's House,

and Blodgett's Hotel, the Treasury Office as built was closer to Hoban's losing competition entry than to Hadfield's winning entry. Hoban was the most successful of the European-trained architects hired by the commissioners in the 1790s, in part because of his pragmatic approach to architectural problems from the viewpoint of a builder; his willingness to accommodate, rather than challenge, the commissioners; and his variations on the theme of the Georgian mansion that were aesthetically acceptable to most people and could be built for predictable sums of money. Moreover, his clients often commented on Hoban's agreeable nature.[39]

Hadfield's aesthetic revenge was slow in coming. About 1823 he designed his last major commission, the Washington branch of the Bank of the United States, a quasi-official institution wherein the government's money was deposited. (fig. I-11) When it opened in June 1824, Hadfield's bank faced the State Office on the northwest corner of 15th Street and Pennsylvania Avenue. The handsome bank displayed well Hadfield's characteristic architectural elements, which had probably been features of his winning design for the executive offices: a clear geometric mass with window and door frames slightly recessed rather than attached to the surface of the walls as at the Treasury Office; second story windows lightly balanced on the belt course; and, large windows throughout allowed abundant light. Comparison of the subtly differing architectural characters of the Branch Bank and the Treasury Office as it was built suggests the effect of the compromises inherent in the collaborative process that was part of creating Washington's official architecture from the beginning. On November 9, 1795, Washington wrote the commissioners that the Capitol's "present plan is no body's, but a compound of every body's," a comment that could easily have been made about the Treasury Office's design process.[40]

I-11 Hadfield's masterpiece was the Bank of the United States directly north of the Treasury Office.

"I Have Not Mate My Estermate:" Building the Treasury Office, 1798–1800

On or soon after May 7, 1798, the commissioners sent the announcement seeking proposals to build the Treasury Office to newspapers in the central states. On May 12 they ordered Hoban to suspend the carpenters' work at the President's House because "our funds are not sufficient for carrying on" both buildings simultaneously. Ten days later contractors were asking to see Lovering's section drawing along with his plan and "bill of particulars." Lovering was among the six contractors who submitted estimates due by June 20. The commissioners acknowledged that they had expected to award him the contract but

his bid of $42,500 was too high. The other five competitors also were local architects, stonemasons, builders, or contractors who already had experience with prominent public or private buildings in the city. Hoban submitted a proposal to build the Treasury Office for $56,000. Since his arrival in the city in 1792, he had been in partnership with Pierce Purcell in a design-construction team that erected many of Washington's private buildings.[41]

Lovering and Hoban also both applied to superintend construction of the Treasury Office soon after Leonard Harbaugh was chosen as the contractor. The commissioners chose Hoban for this part-time position because his faithful superintendence of the President's House was temporarily suspended in favor of erecting the Treasury Office. His contract dated August 21,

1798, required him to inspect workmanship and materials and when defective to report to the board if Harbaugh did not solve the problem. "Mr. Hoban also agrees, on the application of Mr. Harbaugh, to give his advice in any matter relative to the said Executive Office or the quality of materials offered or purchased" for an additional 100 guineas until the building was finished.[42]

The commissioners selected Leonard Harbaugh to build the Treasury Office even though his construction of a stone bridge (1791–94), designed to span Rock Creek at K Street, proved to be faulty. Harbaugh's June 20 letter to the commissioners (he wrote phonetically in the same Pennsylvania Deutsch, or German, that he spoke) may have been in response to allegations brought by one or more of the losing competitors that his bid of $39,511 was so low it must be rigged.

> [F]irst I solemly [sic] Declare that in the undertaking of this Building I have no Combin[e] nor Combination with anny [sic] Man or Set of Menn [sic]. Secontly [sic] I have not Mate [sic] My Estermate [sic] in or out of oposition [sic] to any Man or party—if it is Combin [sic] to be Lone [sic] I can only say this by way of Justification that the principle on which I made it was to ask as Much as I would giff [sic] to others—in case a Decition [sic] of that Nature was left to my Determination.[43]

Harbaugh contracted on June 23, 1798, to begin the walls within a month "agreeably to the annexed plan, Elevation and Section," of which only the elevation survives. On August 10 Harbaugh calculated he would spend $24,800 during the remainder of the building season and the commissioner's part-time paymaster, Thomas Munroe (also the city postmaster), began paying Harbaugh, his subcontractors, journeymen, and suppliers of materials. Few of

these men had worked on the Capitol or President's House and their wages were lower than workmen employed directly by the government. Although identifying nationality based on surnames is fallible, most of the Treasury Office's builders appear to have been Welch, English, German, Scottish, and Irish. The names of two African-Americans, "Negro Jim" and "Negro Frank," are recorded as laborers working for subcontractor Jonathan Jackson in October 1798—two of eleven men named as employed by Jackson that month—but surviving payrolls for the subcontractors are incomplete. Jim and Frank were probably slaves hired out by their masters, since freedmen presumably would have been identified by both their given and surnames. Harbaugh's son, Thomas, was paid increasingly larger amounts monthly in 1799; he may have been a subcontractor himself.[44]

During the early summer of 1798 Hoban and Harbaugh agreed to several minor changes, some solely pragmatic in nature such as moving the privies from under the portico to the basement and replacing king and queen post rafters with partition walls covered with brick to support the roof because the trusses would have obstructed some garret rooms. Others related to the safety and stability of the building, including replacing wood trusses under the first floor with stone pillars and reducing the size of the wall plates because there was too much wood in the brick partition walls. The changes relating to the Treasury Office's design were to reduce the dormer windows in the garret to one per room, but to make them "larger than common," and to lengthen the second story windows for better ventilation. They built four vaulted rooms in the center wing, rather than the six originally specified, because the garret's ceiling was too low for those planned for that floor. On May 20, 1799, Hoban reported on the progress made since mid-November of 1798. The freestone basement walls were finished and ready for the first floor joists and all the building's woodwork except the roof joists dressed and ready to insert as its brick walls rose.[45]

At the end of the second building season the Treasury Office had a wood shingle roof covered with one coat of paint, gutters, and a wood entablature "painted three coats and sanded, and painted over the sanding," to imitate stone. The stone entablature estimated by Lovering to cost $3,757 was struck off his bill of particulars because it was too expensive. Internally little work could be done over the winter months because there was no glass in the windows. The window frames and sashes, however, were in place and their jambs already installed on the first floor. Interestingly, the floor of the garret story was finished first with only the centers laid on the lower floors. The plastering also was done from the top down, the first coat having been applied to rooms in the garret and the second story. The London crown glass the commissioners specified for the Treasury Office could not be made because of the "uncommon" sizes ordered. They finally settled for American plate glass, which was not shipped from Boston until July 21, a month after the commissioners estimated the building would be finished.[46]

The completed Treasury Office had thirty-six rooms. Four were small fireproof storage rooms, ten feet by twelve feet, which flanked the central stairs. All the rest were much larger, typically measuring sixteen feet by twenty-eight feet. The Treasury Office was actually seven and one-half feet longer than Harbaugh contracted for because English émigré surveyor Nicholas King miscalculated its dimensions when he laid out the building's foundations. The error was not noticed until 15th Street was surveyed in 1799 and the building's east end was closer to the street than anticipated. Harbaugh's solution was to build what he called a "platform," a shallow porch approached by stairs on its sides. King's error had far-reaching urban consequences for the neighborhood because in 1836

the Treasury Building's east facade was located adjacent to the sidewalk, its entrance also via a lateral staircase. Had the Treasury Office been set back fifteen feet from the street as planned, it and the Treasury Building would have been framed by gardens rather than determining the streetscape.[47]

"Agreeable to the Heads of the Various Departments:" The Treasury Department Occupies Its Building

On May 24, 1800, Comptroller of the Treasury John W. Steele alerted the commissioners that he had dispatched the Treasury Department's furniture from Philadelphia in charge of clerk Joshua Dawson. "I find considerable difficulty in obtaining hands to assist in arranging the several boxes and cases which are now lying in a scattered situation over the floor of this building," Dawson complained on June 12.[48] Christian Hines recalled more than six decades later that "many of the boxes were marked "Joseph Nourse, Register.""[49]

Secretary Wolcott was receiving mail by June 30 and four days later wrote his wife from his office—"this being a day of leisure"— describing the city's setting as very beautiful and commenting on its lack of amenities, particularly lodging, as he failed to find a room closer than a half mile from his office. President Adams arrived on June 3 to inspect the President's House and public offices, leaving on the eleventh and not returning until November 1. Abigail Adams wrote her daughter on November 21 that William Doughy had solved one of her most pressing immediate needs. "We are now indebted to a Philadelphia wagon for bringing us, through the first clerk in the Treasurer's office, one cord and a half of wood, which is all we have for this house, where twelve fires are constantly required." Wood for heating was unavailable in Washington that winter because the proprietors had earlier cut down all the trees on their lots conveyed to the government—allowed under their agreement with President Washington—to sell as firewood.[50]

It is not clear exactly what the Treasury Office looked like when it was completed in 1800 because the few early views differ or are indistinct. Late in 1799 or early in 1800, King, an architect as well as a surveyor, painted a watercolor from about 6th and C streets, NW, looking northwest. (fig. I-12) In the middle ground is Blodgett's Hotel and in the distance—sketchy, indistinct, and on a small scale—are the President's House and Treasury Office. (The three-story red brick building between them is identified in the margin as Hadfield's house, which stood on the southeast corner of 9th and F streets.) Little can be determined about this southeast view of the Treasury Office except that it was slightly lower than the President's House, two stories tall, had a hipped roof, and the center of its south front was recessed. The recessed south porch is confirmed by the building's footprint on an 1800 map of the President's Grounds. Chronologically the next known view of the Treasury Office is a woodcut of its east end as it purportedly appeared in 1804, but published in *Harper's New Monthly Magazine* in 1872. (fig. I-13) No source dating from 1804 for this woodcut has been identified and an 1817 watercolor, done after the Treasury Office was rebuilt, raises several questions to be considered later.

I-12 Blodgett's Hotel on the right was the preferred model for the Treasury Office, middle distance.

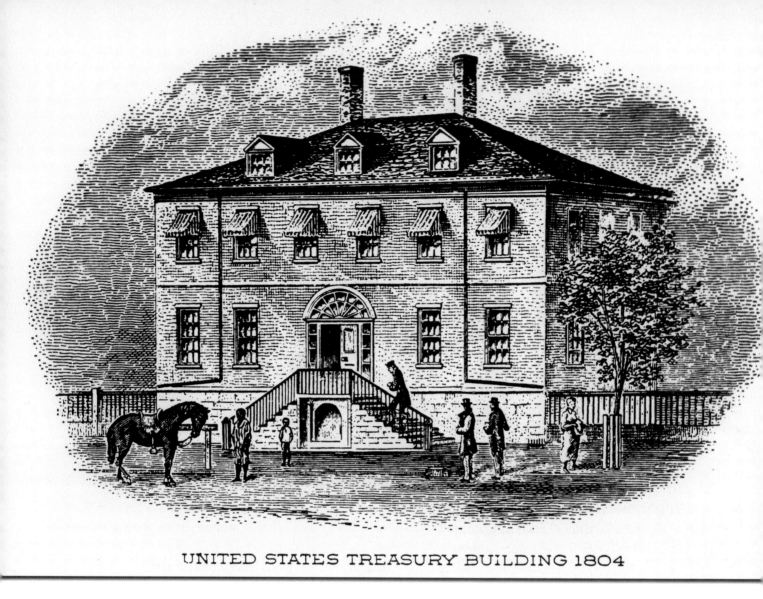

UNITED STATES TREASURY BUILDING 1804

I-13 The engraved view identified as the Treasury in 1804, not published until 1872, is suspect.

The Treasury Office's central block was off-set from its east and west wings with the south entrance to have a columnar portico, but only a triangular pediment that served as the recess's roof was built. Lovering's drawing showed a shallow projecting portico of four slender, unfluted Greek Ionic columns carrying a flat entablature. Had this portico and Hadfield's general design been erected, the Treasury Office would have had the distinction of being America's first Greek Revival building; B.H. Latrobe designed the Bank of Pennsylvania in the spring of 1798 and supervised its construction between 1799 and 1801.

Hadfield designed three simple arched openings set in blind arches for the Treasury Office's south entrance. Lovering's bill of particulars called for three arched openings in the recessed portico, the central door leading to a square vestibule flanked by two small offices. Immediately above them on the second floor was a long room for the storage of warrants. The staircase was located in the projecting central block on the north side, its steps descending towards the south vestibule and central corridor. The 15th Street door, opening onto an eight-foot-wide corridor that ran the length of the building, was used frequently and many believed it to be the Treasury Office's principal entrance.

Offices east and west of the central block were organized into suites of three rooms connected via arched doorways. Fireplaces were in the center of the walls that divided the offices with double or triple tiers of mahogany cases either built-in or set into the recesses between the chimney breasts and the windows. Book and document cases probably lined the other walls in each room. Each office was lit by windows with two sashes, each with twelve panes of glass. In the north-facing room on the second floor occupied by Andrew H. Laub, a clerk in the Secretary's office in 1833, two tables were placed perpendicular to the wall between the windows to take advantage of light falling on his work surfaces. Back-to-back double cases approximately eighteen inches to twenty-four inches high in the middle of Laub's tables were divided into pigeon holes for easy filing and retrieval of papers. There seems to have been a variety of furnishings in the offices, some brought from Philadelphia, some acquired for the new building.

Three additional construction projects completed the Treasury Office. During the fall of 1800, Harbaugh finished off a separate space in the garret for the "Stamper," a function in the Office of Revenue that was abolished in 1802. Harbaugh's final extra job in 1800 was to erect two single-story brick houses for the Treasury Department's messengers ordered by the Commissioner of Revenue. They were located on the north side of the Treasury's square at the corner of 15th and G streets NW, the future site of the State Office. In 1866 Christian Hines recalled that there were "three blocks of small two-story brick houses built north of the old Treasury office … Each block contained three houses—six in all—and were built for the accommodation of the messengers." Hines even remembered their names and that the British destroyed the houses in 1814. The commissioners were so satisfied with Harbaugh's work on the Treasury Office that they contracted with him on August 6, 1799, to duplicate it for the War Office at the same price. Munroe did not

close out his account until the middle of June 1801; $42,263.08 had been expended on building the Treasury Office not counting the messengers houses, which cost $4,622.[51]

During the evening of January 20, 1801, a fire broke out in the Auditor's Office located in the southeast corner of the ground floor. As soon as the alarm was given, heads of bureaus and clerks began removing important documents from their rooms while many citizens joined in fighting the fire, including President John Adams who was "in the line, and was busy in aiding to pass the buckets to and from the burning building." The greatest recorded damage to the building was the breakage of several windows. Auditor Richard Harrison lost the most records but was able to identify them and verify that most could be copied from originals kept by other bureaus.[52]

On arriving at the scene, John Woodside, a clerk in the Comptroller's Office, left the firefighting to others and raced up the stairs to save the books and papers in his office directly above the burning room. Woodside, immediately given the job of building superintendent (a position he held until 1829), traced the cause of the fire to faulty construction behind a fireplace in the partition wall. The previous two days had not been especially cold, but on the afternoon of January 20 "the wind had changed, and blew especially at the time of the fire, cold and violently from the northwest." Woodside was able to determine that "sparks passing through joints one-quarter of an inch in width between the bricks" behind the fireplace ignited wood plugs used to level bricks within the wall.[53] The day after the fire the commissioners:

> Ordered that the Skirting in each Room of
> the two Executive offices at the Backs of the
> several Fireplaces in the adjacent Rooms
> be taken off, and if Blocks of or wooden
> Plugs are in the wall, that they be removed,
> and the vacant spaces left by their removal

as well as by the Skirting be filled up with brick & mortar, provided this measure be agreeable to the Heads of the various Departments.[54]

Hadfield was quick to impute in his March 27, 1801, letter to President Jefferson that Hoban's supervision of the Treasury Office was to blame for the fire. "Had I been permitted to superintend my work & designs in the building of the Executive Offices, that the late unfortunate fire in one of them, would not have happened from the causes, as many supposed & alledged [sic]." He further indicted Harbaugh's cheap construction techniques: "it appears that those buildings, from the manner of their execution will always be subject to similar accidents, if suffered to remain in their present state."[55]

"Bemoaning My Cock Sparrow:" The Treasury Fireproof, 1804–1808

The Treasury Office's four small vaulted rooms for the fireproof storage of documents soon proved to be inadequate for the increasing volume of records needing protection against accidental or intentional loss. Two projects from 1804 coalesced and led to the construction of an outbuilding between 1805 and 1808, designed to be fireproof and called officially the Treasury Fireproof, or simply the "fireproof." During July 1804 Jefferson designed service and office wings to connect the President's House with the executive offices, the latter located about 500 feet east and west of the mansion. The inscriptions on the plan for the wings, drawn on graph paper and found among Jefferson's papers, are in John Lenthall's handwriting, their supervisor of construction. Latrobe painted them in his 1817 watercolor of the south facade of the President's House. (fig. I-14)

Because the President's House was located astride a ridge—its north entrance was a floor higher than the south one—Jefferson planned its wings to be partially submerged along the south side of the hill's edge to visually mask the change in level. The sections to be attached directly to the President's House were for domestic services—a meat house, necessary [privy], servants' room, hen house, and

I-14 The Treasury Fireproof was aligned with the east service wing (right) on the President's House.

stables—were planned for the east side facing the Treasury Office. Pavilions and wide carriage drives were to separate the domestic wings from office wings leading or attached to the Treasury and War Offices. Entrances to all the rooms in the wings were behind colonnades facing south overlooking the river and each room was lit by lunette (semicircular) windows high on the walls of both their north and south sides. The roofs of these wings were to serve as walkways, accessible from the President's House through doors Jefferson cut in the central sections of the Venetian windows on its east and west ends. The domestic wings were completed and are the basis for the White House's present East and West Wing offices, but only a short segment of the office wing for use of the Treasury Department was completed.

Register of the Treasury Joseph Nourse and Auditor Richard Harrison first suggested a separate building for the department's records to Jefferson's Secretary of the Treasury, Albert Gallatin. They initially moved many records from the garret to the basement, fearing their weight endangered the building, but dampness in the new location was detrimental to ledgers and loose documents alike. It was probably Jefferson who suggested Benjamin Henry Latrobe, the architect he had hired in 1803 to complete the Capitol, to be the designer of a fireproof repository as part of the east office wing. On November 21, 1804, Latrobe sent Gallatin drawings, specifications, and estimates for the Treasury Fireproof. The original drawings do not survive, but Nourse had crude copies made for his records; they were printed in *Harper's New Monthly Magazine* in 1872. (fig. I-15) Latrobe estimated costs for two

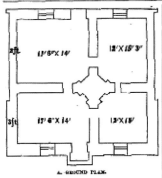

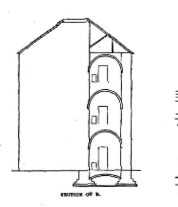

I-15 In 1804 B.H. Latrobe designed a "fireproof repository" for the department's important records.

different designs for a brick building located on the north side of the Treasury Office's square at 15th and G streets. It was to stand between the brick messengers' houses that Harbaugh built just two years earlier. Latrobe estimated a completely fireproof structure with stone framing for doors and windows to cost $9,018.06, or a less expensive version with wood frames for

$7,342.31. Additional costs of $1,877.50 (including the architect's fee of $500) were necessary to complete either design. Latrobe planned a nearly square brick repository with a hipped roof covering three stories, all of its twelve rooms vaulted in brick. Its south front measured thirty-seven feet six inches in width, on axis with and probably about the same width as the Treasury Office's central pavilion. The repository's height of forty feet may have approximated the Treasury Office's height. A decade later Latrobe recalled that he had "proposed to surround a square court north of the Treasury with vaulted buildings," the only evidence of a more extensive Treasury complex planned to cover its entire square.[56]

Gallatin preferred placing the fireproof building north of the Treasury Office, but, Latrobe later recalled, "in Compliance with Mr. Jefferson's wish it was made part of the Colonnade."[57] Because the Treasury Fireproof was constructed as the easternmost section of Jefferson's office wing, the President took a particular interest in its design. On March 1, 1805, Congress appropriated $9,000 for the fireproof, but before completing its design Latrobe rethought Jefferson's ideas concerning the entire executive complex. The architect particularly considered the irregular topography of the President's Square and how to accommodate government officials, the president's family and staff, and visitors who would move through its various parts frequently, but in different ways. Two undated plans of the President's gardens surrounded by a polygonal wall probably were made in May–June 1805, one by Latrobe's young apprentice Robert Mills (fig. I-16), and the second by Nicholas King. (fig. I-17) Both show Latrobe's current idea of building four north-south wings perpendicular to Jefferson's service and office wings, each set connected by a triumphal arch facing what would become Lafayette Square. An undated draft letter from Thornton to Jefferson (following an October 1806 docu-

ment in Thornton's papers), but possibly dated about 1815 discusses Thornton's variants on the architectural development of the landscape between the President's House and the Treasury Office.[58]

Latrobe's intention was to isolate the offices from the hubbub and smells associated with the President's House service areas, to provide better carriage entrances, and to create an impressive ensemble of buildings to fill up the rather barren landscape flanking the mansion. On May 5, 1805, Latrobe sent Jefferson now-lost drawings that showed his ideas about proposed service courtyards. "When the ground around the president's house is dressed, a great variety of convenience will be wanted which cannot be had in the front range of buildings, and which would destroy its great utility as a passage of covered communication between the public buildings." Jefferson approved some of Latrobe's ideas, questioned a few, and rejected others, noting that "the most difficult of all is the adjustment of the new connecting buildings to the different levels of the three existing buildings." Both of the executive offices were outside the low wall, but on the Mills drawing, fifty-nine feet of the original Treasury Fireproof was inside and the thirty-foot 1807 addition outside. With a few quick, strong strokes Latrobe overlaid Mills's rather prissy layout of winding carriageways with strong, dynamic curves that created definite spatial areas for lawns, gardens, woods, and roadways. This landscape, partially completed in 1807, was particularly beautiful when viewed from the Treasury Office. King's survey map showed in sketch form how the

Opposite page, top: I-16 Latrobe's curved drive passed beneath a triumphal arch separating the east wing and repository.

Bottom: I-17 The Treasury (far right) was outside the wall enclosing the President's Grounds on this 1805 plat.

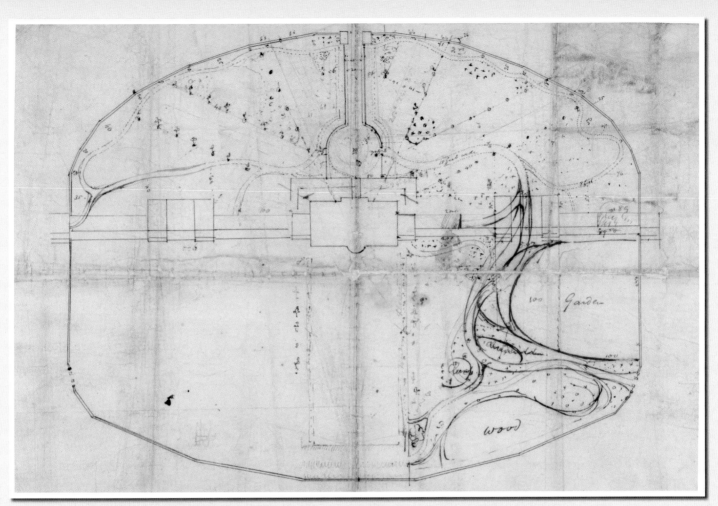

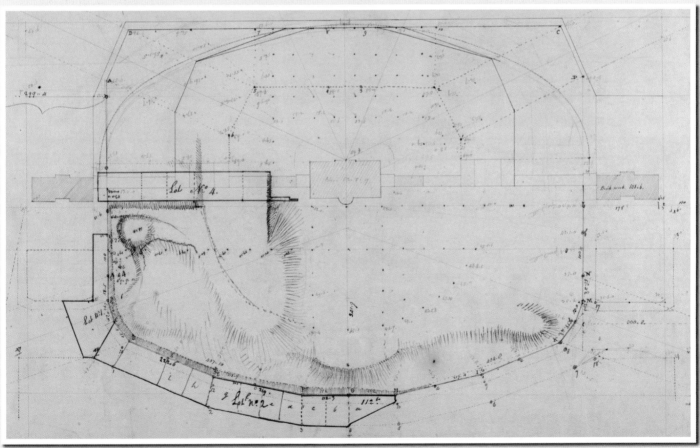

proposed landscape would visually protect vistas from the President's House and ensure privacy within a bustling enclave traversed by a wide variety of people.[59]

In July 1802 Jefferson had written letters of recommendation that introduced Mills to many prominent people during his grand tour to investigate America's architectural heritage. Jefferson noted that the twenty-one-year-old already had considerable experience as an architect in Washington. Sometime late in 1799 or early in 1800, Mills's father had apprenticed him to Hoban, who was superintending the completion of the Treasury and War Offices. About June 1803 Mills entered Latrobe's architectural office as an apprentice and boarded with the Nourses. Familial, professional, religious, and local or regional connections were the underlying network that led to work in Washington during the government's formative years.[60]

In early April 1805 Latrobe wrote Gallatin that he needed to make "a compleat [sic] digest of all the buildings" in the President's House complex before designing the fireproof. The Treasury Office had been built at the edge of a rise that gradually sloped eastward away from the President's House, and the War Office at the edge of an upward slope, a situation that interfered with Jefferson's idea of level wings linking the three buildings. Jefferson wrote Latrobe on May 11, 1805. "Nothing can be admitted short of the terras [sic] of the offices from the Pres.'s House to the pavilions each way being absolutely in the level of the *floor* of the house. How it shall drop off from the last Pavilion to the Treasury, and gain from the West one to the War office is the difficulty of the art which will be worthy of you to conquer." At the end of July, Latrobe was still trying to work out how to seamlessly join the three buildings via the wings, now depending on a survey of the whole area, including the vertical dimensions of the President's House, made by King.[61]

Latrobe and Jefferson separately and together worked with Lenthall who was an active participant in design decisions rather than simply in charge of constructing the service and office wings. Latrobe did work very closely on the fireproof's design with Gallatin for whom he was concurrently designing a lighthouse for the mouth of the Mississippi River and, beginning in 1807, a customs house for New Orleans. Latrobe sent the only surviving watercolor of the fireproof, dated April 27, 1805, to Gallatin with an accompanying description a week later. (fig. I-18) A single eighty-nine-foot-long room was divided into nine bays, the whole supported by a shallow vaulted floor to control rising damp as well as provide a solid foundation. Latrobe noted that its length could be adjusted to come within the $9,000 appropriation. He could not make definitive estimates until he knew the cost of iron-framed lunette windows located between the arches at the tops of the north and south walls. The contract signed in September 1805 called for deleting two bays thus shortening its length to seventy feet. Initially Latrobe had not planned for fireplaces in the room, but two were added on the end walls.[62]

On March 23, three weeks after Congress appropriated $9,000 for the fireproof, Latrobe asked Gallatin if that amount included furniture and if "the papers [are] to be kept in Cases like Bookcases set up along the Walls, as in the Clerks office of the house of representatives, or in open pigeonholes, or in Boxes, and of what size?" Gallatin referred Latrobe's questions to Nourse who replied in detail, his answer probably reflecting how the documents were stored in the Treasury Office's existing vaulted rooms and perhaps its offices as well.[63]

That for the preservation of the public Records, and for the convenience of resorting thereto, a decided preference above all the others is given to their arrangement in

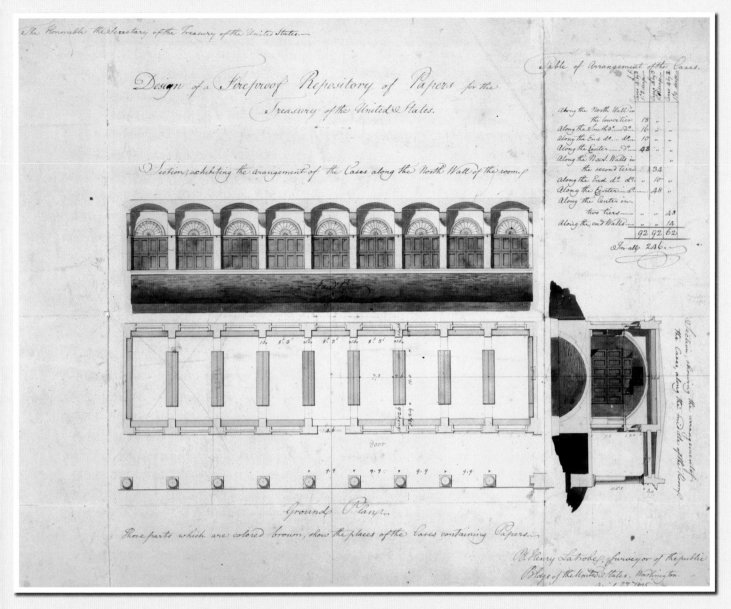

I-18 Latrobe's fireproof repository for the Treasury Department's records was the first national archive.

oblong Cases with Doors like Bookcases. These cases are elevated about 10 inches from the Floor upon a platform of 2 feet 2 inches wide. The size of these cases are:

4 feet wide

3 feet high

1 foot 3 inches deep, and are set against the Wall in a range or tier according to the length of the Room, another range in tier is placed upon them called the second range of cases or tiers, and if the height of the ceiling will admit, a third range or tier, with the use of a ladder.[64]

Nourse went on to suggest these cases could be placed against opposite walls in rooms fourteen feet wide as well as back-to-back on platforms four feet, four inches wide down the center of rooms. This arrangement allowed a passage of about two feet six inches between those lining the wall and those in the center. He based his observations on Latrobe's original design for the Treasury Fireproof, its rooms varying from twelve feet by fifteen feet to fourteen feet by seventeen feet, six inches. For the fireproof that was built, Latrobe designed a storage system that was incorporated into its structure while utilizing Nourse's layout. Latrobe's building was not true vaulting because he used wood and iron in conjunction with brick and stone, a less expensive hybrid system that allowed for larger windows to admit more light for the examination of documents. He set wood beams into the walls just below the windows and ran iron tie rods connecting them across the room. The rods were largely hidden because they were incorporated into the tops of the document cases, serving at the same time to stabilize them.[65]

Latrobe used all of the wall space, except for the single door facing south and the piers supporting the arches, for three tiers of cases of graduated sizes. These wood cases with doors, as well as those placed back-to-back down the center of the room, were organized both horizontally and vertically as Nourse suggested. Latrobe carefully calculated the space between their fronts at three feet, three inches with open doors and suggested that tables to examine papers "should be so made as to form a ladder & stand to get at the upper tiers of cases." In a second letter sent to Gallatin on May 4, Latrobe noted that "Mr. Nourse, in his report, seems to have had in his view the abilities of a Stevadore [sic], rather than the talents of an Architect. His cases seem rather stowed away for a voyage than arranged for commodious reference. I am very anxious that the design should please him, and hope it will."[66]

Jefferson initially misunderstood Latrobe's method of vaulting the fireproof, reading Latrobe's drawings as having a continuous barrel vault running the length of the room. The architect clarified its construction in a letter to Gallatin on May 13, concluding that "oeconomy, [sic] space, and light, render the design submitted to you the most eligible." During the spring and summer of 1805, Latrobe spent much of his time in Iron Hill, Pennsylvania, supervising construction of the Chesapeake and Delaware canal, one of the internal improvement projects sponsored by the Jefferson administration that Gallatin was charged with overseeing.[67]

"Mr. Gallatin has spent an hour with me on his journey to New York," on July 18 the architect noted, the secretary commissioning Latrobe to design a two-story addition on the fireproof building's east end to attach directly to the Treasury Office. Its ground story apparently was intended to serve as a secure vault because it had a single window but no door on its south side and a single semicircular window high on its north wall. When completed, Joshua Dawson, now principal clerk in the Register's Office, could look into the vault through the two windows in his ground-floor office. (fig. I-19) A year later Nourse and Dawson agreed that these windows should be walled up, limiting the vault's entry to a door opening from the fireproof's main room. Although poorly lit, the vault had two fireplaces, most likely intended for burning old currency. "There will probably be stoves to them, but I fear they will smoke do what we will," Latrobe complained to Lenthall.[68]

The upper story of the fireproof's addition was a library directly connected to Gallatin's office designed by Latrobe before the secretary secured Jefferson's approval. Jefferson met with Gallatin on October 15 and the next day wrote Lenthall.

> I spoke with Mr. Gallatin yesterday on the subject of his fire proof offices. I found him desirous of having one room on the level of the upper floor of the Treasury Office. This will so derange the established plan of the buildings that I propose to have a further conversation with him to see whether some measure for accommodating him may not be adopted without destroying the plan of the whole structure.[69]

Jefferson further noted that Gallatin could contribute $1,500 from another fund to add to the $9,000 Congress appropriated. The president wanted Lenthall to use this money "to take off the present roof & cover the whole roof with sheet iron," although Gallatin surely intended the extra money be spent on his library.[70]

The next day Latrobe broke the news to Gallatin. "The president has interdicted your library upstairs … besides regulating *4 mouldings* [sic] *an inch wide each* differently from what I would have done. I am sorry, because I was proud of my whole work and contrivance, and now all is vanished into *thin air*." Latrobe was philosophical about Jefferson's decision, his further comments to Gallatin indicative of how he viewed the president's agile mind and his own disenchantment with Jefferson as a client. "For *my* part, who cannot bend my mind into a hoop to contain all the great and all the little things in the world at once, and with '*equal eye* see a hero perish and a sparrow fall,' am bemoaning my cock sparrow, and must leave it

to you to perform the work of resuscitation, by proper representations."[71]

The arguments Gallatin presented to Jefferson were cogent because he got his fireproof library. It meant blocking up his office windows overlooking the east end of the President's House and installing a central door connecting his office and library. Secretary of State James Madison's office, on the second floor of the War Office overlooking the President's House from the west, was denigrated by British diplomat Sir Augustus John Foster, who commented that "the Secretary of State received Foreign Ministers in a very indifferent little room into which they were ushered by his clerk." Jefferson used the ground floor room in the President's House's southwest corner, intended as the State Dining Room, for his office. Congressmen's desks on the floors of the House and Senate chambers were their offices until the early twentieth century. Gallatin's office/library suite with

I-19 Latrobe added a secure vault between the fireproof and the Office probably to store currency.

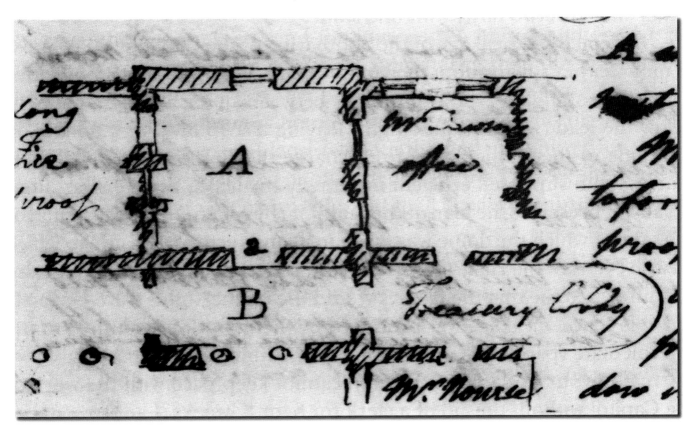

furniture designed by Latrobe and used by six successive secretaries, was more impressive than other rooms provided for government officers, its architectural pedigree having few rivals in Washington. Latrobe proposed a domed ceiling for the library that Lenthall redesigned with a more shallow curvature. "I like your flat dome exceedingly; but it appears to me to require a crabbed center. The brick layers won't complain I think as much as the carpenters." Latrobe used shallow domes to great effect in many of his buildings, an architectural form borrowed from the avant garde English Neoclassicist, John Soane, architect of the Bank of England beginning in 1788.[72]

The Treasury Fireproof soon became the envy of other departmental secretaries and their clerks. In February 1810 Representative Josiah Quincy of Massachusetts introduced legislation in Congress that led to the appropriation on April 28 for "as many fire-proof rooms as shall be sufficient for the convenient deposit of all the public papers and records of the United States, belonging to, or in the custody of the State, War, or Navy Departments." Moreover, Quincy sponsored legislation for "the better accommodation of the General Post Office and Patent Office" (the latter a bureau of the State Department), both of which were outgrowing their accommodations in the War Office. This led to a separate appropriation in 1810 for $25,000 to purchase Blodgett's Hotel where both these agencies moved in 1812. The Treasury Department probably led the way in the preservation of the nation's archives because it was the department that generated the greatest volume of official documents. Moreover, their loss would have the greatest national repercussions because the department's activities touched every facet of the government's civil and military activities.[73]

The second fire at the Treasury Office was much more serious than the 1801 scare, an act of war carried out by the British near the end of the War of 1812. Mordecai Booth, a clerk at the Navy Yard, said the violent summer thunderstorm during the night of August 24, 1814, that saved Washington's public buildings from being piles of ashes, shattered stone, bricks, and molten glass was "the most tremendous storm [he] had ever witnessed." After British General Robert Ross looted, then set on fire the President's House late in the afternoon, he led his troops on to the Treasury Office. Gallatin ordered the evacuation of as many of the Treasury's valuable records as possible before the British began their pillage; his own "official books, papers, trophies, and effects" were saved, but his office furniture went up in flames. Anna Maria Thornton, wife of former commissioner William Thornton— now Commissioner of the Patent Office in the State Department and one of the heroes of the week—described the assault on the Treasury. British torchbearers broke windows then hurled burning poles inside.[74]

Two decades later, Capt. James Scott, a participant in the British firing of the Treasury Office, particularly remembered the difficulties encountered in burning the fireproof.

> The Treasury was next visited, but the specie had been safely conveyed away. The building was fired before the discovery of a strong iron door, that resisted all the efforts made to break it open. It was presumed to be the stronghold and deposit of all the valuables. The window was forced in, and the first officer who descended into the apartment, gave information that it contained several weighty boxes. The flames had driven our men from the passage which communicated with the apartment. Great was the bustle attendant on handing through the window the supposed chests of treasure; our anxiety to extricate them from the flames ceased on finding that the contents would by no means compensate us for our exertions and possible suffocation, and they were left to their fate.[75]

As had been done after the 1801 fire, the chief clerks of each of the Treasury's divisions compiled meticulous records of what had been destroyed for a report to Congress. The losses were serious. For example, Joseph Stretch in the Register's Office reported that "the vouchers and reports on settled accounts, which were contained in upwards of one hundred cases and chests in the fire-proof building, were destroyed." All the settled accounts from the Jefferson and Madison administrations, including those on the construction of the Treasury Office (paymaster Thomas Munroe did not submit Harbaugh's vouchers until June 1801), the Treasury Fireproof, and Jefferson's development of the President's Grounds, seem to have been among those lost. This irony is particularly poignant because Jefferson, Gallatin, and Latrobe built the Treasury Fireproof specifically to protect the department's archives.[76]

"The Workmanship…[Is] Highly Objectionable:" Rebuilding the Treasury Office, 1814–1816

By order of Congress, several architects including George Hadfield were hired in 1814 to examine the ruined public buildings but only Hadfield's report survives. The Committee of the Whole House report from November 21, 1814, noted that all the architects consulted agreed:

> that the walls generally had not been materially damaged, and were not rendered unsafe, or insufficient to rebuild on, conformably either to the former plans, or to some variations suggested, or such as may be adopted as improvements in the rebuilding."[77]

Although the exterior walls of the Capitol, President's House, and executive offices were still standing, none had a roof and in most cases their interiors were either totally destroyed or in such a ruinous state they had to be dismantled before it was safe for workmen to begin rebuilding. The damage to the Treasury Fireproof's structure was negligible but document cases had to be replaced.

Hadfield wrote about rebuilding the Treasury and War Offices.

> These two Buildings in consequence of their having been executed entirely of brick, in the upper structure of the outward walls, have sustained, without material injury, the violence of excessive heat. The apparent and actual damage can be easily corrected by the facility with which bricks can be removed, and replaced in a Building; here also an advantage presents itself from a calamity by affording the opportunity of erecting these Buildings in the interior, of solid materials, and there by render them fireproof; an object often wished in their former state, for the certain preservation of the Public Documents from accidental fire.
>
> The preservation of these Buildings from injury by the weather, may be effected by covering the walls with plank, or Straw, during the ensuing winter.
>
> The expense necessary to restore these Buildings to their former state will be 37,000 Dollars.[78]

Hadfield also calculated that an additional $9,000 for each building would be needed to dismantle and cart away their "ruinous parts."

On February 13, 1815, Congress authorized President James Madison to borrow more than $500,000 from any bank in Washington to rebuild the public buildings. Debates in Congress during the previous months about moving the capital to some new location in the West—Ohio—galvanized local citizens to keep Washington as the capital; they fought to protect their investments of time in creating a settled community and of money in their property. A month later Madison appointed John P. Van Ness, president of the Bank of the Metropolis across the street from the Treasury Office, as well as Richard Bland Lee and Tench Ringgold, both major property owners, as a board of temporary commissioners to supervise the rebuilding. Van Ness's bank loaned the government most of the funds needed and the three men energetically set about organizing the city's rebirth.[79]

When the commissioners advertised for contractors to resurrect the public buildings in the spring of 1815, Mills was one of several architects to respond. But the commissioners called back Latrobe to rebuild the Capitol and Hoban to supervise reconstruction of the President's House and both executive offices. Hoban may well have been the architect who the previous fall had suggested to the congressional committee that variations on its original plan would improve the Treasury Office. His specifications make clear both the extent of the rebuilding and the introduction of new features.[80]

Despite Hadfield's recommendation to the contrary, the Treasury Office's interiors were rebuilt with wood joists and girders, its wood-framed roof covered with cypress shingles. Hoban specified sixteen dormer windows, six on the north, eight on the south, and one at each end, all having twelve "lights," or panes of glass, each measuring ten inches by twelve inches. In October 1819 draftsman William Blanchard drew plans of the three floors of the Treasury Office as Hoban had rebuilt them. (fig. I-20) Hoban redesigned the garret story to include more and better ventilated clerks' offices, eight feet high, by devising an unusual roof structure. In 1833 Washington builder William Archer described Hoban's roof because it contributed to the building's destruction in the disastrous fire that occurred that year.

> The cornice was of wood, and built on the ends of the joists on which the garret floor was laid, and the roof raised. These joists were connected through the whole width of the building, from one side to the other, and formed, as it were, a ventilator through. The cornice did not fit close to the wall, its distance from it varying as much as several inches in some places, and thereby permitting the smoke and flame which issued through the window to pass through to the ceiling joists and the rafters of the roof: it was from this cause alone, evidently, that the fire was communicated to the roof and upper part of the building—the smoke making its escape from various part of the roof at the same time that the fire was confined to the room before mentioned.[81]

The blue areas on Blanchard's watercolor of the third floor show the width of these shafts open to air—essentially two roofs with air passing between them—and the plan shows narrow openings on the outside walls set close to the partition walls, apparently for ventilating individual rooms rather than for light. Hoban did not live to see his clever, humanitarian ventilating system accelerate the 1833 fire, having died in December 1831.

Hoban's specifications called for interior ceilings built of plaster-covered wood lath but the partition walls on the main two stories remained brick and the fireproof rooms on both the main stories had iron doors. Doors in the garret story were to have four panels each with ovolo molding on one side and raised panels on the other, while those on the main floors were divided into six panels with "ovolo and flat pannells [sic] on both sides." Doric columns framed the inside of the north door as well as the door that led from the corridor into the vestibule, giving visitors departing at either of the formal entrances a touch of sober elegance. Blanchard's inscription on his 1819 drawing confirmed that the four columns shown on the south porch were planned but as yet not built.[82]

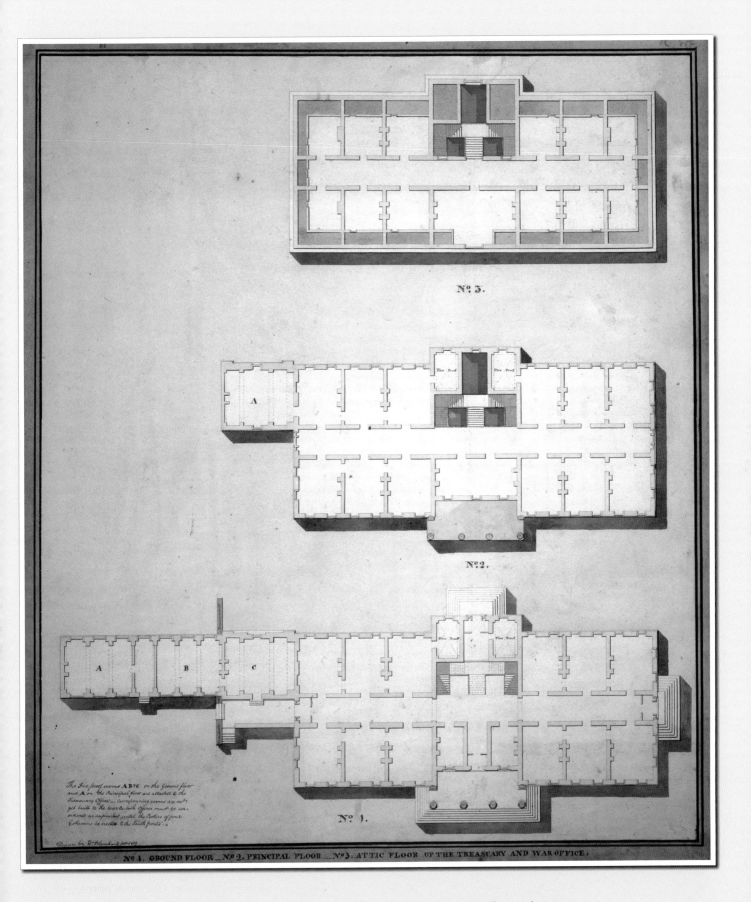

No. 3.

No. 2.

No. 1.

The Fire proof rooms ABYC on the Ground floor
and A on the principal floor are attached to the
Treasury Office. Corresponding rooms are not
yet built to the War & other Offices must be considered accomplished until the Portico of four
Columns be added to the South front &c.

Drawn by H. Blanchard Jan 1799

No. 1. GROUND FLOOR — No. 2. PRINCIPAL FLOOR — No. 3. ATTIC FLOOR OF THE TREASURY AND WAR OFFICE.

I-20 Hoban's rebuilding of the Treasury Office included a novel roof structure to ventilate attic rooms.

Washington house carpenter Henry Smith and New York mason Peter Morte submitted separate proposals to rebuild the Treasury Office, but the commissioners hired them as a team and they signed the same contract on April 14. It took more than eight months to repair the fireproof building even with the help of seven stonecutters from the President's House. Blanchard's 1819 plan of the fireproof shows Hoban added additional security measures to Latrobe's building. A door on the south side of the vault opened onto an enclosed porch that led to the Treasury Office, stairs on the south, and a gate in the President's wall. Hoban also built an internal wall east of the fireproof's entrance and cut a door between its three easternmost bays and the vault. This improvement doubled the size of the most secure storage area while it created additional barriers for future raiders to penetrate.[83]

In late February 1816 Hoban predicted the Treasury Office's completion on the first of April; the new double roof and additional garret offices lengthening its construction time. The final cost of rebuilding the Treasury Office (including the fireproof) was $37,262.14, while the War Office was reconstructed for $31,541.86. Who determined that the shingle roofs of the Treasury and War Offices were a fire hazard is unknown, but between 1818 and 1822 their roofs were covered with slate piecemeal as Congress appropriated funds. Within two years of the Treasury Office's completion, Commissioner of Public Buildings Samuel Lane was criticizing the workmanship. In his January 1820 report to Congress, Lane noted: "It appears the work was done by contract with certain individuals by the former commissioners. The materials employed and the workmanship of a large part of the wood work are highly objectionable, and will require to be renewed within a few years."[84]

"Alteration of Treasury Offices:" Depicting the Treasury Office

Some uncertainty arises about the Treasury Office's exterior appearance in 1800 and 1817 because alterations occurred and the visual evidence is contradictory. In 1815 Hoban replaced all the exterior doors and windows, specifying double doors for the east, west, and north entrances. Each half of the doors was two-and-one-half inches thick with four panels, the double doors framed by "a large fan and sidelights." The double south door had a fan light above it but narrow walls separated the door from the tall arched windows that lighted the rooms on both sides of the vestibule. These specifications for the ground floor seem to replicate, or to nearly replicate, the original construction.[85]

Two changes, however, may have occurred with the windows on the second floor during the rebuilding. They may have been lengthened in 1815, their sills resting on the stone belt course that encircled the structure, or the meeting of belt course and window sills may have occurred in the 1790s when Hoban and Harbaugh agreed to lengthen windows once the building was underway. A similar uncertainty exists with the tripartite Venetian windows—ones that featured a tall, arched center window flanked by lower side lights—in the 1800 building. Did Venetian windows originally light the second floor corridor at its east and west ends or did Hoban add them in 1815?

An 1817 watercolor helps to clarify matters. (fig. I-21) Baron Hyde de Neuville, France's new minister to the United States, forwarded his letter of credence from New York to the State Department in June 1816. Exiled during Napoleon's reign in France, the Baron and Baroness had been living in New York since 1801, where the Baroness painted streetscapes and genre scenes, a pastime she happily continued in Washington until the couple returned to France

I-21 Hyde de Neuville's 1817 watercolor is the best view of the rebuilt Treasury Office's appearance.

in 1821. During the summer of 1817, from one of the windows in her home on the south side of F Street, Hyde de Neuville painted the Bank of the Metropolis diagonally across the street, the former tavern where three years earlier British officers dined by the firelight provided by the burning Treasury Office and President's House.

Hyde de Neuville meticulously recorded the east end and part of the south facade of the Treasury Office on the west side of 15th Street. It had a Venetian window lighting the central corridor on the second story, while the suspect 1804 woodcut had two windows in this area. (see fig. I–13) Hyde de Neuville's image shows a stone belt course immediately beneath the second story windows, while the woodcut placed the belt course between the two stories. Both artists agreed that the east entrance had a fan and side lights but depicted the east porch differently. Hyde de Neuville showed a shallow porch with just a few stone steps on its sides

leading up from the unpaved street, while the woodcut has the entire building sitting higher in relation to the street and, very prominently, an entrance into the basement story in the center of a much deeper porch. Between 1818 and 1820 the State Office was built directly north of the Treasury Office at the corner of G Street. This "1804" view of the Treasury Office might be interpreted as the east end of the State Office done after the grade of 15th Street was first lowered in 1846–47. The State Office, however, had a tripartite window lighting its second story corridor instead of the old fashioned Venetian window on the Treasury Office. Moreover, the State Office was not begun until early 1818, more than six months after Hyde de Neuville painted the view of F and 15th streets from her window.

Hyde de Neuville painted a panoramic view of the President's House in 1821, now flanked by four executive offices, from the southern edge of what within five years would formally become Lafayette Park. (fig. I-22) The just-completed State and Navy offices loom in the foreground, as they rightly should, because they were larger than the two earlier buildings in the background. Moreover, each has its belt course between the two main stories as well as shallow lateral staircases on its ends. Surviving photographs of these two buildings verify that, indeed, they were built with belt courses centered between the windows of the first and second stories, probably because they were not only longer and wider than the earlier office buildings but also taller. Oddly, the belt courses of the Treasury and War offices in the background of the 1821 watercolor are also between the two stories; this may be attributable to the painting's small scale. Hadfield's design called for the higher belt course and this, in conjunction with other verifiable details in her 1817 watercolor, argues that this aspect of the English architect's plan was built at the Treasury Office and almost surely the War Office, as well. It is unlikely Hadfield designed the old-fashioned

Venetian windows; they were surely Hoban's contribution. The lateral staircase was the result of a surveying mistake, albeit a fortuitous one, because as the grade of 15th Street was repeatedly lowered, more steps could be added without projecting onto the street.

In 1830, a year after President Andrew Jackson took office, several improvements were undertaken. In June stonemason John P. Pepper replaced the Aquia sandstone porch on the south with a better quality stone, perhaps in anticipation of adding columns to complete that facade. Robert Mills, who returned to Washington in 1829, was hired by the Treasury Department during the summer of 1830 to design and oversee construction of a privy and "engine house" that sheltered a pump used to operate the water and sewer systems installed on the President's Grounds during the previous two years. Located between the Treasury and State offices, this substantial building of brick and stone and lit by an octagonal cupola was entered through pedimented doors. In October Mills made drawings and estimated the cost of an iron fence to enclose both the Treasury and State offices. Charles Burton's 1830 drawing of the State Office, engraved and published in

I-22 The State Office (left) and the Navy Office (right) were larger than the original two buildings.

Fortress of Finance: The United States Treasury Building

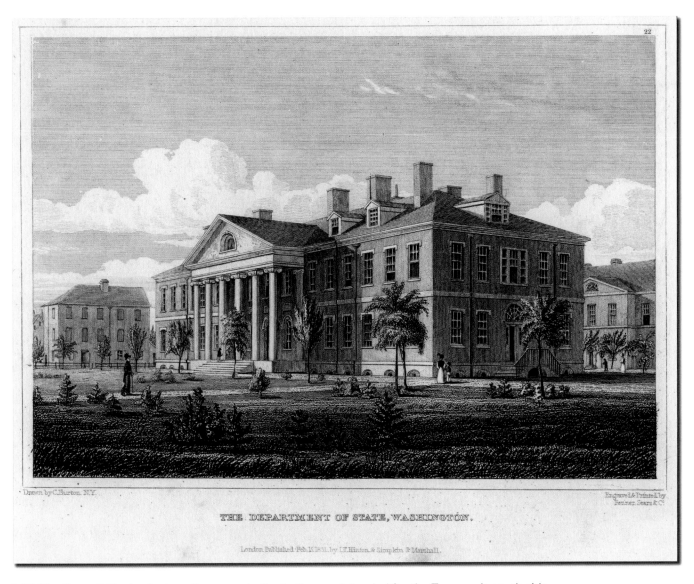

Drawn by C. Burton, N.Y.

Engraved & Printed by
Fenner, Sears & Co.

THE DEPARTMENT OF STATE, WASHINGTON.

London Published Feb. 16, 1831, by I.T.Hinton. & Simpkin & Marshall.

I-23 The State Office's giant portico was similar to the one intended for the Treasury's south side.

1831, shows its predecessor, a wood rail fence, and part of the Treasury Office's projecting north central wing. (fig. I-23) In December 1830 Mills suggested strengthening the single-story portion of the fireproof that he probably worked on as Latrobe's apprentice.[86]

On March 22, 1831, Mills was appointed "Draughtsman of public surveys" in the Treasury Department's Land Office, a position he held until about 1834. His duties there seem to have included consultation on all of the department's architectural and engineering matters. In October 1832 he sent Asbury Dickens, now chief clerk in the Department of State, drawings

and a description of his scheme of cisterns and piping to supply drinking water into the two neighboring offices. Water fountains also would be erected on all four sides of each building and a fire plug installed at the corner of 15th Street and Pennsylvania Avenue. Because his appointment as a clerk was a part-time position, Mills concurrently was making designs for several Washington projects in an effort to establish himself as the city's leading architect. He hoped to succeed Charles Bulfinch who had completed the Capitol and returned to Boston in 1829.[87]

In 1831 Mills made sketches and estimates, "Alterations of Treasury offices," to fireproof

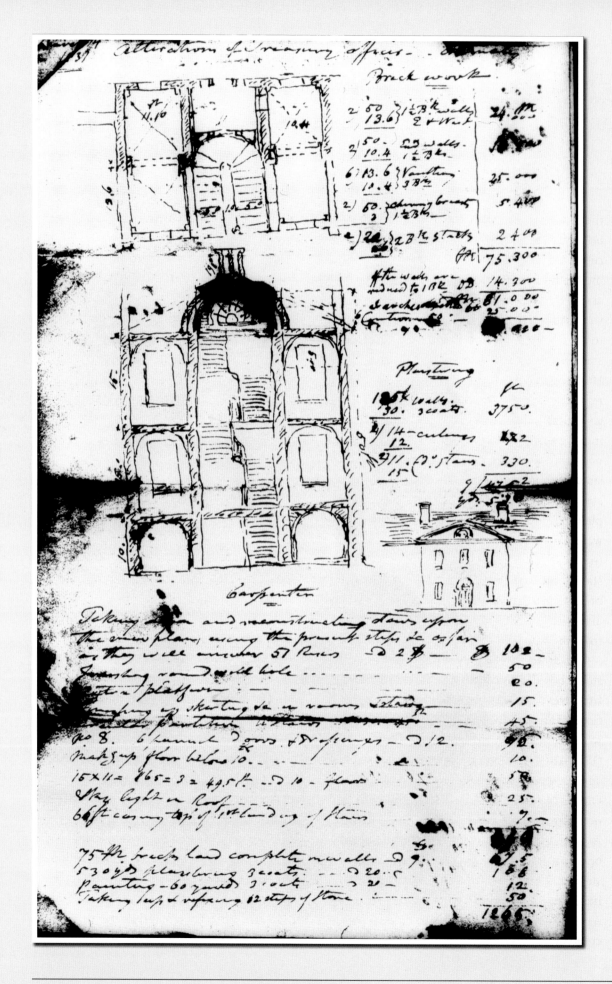

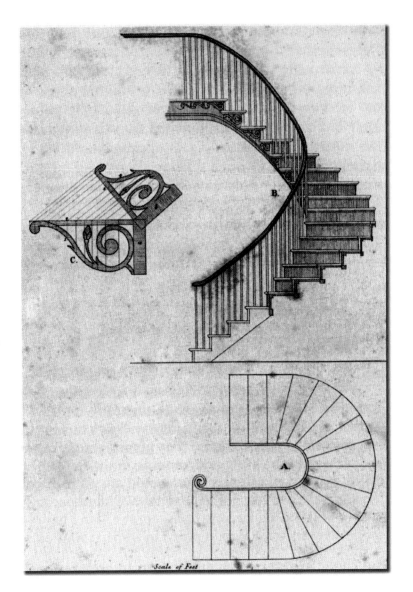

the central wing, double the size of the existing brick vaulted rooms, and erect new ones in the cellar. (fig. I-24) This project involved increasing the thickness of the four brick walls running across the building's width that enclosed the vaulted rooms. A major part of Mills's work was to rebuild Hoban's 1817–19 double, open-well staircase, which probably followed the pattern of Harbaugh's 1798–1800 stairs. Its capaciousness reflected the constant movements of messengers, clerks, and visitors throughout the building. Because Mills's two new fireproof rooms occupied two-thirds of the space where Hoban's staircase had been, he designed a new dog-leg staircase in the middle of the cross corridor. He planned cantilevered treads five feet wide with wedge-shaped boards on a semicircular landing (not built) at the turning point. The curve of the staircase was set within a niche supported by brick arches that were to span the stairwell that also buttressed the new, heavier walls that rose from the basement to the garret.[88]

Mills specified stone treads for the cellar stairs, but planned on a wood staircase, reusing fifty-one of the existing treads for the upper two floors. His model seems to have been the spiral wood staircase in John Tayloe's Octagon House (1798–1800) at the corner of New York Avenue and 18th Street, three blocks from the Treasury Office. In 1805 Owen Biddle published details of such a staircase in *The Young Carpenter's Assistant* (Philadelphia, 1805). (fig. I-25) In borrowing the shape and structure of these staircases, Mills continued his own tradition of including some key motif from notable earlier American sources, apparently integral to his credo of being a thoroughly American architect.

"The Fearless and Indefatigable Exertions of the Citizens:" Conflagration of the Treasury Office, 1833

Many Washingtonians were on the streets during the early hours of Sunday, March 31, 1833, when the Treasury Office was destroyed by fire; taverns were still open at 3:00 a.m. About 2:20 a.m. Charles Pryse was crossing 14th Street on the north side of Pennsylvania Avenue, "between Dr. Jones' and McCarty's tavern," when he saw the smoke. He apparently had his wits about him because when he saw the sash fall out of the room where the blaze started, the room "one sheet of fire," he ran to the Franklin Engine firehouse located at the corner of 14th Street and Pennsylvania Avenue. There he met several people looking for its key, so he "went to Mr. Fuller's, where he knew there was a key; procured the key and a pair of horses, which were immediately put to the engine and driven to the fire by Mr. Fuller." Fuller's American Hotel was on the northwest corner of Pennsylvania Avenue and 14th Street.[89]

The engine arrived about 3:00 a.m. and was hooked to the hydrant on 15th Street between the Treasury and State offices. A second private hydrant across the street belonged to the Bank of the Metropolis. The second engine to arrive, brought from "the west of the city," came about half an hour later, and one from Georgetown "somewhat later." The Capitol's watchman rang the bell at the engine house about 200 yards south of the Capitol as soon as he realized there was a fire. The Capitol's engine arrived at the fire nearly two hours after it began; about ten minutes later the watchman saw the center section of the roof fall and "some water was sent through the hose, but not enough to reach into the building, and was perfectly useless."[90]

While the volunteer firemen were commandeering their equipment, others turned out in numbers to alert officials or fight the fire. William Greer shouted the alarm about 2:30 a.m. when the fire was still in its early stages, then ran to arouse Chief Clerk Asbury Dickins who lived on the north side of F Street between 12th and 13th streets. William M. Steuart also did not attempt to enter the building but went first to the house of the chief clerk in the Register's Office, Michael Nourse, who lived on the west side of 13th Street between E and F streets. His next stop was at Rev. James Laurie's on the south side of Pennsylvania Avenue between 14th and 15th streets, and then on to nearby taverns, "crying fire during all this time." Steuart recognized that Nourse, a Treasury clerk since 1798, and Laurie, a clerk in the Register's Office since 1808, as custodians of the department's impor-

tant archive of settled accounts would want to be informed of the disaster right away.[91]

Abraham Butler, who claimed to be the first person to arrive, observed that the fire was confined to the northwest room adjacent to the central block. Andrew M. Laub, a disbursing officer on the secretary's staff whose duties also included superintending the building, occupied this office. His office was the easternmost of the Secretary's suite of four rooms and shared its east wall with one of Mills's newly extended fireproof rooms. At 6:00 p.m. the previous evening, guard Isaac Goddard did not extinguish the fires in these rooms because Dickens was planning to return after dinner to finish a report—the end of the quarter being that Monday. Dickens's room was between Laub's and Secretary McLane's offices, the three connected by doors perpendicular to the wall adjoining the corridor.[92]

Soon after 2:30 a.m. Butler pounded on the north door, which was opened by a badly frightened Goddard, the fire "then just visible on the roof, probably communicated through the windows by means of the wooden cornice." James Cummings was early to arrive, one of several people who ventured up the stairs to save what records in the second-floor offices they could. Although the west corridor was filling with smoke, he broke open the door into the office of a clerk in the secretary's office, William T. Read, directly across from Laub's room and was able to make three trips out with arms full of books and papers before the corridor filled with flames. Just before 3:00 a.m. Robert P. Anderson, who lived two blocks away—knowing the roof had already caught fire—also ran up the stairs and into the corridor next to Laub's and Dickins's rooms, the latter now on fire. On his way down the stairs he heard the roof fall in one of the rooms. Anderson and others raised a ladder on the building's south side to get into Francis Dickins's office, the middle room across the corridor from those on fire, and all of the men began carrying and throwing books and papers outside.[93]

Daniel Boyd, on arriving at the top of the stairs, turned left into the east wing to save what records he could in the Comptroller's six offices; some doors were locked, others not. Boyd immediately "went down to Mr. Causten's [on 15th Street directly across from the Treasury Office's east door] and procured an axe" and also brought a hose up a ladder to the east end of the second-story. Pryse and the others manning one of the engines carried a spout of two connected hoses to the head of the stairs "to play upon this point, in order to preserve the passage and stairs for the persons employed in removing the books, papers, &c." He thought "their exertions retarded the flames about the stairway, and contributed to the preservation of books and papers, but made no impression upon the roof." Others testified that the amount of water coming from the hoses was simply too little to have any appreciable effect.[94]

When Asbury Dickins arrived shortly before 3:00 a.m., he saw light from flames in his office but nonetheless ran up the stairs to the second floor only to be met by several people who told him that "it was all on fire." Descending the steps, he ordered lights to be brought to the first floor rooms so that people could see to remove documents. Charles Lyons and Isaac Craven first attempted to raise a ladder to windows on the south side but it was not tall enough. They moved the ladder to the fireproof building, climbed onto its roof, hauled the ladder up and put it against the west wall of the secretary's library. Philo Hale removed the frame of the semicircular window high in the center of that wall and the men then lowered themselves down to the mantel about six feet below.[95] Asbury Dickins was the fourth man in and, finding Latrobe's fireproof library room untouched by the fire, he:

> first went to the door communicating with the Secretary's eastern room: the room was full of flame and smoke, and he immedi-

ately shut the door. His first endeavors were to save those things in the Secretary's western room which he thought most valuable, and, with the assistance of his son Thomas and others, … every thing was thrown out. After this he descended the ladder, and assisted in preserving the books, papers, and property.[96]

Dickins estimated he was in the secretary's library from forty-five minutes to an hour, directing the removal of everything portable, including furniture thrown out of windows. A fire hose was then brought through the north window of the library and out the semicircular window on its west side, and water was sprayed though a hole cut in the fireproof's slate roof to forestall the fire's spread. Although its ceiling was vaulted in brick, a wood truss roof above it supported the slates. If the trusses caught fire, the weight and pressure of the falling slates, they feared, would collapse the vaults and fire destroy the mahogany cases and the documents they contained.

Once the fire ignited the roof of the Treasury Office's west wing, it quickly raced eastward and the roof collapsed into the garret but the floor did not immediately cave in. Men were still removing records in second-story offices when the staircase burst into flames, but all safely climbed out windows and descended ladders retrieved from wherever they could be found. Because of the concerted effort of department officials and local residents, some of the furniture and most of the records on the first story and many records in the rooms on the second story east of the central block were carried or thrown to safety.

> Secretary McLane,
>   though not among the earliest, was nevertheless early in arriving at the scene of the conflagration. He soon saw the progress which the fire was making, and from

the wholly inadequate means of checking or subduing it, that the entire building would probably be consumed. His attention was therefore, immediately and almost exclusively, directed to the preservation of the papers and records in the Accounting Offices and in the Register's Office [located on the first floor] … Under the direction of the Secretary, the several collections of papers, books, records, etc., that were made were placed in charge of the clerks or well known and trusty citizens. By these united exertions all the important papers belonging to those offices have been saved. Those belonging to the Treasurer's Office have also been preserved.[97]

Records from the offices of the Secretary, Comptroller, Treasurer, and Register stored in the garret were beyond hope of being saved. In addition, the south pediment room contained the papers used by clerk Samuel C. Potter, who was "issuing the scrip of the revolutionary bounty lands," the vast tracts on the western frontier currently being settled that Congress had granted to Revolutionary War officers a half century earlier. No one involved thought to retrieve records stored in the cellar, perhaps because lights were not available, or they feared being trapped inside a collapsing building. The fate of many documents saved by the firefighters is uncertain. "The Washington [United States] Telegraph says, that on Capitol Hill, the burnt papers were whirling about like autumnal leaves; and from the City Hall and Court House, a person might have walked to the Department, a distance of eight hundred or a thousand yards, entirely on them." By noon on Sunday, McLane agreed to rent a row of five buildings on the south side of Pennsylvania Avenue between 14th and 15th streets within sight and smell of the ruins. By 2:00 p.m. what remained of the department's records and furniture were moved to these temporary quar-

ters or into the fireproof. (fig. I-26) The clerks worked systematically on Monday and Tuesday to get their papers in order and by Wednesday the Treasury Department was again fully operational.[98]

President Jackson ordered a comprehensive investigation to be carried out by the other three departmental secretaries and the attorney general. Many of the men who either witnessed or participated in saving the records, or tried to save the building, were interviewed and their sworn testimonies witnessed by William Cranch, Chief Judge of the District Court. Was the fire caused by negligence in tending a fire in the grate in Laub's room or was it a fault in the building's construction? A hot coal falling and igniting the carpet and then the floor at first seemed likely, but the fireplaces all had broad stone hearths and several men's testimonies cleared the watchman of neglect. Charles L. Coltman, a local builder who had contracted with Mills to work on the 1831 renovations, testified that the fireplaces in the secretary's suite had been retrofitted with coal grates. His statement about how the flues had been rebuilt in the walls eliminated the fireplaces as the fire's cause. William Archer, also a Washington builder, visited the ruin after giving his initial testimony and examined the flues in Laub's room and subsequently all the flues in the secretary's suite and was "satisfied that not a shadow of doubt existed as to the security of the flues" in the walls and ceilings.[99]

The investigation concluded that the cause of the fire was a mystery but it was no secret that the city needed a better water supply system and better firefighting equipment. Some hoses leaked; couplings between hoses from different companies did not match; hoses that did link together were still not long enough to reach Tiber Creek when the water flow from the hydrants dried up; and, the "hydrant near the building [the bank's] had no fire-plug to which the hose could be attached." Moreover, the

I-26 After the 1833 fire the department moved a block southeast to new rowhouses on Pennsylvania Avenue.

Treasury's one ladder was believed by some to have been loaned to Asbury Methodist Church on 14th Street but later found by others leaning against the wall surrounding the President's Grounds. All of the heads of the fire companies, equipped and maintained at the government's expense, noted that their requests for better equipment were never met because of budget limitations. In their testimonies, both Archer and Asbury Dickins stated that the Treasury Office could have been saved if the fire companies had been properly equipped and sufficient water available.[100]

Two years later another major fire occurred at the Patent Office, the former Blodgett's Hotel, resulting in a tremendous loss of government documents. On March 13, 1837, Secretary of the Treasury Levi Woodbury wrote Noland that "the President has directed the appropriation made at the last session of Congress for the purchase of a fire engine and apparatus for the Treasury Building & the enlargement of the engine house to be placed under your direction." At the end of October, the *National Intelligencer* reported on a grand procession of four hundred sixty firemen, members of seven fire companies, to show off their new equipment. The Franklin Fire Company's engine was drawn by "Gov. [Treasury Secretary] Woodbury's beautiful span of bays, elegantly caparisoned." Later nineteenth-century fires in the city were not as serious as those in the 1830s simply because volunteer firemen were more plentiful and much better equipped.[101]

In its coverage of the investigation, widely reprinted, the *National Intelligencer* reported "all the Revolutionary War records which were in the Treasury Building before the fire, are preserved," but that inaccuracy may have been part of the department's minimizing of the fire's seriousness. The fate of these sacred documents was of the greatest concern to the public. A circular signed by McLane on April 12, 1833, asked all government officers around the country, as well as private citizens, to copy letters sent to or from the Secretary of the Treasury "from the Establishment of the department until the 31st of March" (with some stated exceptions), in order to reconstruct the department's central files. The biggest immediate problem was outstanding bills with their accompanying vouchers and it took some time to reconstruct and pay these. The losses, however, reverberated for decades. Revolutionary War veteran John Leach, born in 1759 in a house that then stood in the middle of what became Washington Circle, was unable in his old age (he lived to 103) to get a pension because his enlistment roll was "presumed to have been burnt in the Treasury building along with other papers," the *National Intelligencer* reported in 1862.[102]

The 200 to 300 men who were at the scene of the March 31 fire, many putting themselves in dangerous situations, knew the importance of the Treasury Department's records. So did the arsonists, brothers Richard and Henry White, who were hired by someone to destroy the evidence of a fraudulent pension claim. Their crime was discovered two years after the fire through an informer, William Hicks, who alerted Henry Dilworth Gilpin, the U.S. Attorney for Pennsylvania. In March 1836 a District of Columbia grand jury indicted the White brothers, Richard arrested in New York and brought secretly to Washington in April. John Kelly, Deputy Marshall of Ohio, pursued Henry

White to New Orleans, arrested him on July 21 and delivered him to Washington's district attorney, Francis Scott Key.[103]

Henry White admitted guilt, saying he entered the Treasury Office and placed a combustible chemical mixture in several desks while his brother remained outside on watch. On January 17, 1837, Henry White was sentenced to ten years in the penitentiary. Richard White was tried four times, in December 1836, January 1837, May 1837, and June 1838, the first three trials resulting in hung juries because the two-year statue of limitations expired before Richard's arrest and the last in acquittal because the jury found him innocent. During Richard's trials, avidly reported in the *National Intelligencer*, it came out that not only the defendants, but their accusers as well, were habitual petty criminals. Moreover, one witness quoted Richard as saying "that but for Harry's bad management he would have made something handsome; (for it seems that Henry fired the wrong apartment, and that the papers intended to be burnt, being in another room, were rescued from the flames)." As a result of Richard's verdicts, President Jackson asked Congress to revise the laws on the destruction of public property and "to repeal entirely the statute of limitation in all criminal cases."[104]

The *New Orleans Bulletin* reported in June 1836 that Mr. Hubbard, "a person charged with having set fire to the Treasury Building in Washington, some three years since, was arrested on June 9, while in the New Orleans Post Office, by an officer from New York." In February 1837 *The Huntress* took the *Congressional Globe* to task for prejudicing Richard White's trial by claiming that he confessed. The *Huntress* further claimed that Robert Temple of Vermont, who practiced frauds against the government by collecting false pensions arising from war claims, was actually behind the Treasury Office's fire. Henry was pardoned in 1841 because "circumstances have come to light, which make it very doubtful whether White was guilty." No one was subsequently tried as the fire's instigator.[105]

In early April 1833, immediately after the fire, Secretary McLane asked Robert Mills (who is not recorded as having witnessed it) for "a 'minute description of the Old Treasury building, with the chimneys, number of Rooms, and how occupied, with fire places and fixtures, accompanied with a Diagram,' shewing [sic] the plan of every floor, as they were previous to the fire." Mills's plans of the first, second, and garret floors (figs. I-27, I-28, I-29) accompanying his April 6, 1833, report, are among the most valuable records concerning the architectural development of the Treasury Office and Treasury Fireproof. They indicated not only the vaulted rooms, but the placement of windows, doors, and fireplaces and the internal arrangement of most of the building, including significant changes Mills made to the central block in 1831. Very importantly, Mills recorded on his drawings the names and functions of the occupants of each of the rooms in 1833, helpful in understanding the bureaucratic hierarchy within the department.[106]

Mills was quick to note in his report that records stored in the four vaulted rooms in the Treasury Office and all those in the fireproof wing survived. The Treasury Fireproof that incorporated the Secretary of the Treasury's library was intact, as were "a few small rooms adjoining the centre block of the building, on the north side, which, from being vaulted, escaped comparatively the general destruction; the wooden cases fixed against the walls here are still standing uninjured." Moreover, it is likely that Mills's thickening of the walls of the western fireproof room in the Treasury Office contributed to the survival of the staircase long enough for many records to be carried down from the second floor. In April 1833 he not only recommended complete vaulting for the future building to replace the Treasury Office,

but suggested iron doors between all rooms and into halls, and even "sheet iron" filing cases. Mills's recommendations became standard in the construction of the government's customs houses, courthouses, post offices, assay offices, and other buildings containing important archives, beginning with his own design in June 1833 for the New London, Connecticut, Custom House. In his 1833 annual report, Roger B. Taney (McLane's successor as Secretary of the Treasury) was more circumspect in approaching Congress about funding a new building. "It will become necessary to provide another building, and the loss already sustained in the documents and records of this office show the propriety of erecting it upon a different plan from the former one, and of placing the archives of the Government in a situation less exposed to danger."[107]

Many lessons were learned during the Treasury Department's first thirty-three years in Washington. Oliver Wolcott's request in 1796 for forty rooms, although not provided in the Treasury Office itself, was supplemented by messengers' houses and the fireproof because the department needed a variety of spaces to function efficiently. As the country expanded, the Treasury Department's services to the rest of the government expanded disproportionately because the many people who worked for the government, creating the physical infrastructure of roads, canals, waterways, and public buildings and the governing structure at the ports, county seats, and post offices in each of the new states and territories, had to be paid. The Treasury Department's central bureaucratic offices, so interdependent on its system of checks and balances that ready access to each other was crucial, required a large building responsive to its methods of operating. The loss of records in three fires had been disruptive as well as destructive. The need for a fireproof building that protected not only stored records but also ledgers that were consulted daily, and papers left on desks, was finally acknowledged

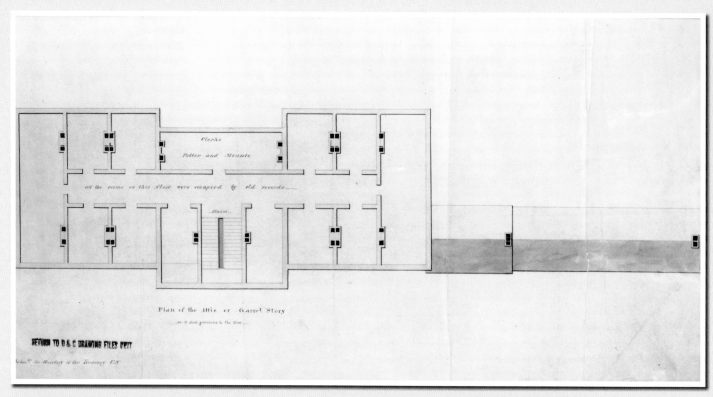

I-27 After the fire Mills made detailed drawings of the Treasury Office to aid in determining its cause.

I-28 Newly built coal grates in the secretary's suite were initially supposed to be the fire's source.

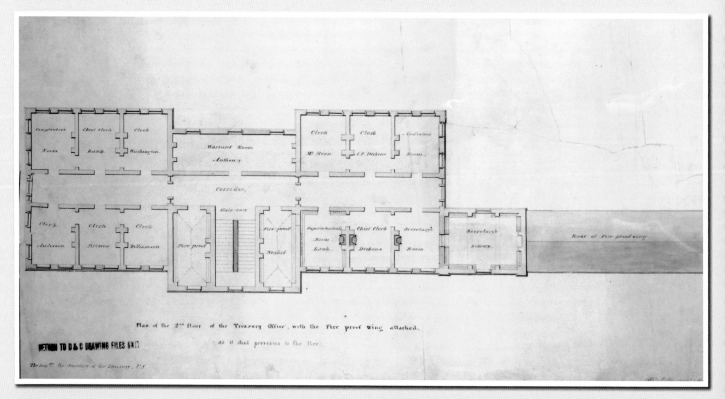

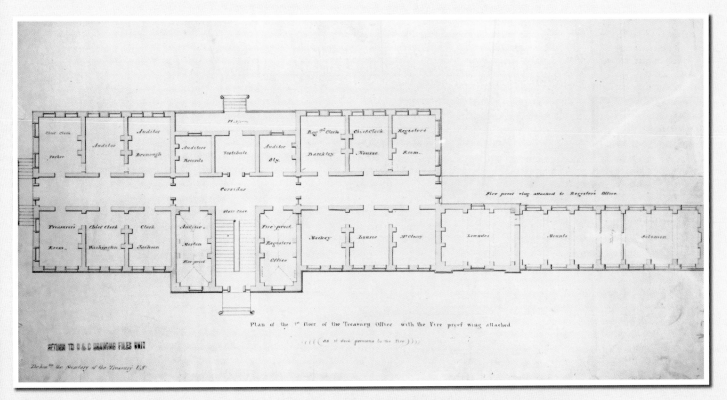

I-29 Most documents stored in the fireproof survived but losses were extensive in the main building.

by many, rather than a few. The Treasury evolved into the most powerful of the executive departments, its officers dealing with national and international financial institutions housed in marble temples of fortune. The country's prestige demanded a bigger and better Treasury building, a temple emblematic of national prosperity and financial stability. The challenge was convincing Congress to sanction and fund such a building.

Endnotes, Chapter One

1 Hamilton to Edward Carrington, May 26, 1792, in Harold C. Syrett, ed., *The Papers of Alexander Hamilton* (New York: Columbia University Press, 1966), 21:442. Abby L. Gilbert, "Department of the Treasury," in George T. Kurian, comp., *A Historical Guide to the U.S. Government* (New York: Oxford University Press, 1998), 581.

2 Gilbert, "Treasury," 581.

3 Jacob Ernest Cooke, *Alexander Hamilton* (New York: Charles Scribner's Sons, 1982), 73.

4 Ibid.

5 Noble Cunningham, *The Jeffersonian Republicans, The Formation of Party Organization* (Chapel Hill: University of North Carolina Press, 1957), 98–9.

6 Gilbert, "Treasury," 583.

7 Edgar J. McManus, "William Harris Crawford," in John A. Garraty and Mark C. Carnes, eds., *American National Biography* (hereafter cited as *ANB*), New York: Oxford University Press, 1999), V:713. "Rooms Proposed to be occupied," Estimates and Statements by the Register of the Treasury, 1791–1858, entry 28, (hereafter cited as entry 28), 12:51; Records of the Bureau of the Public Debt, Record Group 53, (hereafter cited as RG 53); National Archives at College Park, MD (hereafter cited as NACP).

8 U.S. Treasury Department, *The United States Treasury Register* (Washington: Government Printing Office, 1883), vols. 8–11.

9 Donald Jackson and others, eds., *Diaries of George Washington* (Charlottesville: University Press of Virginia, 1976–1979), V:165.

10 Commissioners to White, February 5, 1796, Records of the Office of Public Buildings and Public Parks of the National Capital, Letters Sent, entry 6, RG 42 (hereafter cited as RG 42), National Archives Building, Washington, DC (hereafter cited as NAB).

11 Ibid. and Commissioners to John Adams, April 18, 1798, entry 6, RG 42, NAB.

12 C.M. Harris, ed., *Papers of William Thornton, 1791–1802* (Charlottesville: University Press of Virginia, 1992), 372. White to Commissioners, January 13, 18, and 20, 1796; entry 1, RG 42, NAB.

13 White to Commissioners, January 18, 1796; Alexander White, printed circular, January 21, 1796; White to Commissioners, two letters, January 23, 1796; all entry 1, RG 42, NAB.

14 White to Commissioners, January 31, 1796, entry 1; Commissioners to White, February, 5, 1796, entry 6; both RG 42, NAB.

15 Wolcott to White, February 1, 1796, entry 1, RG 42, NAB. "Extract from the Report of the Committee for the Government's Removal to Washington," *Records of the Columbia Historical Society* (hereafter cited as *RCHS*) 9 (1906): 228–30.

16 Ibid. and White to Commissioners, May 9, 1796, entry 1, RG 42, NAB.

17 Commissioners to Washington, October 1, 1796, entry 6, RG 42, NAB.

18 Washington to Commissioners, October 21, 1796, "The Writings of George Washington Relating to the National Capital," *RCHS* 17 (1914): 167–8.

19 Harris, *Thornton*, 458.

20 Commissioners to Washington, January 25, 1797, entry 6, RG 42, NAB.

21 "Writings of Washington," *RCHS* 17 (1914):185, 189, 196.

22 Howard Colvin, *A Biographical Dictionary of British Architects, 1600–1840* (New Haven: Yale University Press, 1995), 443–4.

23 Commissioners to Lovering, November 18, 1797; Commissioners to Members of Congress, November 25, 1797; Commissioners to Hadfield, January 12, 1798; Commissioners to Lovering, May 22, 1798; all entry 6, RG 42, NAB.

24 White to Commissioners, March 8, 1798, entry 1, RG 42, NAB.

25 Madison to Jefferson, April 15, 1798, in Gaillard Hunt, ed., *The Writings of James Madison* (New York: G.P. Putnam's Sons, 1906): 6:318. White to Commissioners, March 11, 1798, entry 1, RG 42, NAB.

26 Commissioners to Adams, March 15, April 18 and 20, May 7, 1798, entry 6, RG 42, NAB. "Writings of Washington," 199–200.

27 Commissioners' draft soliciting bids, May 7, 1798, entry 6, RG 42, NAB.

28 Commissioners to stonecutters, April 16, 1798, entry 6, RG 42, NAB. The commissioners' inept handling of labor issues relating to the public buildings is examined in detail in Robert James Kapsch, "The Labor History of the Construction and Reconstruction of the White House, 1793–1817," (PhD diss., University of Maryland, 1993), 254–307.

29 Commissioners' draft, May 7, 1798, entry 6, RG 42, NAB.

30 Hadfield to Commissioners, May 14, 1798, entry 1, RG 42, NAB. Commissioners to Hadfield, May 15, 1798, entry 6, RG 42, NAB.

31 Hadfield to Commissioners, May 16, 1798, entry 1, RG 42, NAB.

32 Commissioners to Hadfield, May 18, 28, 1798, entry 6, RG 42, NAB. Hadfield to Commissioners, May 29, 1798, entry 1, RG 42, NAB. Pickering to Commissioners, n.d., [c. June 13–15, 1798,] Timothy Pickering Papers, Massachusetts Historical Society, microfilm reel 8.

33 Harris, *Thornton*, 454–62. Commissioners to Pickering, June 25, 1798; Commissioners to Hadfield, June 18, 1798; both entry 6, RG 42, NAB. Pickering to Commissioners, [c. June 13–15, 1798], Pickering Papers, reel 8.

34 Commissioners to Pickering, June 25, 1798, entry 6, RG 42, NAB. George Hadfield, Petition, January 19, 1821, Reports of Committee on Expenditures on Public Buildings, entry 11.52, Records of the U.S. House of Representatives, RG 233, NAB.

35 Hadfield to Jefferson, March 27, 1801, Thomas Jefferson Papers (hereafter cited as Jefferson Papers), General Correspondence, reel 23, Library of Congress. "We are happy to hear," *Washington Federalist,* May 16, 1803, 2. "New Jail in Washington City is Completed," *National Intelligencer,* February 11, 1803, 2. George Hadfield, Hand-drawn plan of President's Grounds, 1808; G3852,W46 1828 [misdated by cataloguer], W8 Vault, Geography and Map Division, Library of Congress. Receipted Accounts, entry 19, RG 42, NAB.

36 Lovering to Commissioners, July 10, 1798, entry 1, RG 42, NAB.

37 Ibid.

38 White to Commissioners, January 31; February 15, 1796, entry 1, RG 42, NAB. Margaret Burri, "A New View of Blodgett's Hotel," *Washington History* 2 (Spring 1990): 103–06.

39 William Seale, *The President's House* (Washington: White House Historical Association, 1986), I:22–36.

40 "Writings of Washington," 148.

41 Commissioners' draft of newspaper advertisement, May 7, 1798; Commissioners to Hoban, May 12 and 22, 1798; Commissioners to Lovering, June 23, 1798; all entry 6, RG 42, NAB. Martin I.J. Griffin, "James Hoban. The Architect and Builder of the White House and the Superintendent of the Building of the Capitol at Washington," *American Catholic Historical Researches* 3 (1907): 45. The contractors submitting estimates for the Treasury Office were invited to compete for the War Department contract the following year. Commissioners to Lovering, September 8, 1798; Commissioners to Hoban, Blagden, Harbaugh, Lovering, Thomas Jones and Isaac Polock, July 23, 1799; both entry 6, RG 42, NAB. Lovering to Commissioners, June 21, 1798; entry 1, RG 42, NAB.

42 Griffith, "Hoban," 45. Kapsch, "Labor History," 269; 385. Allen C. Clark, *Greenleaf and Law in the Federal City* (Washington: Press of W.F. Roberts, 1901), 143.

43 Harbaugh to Commissioners, June 20, 1798, entry 1, RG 42, NAB.

44 Harbaugh to Commissioners, June 20, 1798, entry 1, RG 42, NAB. John Ball Osborne, "The Removal of the Government to Washington," *RCHS* 3 (1900): 144–5. Harbaugh to Commissioners, August 15, 1798, entry 1, RG 42, NAB. Miscellaneous payrolls from unidentified National Archives source, photocopies in the files of writer Bob Arnebeck (Essex County, NY).

45 Harbaugh to Commissioners, July 8, 1799; Hoban to Commissioners. May 20, 1799; both entry 1, RG 42, NAB.

46 "Report of James Hoban," *Federal Gazette and Baltimore Daily Advertiser,* December 17, 1799, 2. Charles F. Kupfer to Commissioners. July 21, 1800, entry 1, RG 42, NAB. Glass shipped was four boxes of 140 squares 18 ¾ x 14 ¼ inches and one box of 34 squares 18 ½ by 14 ½ for the lower story and five boxes of 150 squares 18 ¾ x 15 ¼ and six boxes of 210 squares 18 ½ by 13 ½ for the upper story.

47 Commissioners to Charles Lee, May 20, 1800, entry 6, RG 42, NAB. On March 9, 1802, Harbaugh explained that this error, as well as the losses in the fire at his shop, left him $1,000 in the red; on April 9 he was paid an additional $691; entry 1, RG 42, NAB.

48 Steele to Commissioners, May 24, 1800, entry 1, RG 42, NAB.

49 Christian Hines, *Early Recollections of Washington City* (Washington: Chronicle Books, 1866), 12.

50 Wolcott quoted in "Viator," [Joseph B. Varnum, Jr.], *Washington Sketch Book* (New York: Mohun, Ebbs & Hough, 1864), 91–93. Adams quoted in Mary S. Lockwood, *Historic Homes in Washington* (New York: Belford Company, 1889), 46.

51 Voucher 11,800, October 24, 1800; voucher 12,226, November 10, 1800; Records of the Accounting Officers of the Department of the Treasury, entry 6.5, RG 217, NACP. Hines, *Early Recollections,* 74. Osborne, "Removal," 146. Thomas Munroe, Commissioners' Ledgers, 1791–1815, 90, entry 14, RG 42, NAB.

52 Arnebeck, *Fiery Trial,* 612–3.

53 *American State Papers* (hereafter cited as *Am. St. P.*), 10, *Miscellaneous* I:248–9.

54 Commissioners to Hoban, January 21, 1801, Proceedings and Letters Sent, entry 21, RG 42, NAB. *Am. St. P.,* 10, *Misc.* I:241–3.

55 Hadfield to Jefferson, March 27, 1801, Jefferson Papers, Library of Congress.

56 "United States Treasury Department," *Harper's New Monthly Magazine,* 262 (March 1872):481–498. A clerk in the Register's Office copied Latrobe's drawings and estimates into Joseph Nourse's "Estimates and Statements," following a copy of letter from Nourse to Gallatin, March 27, 1805, vol. 11, entry 28, RG 53, NACP. Jeffrey A. Cohen and Charles E. Brownell, *The Architectural Drawings of Benjamin Henry Latrobe* (New Haven: Yale University Press, 1994), II:491–2.

57 John C. Van Horne and others, eds., *The Correspondence and Miscellaneous Papers of Benjamin Henry Latrobe* (New Haven: Yale University Press, 1986), II:34.

58 C.M. Harris, "The Politics of Public Building: William Thornton and President's Square," *White House History* 3 (Spring 1998): 57–8.

59 Ibid., 62–7, 67–8.

60 "U.S. Treasury," *Harper's*, 491–2. H.M. Pierce Gallagher, *Robert Mills, Architect of the Washington Monument, 1781–1855* (New York: Columbia University Press, 1935), 14, 127, 185.

61 Edward C. Carter II, ed., *The Papers of Benjamin Henry Latrobe* (Clifton, New Jersey: James T. White & Company for the Maryland Historical Society, 1976), fiche 39/B5. Van Horne, *Latrobe Correspondence,* II:68. Carter, *Latrobe Papers,* fiche 42/B10.

62 Ibid., fiche 41/D3, 41/E13. Michael W. Fazio, "Benjamin Latrobe's Designs for a Lighthouse at the Mouth of the Mississippi River," *Journal of the Society of Architectural Historians* 48(September 1989):232–246. Carter, *Latrobe Papers,* fiche 39/F7.

63 Van Horne, *Latrobe Correspondence,* II:31.

64 Nourse to Gallatin, March 27, 1805, 11:21*ff*, entry 28, RG 53, NACP.

65 Latrobe to Gallatin, May 13, 1805, in Carter, *Latrobe Papers,* fiche 39/G9.

66 Latrobe to Gallatin, May 4, 1805, in Carter, *Latrobe Papers,* fiches 39/F2, 39/F7.

67 Van Horne, *Latrobe Papers,* II:69.

68 Carter, *Latrobe Papers,* fiche 41/E13. Van Horne, *Latrobe Correspondence,* II:470–1. Carter, *Latrobe Papers,* fiche 41/F2.

69 Jefferson to Lenthall, October 16, 1806, Jefferson Papers, Library of Congress.

70 Ibid.

71 Latrobe to Gallatin, October 17, 1806, Van Horne, *Latrobe Papers,* II:275.

72 Van Horne, *Latrobe Correspondence,* II:273. Michael W. Fazio and Patrick A. Snadon, *The Domestic Architecture of Benjamin Henry Latrobe* (Baltimore: The John Hopkins University Press, 2006), passim. Lee H. Burke, *Homes of the State Department, 1774–1976* (Washington: Department of State, 1976), 29.

73 *Annals of Congress,* 11th Cong., 2d sess., 1427–8, 1704, 1771–2. [Irving Atkins], "Description of the National Archives Building," n.d., partial MSS, copy on deposit in Curator's Office, Treasury Department.

74 Anthony S. Pitch, *The Burning of Washington: The British Invasion of 1814* (Annapolis: Naval Institute Press, 1998), 127. *Am. St., P.,* 10, *Misc.* II:248.

75 James Scott, *Recollections of a Naval Life* (London: Richard Bentley, 1834), III:305.

76 *Am. St. P.,* 10, *Misc.* II:250.

77 Hadfield, Report to Congress, October 13, 1814, entry 1, RG 42, NAB.

78 Ibid.

79 Mary Jane Dowd, comp., *Records of the Office of Public Buildings and Public Parks of the National Capital, Record Group 42.* (Washington: National Archives and Records Administration, 1992), 27–8.

80 Mills to Commissioners, March 8, 1815; and Hoban, "Particular Description of the Materials," [April 14, 1815]; both entry 1, RG 42, NAB.

81 President of the United States, *Burning of the Treasury Building,* 23rd Cong., 2d sess., 1841, H. Doc. 22, 25.

82 Hoban, "Particular Description," 1815.

83 Contract of Commissioners with Henry Smith and Peter Morte, April 14, 1815, Commissioners Contracts, entry 16, RG 42, NAB. Commissioners to Hoban, April 22, 1815, entry 21; Hoban to Commissioners, July 1, 1815, entry 1; Commissioners to Madison, November 11, 1815, entry 6; both RG 42, NAB.

84 Hoban to Commissioners, February 26, 1816, entry 1, RG 42, NAB. Richard Harrison, Auditor, voucher 32,980, September 19, 1816, entry 347, RG 217, NACP. Lane to Thomas W. Cobb, January 5, 1820, Reports of Committee on Expenditures on the Public Buildings, entry 13, RG 233, NAB.

85 Hoban, "Particular Description," 1815.

86 John P. Pepper, June 21, 1830, Voucher 57,585, entry 347, RG 217, NACP. Mills, Various estimates and contracts, c. August 1830, Papers of Robert Mills, South Carolina Historical Society. A December 1830 sketch of Mills's fireproof vault, illustrated in the 1989 issue of *Prologue* as located in the Cartographic and Architectural Archives, cannot be found.

87 Mills to Dickens, March 22, 1831, RG 42, entry 1, NACP. Asbury Dickens had an unusually peripatetic bureaucratic career. He served as Chief Clerk in the Treasury Department for several years before being appointed Chief Clerk in the State Department in 1833. On December 12, 1836, Dickens was elected Secretary of the Senate. "Asbury Dickens," *National Intelligencer,* December 13, 1836, 3. Mills to Dickens, October 11, 1832, entry 1, RG 42, NAB.

88 Mills, Estimates and certification of renovation, Sept. 21, 1831, Correspondence of Robert Mills, 1830–31, Gift Collection Records, RG 200, NACP.

89 *Burning of the Treasury Building,* 30–2.

90 Ibid., 31, 44–5.

91 Ibid., 18, 33.

92 Ibid., 17, 14–6.

93 Ibid., 17, 19–20.

94 Ibid., 36–7, 30–1.

95 Ibid., 28, 35–6.

96 Ibid., 28.

97 McLane to Jackson, April 12, 1833, Miscellaneous Letters to President, A Series, entry 3, RG 56, NACP.

98 *Burning of the Treasury Building,* 41–6. "The Fire at the Treasury," *Workingmen's Advocate* 4 (April 6, 1833): 2.

99 *Burning of the Treasury Building,* 44, 47–8.

100 Ibid., 36.

101 Woodbury to Noland, March 13, 1837, entry 1, RG 42, NAB. "Local Affair," *National Intelligencer,* October 30, 1837, 2.

102 "A Serious Disaster," *National Intelligencer,* April 1, 1833, 1. "Old John Leach," *National Intelligencer,* July 3, 1862, 3.

103 Donald J. Lehman, "Treasury Building, Washington, D.C., Part I. The First Treasury, 1800–1833," 58–69, typescript, 1967, photocopy in the Office of the Curator, Treasury Department.

104 "New Orleans Bulletin," *National Intelligencer,* June 27, 1836, 2. "The Burning of the Treasury Building," *The Huntress* 1 (February 25, 1837): 13. "A Hard Case," *American Masonic Register and Literary Companion* 2, 52 (August 28, 1841): 416.

105 "Trial of R.H. White," *National Intelligencer,* May 2, 1837, 2. See also "Important Trial for Burning the Treasury Building," December 26, 1836, 2; "Second Trial of R.H. White for Burning the Treasury Building," January 14, 1837, 2; "Henry White," January 28, 1837, 2; and "Richard H. White Acquitted," June 15, 1838, 2; all in *National Intelligencer.* President of the United States, *Punishment of Incendiaries*, 24th Cong., 2d sess., 1837, H. Ex. Doc. 85, 1.

106 Mills to McLane, April 6, 1833, Personnel Folders of Notable Treasury Employees, 1822–1940, entry 213, RG 56, NACP.

107 Ibid. and Secretary of the Treasury, *Report on the Finances*, 23rd Cong., 1st sess., 1833, S. Doc. 9, 385.

"The House That Jack Built:"
The East Wing, 1836–1842

Chapter Two

"So Many Conflicting Interests:" Robert Mills Designs the Treasury Building

Impressive architectural scale and meaningful historical prototypes were fundamental to Robert Mills's thinking about Washington's second wave of public buildings begun in the early 1830s. No less a visionary than L'Enfant, Mills proposed five structures proportioned to the city's 1791–92 plan. In terms of sheer size, the most notable was the Washington Monument (1845–1888), its planned height 600 feet and the diameter of its circular base 250 feet. In his Treasury Building designs, Mills sought to realize his dictum that "the character of a nation is judged of by the character of its public buildings." It was the first of three massive and impressive federal office buildings he designed and saw built between 1833 and 1842, the second being the Patent Office on a two-block square between 7th and 9th streets NW and the third the General Post Office on the north side of E Street between 7th and 8th streets NW. The price of Mills's success convincing public officials that Washington's public buildings should reflect the nation's progress in the arts and technology, and symbolically its political achievements, was his public humiliation at the hands of a few ambitious congressmen for their political gain.[1]

Mills recalled two decades later that, soon after the destruction of the Treasury Office in April 1833, "at an early period before the meeting of Congress, I prepared and submitted plans for [a building] to President Jackson, predicated upon a *new* site for the executive offices, which should allow for a building large enough to accommodate all these offices under one roof." Mills's cursory description of this design noted it was to have been located on Lafayette Square, "the building occupying three sides of the same—the north, west, and east, leaving the south side open—thus forming a hollow square." Mills drew on his first-hand experience as a part-time clerk in the Treasury Department's Land Office when he urged Jackson to consolidate all the executive departments in a single, fireproof building on a scale that would house the rapidly increasing bureaucracy. Helping the government operate more efficiently and, in the long view, build more economically and safely were central to Mills's planning of the Lafayette Square complex.[2]

Considering its prime location immediately north of the President's House, Lafayette Square was still relatively undeveloped when Mills made his proposal in 1833. The section of the President's Grounds north of Pennsylvania Avenue was officially named Lafayette Square in 1824 to commemorate the Marquis de Lafayette's triumphal tour of America. It was graded and enclosed by a picket fence two years later. Although Mills's drawings for his Lafayette Square complex have not been located, his design was admired by one of his principal rivals, the Philadelphia architect Thomas U. Walter. In 1838 Walter praised Mills's multi-departmental building covering the square's seven acres. "Were buildings constructed on this ground according to the design furnished by your Architect … the effect would be far superior to any thing of the kind in the world, and no nation on earth could boast a structure equaling it in adaptation to governmental purposes." Walter proposed in 1838 that the government purchase all the properties facing the square, erect entrance lodges at the corners

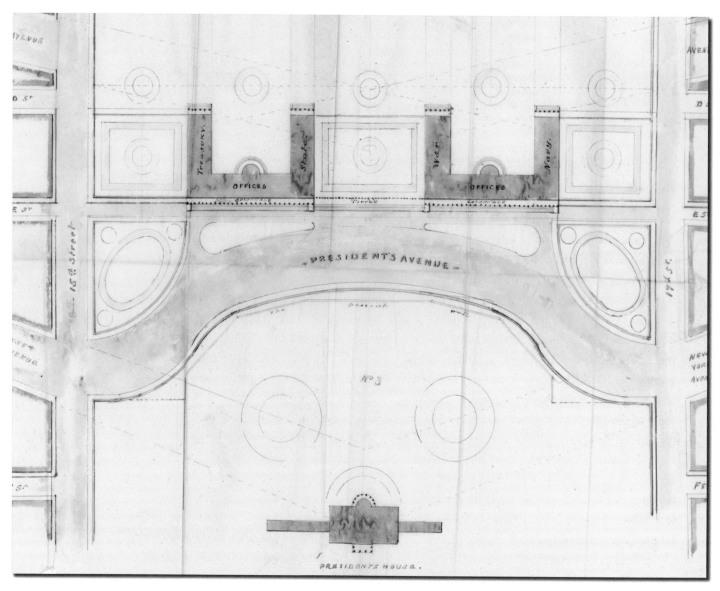

II-1 In 1834 Mills proposed two massive executive office buildings south of the President's House.

of F, 15th, and 17th streets, and enclose the expanded executive enclave with an ornamental iron railing. Walter had not yet had Mills's experience with the political conflicts, intense personal and social competition, and economical mindset of congressional committee members who controlled not just the funding of buildings proposed by and for the executive branch, but to a large extent their designs as well.[3]

In 1833 Jackson submitted Mills's Lafayette Square design to Congress where it was considered by the House Committee on Public Buildings. Because part of Mills's task was to persuade Congress to accept the design, he met with the committee several times to explain his thinking. Opposition by the square's landowners led Mills to make a second design in 1834 that placed all four executive offices south of the President's House, a scheme that recalled L'Enfant's 1792 plan for their location. The single surviving site plan shows two massive U-shaped buildings south of the President's House, their spines twice the length of the presidential mansion and each of the four north-south wings slightly longer than the President's House's 160-foot-long main facades. (fig. II-1) Each had colonnades of thirty columns facing the President's House and porticoes fronting their wings facing the Potomac River, but the site's low elevation ensured that views of the

President's House from all directions would remain open.

Two decades later Mills described these buildings.

> The grand front would have been to the President's House, ranging from 15th to 17th streets, with an open space in the centre equal to the front of the President's House, to form a vista to the river, &c… This would have proved an admirable site for these buildings, looking down the broad Potomac, and fronting south and north.[4]

President Washington purposefully placed the executive offices within the presidential precinct to facilitate the workings of the executive branch. In 1810, when the Patent Office (part of the State Department) had outgrown its allotted quarters in the War Office, and the General Post Office had endured a decade of cramped quarters, Congress invested $25,000 to purchase the former Blodgett's Hotel midway between Capitol Hill and the President's House to accommodate them. A new Patent Office was part of congressional thinking in the early 1830s, even before Blodgett's Hotel was destroyed by fire in December 1836. Congressman Jarvis saw the advantages of housing the executive departments in a single structure, but also understood the political reality of each department guarding its own autonomy.

> That great convenience would result from this change to the public at large, to the members of Congress, and to the officers employed, cannot admit of doubt; but so many conflicting interests would be set in motion by any proposition of this kind; and so many obstacles would be interposed, that it was determined, after mature deliberation, to relinquish what might be considered the best plan for one that was of more easy attainment; and it was therefore

concluded to recommend that the location of the [executive] buildings should not be disturbed.[5]

Mills was not the only architect presenting plans to Jackson and the House committee for the new executive buildings. Two alternate designs for Lafayette Square by Alexander Jackson Davis of the New York firm of Town & Davis survive among Davis's drawings. (fig. II-2) The simplest is a large rectangle divided by two internal arms to make four courtyards, a rotunda vestibule at the crossing of the arms. It is titled "Study for the four Departments at Washington, Lafayette Square," dated 1832 and inscribed "at the suggestion of Pres. Jackson," the date and inscriptions possibly added later in Davis's life. For his second, more complex design, Davis proposed massive and expensive corner pavilions but retained the same general plan. During his extended visits to Washington in the early 1830s, Davis was frequently Mills's guest and they are known to have freely discussed various public buildings under consideration by Congress.[6]

None of the drawings made by Mills in 1835–36 for the several variants he explored for the Treasury Building's 15th Street site are known to survive, with a single possible exception. An undated sketch in his c. 1836–40 journal shows four buildings attached to the east and west of the President's House, all five buildings connected by colonnaded loggias. (fig. II-3) Mills rejected this railroad-car arrangement of increasingly larger structures as too intrusive on the privacy of the residents of the President's House. Moreover, they dwarfed it, as the end wings (the easternmost, presumably the Treasury Building) were 100 feet longer than the President's House.[7]

As the House Committee continued to weigh the options, another of Mills's arch rivals, William P. Elliot, Jr., published a description of his own design for the 15th Street site in the

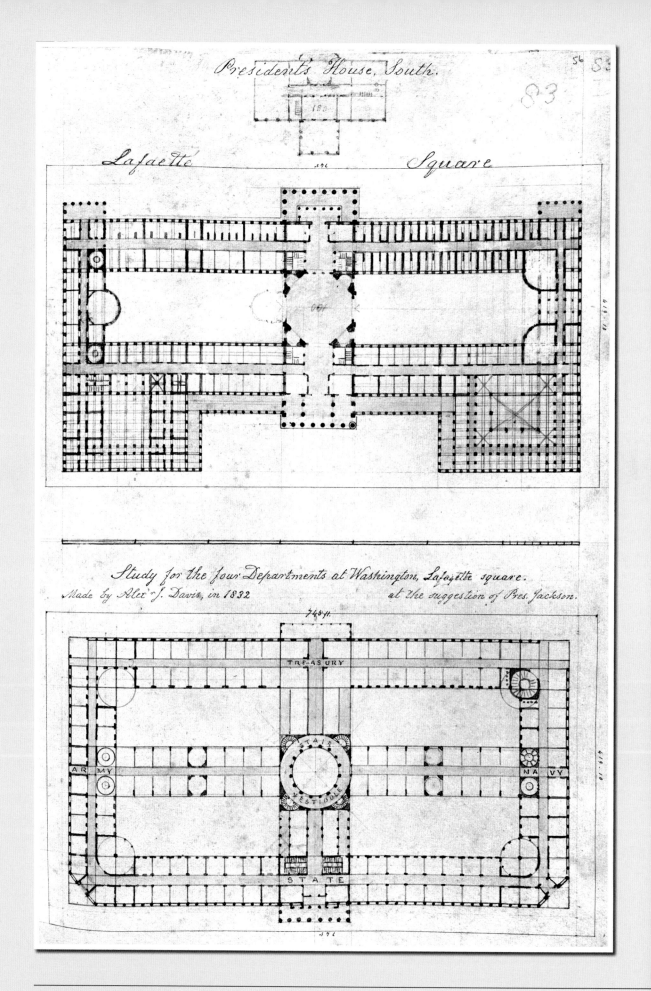

President's House, South.

Lafaette *Square*

Study for the four Departments at Washington, Lafayette square.
Made by Alex'r J. Davis, in 1832 *at the suggestion of Pres. Jackson.*

TREASURY

STAIR

ARMY

NAVY

VESTIBOLE

STATE

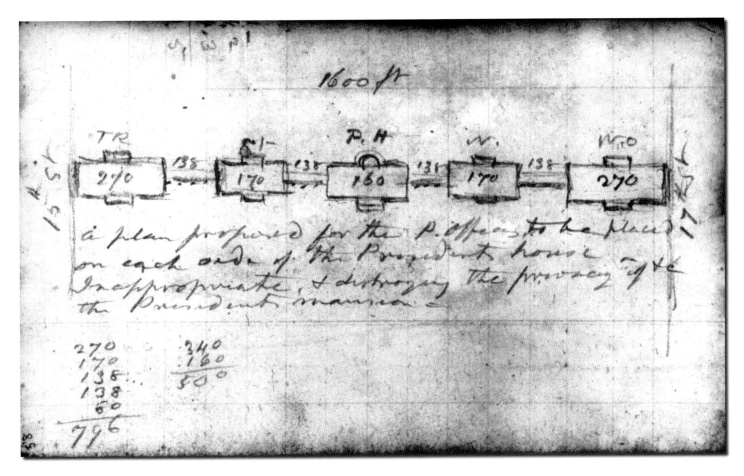

a plan proposed for the P. Offices to be placed on each side of the President's house. Inappropriate, + destroys the privacy + c the President's mansion.

II-3 Mills briefly explored attaching new lateral offices east and west of the President's House.

February 13, 1835, issue of the *National Intelligencer.* This initiated an acrimonious exchange of letters with each architect accusing the other of plagiarism and professional incompetence. The executive office building Elliott described resembled in plan Mills's third design enough to anger the older architect. Elliott proposed a U-shaped brick and granite building, its spine extending 286 feet on 15th Street with its two 160-foot wings facing the President's House, each entered through porticoes with six Ionic columns approached by fifteen steps. (Mills planned his E-shaped building to extend 457 feet along 15th Street, with each of its three wings 190 feet long.) Elliot's Treasury was to be fireproof, the vaulted floors in its 148 rooms separated by cast iron joists (unlike Mills's preferred self-supporting groin vaults built exclusively with bricks and mortar).[8]

Opposite page: II-2 Like Mills, A.J. Davis designed monumental executive office buildings for Lafayette Square.

Congressman Jarvis recognized that Washington's government buildings needed to compete architecturally with increasingly more sophisticated buildings elsewhere. "The public edifices in the capital of our confederated republic ought not to be inferior to those erected for federal or State purposes in our large commercial cities; and if not in advance of public opinion, they ought at least to keep pace with it." Jarvis concluded that a new consolidated Treasury and State departments building should be erected east of the President's House, with a duplicate to house the War and Navy departments to its west. Choosing to fund multiple executive buildings on several sites, rather than sanction a single massive building north of the President's House, changed the city's pattern of domestic and business development. It also curbed what Congress may have perceived as evidence of Jackson's excessive need to express the executive branch's power. Had either of Mills's first two designs for the consolidated executive offices been built, the executive enclave would have dwarfed the Capitol. [9]

On July 4, 1836, the sixtieth anniversary of the signing of the Declaration of Independence and the last day of the first session of the 24th Congress, the legislators passed an act authorizing Jackson "to cause to be erected on or near the site of the former treasury building, or on any other public lot he may select, a fire-proof building of such dimensions as may be required for the present and future accommodations of the Treasury Department, upon such plan and of such materials as he may deem most advantageous." The appropriation was for $100,000 and a proviso added that the Aquia sandstone used in the construction of the Capitol and President's House be used if "a cheaper and more suitable material cannot be obtained" with the exception of the foundations which "shall be of the hardest and most solid rock."[10]

Mills and Elliot immediately presented Jackson with letters of recommendation, as well as letters outlining their qualifications; two days later on July 6, Jackson chose Mills's design for the Treasury Building and Elliot's for the Patent Office and hired Mills to oversee the construction of both buildings. (fig. II-4) He was to work with William Noland, who was already functioning as the Commissioner of Public Buildings. Elliot complained that on July 5 Mills waited at the President's House in readiness to revise his Treasury Building design to accommodate the General Post Office because he "had been recently employed by General Jackson to make drawings for the Hermitage." The Washington correspondent for the *Charleston Courier*, on learning that Jackson had appointed Mills the architect of public buildings, lauded the native South Carolinian's talent and accomplishments, and added: "Mr. Mills derives an additional claim to the office, from the circumstance that he has

II-4 Robert Mills played a key role in the Treasury Office and designed the Treasury Building.

been the victim of a too implicit confidence in former promises."[11]

One of the Treasury Building's most enduring legends describes Andrew Jackson impetuously selecting the site for the Treasury Building, thrusting his hickory cane in the ground on July 6, 1836, and proclaiming: "Put the building right here!" The legend portrays Jackson as simultaneously arrogant and ignorant, because the Treasury Building's southern end shuts off the reciprocal vistas along Pennsylvania Avenue between the Capitol and President's House. But even before the site was chosen, and well before additions to the Treasury Building blocked the view, a pre-existing problem with L'Enfant's planned vista was attributed to a blunder by the city's founders. The problem arose simply because Washington reduced the size of L'Enfant's proposed President's House and moved it further north with no corresponding reduction in the scale of its grounds.[12]

The real decision-making in 1836 was considerably more complex than popular accounts first published nearly four decades after the event portrayed. That Jackson personally chose the Treasury Building's location is verified by two nearly contemporary accounts, but challenged by other participants, including Mills, nearly a decade later. No record has been found of a formal cornerstone ceremony and no cornerstone has ever been discovered.

On July 8 Jackson wrote Secretary of the Treasury Levi Woodbury inquiring about the department's space needs. He asked him to provide "the number of rooms that may be necessary for the Treasury" and "to give the number he may think necessary to build the south wing to the Treasury, as per Mr. Mills's plan." Woodbury replied that the Treasury Department needed fifty-four rooms and the Land Office thirty-six, adding that the three wings should each contain thirty-six rooms. "Which would leave a surplus of eighteen rooms, or six in each wing, or six in the centre in [the] third story, for papers, records, etc., and to accommodate Solicitor of the Treasury, if necessary. This would not, perhaps, be too much, if the present fire-proof be removed." Jackson endorsed the letter: "Let the foundation be laid accordingly, for centre and north and south wing." Because the existing State Office "by being somewhat altered, was to form the north wing," and its east side was immediately contiguous to 15th Street, the spine of the new Treasury Building was accordingly brought up immediately adjacent to 15th Street, rather than set back fifty feet as Mills preferred.[13]

Noland, who witnessed Jackson's selection of the site, wrote Speaker of the House James K. Polk at the end of September 1837 that "Ex-president Jackson, after an examination of the ground, in company with his Cabinet, selected the site on which the new Treasury is now being erected as the most suitable one." Robert Brown, superintendent of the Treasury's stonemasons,

in response to questioning during the 1837–38 congressional investigation, gave valuable information about the issues which most concerned those involved.

> The President of the United States did designate the Site on which the new Treasury Building is now being erected, but I dont [sic] know that the Precise location was pointed out by him further than with an understanding that it was to be erected with a view to Preserve the present State Department and to case it with Stone to make it uniform with the new Building. I believe that he was made acquainted with its full extent on 15th Street, but I dont [sic] know that he was made acquainted with its full depth West from said Street, however he saw the Stakes drove in by which the foundation was taken out.[14]

Did either Jackson or Mills deserve the opprobrium history has heaped upon them for closing the vista between the city's executive and legislative landmarks? In 1845 while Congress was debating new buildings on the west side of the President's House for the War and Navy departments, Mills urged that their combined mass replicate the Treasury and State department building on the east. He argued that L'Enfant planned vistas of the central sections of the President's House be framed by buildings on both sides of Pennsylvania and New York avenues. Furthermore, the encroachment of one corner of the Treasury Building's south wing was because of "an oversight on the part of the committee of the House that determined the site, and the extent of building which should be constructed on it … In the future extension of the Treasury building north, its colonnade may be carried on to fill up the entire space, or to touch the south line of the New York avenue."[15] (fig. II-5)

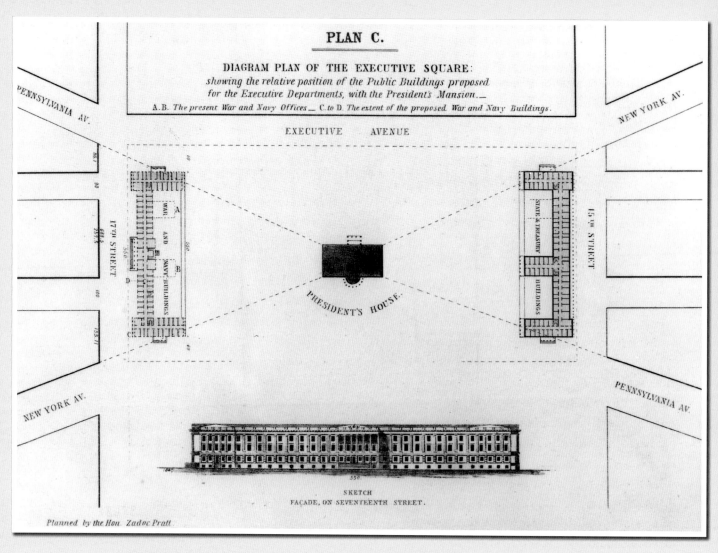

PLAN C.

DIAGRAM PLAN OF THE EXECUTIVE SQUARE:
showing the relative position of the Public Buildings proposed for the Executive Departments, with the President's Mansion.—
A.B. *The present War and Navy Offices.— C. to D. The extent of the proposed War and Navy Buildings.*

EXECUTIVE AVENUE

PENNSYLVANIA AV.

NEW YORK AV.

17TH STREET

WAR AND NAVY BUILDINGS

A

B

PRESIDENT'S HOUSE.

STATE & TREASURY BUILDINGS

15TH STREET

NEW YORK AV.

PENNSYLVANIA AV.

SKETCH
FAÇADE, ON SEVENTEENTH STREET.

Planned by the Hon. Zadoc Pratt.

II-5 Open vistas of the President's House from the two avenues was symbolically critical to many.

In 1854 Joseph B. Varnum, Jr., recognized the east wing's actual siting fault, the offset of its 15th Street entrance staircase with F Street.

> [The Treasury Building] is so badly situated as to ruin its appearance, and entirely exclude from view the President's house, and to obstruct the distant and beautiful prospect from the East room of that edifice, through the line of F street. The building, although nearly four hundred feet in length, will scarcely be visible except from the street immediately before it; and the three finest porticoes will front upon the President's kitchen garden.

Varnum argued that if the sites for executive offices south of the President's House shown on L'Enfant's map had been followed, "it would have preserved a distinct view of the President's house in every direction," although he did not complain about obstructing Pennsylvania Avenue's reciprocal vistas. In fact, the southern termination of the east wing was north of the avenue's sightline.[16]

The earliest known published accounts of the story that Jackson used his cane to designate the site appears thirty-eight years after the supposed act in Mary Clemmer Ames's *Ten Years in Washington* (1874) and George Alfred Townsend's *Washington Outside and Inside* (1874), followed a decade later by Joseph West

Moore's account in *Picturesque Washington* (1884). While the tale may be apocryphal, it endures because at its heart are two inescapable facts—Jackson picked the site and, on that site, the Treasury Building interrupts one of the key urban vistas in America. Yet, it is the Treasury's south portico, not any part of Mills's east wing, which fills the west end of the Pennsylvania Avenue vista. Thereby hangs another tale.[17]

"To Aid in Forming the Plans:" Prestige, Permanence, and Power

Each of America's Greek revival architects who worked during the first six decades of the nineteenth century treated their ancient models differently. For his three Washington office buildings, Mills followed the eclectic design principles taught him in the first decade of the nineteenth century by Benjamin Henry Latrobe at the Capitol. Latrobe taught Mills to combine Roman structure with Greek columns to achieve monumentality externally and internally. Roman fireproof construction tied outer masonry walls inextricably to brick inner ones as well as to brick vaulted ceilings supporting brick floors of the rooms above them. Mills steadfastly adhered to vaulted construction, even when iron was introduced as a modern and less expensive form of fireproof construction. He also imitated Latrobe's use of plain Greek (rather than ornate Roman) columns to determine the scale of his federal offices and, as Latrobe had done at the Capitol, intended them to convey meaning. Mills's fusion of structure with internal space, coupled with the lofty classical proportions established by the columns, resulted in monumental buildings. (fig. II-6) This accomplishment was shared by only a few other American architects who also never visited Europe but learned their technical skills through architectural treatises and developed their innate talents via interpretations of classical revival buildings erected in America.

II-6 The beauty of Mills's interiors is the interaction between the shapes of form and of space.

Latrobe's Capitol was Mills's touchstone for Washington's second generation of federal buildings, its Greek Doric Supreme Court finding a counterpart in the Doric Patent Office; the Greek Ionic used in the Senate chamber replicated in the Treasury Building; and the Greek Corinthian of the House of Representatives changed to a Roman Corinthian for the General Post Office. In addition, Mills's ancient orders were applied to three different classical building types: his Treasury Building's east front is based on a Greek stoa or business complex (see frontispiece); the portico of the Patent Office took the form of a temple end; and the General

Post Office was based on a Renaissance palace. Moreover, in all three instances, Mills quoted from the most famous of ancient buildings. The Ionic order Mills chose for the Treasury Building was derived from the Erectheum on the Acropolis in Athens. (fig. II-7) The Patent Office's portico replicated the dimensions and Doric columns of the gable end of the Parthenon, the Temple of Athena on the Athenian Acropolis. When he learned that Congress would allow him to build the General Post Office of marble, Mills changed a more common Corinthian capital prototype to that used on the Temple of Jupiter Stator, the first marble temple built in Rome.[18]

To complete this symbolic urban conceit, Mills suggested in 1841 that the Smithsonian Institution be based on some medieval model, his own medieval revival design winning second place in the competition held five years later. Mills's drawing entered into the competition for the Washington National Monument in 1836 has not survived but it may have been similar to the 600-foot-tall Egyptian obelisk surrounded by a colonnaded base the Washington National Monument Society chose in 1845. With these five buildings, Mills brought to Washington a museum of architecture that quoted from the greatest of European examples; he probably intended to further Jefferson's agenda begun at the University of Virginia, his "academical village" being composed of great ancient (and one eighteenth-century) buildings to teach the students ancient history and its meaning through its architecture. How much more meaningful, Mills may have felt, to create a museum of national architectural exemplars—rooted in the Capitol—that tied America's diverse population to its European and African antecedents. Throughout his career Mills consciously revived earlier American models or incorporated specifically American symbols in his quest to foster "American" architectural traditions.

George Hadfield's plan for the Treasury Office may have contributed to Mills's organization of the Treasury Building's internal spaces; both were rooted in European double-loaded corridor plans. Central corridors flanked by cubic office rooms entered by single doors were lit as well as ventilated by two tall windows. This arrangement was probably derived ultimately from Renaissance hospital plans that had been developed to maximize ventilation in large public buildings. Traditionally, each doorway of the Treasury's offices, as well as those in other nineteenth-century federal buildings, had two doors, the inner one was solid wood while the outer had double swinging louvered doors open at the top and bottom. During the hot months, windows were kept open, as were the inner doors, the louvered doors ensuring privacy while at the same time allowing air to circulate across each wing's width.[19]

Contemporary descriptions did not praise the old Treasury Office because it was a strictly utilitarian building erected as inexpensively as possible. Had Hadfield superintended his winning design, even within a stringent budget, it would have had greater architectural presence than what was built, but too many participants with conflicting agendas had spoiled its promised quality. Mills was determined to ensure the architectural integrity of his designs for Washington's second generation of federal buildings by retaining oversight of their construction. He spent the previous three decades preparing himself to meet the technical, intellectual, and political challenges of being the federal architect of public buildings. He would dedicate the next two decades of his life fighting to salvage the basics of his visionary designs—permanent construction, monumentality, dignified spaces, national symbolic content—to realize the core

Opposite page: II-7 Tightly wound volutes and a wide necking band distinguish the Ionic capitals of the Erectheum.

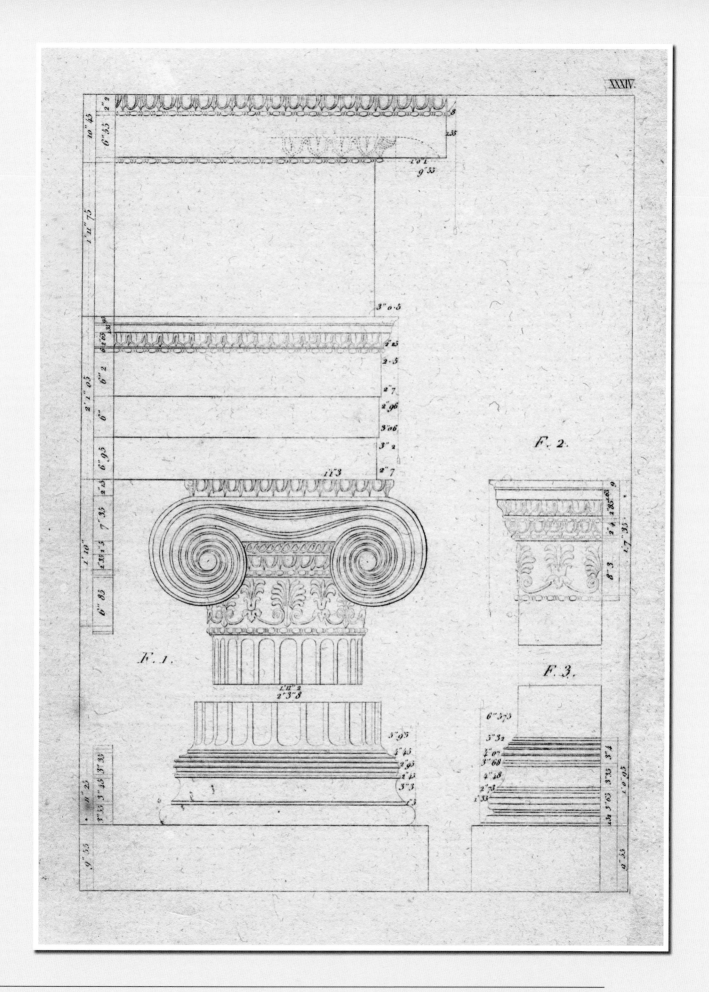

F. 1.

F. 2.

F. 3.

of his idea of making Washington America's national capital architecturally capable of competing with great European cities.

Mills and Noland began superintending the Treasury Building and Patent Office concurrently during the summer of 1836, originally working with only one clerk turning Noland's drafts into finished contracts, keeping the accounts, and preparing contractors' vouchers for payment. Noland's duties outlined in President Jackson's letter of appointment required him "to superintend generally the detailed modifications of plan for [the two buildings], the advertising & forming of the Contracts, and the whole disbursements thereon." Mills's responsibilities were equally general in nature: "as architect to aid in forming the plans, making proper changes therein from time to time, and seeing to the erection of said buildings substantially, in conformity to the plans hereby adopted, which are in general outlines to be, as to the Treasury building that plan annexed by said Mills."[20]

Mills had wide latitude in modifying the approved design, but all changes had to be approved by Noland. On July 9 Jackson approved the salaries for Mills and the superintendents, Mills to be paid $1,800 per year, stonemason Robert Brown, $1,600, and a clerk $900, while the foremen of the bricklayers earned $3.50 per day and the carpenters $4.00 per day. The Capitol and President's House were built by skilled artisans and laborers hired by the day, overseen by superintendents of stonemasons, bricklayers, carpenters, and laborers who were on the government payroll. The experiment of contracting with the lowest bidder to erect the executive offices in the late 1790s and rebuilding them late in the second decade of the nineteenth century may have been abandoned in the 1830s because their construction proved to be inferior. Part of the 1830s debate about the Treasury and Patent office buildings was aesthetic, part was fiscal, and part was political with all three issues usually entangled.

The collaboration between Mills and Noland was a success as together they faced labor problems, inferior materials, and a major congressional investigation that halted construction for several months in 1838. By July 12, 1836, Noland was advertising for bricks, granite for the foundations, and wood to build scaffolds. On August 1 enough of Mills's working drawings had been completed for Noland to contract for stone, a difficult beginning because it was mid-way in the building season and the best workmen were already committed to projects elsewhere. In mid-September Robert Brown, the superintendent of the stonemasons, traveled in Baltimore, Philadelphia, and New York looking for skilled workmen willing to move to Washington. "[S]uch was the difficulty of procuring masons, that, after every effort was made to obtain them, their number, for the greater part of the season, barely exceeded half the force which we could have employed to advantage," Mills reported at year's end. Brown apparently had promised them two-to-three years of steady work to entice them to move to Washington.[21]

Mills's education and professional experience convinced him that truly fireproof construction required stone exterior walls coupled with plastered brick interior walls that supported brick vaulted ceilings, their upper surfaces becoming the floors of the story above. Mills achieved very strong brick bonds and was able to reduce the thickness of walls and vaults by using hydraulic cement, normally used by engineers when building canals and bridges because it hardens under water. By the end of the season, "the front range of rooms [was] brought up to the springing line of the groin arches, several of which are turned and laid in hydraulic cement."[22]

During the 1837–38 investigation, Mills was criticized for this transfer of technology because the vaults seemed visually to be floating above each room and, therefore, might induce anxiety. He had calibrated his dimensions and loads so carefully and was so sure of his vaulting technique that he placed stone balls in the corners of each room as springing points of the vaults. One of the outcomes of the investigation was the insistence that Mills build square posts in these corners so that the vaults would appear to be solidly connecting ceilings to floors. The interior brick walls, vaults, and window reveals were plastered to mitigate the passage of moisture from the exterior. Aesthetically, the smooth, painted walls decorated solely by fireplaces accentuated their volumetric character. Their plainness satisfied Mills's congressional critics who may or may not have realized their architectural power.

Although the foundations were not begun until August, 460 feet had been completed along with much of the basement story of both the spine and central wing. Moreover, workshops had been erected so that during the winter months the masons could cut and dress the large quantity of granite and sandstone collected at the site. Mills reported that a total of $43,837.48 was expended on the Treasury Building in 1836. His detailed estimate for 1837 was $308,973, from which he subtracted $51,406 left from the 1836 appropriation. He asked for an additional $100,000 for the foundations of the south wing, for, as he explained to President Martin Van Buren soon after he took office in March 1837, these foundations "as high up as the water table line" should be built during 1837 "to prevent a fracture in the walls when this building shall be ordered to completion." Because the south wing had been designated for the General Post Office and no specific appropriation had been made for that department, Van Buren declined to act on Mills's suggestion.[23]

"Taking Down the Walls of the New Treasury Building:" Congressional Investigation, 1838

Shortly after Mills's annual report was published in December 1836, William P. Elliot forcefully and publicly criticized the Treasury's siting and Mills's design, the opening volley that led to a rancorous congressional investigation begun ten months later.

[T]he construction of burrows for the clerks—narrow and dark passages—a useless and expensive colonnade of forty-two columns, which support nothing but an entablature, shutting out light and air, and totally inconsistent with the inclination of the street—the bases of the columns at one end being six feet above the established gradation of the pavement, and eighteen feet at the other.[24]

In February 1837 the primary player in the investigation, Massachusetts Congressman Levi Lincoln, a Whig who had recently been appointed chairman of the House Committee on Public Buildings and Grounds, questioned Mills about the relative merits of building with brick and sandstone. Mills ran an experiment and concluded that "brick under common circumstances will absorb twice as much water as the Free stone." Lincoln was to become Mills's nemesis as his crusade ostensibly to save the government's money turned into a partisan and sectional battle that endangered the entire project. Mills's reputation among his professional colleagues was injured and major labor problems erupted when the workmen who had relocated with the promise of extended employment on the Treasury and Patent Office Buildings were laid off.[25]

The 1837 building season was waning when Congress called for a site plan, design drawings, and report concerning the future of the State Office. Originally it was planned to incorporate the existing building but, since its exterior would have to be encased in stone and its interior rooms vaulted to make them fireproof, Mills noted that "no plan of operation has been adopted, and the whole subject lies open for future examination and decision." During the previous four years, Mills used data compiled by the Treasury's bureau heads to determine space needs, which he then had to fit onto the site's available space yet stay within the building's budget. He noted that the building line was thirteen feet back from 15th Street and that the Treasury's length was to ensure that it did not encroach on the "private enclosure of the President's mansion." His drawings proved, Mills asserted, that he had been careful to keep the major vistas of the President's House along the avenues open as the "ingenious" L'Enfant

had planned them to be. One sketch plan, dated October 1837 in Mills's notebook, shows one solution of how to incorporate the existing State Office into his E-shaped building but foresaw a duplicate located west of the President's House, its three wings to house the Departments of War and Navy as well as the Corps of Engineers.[26] (fig. II-8)

The House committee was not satisfied with Mills's general answers and on October 14 decided to ask President Van Buren for more definite answers about the comparative costs of adapting the State Office or building a new fireproof wing on its site. At issue were the amount of space devoted to document storage versus offices; a breakdown of what had already been spent in comparison to the amount needed to finish the Treasury Department's portion of the complex; and a tabulation of the amount of office space required by each of the executive departments and their sizes. The House committee's rigorous questions prompted the

II-8 In 1837 State and Treasury were to share the Treasury Building with the General Post Office.

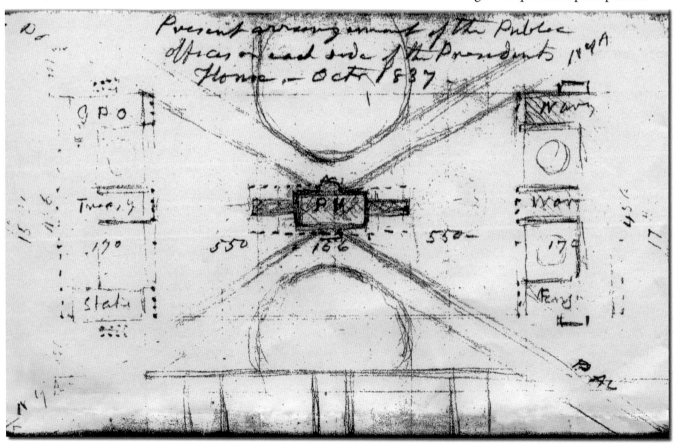

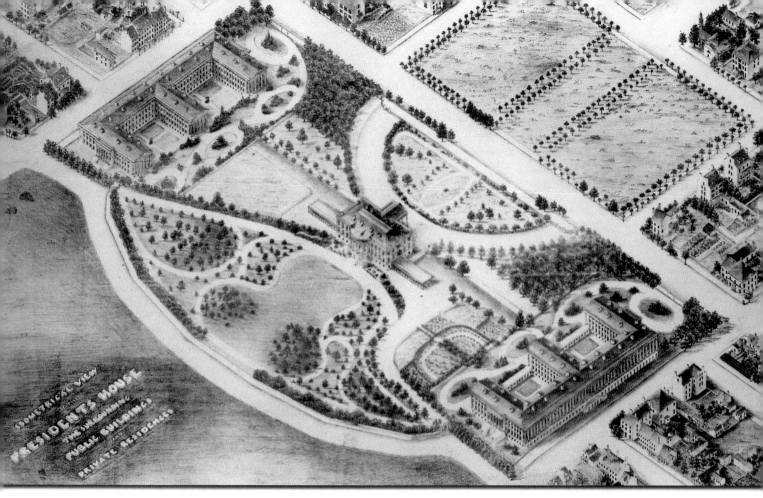

GEOMETRICAL VIEW
OF THE
PRESIDENT'S HOUSE
WITH THE SURROUNDING
PUBLIC BUILDINGS
AND
PRIVATE RESIDENCES

II-9 Mills hoped two E-shaped buildings would foster the bucolic setting of the President's House.

Senate on December 19, 1837, to create its own three-member committee on public buildings. Two days later, in his introduction to Mills's more detailed report, Van Buren reiterated that the congressional act of July 5, 1836, had not authorized the Post Office and invited Congress to review the increasing office needs of the expanding government.[27]

In July 1836 Secretary of the Treasury Levi Woodbury asked for ninety rooms for the Treasury Department; eighteen months later he wanted 132 excluding "all the bureaus connected with the Treasury Department, whose places of business can more conveniently be in the buildings occupied by other departments, the accounts of which they supervise." The other executive departments needed a total of 201 rooms ranging in size from small document storage rooms to impressive office suites sixty feet in length; they all wanted new, more spacious offices that were fireproof. Along with three lost plans detailing the various site restrictions, in December Mills also prepared a large

perspective drawing for display in the House to help members visualize how the E-shaped building would appear should they choose to fund the entire complex.[28] (fig. II-9)

Mills designed the office cubicles on the Treasury's east side to be twenty-one feet by fifteen feet, while those in the center wing measured seventeen feet by nineteen feet. In addition, he planned two large (fifty-four feet by fifteen feet) and eight small (fifteen feet by ten feet) rooms and the "vaulted gallery" 340 feet in length under the colonnade, which he apparently thought might be used as an outdoor room, perhaps for ceremonial occasions. For reasons he did not explain, Mills spent only about half of the 1837 appropriation and had nearly $157,000 on hand for the 1838 season. In answer to one of the committee's queries, he calculated that there would be little difference in cost between demolishing the State Office and building anew or gutting it to make it fireproof and aligned with the east wing.[29]

Although the pragmatic issues of the number of offices and their cumulative cost were always present in Mills's thinking, it was the architectural appearance of his building, especially in relation to the President's House, that underlay his December 1837 designs, as it had those of the previous four years. "Independent of the advantages which this arrangement offers for the transaction of the public business, the effect of such a combination of buildings, properly disposed, would be both imposing and grand," he averred. Mills did not have the verbal gift of fulsome description that might well have swayed many Congressmen unfamiliar with architectural quality and taste. He was unable to comprehend that what was manifestly clear to him in graphic form was meaningless to many others. Mills repeatedly referred committees and individuals to appended drawings, which are now lost, but the evidence of his few remaining pencil sketches and watercolors for the Treasury Building show that he was not an accomplished, up-to-date draftsman with the ability to render three dimensions convincingly. The truth of his architectural quality was in his actual works.[30]

Mills continued to work directly with the House Committee on Public Buildings in the new year, calculating for them the cost of dismantling and reusing the materials on a new site that he rather disingenuously calculated as a loss of only $2,265.79 (even though more than $200,000 had been spent) because he was so anxious to build one or two imposing buildings north or south of the President's House. He even suggested the government should buy the squares east and west of Lafayette Square as a fourth possible location for the executive offices to mollify those who wished to protect the President's House's extended garden setting. During the same period, Levi Lincoln set in motion a thorough inquiry, asking Robert Brown, superintendent of the bricklayers, questions similar

to those that had been put to Mills. Brown recounted his memories of Jackson's choice of the site and Mills's design as well as various construction dimensions and details relating to the building's solidity. He reported that Mills added nine inches to the building's height after Jackson approved the design, that he intended to have 15th Street graded after the building was finished to improve the site, and that iron bars were imbedded in the walls only when Mills thought them necessary.

> I differed in opinion with the architect relative to the thickness of the walls, but I believe they are as firmly constructed as it is possible to construct walls of the same materials and thickness, and I believe they are sufficient to resist the lateral thrust of the arches without settling or cracking and resist the horizontal pressure of the Superincumbent weight. [T]here is [sic] strong iron bars let into the back of the Pilasters in all cases as the springing of the arches from 16 to 18 feet long and let into the block of Stone in the cross walls which entirely takes the lateral or horizontal thrust of the arches off the external walls.[31]

Brown's testimony was direct and honest, calculated neither to exonerate nor blame Mills. The architect, however, was "mortified" by Congressman Lincoln's questioning of his professional abilities, referring Lincoln to the entry on him in William Dunlap's *History of the Rise and Progress of the Arts of Design in the United States*, published in 1834. "The many years experience which I have had in works of this character, should have shielded me from professional defamation, in the present case, and obtained for me the confidence of all." Without naming him directly, Mills makes it clear that he believed Lincoln had been influenced by Elliot's malicious public and private attacks against him. "Who has attempted to defame my

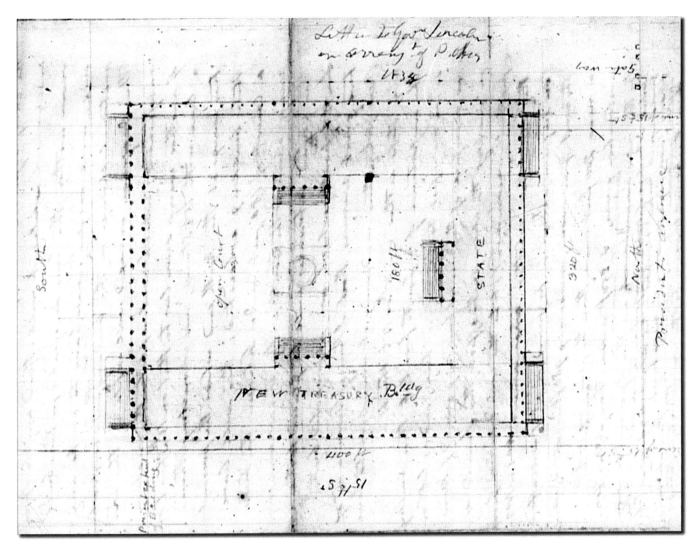

II-10 Another Mills proposal was a long U-shaped building surrounded by colonnades on all four sides.

professional reputation? I know of but one, and he has no qualification to judge in the matter, having not the smallest degree of experience in building—and beside, this individual has resorted to every means to injure my professional standing." Mills continued to prepare drawings for an "abridged plan" while he promoted alternate sites, particularly the one south of the President's House.[32]

It is very evident that from the *Mall*, the view of all these buildings, together the Presidents house, in the center retreating to the high grounds, the two blocks of office buildings in a row & each forming a hollow square & with wings spreading 400 ft. each centered & flank'd by lofty Porticos, the whole connected together by an arcaded terrace spreading upwards of 1500 feet,

would present a spectacle, a tout ensemble, not to be surpassed.[33]

During the second week of January, Mills made a more exact survey of 15th and 17th streets below E Street as well as the meadow between them and concluded that two office buildings south of the President's House could be separated by 670 feet to protect its vistas whether looking north or south. A week later Mills sent Lincoln a description and sketch plan for an alternate solution to the 15th Street site that would preserve the vistas, incorporate both the Treasury Building and State Office, and provide enough office space for all the executive offices. (fig. II-10) His new proposal was for two 400-foot-long parallel wings, the Treasury Building on 15th Street and a new one along 15½ Street adjacent to the President's House grounds, with no entrances on their outer walls but with steps at their north and south ends. A new wing replacing the State Office would connect them on the north end, while the south end would be left open. Each wing would have a central portico opening onto the 180-foot-wide central courtyard. Mills planned to surround the entire rectangle, including the open south end, with a colonnade. This variant on his Lafayette Square design seems to have never been seriously considered, probably because the continuous colonnade would have been a red financial flag, as well as further evidence of Mills's grandiosity to the Congressmen who would have preferred a simple, new brick building.[34]

While Mills's reaction to attack was to first defend himself and then quickly suggest several viable alternatives, Lincoln's response was a lateral attack by consulting an architect with credentials comparable to those of Mills whose professional opinions (unlike those of Elliot) could not be questioned. Because the act of July 4, 1836, authorizing the Treasury Building had given then-President Jackson complete control in the selection of architect, site, and design, Lincoln sought Van Buren's approval to have "some distinguished and skilful [*sic*] Artist, unprejudiced by any predilection, or preferences" examine the Treasury Building. On January 11, 1838, Lincoln wrote the Philadelphia architect Thomas U. Walter asking him to make a "Survey of its present work, with a view to the benefit of our opinion as for the fitness of the site selected for the location of the Edifice, and also, the adaptation of the plans to the object and uses for which it is to be erected." Lincoln's letter to Van Buren the same day made clear his suspicion that Mills was misrepresenting the situation concerning the new and existing buildings because both the horizontal and

vertical positions of the earlier building were not congruent with Mills's new construction. Moreover, he claimed, repeated visits to the site had convinced committee members that the vista between the Capitol and President's House would at the very least be compromised. These feelings about maintaining open views around the President's House reveal a real appreciation of L'Enfant's conception of Washington as a garden city when its urbanization was just beginning.[35]

Walter's success as the architect of Philadelphia's Girard College complex (1833–48) was widely known when he arrived in Washington on January 22, 1838. At that time Congressman Lincoln expanded Walter's responsibilities to include a survey of the Patent Office and his observations on the stability and architectural effects of both it and the Treasury Building. Walter professed great respect for Mills's architectural abilities (whom he did not meet while in Washington) and expressed some distaste at critiquing the elder architect's buildings. Nonetheless, by the twenty-ninth he had composed a thirty-page report focusing on the Treasury Building's site, structural stability, internal organization, and architectural appearance. He found that the Treasury's siting "materially interfered" with the city's plan because the President's House would be partially masked by the oblique view of the Treasury's southern end. Moreover, it was cramped on its site and 15th Street's fourteen-foot grade difference meant the north end of its basement was buried while the southern one was "entirely out of the ground." Walter, the son of a stonemason and particularly well known for designing marble buildings, considered that the Treasury's two-foot three inch-thick walls were "entirely too thin" and recommended that they should have been at least three feet six inches thick. He criticized Mills's sparse use of iron (limited to occasional bars to connect pilasters), claiming that clamps and dowels should have been used throughout

to tie interior brick walls to exterior stone ones. Walter also felt that the three compartments of groin vaults in Mills's fifty-four-foot-wide central vestibules on all the floors facing 15th Street did not have proper counterweights to resist lateral pressure.[36]

As to fitness to its purpose, Walter agreed with other critics that the basement was too dark and damp for offices and thus must be relegated to document storage. Because the third-story windows were half the size of those on the lower floors, and tucked up under the colonnade, he considered them useless to light offices. Nearly half of the 150 rooms (out of the 132 rooms the Secretary of the Treasury needed), Walter felt, were not suited for their purpose. The corridors at only nine-and-one-half feet wide, and lit only at their ends, were too narrow and the office rooms too small for three clerks. Walter was particularly outspoken in his criticism of Mills's design. "This I consider as by no means creditable to the nation." He disapproved of the colonnade's length unbroken by any kind of portico and the inclined plane of its base. Although no elevation of Mills's original or modified designs survive, an engraved view (see fig. III-4), probably based on a lost Mills drawing, shows he decided to terminate the colonnade with the solid ends of the north

II-11 Walter's 1830s alteration of the east facade introduced porticoes and Corinthian columns.

and south wings, their end walls articulated with engaged columns to carry on the vertical rhythm established by the colonnade. "The abrupt termination of the flank portico will also be objectionable, it will always present an unfinished appearance, and the building will look as it if had been surrounded by columns, which (by the way) would have given a much better architectural effect," Walter contended.[37]

A perspective watercolor found among Walter's papers is an intriguing mystery. (fig. II-11) It might be Walter's plan for the building sent or brought to Washington in the early summer of 1836, when several unknown architects hoped to be chosen to design at least one of the newly proposed public buildings. Experts agree that the drawing's style dates from the 1830s and that it was done by Walter, although two mutilations in the lower right corner removed all identifying information. More likely it shows Walter's proposed improvements in 1838 to Mills's 15th Street colonnaded facade. He replaced Mills's central staircase by a shallow portico and added equally shallow pavilions at each end, yet retained Mills's colonnades between the three projections. The upper stories were supported by a rusticated basement entered via ten doorways and adequately lit by twenty-one large windows. The oddity of the design is that Walter's columns have Greek Corinthian capitals, inappropriate because the President's House was Ionic and the Treasury Building should be either that order or a lower one according to the strict dictates of the classical language of architecture. (Mills's colonnade was not begun until 1840.) In addition, Walter topped his building with Greek antefixes rather than a balustrade (see pp. 214–218 for further discussion of such cornices on the Treasury Building).

All of Walter's conclusions, except his promotion of Mills's initial plan for a single building on Lafayette Square, reinforced earlier criticisms by Elliot and others. Walter recognized, however, that circumstances determine results in architecture.

> I have given my whole attention to the works themselves without having any of the circumstances which induced him to adopt the arrangements of which I am speaking thus freely. I am well aware of the difficulties that our architect has to encounter in defending his plans from innovation, not unfrequently [sic] even after they are adopted; and I shall not be surprised to learn that all the errors and deficiencies I have been under the painful necessity of naming, have been committed at the instance of others, and against the better judgement [sic] of the Architect.[38]

It took Mills three weeks to compose his lengthy rebuttal of Walter's report and, notwithstanding the latter's attempts at flattery, Mills referred to him as the "umpire" and counter attacked vigorously. "*Had I* exercised any control over the location of the building, the ground now occupied by it would never have been selected by me," was his opening salvo against the former congressional committees that had determined that the Treasury Building be erected on the site of the burnt Treasury Office. "Owing to the demands, for office room, by the departments intended to be accommodated on the chosen site, and wishing to avoid too great an infringement upon the President's Square, the present position, arrangement, and extent of plan were necessarily decided upon and resulted in shutting out the view of the President's house, from F Street," the last point one that Walter made. Mills's response to the closure of the F Street view is curious. "Indeed it is not evident, why, the natural disadvantages of the site, should be added the sacrifice of public utility to a mere *point de vue* from that street." As to the more politically and emotionally volatile issue of the Pennsylvania Avenue vista, Mills maintained as he always had that "the diagram plan shews [sic] that the North line of the Pennsylvania Avenue extended out towards the President's house, will cut only a few feet off the South-West corner of the Treasury building, which will affect the vision but little, in the width of the Avenue, between the Capitol and President's house." Yes, Mills agreed that the grade of 15th Street was an unfortunate circumstance but one that he had stated would be modified, repeatedly including its re-grading in his estimates.[39]

Mills then recounted at length and with great warmth his experience over the previous three decades in designing and erecting fireproof buildings, including the Fireproof Records Office in Charleston, the Lunatic Asylum in Columbia, South Carolina, and his four New England Customs Houses for the federal government. "[W]here I have thrown arches over rooms of larger dimensions than those of the Treasury, and from walls not more than two-thirds the thickness of the Treasury walls, none of which have failed. One single fact of this nature will compete with volumes of theory." Walter's dependence on theoretical models of dynamics in the face of Mills's experience was especially

II-12 The Paris Bourse's peripheral colonnade inspired Mills's similar design for the Treasury.

hurtful because Mills recognized his own contributions to the American practice of architecture. "[M]y system has some merit in it, and I have gained for the profession an important advantage, namely: to economize in the construction of fire-proof structures, and remedy the evil of very thick walls in such buildings."[40]

Mills used the size of the rooms in the State Office to determine those in the Treasury Building and noted that of the 129 required for immediate use (he gives differing numbers of rooms in several letters) those on the basement's west side were above ground and would be dry, while those on the east were destined for document storage. He conceived of the third story with its smaller windows but "lofty elevation" as substitute attic rooms and if they were found to be too dark for offices once they were in use, skylights could be inserted. "But even admitting that the front Attic rooms next the colonnade, be used for records only, there will still remain 114 suitable apartments for business." The corridors, Mills felt, were sufficiently wide as passages; the wide ones in the State Office and the destroyed Treasury Office were so spacious that they had been subdivided for small offices.[41]

Mills displayed his architectural erudition when confronting Walter's criticisms of his Treasury Building design. Mills was not unique among his professional contemporaries in America for his broad knowledge of ancient and modern European architecture gleaned solely from engraved and textual sources. His display of that learning in his own written communications, however, was quite unusual. In response to Walter's opinion of the Treasury colonnade's aesthetic worth, a matter of "arbitrary rules of taste," Mills cited notable Renaissance and Neoclassical buildings with extended colonnades. "The Bourse, in Paris (fig. II-12), which has extended and unbroken colonnades, is regarded as the most magnificent of modern structures; the Louvre has been admired and often celebrated for its extended and lofty colonnade, elevated upon a *high basement*." In addition, Mills cited an English writer who bemoaned the pediment in the center of the Louvre colonnade (1678–88) as its one defect. (fig. II-13) Early in his career Mills argued in favor of a triumphal column for

II-13 Mills acknowledged vying with the famous Louvre colonnade in his 15th Street range of columns.

the Baltimore Washington Monument because there was none in America. In 1838 he noted that "we have no colonnade of any extent in our country, and must form our judgement [*sic*] as to its merits, from those abroad, if we have not professional skill to judge for ourselves."[42]

His sarcasm was never more acerbic than when he responded to Walter's demeaning of the double-ramped staircase leading from the sidewalk to the main story in the middle of the colonnade. Mills planned the Treasury Building's main entrances to be at its north and south ends, claiming that it "was to avoid the appearance of steps on the front (which was adviseable [*sic*] for the effect of the colonnade) that the disposition of the side steps was introduced." Mills further claimed that "a similar arrangement of steps to the colonnade of the Artemisium [*sic*] of Ephesus" justified its use on the Treasury Building's long east front. "It is an unfortunate circumstance for the storied fame of the Architect,

Dinocrates, that his ideas should not meet with Mr. Walter's approbation," was Mills's final shot. The earliest architectural treatise that illustrated such a staircase on the Temple of Diana at Ephesus, the largest temple in antiquity, was its hypothetical reconstruction by Fischer von Erlach in his *Entwurf einer historischen architektur* (1721; *A Collection of Historical Architecture*), engravings of the world's greatest architectural achievements. (fig. II-14) Whether or not Mills had seen a print of von Erlach's plate (no copy of the book is known to have been in an American library at that early date), he almost surely knew the rather naïve copy of that plate which appeared in Robert Mayo's *A New System of Mythology* published in Philadelphia in 1815–19.[43] (fig. II-15)

Opposite page, top: II-14 Erlach's 1722 reconstruction of the Temple of Diana suggested the Treasury's lateral staircase.

Bottom: II-15 Mills may well have known Mayo's 1815 version of Erlach's print published in Philadelphia.

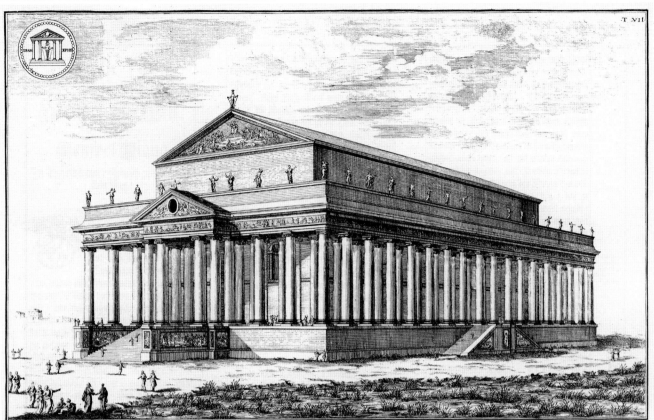

T.VII

Der Tempel Diana zu Ephesus, woran gantz Asien, 220 Jahr gebauet, hatte in der Länge 425. Schüh; In der Breite 220 Sch.; In allen aus und inwendig 127 Säulen von 60 Sch: Höhe und Ionischer Ordnüng. Wie das Vestibulum auf angeführter medaille und die rudera auswesen.

Le Temple de Diane d'Ephese, L'ouvrage de toute l'Asie pendant 220 ans. Il avoit 425. pieds de longueur, et 220 pieds de largeur. On y comtoit dedans et dehors en tout 127. Colones de 60 pieds de haut. La medaille ci jointe, qui represente son vestibule, fait voir aussi bien que les ruines, que l'ordre en a été Ionique.

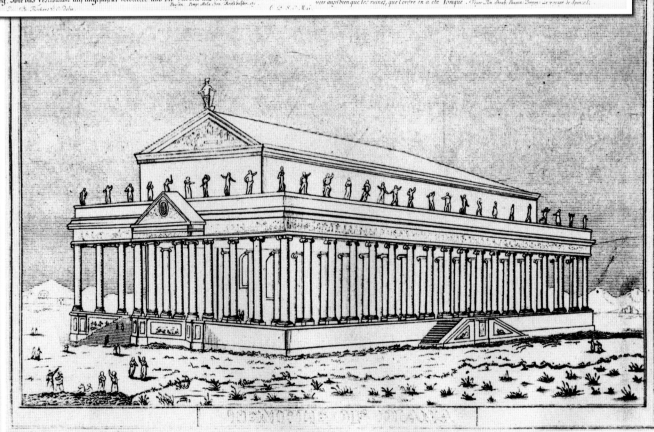

Throughout his rebuttal to Walter's report, Mills repeatedly cited congressional actions documented in official reports created during the previous five years to explain his decisions. He concluded his very able self defense by noting: "Should the committee recommend the taking down and removing the building from its present site, the cause will not be found to arise out of any defect in the structure itself, as I have shewn [sic], but on the unsuitableness of the site, and the obstruction it gives to the views to and from the President's house. These drawbacks I could not control; I was hemmed within certain limits, and [by] these compelled to move." Walter, a Philadelphian, may not have realized the risks of questioning former actions of congressmen, but Mills certainly should have. Lincoln responded to both their reports by seeking Van Buren's approval to hire the Boston architect Alexander Parris for a third evaluation because of the "unfortunate difference of opinion" between Mills and Walter as well as other artists.[44]

Parris, who had commanded an engineering corps during the War of 1812 and been involved in several engineering and architectural projects for the federal government in New England, was in Washington in late February 1838 for one of his periodic southern winter trips looking for work. Like Walter, Parris had extensive experience designing and erecting stone buildings with brick interior walls. Whereas Lincoln had directed Walter to consider four questions about the Treasury Building, he gave Parris specific instructions relating to six possible faults: how its colonnade, windows, and walls would mesh with the State Office; if the dimensions and lighting of the corridors was sufficient; whether the basement rooms would have enough light and be sufficiently dry to be occupied by clerks; if Mills's method of construction was strong enough to withstand adverse weather conditions as well as normal weights and pressures; and, whether the 15th Street entrance steps relative to

their direction, dimensions, arrangement, and appearance were viable.[45]

Parris, who also was asked to suggest solutions to any problems he encountered, accompanied his report of March 15, 1838, with two plans illustrating the impossibility of connecting the exterior and interiors of the State Office with the new Treasury Building. (fig. II-16) The former must be removed, the same conclusion Walter came to. Moreover, Parris considered the corridors too narrow for the building's number of workers and visitors; the basement "too dark for the occupation of Clerks, and too damp, when closed, for the deposite [sic] of papers;" and the attic windows too small to adequately light rooms for clerks. Parris apparently was given a copy of Walter's report because he agreed with his assessment of Mills's construction of the walls and vaults, suggesting "cast iron beams with brick arches be substituted for the groined arches," noting he had recently constructed such floors at the Boston Navy Yard. As to the 15th Street entrance, Parris confessed he was at a loss for an answer, "nor [did he] see any remedy for the disagreeable appearance owing to the grade of this street." He went on to say that the "most elegant structure that art can devise may present an ordinary appearance in an unsuitable location." Parris concluded with a discussion of Mills's method of constructing the Treasury and Patent Office Buildings, citing several of his own solutions in New England buildings. He regularly used cast iron to solve structural problems, certainly the cutting edge of building technology during the previous decade.[46]

Bowing gracefully to the inevitable, Mills wrote Van Buren and Lincoln about "disposing of the present building erecting for the Treasury, looking forward to the final removal of the building when other buildings on the new site shall have been prepared." He suggested roofing it above the second floor and using it temporarily for the Treasury Department to secure its records because several years might elapse

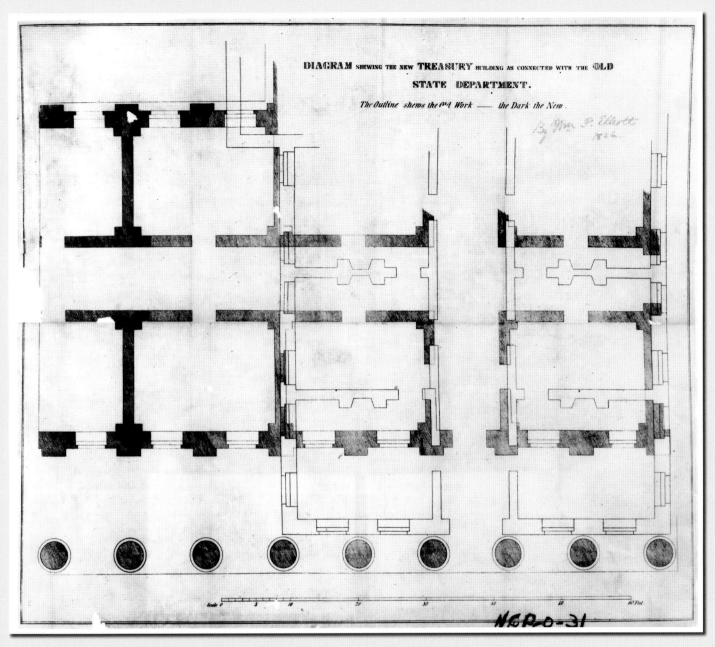

DIAGRAM SHEWING THE NEW TREASURY BUILDING AS CONNECTED WITH THE OLD
STATE DEPARTMENT.

The Outline shews the Old Work —— the Dark the New.

II-16 Alexander Parris demonstrated the difficulty of salvaging the existing State Office.

before a new building could be erected. Mills used the opportunity to suggest that future buildings be erected of a better material than the Aquia, Virginia, sandstone he had been required by law to use. Lincoln's response to was to recall Walter to consult about an appropriate site for a single office building for all the departments and to garner congressional support for such a startling change in direction.[47]

In mid-January 1838 Lincoln did not wait until he heard whether Walter agreed to his ini-

tial examination of the Treasury Building but immediately called a Committee of the Whole House to vote on a bill calling for the "removal of the walls of the Treasury building, and for the erection of a fire-proof building for the Post Office Department," apparently in response to Mills's alternate proposals that the Treasury Department be located in a large office complex either north or south of the President's House. The bill was defeated 99 to 70, but it was only the first skirmish in a major battle. On March

29 Lincoln reported a bill, "New Treasury and Post Office Buildings," that published Walter's and Parris's reports, letters attesting to their credentials, and Mills's correspondence with the committee.[48]

Mills felt the report so unfairly damaged his reputation that he wrote Speaker of the House Francis W. Pickens (a fellow South Carolinian) and the House members. "The object of these reports appear evidently intended to influence the vote of the house ... for removing the Treasury building to some other site by conducing the idea that the walls are inadequate to sustain the arches with which they are charged, when, in fact, *I have proved both by theory and long practice, that if there is any fault, these walls are unnecessarily thick for this object.*" Mills further noted that the report was interpreted to state that "the walls of this building are cracked, that the arches are spreading, in fact, that the whole edifice is tumbling to pieces; when, on the contrary, not a crack is to be seen in any of the walls, not the least spreading or giving in the arches," a fact that could be verified by the many members of Congress who had visited the construction site. Yet, the brief reporting (rather than reprinting) of his letter in the *Journal of the House of Representatives* was so bland—"which reports are calculated to injure him in his professional business and character, and denying that there is any foundation for said reports"—that the public was left with the impression that, in fact, the Treasury Building was falling down.[49]

Plain-speaking Arkansas Democrat Archibald Yell protested Lincoln's bill for an appropriation to dismantle the Treasury Building when it was again presented in mid-April on the grounds that it was the "commencement of another scheme for a splendid and a profligate Government" directly opposed to Jackson's and Van Buren's principles. The bill, Yell maintained, "is intended and designed for political effect: it has been conceived in a settled determination to get up a wasteful expenditure of the public funds, for the purpose of enabling the opposition of the Administration to raise the watchword of alarm, preparatory to a deafening outcry of profusion and prodigality against this Administration." Yell either simplified a complex situation or saw directly to its heart.

> As for the new Treasury building, Mr. Chairman, what are the objections raised against it, that call for its demolition? Why, sir, it is said that it stands in the way of the President's mansion! It is guilty of the monstrous crime of hiding the President's House from the view of *some gentlemen* who hold seats in the other end of the Capitol. It impedes their vision, and, forsooth, they cannot see that building, for the occupancy of which their hearts palpitate, and all their aspirations are breathed by midday, and on which their dreams are based at the midnight hour. [Loud laughter and approbation.][50]

The next day, Virginia Whig John H. Fulton submitted the same thirty-six-page report to the Senate that Lincoln submitted to the House on March 29 that called for the Treasury to be dismantled and the materials to be used to construct a new Post Office. Fulton was the chairman of the Senate's Committee on Public Buildings, formed when the issue became so volatile. A joint committee soon followed. That same day, April 17, 1838, Lincoln gave a lengthy speech in which he refused to blame Jackson (even Whig congressmen criticized the hero of New Orleans at their own peril) but repeatedly and viciously maligned Mills. "In the judgment of the committee, *with the architect,* and *with him alone,* rests the fault for whatever cause of complaint justly exists." He used the original law, Walter's and Parris's reports, as well as other information gathered by him to denounce Mills as both a liar and an incompetent archi-

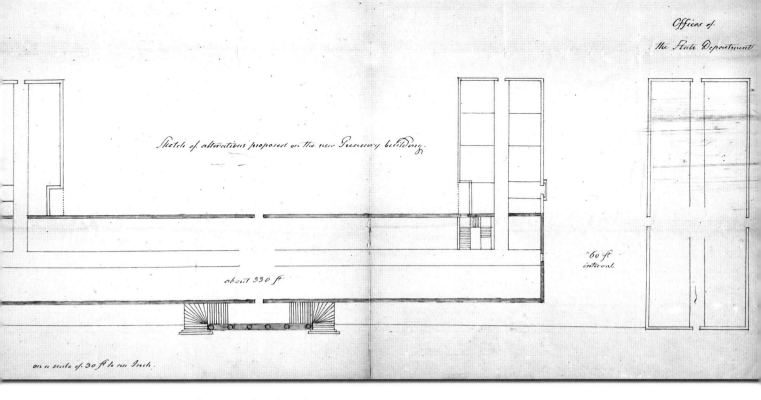

Sketch of alterations proposed on the new Treasury building

about 330 ft

60 ft interval

on a scale of 30 ft to an Inch.

II-17 Bulfinch suggested replacing Mills's colonnade with a portico and adding short end wings.

tect. He wrote Van Buren the same day that the joint committee agreed unanimously that some architect other than Mills should carry out the recommended changes to the Patent Office but made no mention of the Treasury Building.[51]

Within four months Lincoln changed from being Mills's apparent ally by securing him the commission for a magnificent office building on Lafayette Square or double buildings south of the President's House, to a malicious and seemingly vindictive enemy bent on the architect's destruction. Van Buren's reaction to Lincoln's recommendation that Mills be replaced as the architect of public buildings was to create a Board of Commissioners of Public Buildings composed of the secretaries of Treasury, State, and War. They wrote Lincoln asking if the 25th Congress during its second session was likely to pass a law suspending work on the Treasury Building because they must proceed with directing its completion if no such legislation was anticipated. Lincoln replied that the "Committees have no other or better means of Judging, than the Commissioners themselves."[52]

The third and last notable American architect to critique Mills's design was Charles Bulfinch, who retired to Boston a decade earlier after having spent twelve years in Washington

as the architect of the Capitol. At the beginning of May, he replied to a now-lost letter from his son-in-law, Washington attorney David A. Hall, who had sent the architect the lengthy congressional reports. From them Bulfinch made a long-distance assessment of the architectural problems involved, first expressing shock that "any Committee or agent of the government would sanction designs so extravagant" and unsuitable for their use as office buildings. Because he found Mills's design "incongruous," Bulfinch favored the Walter-Parris interpretations but considered the Lafayette Square consolidated offices "quite visionary" and delicately probed whether he himself might be called back to Washington to complete the Treasury. Bulfinch included a sketch of how to resolve the problem of marrying the new Treasury Building to the old State Office that included widening the spine by eliminating the colonnade and proposing lateral steps to approach a new portico on its sides. (fig. II-17) Hall turned Bulfinch's letter over to Lincoln who must have replied indicating that Bulfinch might be considered as the Treasury's new architect because the architect wrote Lincoln six weeks later describing his proposed design for a new building based on the old Treasury Office.[53]

During May and early June of 1838, the battle continued on two fronts, the executive and legislative, with the most vociferous activity occurring in the halls of Congress, while the Board of Commissioners and the Office of Public Buildings were kept busy gathering information requested by either House or Senate committees. Mills himself was silent, either having discovered himself—or been advised—that all his explanations had been and probably would continue to be used against him. As three of the most powerful men in the executive branch, the board of commissioners almost certainly worked subtly behind the scenes to influence individual members of Congress. Former President John Quincy Adams, now a Whig member of Congress from Massachusetts and the only diary keeper known to have commented privately on the affair, was Lincoln's ally.

On May 19 Lincoln offered a resolution asking that a half day be set aside to debate taking down the Treasury's walls; however, it was defeated 77 to 67. He was more successful a week later when he added erecting a Post Office to the bill, the vote being 98 in favor and 46 opposed. The outcome of that debate was the resolution to direct Commissioner of Public Buildings Noland to produce a detailed accounting of all the monies spent on the Treasury Building, itemized according to kinds of materials and branches of labor. On June 8 Adams noted in his diary that Lincoln had called one of the New England collectors to testify about the poor construction of one of Mills's customs houses erected there. "Cushing was irresistibly facetious, and while up, gave his advice to take down the embryo palace of the Treasury Department and build a plain brick fire-proof republican work house for the Department in its place."[54]

Mills finally found his defender in George M. Keim, a Democratic Congressman from Pennsylvania, who on June 8 demolished Walter's seemingly unassailable reputation while presenting reasoned arguments to finish the Treasury Building according to Mills's design. He began his speech with an apology to House members "for an attempt to solicit their attention upon a subject of comparatively so little interest to them" and went on to accuse the opposition of party bias, observing "that a latent propensity is apparent throughout to confer odium upon the past and present Administration. Indeed, with all the smooth denials of the gentleman from Massachusetts [Mr. Lincoln,] his indirect and apologetic language for the state of things, was the first inducement to invite my attention." Keim dismissed the witty quip of his fellow Pennsylvanian, John Sergeant—"instead of falling [the Treasury Building] was rising to ruins"—as wishful thinking as he restated the most salient facts about its construction drawn from the same congressional reports as his opponents had used to malign it. Adams maintained that "Keim looks at this object, and all others, through the smoky lens of party politics, and stands by the wretched bungler in architecture, Mills, because he was recommended by Mr. Jefferson."[55]

As a Pennsylvanian, Keim was familiar with the will and intentions of Stephen Girard to found a home and school for orphans that resulted in Walter's designs for Girard College, the complex that led Lincoln to invite Walter's professional opinion on the public buildings. Girard, who "from his general regard for economy, and his antipathy to useless and unnecessary expenditure, never projected, either in the spirit or the letter, a building such as is Girard College," in Keim's judgment. "[H]owever beautiful and strictly in good taste may be the design in the abstract, it is, in this particular, an open and plain violation of the last will and testament of Stephen Girard. So much, by way of digression, as to the skill of Mr. Walters, and the independent and faithful manner in which he exercises it."[56]

Keim, who pursued classical studies and attended Princeton College, repeatedly defended Mills "whose character in every respect has been fully established from the time of Mr. Jefferson" personally and professionally. "The veracity of Mr. Mills, with his most exemplary character, are too well established in this community to be impugned... The filthy slang of the billingsgate school ill becomes any censors of public taste, and our own infirmities should induce us not to investigate those of others, particularly when so much ill would result to the comforts and happiness of an interesting family." Keim's most valuable addition to the debate was his understanding of Mills's Treasury design as an inventive contribution to the long history of classical architecture. "If science is progressive, so should the polite arts keep pace with them, and American architecture become a new school, in which might predominate as a characteristic feature, the principles of economy, simplicity, and convenience," Keim asserted. Moreover, "instead of making [Washington] the counterfeit imitation of 'the Eternal City,' would it not be conducive to our better interest if the same simplicity were preserved which the spirit of our Constitution inculcates ... Utility is emphatically the American order, and look where you may, it will be found to be consonant with the feelings, as it is compatible with American taste." Keim thus equated the Republican simplicity of Mills's Treasury and the attitude of the Jacksonian Democrats towards expenditure on public buildings in contrast to Whig profligacy in their willingness to tear down a building in which the government had invested more than $200,000.[57]

After Keim's speech and those of others on June 8, a vote was taken to let the motion to remove the Treasury "lie on the table" (a legislative strategy to avoid a vote on any particular

motion) and it passed 88 to 82. Motions to reconsider that victory for Mills began the next day with the final assault mounted two days later when Henry H. Wise of Virginia declared that he was indifferent whether the building stood or fell during the rest of Van Buren's administration. "[T]his Treasury building is the House that Jack built; it is a monument of the inability and stupidity of the Administration; and I am reminded to inquire, where is the malt that once lay in the House that Jack built. It is all gone; the rats have eaten it; and yet we are called upon to vote more malt to be placed in this House that Jack built, to be devoured by the rats and cats of the Administration." Wise had interrupted Archibald Yell (the first congressman to ask for an accounting of expenditures on the Treasury) who was opposed to tearing down the Treasury's walls but was concerned about erecting such an expensive building when there was a substantial national debt.[58]

When all the congressional shouting was over on June 11, the Board of Commissioners quietly wrote Noland: "It being sufficiently apparent the new Treasury Building is not to be removed or altered by any Act of Congress, you will cause the work on that Building to be resumed tomorrow and carried on with all convenient dispatch. Any new directions needed or any questions proper for us to settle, you will please to call our special attention to from time to time as they arise." The following day, the Joint Committee on Public Buildings recommended that the work go forward, but with Alexander Parris replacing Mills and some to-be-named superintendent replacing Noland. On June 23 a House Resolution asked Van Buren several questions about the executive department's future plans for completing the building and requested that "a definite and descriptive plan of the elevation and dimensions of the Treasury building" be laid before the House, including full costs, drawings Mills sent the Board of Commissioners four days later. Mills responded that he would "give a temporary finish to the present structure at each end, and without affecting the walls of the present State Department building," until Congress directed that the north and south wings be built. Moreover, the "plan marked A will show in what manner the south wing may be drawn in so far as not to interfere with the line on Pennsylvania avenue." Mills's second drawing indicated how the re-grading of 15th Street would improve the building's appearance. Although these drawings are lost, from Mills's descriptions they duplicated at least one set that he previously sent to Congress.[59]

"Great Distress Would Result:" The Treasury Workmen

The political power of the Treasury Building's workforce, combined with Keim's reasoned review of its history, brought the congressional investigation to a halt. At the beginning of the 1837 season, the laborers lobbied Noland to change the regulations, established in 1816, that set their hours "from the 20th of March to the 22d of Septr from 6 in the morning to 6 at night with one hour to breakfast and one to dinner, from the 22d of Septr to the last of Octr. from sun to sun, from the first of Novr. to the first or middle of March to go to work in the morning at one hour after sun rise, and work to sun down with one hour to dinner." Their goal was to establish a uniform 10-hour day to conform to the hours the skilled mechanics—masons, stonecutters, bricklayers, carpenters, and painters—worked. Mills solicited information from architects and contractors about wages paid in Philadelphia and Baltimore and learned that although Washington's laborers worked longer days they were paid more.[60]

The laborers' petition was denied, but the following year—in mid-February 1838—the laborers went directly to Congress asking for legislation to include them in the "ten hour system," claiming they worked three hours more per day during the summer than the trained artisans on the same job sites. At the beginning of May they followed up with a petition to President Van Buren that he referred to the new Board of Commissioners of Public Buildings who advised Noland to negotiate lower wages for fewer hours. While awaiting an anticipated congressional report, Noland noted: "It is little remarkable that any of the laborers in the employment of Government should be discontented, when there are so many poor men imploring to work and anxiously waiting for the first vacancies that may occur." Lincoln's draft of the congressional report dated May 11 pointed out that the petitioners were all freemen who understood at the time they sought work the hours and rates of compensation; he further remarked that they were fortunate to have "found occupation during a period of great pressure and want."[61]

While Congress was still considering the laborers' petition for ten-hour workdays, Van Buren ordered construction on the Treasury Building halted until Congress decided its fate. On May 5 Noland began laying off skilled mechanics as well as common laborers. A week later Lincoln tried to use the workmen's plight to push his bill through the House, noting many of them "had large families dependent upon their support and daily bread, and consequently great distress would result, unless this subject [dismantling the Treasury Building] was early acted upon." In the meantime, the workmen organized themselves. On June 19 Adams presented a petition to the House signed by seventy-eight mechanics who requested they be paid while work on the Treasury Building was suspended. They pointed out: "many of [us] have removed our Families from a distance, and have no other means of support than our daily labour [sic], and knowing that it has been the constant practice of Government to grant furloughs to its officers of large Salaries, and continue their pay." Other petitions signed by smaller groups of workmen sent to both houses of Congress and directly to Lincoln soon followed. Collectively, they helped end Lincoln's investigation.[62]

By stopping the work, Van Buren took a risk, calculating that the workmen's ire (and its ripple effect nationally) would push Congress to vote for the Treasury's completion. Lincoln understood that he had been out-maneuvered but blamed Noland, claiming the building commissioner had promised the workmen speedy reemployment at the time he let them go. Noland replied: "Whether the workmen were encouraged to expect a resumption of the work immediately after its interruption, I am unable to say. It was generally believed, that Congress knowing the situation of the Workmen, would decide promptly on the subject; and this may have encouraged them to expect a resumption at an earlier date than the 11th of June." These varied surviving documents suggest that halting the Treasury's construction (with all its attendant labor problems) was the only way the executive branch found to circumvent Congressman Lincoln. During June and July Noland and the various superintendents processed the workmen's claims for lost wages, some for as many as twenty-five days, which Congress reluctantly agreed to pay. The investigation's monetary cost was measurable while the silent damage to Mills's reputation and to the public's perception of the Treasury Building's quality was incalculable. For the remainder of the project, Noland was the central clearing house for information and policy decisions among the President, Congress, the superintendents of workmen, the Board of Commissioners of Public Buildings, and Mills who abandoned his lengthy explanatory letters to congressmen and wrote only cursory notes or reports to Noland.[63]

"Discovered in the Neighborhood of Washington:" Etruscan Mantels

In mid-July 1838 the Treasury Building's offices were finished to the point that Mills began to think about the fireplace mantels. He originally planned "plain, neat marble Mantles" for about 100 rooms costing between $20 and $25 each. For the Secretary's office as well as those of heads of bureaus—twelve rooms—Mills planned more elaborate mantels costing four times as much. During the early 1830s Mills and his family befriended Ferdinand Pettrich, the expatriate Dresden-born sculptor who had been a student in Rome of the notable Danish sculptor Bertel Thorvaldsen. Pettrich "discovered in the neighborhood of Washington, a clay possessing uncommon properties of hardening and capable of being moulded [sic] into classic forms, as well as ornamental with designs similar to the ancient Etruscan Vasses [sic]." He convinced Mills that he could make both plain and ornamented mantels for the Treasury in the "Etruscan style" at a savings of between twenty and fifty percent. Mills knew of no earlier experiment in America to make composition stone mantels although imported Coade stone mantels (made from clay mixed with glue), such as those in the parlor and dining room at Washington's Octagon House, were admired. On August 1 the Board of Commissioners authorized Noland to contract with Pettrich for all the mantels "on the condition that one be burnt and that it then meets the expectation of the architect and the approval of the Superintendent."[64]

In mid-October Mills reported that Pettrich's considerable preparatory work was finished and four plain and four "figure" mantels were ready for burning. He further predicted that Pettrich would be able to make twelve mantels per week. In reality, Pettrich ran into difficulties during the firing process and, by the end of January 1839, he had completed

II-18 Pettrich added Etruscan mantels to Mills's use of the major classical orders in his buildings.

the twelve ornamental mantels for which he was paid $75 each before being released from the rest of his contract. The Treasury Building has nine surviving Etruscan mantels, all seemingly made of cast iron, their caryatids primitive figures derived from pre-Roman Etruscan art. (fig. II-18) Publication in the January 1839 issue of the *North American Review* of a translated précis of Giuseppe Micali's pioneering 1832 book on the history of the Etruscan people certainly would have excited both the architect and the sculptor. If the decorative design for the mantels originated with Mills (most likely), he would have been adding to his and Latrobe's compendium of architectural elements derived from the classical world.[65]

Appropriations in 1839 essentially completed most of the Treasury Building's interiors,

with only $9,525 needed in 1840 to finish stairs and their iron railings, woodwork, and plastering. In 1840 the House, on the advice of its Committee on Ways and Means, exercised its ultimate power by withholding the requested $105,000 appropriation to erect the colonnade along 15th Street, the center wing's portico facing the President's House, and the outbuildings. Because the colonnade was such an imposing and expensive architectural feature, it again became the lightening rod that attracted criticism. For the first two months of 1840, the men worked "on the credit of the government, under an agreement made with the [Board of] Commissioners of Public Buildings, that we were to have employment 'until an appropriation was made for the Treasury Building.'" On March 1, Noland finally suspended approximately half

Fortress of Finance: The United States Treasury Building

the stonecutters, retaining the married men to do piece work by the day but discharging the single men. On Saturday evening, March 9, the unmarried stonecutters met and factiously passed three resolutions because "we have been informed by the superintendents that if we will marry they will find employment for us." Their first resolution was that the action of "the superintendents of the Treasury Building *is perfectly just and fair,*" the second that the stonecutters resolved to call "upon the ladies of this city to assist us in our laudable design," and the third to appoint their secretary to accept the ladies' proposals. The stonecutters' entire paid newspaper notice that concluded with "Wives Wanted!" was either their own strategy to use public opinion to force the congressional appropriation or it was an elaborate ploy undertaken with Noland's knowledge and consent.[66] (fig. II-19)

On the last day of April, the House began considering the 1840 appropriations for the Treasury Building. The Committee on Ways and Means inserted $51,000 in place of $105,000 "to make it comfortable to the occupants" because of "the ornamental work it was not deemed prudent to progress with at this time." Physician and Pennsylvania Democrat David Petrikin argued for the full appropriation, noting $53,000 was due the workmen for their labor during the previous four months. Lincoln was not about to fall in the same trap twice. "[I]t would be doing crying injustice to the mechanics, to whom more was due than was proposed to be appropriated. It would be improper to discharge them, considering the nature of the circumstances under which they were brought here." He proposed this amendment "including the arrearages due for materials furnished, and labor performed on the said building, certified by the Commissioner of Public Buildings to amount, on the 15th of April, 1840, to the sum of $53,194.06, [within] the [total] sum of $105,000." When discussion of the mat-

AN ADJOURNED MEETING OF THE UN-married Stone-Cutters from the Treasury Building was held this evening, March 9, when the committee appointed on the 7th instant to draught a preamble and resolutions, reported the following, which were unanimously adopted:

Whereas we, the unmarried Stone-Cutters formerly in the employ of Government, at the Treasury Building, have been suspended from the said employ, the said suspension having taken place in consequence of our being in a state of single blessedness; and whereas we have been informed by the superintendents that if we will MARRY they will find employment for us: Therefore, be it

Resolved, That the resolution adopted by the superintendents of the Treasury Building *is perfectly just and fair,* and that we endeavor to furnish ourselves with the necessary requisition.

Resolved, That, for the purpose of furthering the foregoing resolution, an advertisement be placed in the National Intelligencer calling upon the ladies of this city to assist us in our laudable design.

Resolved, That the Secretary be authorized to receive proposals, and that he do report the same to a meeting of this body on Saturday evening next.

On motion, adjourned.
WATSON KIRKHAM, Chairman.
JOHN M. TAGGART, Secretary.

WIVES WANTED !

The subscriber has been authorized to issue an advertisement for wives for the Stone-Cutters at the Treasury Building who still remain unmarried. They are about 28 in number, and between the ages of 23 and 35 years. A good opportunity is now offered to those young ladies who wish to enter the matrimonial state.

Applicants must be between the ages of 17 and 33 years, of good moral character, and good disposition. Applications sent through the Post Office, before Saturday next at 12 M., addressed to the subscriber, will be thankfully received, and immediately attended to.   JOHN M. TAGGART, Secretary.
WASHINGTON, MARCH 10, 1840.

II-19 Unmarried stonecutters, suspended in favor of retaining married ones, protested humorously.

ter resumed on May 1, Congressman Adams "defended [Lincoln's] amendment with much animation. He contended that Government was bound in honor and, by every consideration of justice and equity, to pay these laborers for the work they had performed." Other Congressmen argued that the mechanics continued to work knowing there had been no appropriation, but Lincoln repeatedly supported the full $105,000 appropriation, even stating that since Mills had asked for that amount "there was no good reason why it should not be appropriated." The full amount was appropriated, the vote being 80 to 43, but the workmen spent much of the remainder of the year fighting to collect their back pay.[67]

"The Only Ornament to the Building:" The Treasury Colonnade

An extensive colonnade for the Treasury Building was an obsession with Mills. It is likely that his 1833 proposal for a Lafayette Square building included a colonnade similar to those he designed for the 1834 project and the 1836 accepted design. Judging from the later versions, the 1833 colonnade would have encircled three sides of the complex, perhaps have even spanned its 650-foot-wide open side that faced south. Orientation was not Mills's concern. Rather, impressive architectural effect was his goal because he considered an expensive colonnade of unprecedented length a necessary expression of the Treasury Department's prominent role in the national government and pervasive presence in American life. Mills almost surely designed porticoes for the ends of the east and west wings that overlooked the President's House's north portico. In fact, the 15th Street design President Jackson approved in 1836 seems to have varied from Mills's Lafayette Square design only in its reduced scale and the addition of a central wing to make it an E-shaped rather than a C-shaped building.

Mills believed that the visual effect of viewing the colonnade along 15th Street from Pennsylvania Avenue to G Street "will be far from being disagreeable. The eye will always accommodate itself to natural obstacles in connection with artificial objects. The level line, which we will give for our front, will be traced by the eye as it rises the plane the whole distance, and when looking at the facade from each end, the perspective will accommodate the tout ensemble, and the eye will be satisfied to be deceived." Adapting this tenet of picturesque landscape design to enhance the monumental effect at one of the city's two most important Neoclassical enclaves was a brilliant solution to Washington's rolling terrain and much appreciated by later generations. Mills constantly sought comparisons with other cities and other great buildings for all of his major Washington buildings.

> We have no Colonnade in this country by which we can draw a comparison, and there is none in Europe, not even that of the Louvre, that will exceed it in extent.
>
> Our Colonnade constitutes the only ornament to the building, and its utility is obvious; every part of the structure is rigidly plain; even the pilasters cuts into and form a part of the strength called for in the fire proof system of construction.[68]

The Treasury's column capitals were begun well before the shafts were raised, probably because their carving took upwards of a month each to complete. Between the fall of 1837 and the following spring, Pettrich sculpted the capitals for about $100 each; each month he was able to rough-carve one while doing the finishing work on two others.[69] Mills's choice of richly decorated Ionic capitals based on those on the Athenian Erectheum was well within the tradition of American Greek Revival architecture. The Erectheum model (see fig. II-7) was characterized by tightly wound volutes connected by a gently-sloped stone bridge that might be likened to the ends of a bolt of cloth wrapped around two poles, its bridge relaxed while its "spool ends" were under tension. (fig. II-20) The second characteristic unique to the Erectheum's Ionic capitals was its wide necking band of alternating stylized anthemion leaves and flowers, the most sculpturally elaborate example of the Ionic order found in Greek architecture.

Within the traditions of classical usage chronicled by the Roman architect Vitruvius (*c.* 90 to *c.* 20 B.C.), Corinthian columns were reserved for the most significant buildings in a city while Ionic ones were used for the buildings in the second tier of importance. In Washington, the Capitol is a Corinthian building and the President's House an Ionic one, choices made by

II-20 Pettrich carved the Treasury's sandstone Ionic columns at the rate of about one per month.

Washington and Jefferson to indicate the relative importance of the legislative and executive branches of government. Ionic capitals were appropriate for the Treasury Building because it was part of the complex associated with the Ionic President's House.

The east colonnade itself was not raised until 1840–42, each column composed of six separate drums stacked atop one another with iron rods aligning their centers. Following classical precedent, the shafts bulged slightly at their mid-points before diminishing in diameter at their tops just below the capitals. Following both ancient and modern practice, fluting of the Treasury colonnade's shafts from top to bottom was done once the drums were *in situ* and the capitals and entablature they carried were securely in place. Pettrich's deep undercutting of all the capital's sculptural details—almost to the point of crudeness—assured that they could be seen distinctly from the ground below, especially important because Mills and Pettrich realized that the Aquia sandstone's brown hue deepened with age and exposure to the elements.

In mid-August 1842 Mills reported to Noland that contracts had been executed to complete the east front with the balustrade put

in place, the colonnade's ceiling finished with plastered panels, and marble flagging cemented in place on its floor. Mills designed an ornate iron railing, its acanthus motif based on the capitals above, to enclose the colonnade's terrace. "In the design of this railing it was contemplated to terminate that surmounting the blocking of the steps with cast iron tripods for lamps and provision should be made for these to make a suitable finish to this railing." Lamps atop tripod posts at the top of the entrance stair lighted the way for employees and visitors alike.[70] (fig. II-21)

In 1851 Vermont's prominent Neoclassical sculptor Horatio Greenough, who spent much of the past quarter century working in Florence and was a purist about how classical architectural prototypes were to be reinterpreted in America, objected to Mills's integration of the railings with the colonnade.

> What shall we say of the balustrades, where massive iron bars have been driven bodily into the columns as though a column in a first-class building might be treated like a blind wall in the basest structure, and that, too, without a shadow of need? ... Do not such absurd and ignorant malpractices look as if a barbarous race had undertaken to enjoy the magnificence of a conquered people, and not known how to set about it?[71]

Two years later, local columnist Ben Perley Poore characterized the colonnade as a "velvet vest, with no pockets, and a flimsey [*sic*] cotton back—all show." What Mills conceived of as a timeless architectural gesture to express America's economic stability linked to its political system others saw as a pompous, hollow gesture.[72]

Building the colonnade was a national architectural achievement with various local consequences. (fig. II-22) In the dim morning light of February 23, 1842, soon after seven stone carvers were positioned to begin their

LADY CLERKS LEAVING THE TREASURY DEPARTMENT AT WASHINGTON.—[SKETCHED BY A. R. WAUD.]

day's labor fluting the columns, part of the scaffolding collapsed. Five men saved themselves by clinging to planks and ropes until they could be rescued, but Washingtonian Samuel Walker and Georgetowner Francis G. Beatty fell thirty-five feet to pavement. Both survived but were badly crippled and in May began seeking government pensions. It was not until August 13, 1842, that the Senate considered settling their claims, offering each of the men $500, but adjourned without a final vote. Beatty and Walker were still seeking compensation in 1850.[73]

Even before the Treasury Building's three light-colored granite wings got underway in the mid-1850s, the color of Mills's colonnade was an issue. Mills himself objected to using the Aquia sandstone to construct both the Treasury Building and Patent Office because its porous surface required periodic painting to repel moisture and protect it from disintegrating. Greenough reported in 1851 that the Treasury Building was painted in three shades of gray, the granite basement one color, the columns a second, and the wall behind the colonnade a third. "Even the lampposts have been daubed with divers tints, like a barber's pole," Greenough complained. By 1864, after the granite west wing was completed, the colonnade's dinginess prompted one Washington commenter to note that "it will become necessary to paint the colonnade to resemble granite."[74]

Opposite page, top: II-21 Mills's monumental colonnade changed Washington's streets from suburban to urban in character.

Bottom: II-22 At least two 19th century re-gradings of 15th Street improved the east colonnade's appearance.

The engineers and architects who erected the south and west wings preferred more permanent solutions to what they considered defects in Mills's colonnade. In 1855, six months after Mills's death, engineer Alexander Bowman suggested that a central eight-column portico to project twelve feet in front of the colonnade be built to conform to the central porticoes on the other facades. The problem was the wing's position immediately adjacent to the sidewalk; three blocks of 15th Street would have to be narrowed considerably or the corresponding properties on its east side purchased by the government. Eight years later Isaiah Rogers, supervising architect of the west wing, agreed with the concept of an east central portico to match the rest of the building but proposed one with ten columns to be more in proportion with the east facade's great length. Rogers solved the problem of acquiring more land on the east by simply removing the colonnade altogether, designing a shallow central portico with three staircases passing between the central ones and reducing the columns on the corner pavilions from four to two. (fig. II-23) Rogers's central portico columns were either engaged, i.e., attached to the wall, or the portico was very shallow. The removal of Mills's colonnade (and the recession of Rogers's central portico) would have allowed for a broad areaway between the facade and sidewalk along 15th Street.

Rogers's solution to the downside of his proposal—dismantling document storage rooms in the attic story and the drafting room that partially extended over the colonnade—

was to heighten the third story while building a new attic story behind a high, solid entablature. Although the south, west, and planned north wings had dramatically increased the building's number of offices, they could not keep pace with the department's rapidly expanding space needs. Rogers's 1865 solution was not seriously considered until two years later—his successor A.B. Mullett proposed to retain the colonnade but shift three blocks of 15th Street eastward in order to provide the Treasury Building with a proper landscape setting. In 1871 Mullett tried again to acquire land to make the east facade conform to the rest of the building's architectural character; in 1876, when another proposal was suggested, the Senate Committee on Public Buildings decided that the government was too poor to buy the properties valued at $1,039,674.[75]

"Treasury Relicts:"[76] Replacing the Colonnade

The Senate Park Commission's 1901–02 proposed beautification of Washington's monumental core included dozens of new white marble buildings planned to be Neoclassical in style to complement the city's founding architectural monuments. During the spring and summer of 1902, President Theodore and First Lady Edith Roosevelt personally directed Charles F. McKim's expensive renovations and additions to the President's House, officially renamed the White House at this time. These initiatives led to the east colonnade's refurbishment and eventual replacement. The Treasury Building was "visited by more persons than any other public building in Washington, with the possible exception of the President's House." Visitors approaching the President's Grounds from the Mall or along Pennsylvania Avenue were first greeted by the Treasury Building's stately south facade but were quickly dismayed by the unsightly, if not grimy, east colonnade. Unlike the Treasury Building's mid-

Victorian granite wings, the East Wing's porous sandstone walls and colonnade could not be cleaned with soap, water, and brushes. Rather, the sandstone's crevices had collected decades of urban grime, especially soot from the coal-burning fireplaces and furnaces that warmed the homes and offices of nineteenth-century Washington. Moreover, deterioration of the soft stone led to pieces of the entablature falling.

In September 1902 steel girders and a metal ceiling replaced the colonnade's wood beams and plaster ceiling to ensure the safety of the one thousand tons of files stored in the partial attic and to increase this storage space by thirty percent. At the same time, the entire building got a new roof. In the fall of 1902 Secretary of the Treasury Leslie Shaw also decided to use departmental funds rather than await another congressional appropriation to clean the nearly black columns.[77]

"All day," on November 22, 1902, "a puffing six-horse-power engine pumped blasts of air through pipes, and sand through tubes to be manipulated high in the air upon the swinging scaffolds." By 9:00 a.m. when Treasury clerks were hurrying to work, "one column was already as white and clean as the Washington Monument." Two more were finished by noon as thousands of spectators from all over the city came during their dinner hours to watch the building's transformation. Colonel Theodore Bingham, Superintendent of Public Buildings and Grounds, believed in the English "anti-scrape" school of thought promoted by the architectural writer John Ruskin. "The discoloration of age and weather renders a building uniform in appearance, and it is not necessarily objectionable. It is not necessary that our great buildings here should look as though they were built only yesterday," declared Bingham.[78]

Cleaning the colonnade was considered only a stopgap measure, perhaps one that would impress legislators that a completely light-colored Treasury Building would dramatically improve the cityscape viewed by thousands of annual visitors. The 1902 sand blasting either revealed or hastened the sandstone's disintegration, but any hope of a congressional appropriation to replace the entire east facade soon were dashed. Many new necessary government building projects in the wake of the publication of the Senate Park Commission's report were competing for funds. The Treasury Department continued to seek its own temporary solutions to improve its aging and unsightly face exposed to a new Washington increasingly composed of grandiose marble or limestone public and private buildings.[79]

In 1903 the department's second attempt to consolidate the crumbling stone and improve the colonnade's appearance was to fill lost portions on one column with a stone-colored cement followed by coating the whole with a solution impermeable to water. Two years later a Treasury stonemason, Mr. Bruce, was paid $2,000 for the use of his own invention, a "mysterious blue-black liquid," to clean the granite exteriors where grease and soot had accumulated as much as an inch thick in some places. Bruce's liquid, however, was ineffective in cleaning the pitted and discolored sandstone.[80]

> The building now appears in four shades, ranging from light gray to very dark gray. The foundation stones and the finely cut lamp and fence posts about the buildings are almost white. The same color obtains on the lower part of the magnificent Ionic pillars, as far up as a man can reach. The upper part of the pillars is medium gray, or about the same as they were after the sandblast of two years ago. The granite of the Treasury walls above the great columns is discolored by smoke from soft-coal furnaces.[81]

After large chunks of the cornice had been falling for years, safety concerns convinced

Congress in 1907 to appropriate $360,000 to replace the sandstone. The east wall was taken down during the summer and refaced with granite but the colonnade was not dismantled until a year later. Supervising Architect James Knox Taylor's specifications stipulated that Mills's thirty columns be replicated with granite monoliths wrought by hand rather than machine carved. The contract with the Philadelphia masons, Edwin A. Gilbert Company, stated that six of the Milford, New Hampshire, granite columns had to be in Washington and six others quarried and ready for shipment before the work of installing the new colonnade could begin. Each of the new columns cost $4,000 to $5,000 to quarry and carve, weighed twenty-eight tons, and stood thirty-nine feet tall including their bases and capitals. Taylor's goal was to have the new colonnade in place by March 1909, in time for the inaugural parade that marched up 15th Street before turning left on Pennsylvania Avenue and passing in front of the presidential viewing stand. Despite the bankruptcy of the contractor, a delivery truck stuck in asphalt softened by the heat of an August day, and defective columns, he nearly met that deadline.[82]

"Early in the afternoon," on August 4, 1908, "the riggers at work on the building fastened a great chain around the top of the gigantic pillar of stone, the foreman waved his hand, and the engineer pulled a lever. As easily as if it were a bamboo rod the 28-ton monolith was lifted by the derrick into the air, where it swayed gently back and forth." A cement bed had been readied and the column shaft without its capital was slowly lowered into position "and then everyone on the job heaved a sigh of relief." (fig. II-24) It had taken several months to erect the derrick to lift the columns and many skeptics doubted it could do its job. In fact, the difficult part of the work "was tearing away the old cornice and making ready for the new stones," because the original colonnade and its entablature were not

EAST FRONT
TREASURY DEPT.
1ST COLUMN
30 TON
AUG 4th 1908.

II-24 Mills's sandstone columns were replaced by granite monoliths to unify the building's exterior.

Fortress of Finance: The United States Treasury Building

REPAIRS EAST FRONT U.S. TREASURY
APRIL 2nd 09.

dismantled all at once, but the new replaced the old section by section.[83]

Only three columns were delivered in August 1908 and all three had "undesirable markings" that led experts in the Supervising Architect's office to send a Smithsonian geologist to examine the quarry and question whether the government should accept them. When the final column arrived in late February 1909, it was rejected because of an eleven-foot crack, although Taylor wanted the colonnade finished in time for the inaugural. The last column "wrapped in two large American flags and quantities of red, white, and blue bunting" arrived in mid-May. The new colonnade was not just made of a more durable material than its

II-25 After each shaft was put in place, the capitals were raised and a new entablature erected.

predecessor, it was a more academically correct version of the columns used on the Erectheum, such historicism a hallmark of early twentieth-century classicism. The total cost of replacing the east front was about $350,000, bankrupting the first granite contractor and nearly ruining the second.[84] (fig. II-25)

Peter Holscher, the Washington builder in charge of removing the old colonnade, reused part of the sandstone cornice in at least two houses he was erecting at 15th and Decatur streets, NW. Most historic preservation in America until the last quarter of the twentieth century meant the reuse of historic salvage either for pragmatic purposes or to keep historic memory alive. The larger recycling effort focused on the columns themselves. Taylor and the Supervising Architect's staff, who considered Mills their founding father, were determined to re-erect the columns in some Washington park, possibly as part of a bandstand in Potomac Park west of the Washington Monument. In June 1908, after the first of the original columns had been taken down, Colonel Charles S. Bromwell, in charge of the Office of Public Buildings and Grounds, succinctly explained his office's position. "The columns are rather too large for an ordinary structure, and it is not worth while to put up an expensive structure for the sake of preserving them." As the column drums were lowered, they were immediately moved to a nearby vacant lot in West Potomac Park at the corner of 17th Street and Constitution Avenue, southwest of the Treasury Building.[85]

Although many Washingtonians were keenly interested in the fate of the columns, for the next decade various schemes for their reuse failed because they were not linked to adequate public or private funding. Ideas ranged from their placement in parks or lining Executive Avenue between the White House and the Treasury Building; installing them along the south side of Lafayette Park to form a permanent court of honor facing the White House; lining Washington's streets by placing one on every other corner on Pennsylvania Avenue between the Capitol and Treasury; outlining the semicircular court in front of Union Station; surrounding the proposed Lincoln Memorial with them; or forming a semicircle south of the Capitol for shelter during inaugurations.[86]

In July 1908 the Washington Architectural Club announced a competition for the best design utilizing all thirty columns. The first competition was invalidated, partially because the only two schemes were expensive and Con-

gress had not appropriated funds. One of Washington's most prominent Beaux-Arts architects, George Oakley Totten, Jr., won the second competition. His proposal using fourteen columns to outline both semicircular ends of an exiting sunken garden 600 feet in length on the south side of West Potomac Park was favorably received because it was inexpensive and well-designed. (fig. II-26) In 1909 Buildings and Grounds Commissioner Colonel Spencer Cosby also was unsuccessful convincing Congress to appropriate the estimated $15,000 to $20,000 to reuse the columns in West Potomac Park or elsewhere in the city.[87]

In March 1911 the columns were sold to contractor Martin McNamara who bid below the cost of removing the columns in hopes of saving them from destruction. The People's Garden Association was joined by nearly all of Washington's neighborhood associations in promoting Totten's 1909 design, with McNamara declaring unequivocally: "I shall see that the columns are not broken up for paving stones." Cosby personally supported Totten's design. "I hate to see the columns destroyed, because of their historic value, but the Treasury Department has no money to spend for setting them up, and I have no money at my disposal for such a purpose." The unacknowledged enemies of Totten's scheme may well have been the surviving members of the Senate Park Commission, Daniel Burnham and Frederick Law Olmsted, Jr., who had a vested interest in seeing that their scheme for placing the Lincoln Memorial and the Reflecting Pool in West Potomac Park be carried out as they planned it.[88]

The intense spate of public furor worked and, on March 24, 1911, New York Representative William Sulzer, a Democrat, announced he would introduce a bill to fund reuse of the columns in West Potomac Park. McNamara also sought to interest Washington's Chamber of Commerce and its Board of Trade. Immediately, Mary Henderson, wife of former Senator

STADIUM EFFECT WITH OLD TREASURY COLUMNS.

—Geo. Oakley Totten, jr. designer.

Inexpensive and artistic design which won a prize of $50 in a competition held by the Washington Architectural Club.

II-26 Several efforts to save and reuse the original columns in Washington, or elsewhere, failed.

John B. Henderson, who was instrumental in developing Meridian Hill into a socially prominent neighborhood, vowed to buy the columns and erect them on the grounds of her estate at 16th Street and Florida Avenue, NW. Yet, two days after Henderson's declaration, McNamara was considering breaking the columns up and using them to build a rip-rap wall along the river front, no explanation for his change of plans proffered. New York hotel owner Charles N. Vilas made a last-ditch suggestion that the columns be shipped around the country to be erected either at the homes or gravesites of every former Secretary of the Treasury.

McNamara owned the Treasury columns for less than a month, but managed to excite a great deal of public comment about their fate before he sold them to Washington attorney William W. Bride, who "seriously consider[ed] selling the historical relics to some prominent Boston people, who contemplate placing them around the Bunker Hill monument." About 1916 his son Cotter T. Bride gave four of the columns to Lincoln, Nebraska, the hometown of William Jennings Bryan whom Bride supported in his presidential bid. They were erected as a formal entryway to a public park in 1916, removed in the 1950s, then re-erected as a picturesque ruin in Pioneers Park in 1976. (fig. II-27) The piebald appearance of all the surviving column fragments helps explain why only diehard historians valued saving them for posterity.[89]

"An excitable person was certain that German Zeppelins were bombing the Capital," was one explanation for the explosions heard throughout the day and night of January 14, 1918. It was not Zeppelins, nor ice being broken up to save Potomac River bridges; it was the last remnants of the Treasury colonnade being dynamited.[90]

Conclusion

Throughout his entire career as a public architect, Mills's intense patriotism was expressed through several visionary architectural projects. He intended his Washington buildings—informed by advancing technology and often limited by unsuitable building materials, scarce skilled workmen, and few sympathetic clients—to contribute uniquely American advances to European and African architectural traditions. When he chose his models from amongst the greatest of historical architectural precedents, Mills was expressing his era's belief in the nation's achievements and continuing glory. The trial by fire he endured while designing and erecting the Treasury Building from 1833 to 1842 seems to have been the most intense professional hostility he experienced during his fifty-five-year career. The history of the Treasury Building's colonnade alone demonstrates that Mills's visionary goal was not again truly appreciated until early twentieth-century Beaux Arts classicism revived a broad range of European models to invigorate American architecture. As faulty as the colonnade's sandstone and the crudeness of its sculpture were, Mills's grandiose architectural gesture represented the confidence of his era in America's destiny, which he linked directly to the Treasury Department via its building.

II-27 Most of Mills's sandstone columns were dynamited; four were moved to Lincoln, Nebraska.

Endnotes, Chapter Two

1   The War & Navy Departments Building was Mills's fourth design. Secretaries of War and Navy, *Additional Buildings for War and Navy Departments,* 27th Cong., 3d sess., 1843, H. doc. 85, 16. Mills's fifth building was his design for the Smithsonian Institution. Although he lost the competition for the Patent Office to William P. Elliot, Mills was placed in charge of its construction and his alterations brought it close to his own submission. Douglas Everett Evelyn, "A Public Building for a New Democracy: The Patent Office Building in the Nineteenth Century," (PhD diss., The George Washington University, 1997).

2   Robert Mills, "The Public Buildings," *Washington Union*, March 29, 1854, 2.

3   Walter to the House Committee on Public Buildings and Grounds (hereafter cited as HCPB&G), January 29, 1838, HR25A-D20.4, RG 233, NAB.

4   Mills, "Public Buildings."

5   House Committee on Public Buildings, *New Executive Buildings,* 23d Cong., 2d sess., 1835, H. Rep. 90, 1-2.

6   Alexander Jackson Davis, June 2–9, 1832, in A.J. Davis Diary, 1828-53, Manuscripts and Archives Division, New York Public Library.

7   [Robert Mills], "1836-1840 Journal," Papers of Robert Mills (hereafter cited as PRM), Manuscript Division, LC.

8   Evelyn, "Patent Office," 1997. Elliot to Jarvis, February 18, 1835, entry 1, RG 42, NAB. Elliott, "Description of the plan for the proposed new fireproof public buildings," *National Intelligencer,* February 13, 1835, 1-2.

9   *New Executive Buildings,* 2.

10   Richard Peters, ed., *The Public Statutes at Large of the United States of America,* (Boston: Charles C. Little and James Brown, 1846), 115.

11   Mills to Jackson and G. W. B. Towns to Jackson, July 4, 1836, "Robert Mills," entry 213, Notable Treasury Employees (hereafter cited as entry 213), RG 56, NACP. "William Parker Elliot's Diary," in Patent Centennial Celebration, *United States Bicentennial Edition of Proceedings and Addresses of the American Patent System* (Washington: Press of Gedney & Roberts Co., 1892). "From Our Correspondents," *Charleston Courier,* August 6, 1836, 2.

12   Mary Clemmer Ames, *Ten Years in Washington, Life and Scenes in the National Capital* (Hartford: A. D. Worthington & Co., 1874), 304. Anne Newport Royall, *Sketches of History, Life, and Manners, in the United States* (New Haven: Privately printed, 1826), 135.

13   *Message of the President of the United States,* 27th Cong. 1st sess., 1841, S. Doc. 123, 11-2.

14   Robert Brown, Testimony before HCPB&G, [1838], HR25A-D20.1, Records Relating to Public Works, entry 19 (hereafter cited as entry 19), Records of the United States House of Representatives, RG 233 (hereafter cited as RG 233), NAB.

15   House Committee on Public Buildings and Grounds, *National Edifices at Washington,* 28th Cong., 2d sess., 1845, H. Rep. 185, 20.

16   Joseph B. Varnum, Jr., *The Seat of Government of the United States* (Washington: R. Farnam, 1854), 39.

17   Ames, *Ten Years in Washington,* 304. George Alfred Townsend, *Washington Inside and Outside* (Hartford: James Betts & Co., 1874), 561. Joseph West Moore, *Picturesque Washington* (Providence, J.A. & R.A. Reid, 1884), 175-6.

18   Pamela Scott and Antoinette J. Lee, *Buildings of the District of Columbia* (New York: Oxford University Press, 1993), 154-7, 189-93.

19   In 1831, the Philadelphia architect John C. Trautwine used the double-pile plan for his Wills Hospital design. Jeffrey A. Cohen, *Drawing Toward Building* (Philadelphia: University of Pennsylvania Press, 1986), 74-5.

20   *Message of the President,* 1841, 11-2.

21   Franck Taylor, August 25, 1836, Voucher 70925, Office of the First Auditor, Miscellaneous Division, Miscellaneous Treasury Accounts, entry 347 (hereafter cited as entry 347), Records of the Accounting Officers of the Department of the Treasury, RG 217 (hereafter cited as RG 217), NACP.

22   Mills to Dickerson, October 8, 1836, Records of the Office of the Secretary of the Navy, Miscellaneous Letters Received, entry 2.1, Naval Records Collection of the Office of Naval Records and Library, RG 45, NAB.

23   *Message of the President of the United States,* 24th Cong. 2d sess., 1836, H. Ex. Doc. 10, 2-3. Joan M. Dixon, *National Intelligencer, Newspaper Abstracts, 1836-1837* (Bowie, MD: Heritage Books, Inc., 2001), 289. Mills to Noland, December 28, 1836, entry 1, RG 42, NAB. Mills to Van Buren, March 27, 1837, Martin Van Buren Papers, Manuscript Division, LC.

24   "To The Editors," *National Intelligencer,* December 12, 1836, 2

25   Mills to Lincoln, February 22, 1837, PRM, Manuscript Division, LC.

26   *Congressional Globe,* 25th Cong., 1st sess., 1837, 331-7. Mills to Noland, September 28, 1837, HR 25A-D20.1 and Mills to HCPB&G, October 11, 1837, HR 25A-D20.1, both entry 19, RG 233, NAB.

27   *Message of the President,* 1841, 12.

28   Draft Senate resolution, December 19, 1837, HR 25A-D20.4, entry 19, RG 233, NAB.

29   President of the United States, *Treasury Building,* 25th Cong., 2d sess., 1837, H. Ex. Doc. 38, 2-3.

30   Mills to HCPB&G, December 28, 1837, HR 25A-D20.1, entry 19, RG 233, NAB.

31 Brown, Testimony, [1838].

32 Mills to HCPB&G, January 3, 1838, HR 25A-D20.1, entry 19, RG 233, NAB.

33 Mills to HCPB&G, January 8, 1838, PRM, Manuscript Division, LC.

34 Mills to HCPB&G, January 13, 1838, HR.25A-D20.1, entry 19, RG 233, NAB. Mills to Lincoln, January 20, 1838, entry 1, RG 42, NAB.

35 Lincoln to Walter and Lincoln to Van Buren, January 11, 1838, both HR 25A-D20.1, entry 19, RG 233, NAB.

36 House Committee on Public Buildings, *New Treasury and Post Office Buildings,* 25th Cong., 2d sess., 1838, H. Rep. 737, 2-10.

37 Ibid., 14.

38 Ibid., 22.

39 Mills to HCPB&G, February 21, 1838, HR25A-D20.4, entry 19, RG 233, NAB.

40 Ibid.

41 Ibid.

42 Ibid.

43 Ibid.

44 Ibid. and Lincoln to Van Buren, February 28, 1838, HR 25A-D20.4, entry 19, RG 233, NAB.

45 Lincoln to Parris, [March] 1838, HR25A-D20.1, entry 19, RG 233, NAB.

46 Parris to HCPB&G, March 15, 1838, HR25A-D20.1, entry 19, RG 233, NAB.

47 Mills to Lincoln, March 20, 1838 and Lincoln to Walter, March 21, 1838, both HR25A-D20.4, entry 19, RG 233, NAB.

48 *House Journal,* 25th Cong., 2d sess., January 14, 1838, 901. *New Treasury,* 1838, passim.

49 Mills to Speaker of the House and HCPB&G, April 2, 1838, HR 25A-D20.1, entry 19, RG 233, NAB. *House Journal,* 25th Cong., 2d sess., April 4, 1838, 699.

50 *Congressional Globe,* 25th Cong., 2d sess., 1838, 274-5.

51 Committee on Public Buildings and Grounds, *In the Senate of the United States,* 25th Cong., 2d sess., 1838, S. Rep. 435. *Congressional Globe,* 25th Cong., 2d sess., 1838, 312-3. *Congressional Globe,* 25th Cong., 2d sess., 1838, 336-41. Lincoln to Van Buren, April 17, 1838, HR 25A-D20.4, entry 19, RG 233, NAB.

52 John Forsyth, Levi Woodbury, and Joel R. Poinsett to Lincoln, April 28, 1838 and Lincoln to Forsyth, Woodbury, and Poinsett, April 30, 1838, both in HR 25A-D20.4, entry 19, RG 233, NAB.

53 Bulfinch to Hall, May 5, 1838 and Bulfinch to Lincoln, June 16, 1838, both in HR 25A-D20.4, entry 19, RG 233, NAB.

54 *House Journal,* 25th Cong., 2d sess., May 19, 1838, 905; June 2, 1838, 1015; and June 6, 1838, 1041. Charles Francis Adams, *Memoirs of John Quincy Adams* (Philadelphia: Lippincott Bros., 1876), 10: 20-1.

55 *Congressional Globe,* 25th Cong., 2d sess., 1838, 418-9. Adams, *Memoirs,* 14.

56 *Congressional Globe,* 25th Cong., 2d sess., 1838, 419-20.

57 *A Biographical Dictionary of the American Congress, 1774-1949* (Washington: Government Printing Office, 1950), 1396. *Congressional Globe,* 25th Cong., 2d sess., 1838, 420-1.

58 *House Journal,* 25th Cong., 2d sess., June 8-9, 1838, 1052-4; 1058. *Congressional Globe,* 25th Cong., 2d sess., 1838, 371-2.

59 Forsyth, Woodbury, and Poinsett to Noland, June 11, 1838, entry 1, RG 42, NAB. Resolution, Joint Committee on Public Buildings, June 12, 1838, autograph copy, entry 1, RG 42, NAB. *New Treasury Building,* 25th Cong., 2d sess., 1838, H. Ex. Doc. 447, 3.

60 Brown to Noland, February 14, 1837, HR 25A-G17.7, entry 19, RG 233, NAB. William Strickland to Mills, April 6, 1837 and William Stuart to Mills, April 6, 1837, both in entry 1, RG 42, NAB.

61 Laborers to the House of Representatives, Petition, February 14, 1838, HR 25A-G17.7, entry 19, RG 233, NAB. Board of Commissioners of Public Buildings (hereafter cited as BCPB) to Noland, May 5, 1838 and Noland to BCPB, May 7, 1838, both in entry 6, RG 42, NAB. Lincoln, autograph draft report of HCPB&G, May 11, 1838, HR 25A-G17.1, entry 19, RG 233, NAB.

62 Noland to Lincoln, June 27, 1838, entry 6, RG 42, NAB. *Congressional Globe,* 25th Cong., 2d sess., 1838, 383.

63 Noland to Lincoln, June 29, 1838, entry 6, RG 42, NAB. Three letters from the superintendents of workmen to Noland, all dated June 28, 1838, in HR 25A-G17.1, entry 19, RG 233, NAB. Draft of Joint Resolution, 25th Cong., 2d sess., H. Rep. 27, July 7, 1838, in entry 1, RG 42, NAB.

64 "Pettrich, the Sculptor," *National Intelligencer,* April 25, 1836, 2. Noland to BCPB, July 26, 1838, Mills to Noland, July 20, 1838; Brown to Noland, July 28, 1838; Mills to Noland, July 30, 1838; and BCPB to Noland, August 1, 1838, all in entry 1, RG 42, NAB.

65 Mills to Noland, October 18, 1838, Noland to BCPB, January 28, 1839, both in entry 6, RG 42, NAB. Giuseppe Micali, "Storia degli Antichi Popoli Italiani, *North American Review* 52 (January 1839): passim.

66 Mills to Noland, [November] 1839; Noland to BCPB, February 8, 1840; James Hoban [attorney and son of the architect] to BCPB, February 1840; and twenty-eight stonecutters to the Senate and House of Representatives, [June] 1840; all in entry 6, RG 42, NAB. "An Adjourned Meeting," *National Intelligencer,* March 11, 1840, 2.

67 *Congressional Globe,* 26th Cong., 1st sess., April 30 and May 1, 1840, 370-1. Commissioner of Public Buildings, *Workmen on the Public Buildings,* 26th Cong., 1st sess., 1840, H. Doc. 250.

68 Mills to HCPB, October 11, 1837, entry 6, RG 42, NAB.

69 Pettrich, October 2. 1837, voucher 73262; November 1, 1837, voucher 73572; December 1, 1837, 73626; January 1, 1838, voucher 73842, all in entry 347, RG 217, NACP.

70 Mills to Noland, August 19, 1842, entry 6, RG 42, NAB.

71 Horatio Greenough, *Aesthetics at Washington* (Washington: John T. Towers, 1851), 12-3.

72 Ben Perley Poore, "Waifs from Washington," *Gleason's Pictorial Drawing Room Companion* 4 (February 5, 1853): 97.

73 "Distressing Accident," *National Intelligencer,* February 25, 1842, 3. *Senate Journal,* 27th Cong., 1st sess., August 13, 1842, 574. *Senate Journal,* 31st Cong., 1st sess., August 14, 1850, 558.

74 Greenough, *Aesthetics,* 11-2. "Viator," *Washington Sketch Book,* 196.

75 "Forty-Fourth Congress," *New York Times,* April 13, 1876, 2. Roose's *Companion and Guide to Washington and Vicinity* (Washington: Gibson Brothers, 1876), 56. Secretary of the Treasury, *Report on the State of the Finances,* 40th Cong., 2d sess., 1868, H. Ex. Doc. 2, 185–6. "Safety of Treasury Files," *Washington Post,* September 6, 1902, 3.

76 "Column Plans Indorsed," *Washington Post,* March 23, 1911, 3.

77 "Power of Sand Blast," *Washington Post,* December 7, 1902, 31. "Replacing Old Pillars," *Washington Post,* May 31, 1908, 12.

78 "Treasury Pillars White," *Washington Post,* November 22, 1902, 12. "Thousands Watch It Whiten," *Washington Post,* November 23, 1902, 12. "Youthful Look Not Desired," *Washington Post,* November 27, 1902, 12.

79 "Power of Sand Blast," *Washington Post,* December 7, 1902, 31.

80 "Treasury Pillars Crumbling," *Washington Post,* July 25, 1903, 3. "Cleaning Treasury Stone," *Washington Post,* August 7, 1905, 3. "Treasury Looks New," *Washington Post,* September 24, 1905, E8. "Treasury's New Dress," *Washington Post,* August 11, 1905, 4.

81 "Cleaning Treasury Stone," *Washington Post,* August 7, 1905, 3.

82 "The Last Section of the Old Treasury Building Will Soon Be Demolished," *Washington Post,* April 14, 1907, M3. "Removing Old Pillars," *Washington Post,* May 31, 1908, 16. "Sandstone is Dead," *Washington Post,* June 7, 1908, E8. "Noise Annoys Clerks," *Washington Post,* June 12, 1908, 5.

83 "Huge Monolith May Be Defective," *Washington Post,* August 9, 1908, E3.

84 "New Columns for Old," *Washington Post,* August 11, 1908, 6. "Treasury To Be Ready," *Washington Post,* February 21, 1909, F3. "Big Column Rejected," *Washington Post,* February 24, 1909, 5. "Huge Monolith in Place," *Washington Post,* May 20, 1909, 12.

85 "Pillars for Band Stand," *Washington Post,* June 16, 1908, 15.

86 "Told in Departments," *Washington Post,* July 17, 1908, 5. "Pillars for Band Stand," *Washington Post,* July 19, 1908, 15. "Use for Treasury Columns," *Washington Post,* July 26, 1908, 10. "Uses for Treasury Pillars," *Washington Post,* July 31, 1908, 14.

87 "Design for Old Columns," *Washington Post,* August 23, A3. "Use for Old Columns," *Washington Post,* October 11, 1908, R1. "Washington (D.C.) Architectural Club," *Inland Architect* 53 (November 1908): 64. "A Suggestion for Potomac Park," *Washington Post,* March 19, 1911, E4.

88 "Park to Get Columns," *Washington Post,* March 21, 1911, 3. "Historic Columns May Go," *Washington Post,* March 22, 1911, 3.

89 "Boston May Get Pillars," *Washington Post,* April 19, 1911, 14. James L. McKee and Arthur Duerschner, *Lincoln, A Photographic History* (Lincoln, Nebraska: Bicentennial Commission, 1976), 165. A. C. Lieber Memorandum, December 28, 1950, Curator's Files, U.S. Treasury Department.

90 "Former Treasury Columns Blown Up," *Washington Post,* January 15, 1918, 8.

"Massive Quadrangle of Granite:"[1]
The South Wing, 1852–1860

Chapter Three

"Every Year Demanding Increased Accommodation:" Planning the Treasury Extension

The fourteen years spent erecting the Treasury Extension's three massive wings from 1855 to 1869 were interrupted by the Civil War, halted when Congress cut off funding, and delayed by labor unrest and shortages of materials. This intermittent progress was surpassed by the nineteen years it took to settle on a master plan after the east wing was completed. Once the design was chosen and the superintending architect and engineer selected, the extension's initial construction moved forward quickly because the latest technologies available from iron I-beams to steam engines to photography were adopted to save time and money. The "Boston Granite Style"—an old material but a new way of locking the building blocks together—was imported from New England, changing the building's character from monumental to fortress-like. Other concurrent government buildings influenced, and were influenced by, the Treasury Extension in matters of design and technology, the interchange sometimes collegial but more often competitive as architects and engineers vied to have the decisive voice in determining the course of government buildings.

During 1836–37, when the foundations for the east wing were being built, Mills repeatedly warned that those for the south wing should be laid concurrently to ensure the structural stability of the whole, principally because the south's foundations had to be deeper in response to the sloping site. In Mills's December 1841 description of his E-shaped plan to complete the Treasury Building, he attempted to minimize some aspects of the east wing that had been criticized during the 1838 investigation and its aftermath. (fig. III-1) He noted that the future five porticoes would be the main entrances, while the one on 15th Street would be merely the business entrance. He planned the future wings to have wider corridors and conceived of the terraces connecting them as part of the circulation system between bureaus. Aesthetically, Mills was thinking of views from many Treasury offices to the President's House and its grounds, or to Lafayette Square or, at the very least, of a fountain in a courtyard. Pragmatically, he was considering unimpeded circulation of air and abundant light to offices throughout the day to aid Treasury clerks in carrying out their work. Moreover, Mills's E-shape offered occupants of the President's House a faceted and open facade to diminish somewhat the Treasury Building's huge presence adjacent to the house's grounds.[2]

Expansion of the Treasury Building gathered momentum in 1842. In February the House Committee on Public Buildings asked Secretary of the Treasury Walter Forward to determine if the Treasury bureaus were adequately housed in the east wing. All of the bureau heads reported that they needed more space. "The continually accumulating masses of documents, books, papers, etc., are every year demanding increased accommodation, and the duties are such as to require a very great amount of cases and other office furniture of more than ordinary dimensions."[3]

On April 1, 1842, Massachusetts Representative Charles Hudson reported on the Treasury Building for the Committee on Public Expenditures.

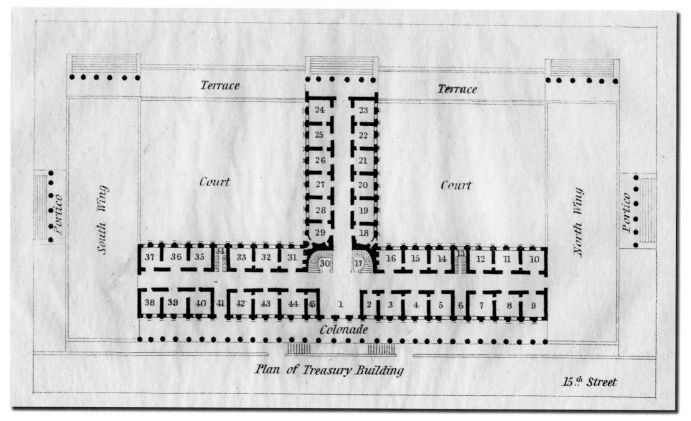

III-1 By 1841 Mills's hoped-for E-shaped Treasury Building was reduced to the spine and central wing.

At one time arrangements were made for 108 rooms, and at another time 132 rooms were required. Thus a scene of confusion, neglect, and official mismanagement, seems to have prevailed, which must have enhanced the cost of the building, and at the same time, rendered the internal arrangement injudicious and inconvenient, as it is now pronounced to be.[4]

Mills was made to share the blame for perceived management deficiencies but shouldered solely the responsibility for the Treasury Building's design. "There seems, from the first, to have been a sort of covert design to erect a magnificent edifice, much larger and more expensive than Congress had anticipated." William Noland, the commissioner of public buildings who superintended the entire work, vigorously defended his and Mills's contributions, noting that each had reacted to both presidential and congressional dictates in all their decisions.[5]

In June 1842 Secretary Forward again surveyed his bureau heads about additional office space. Twenty-five new rooms were needed, twelve of them for the General Land Office, which had been created in 1812 and not integrated into the Department of the Interior until it was formed in 1849. Mills's estimate of $265,000 to build the south wing spanning two years was balanced by the expenditure of $20,000 spanning six months to alter the east wing's basement story to make it habitable as offices rather than for storage of documents. W.W. Boardman, the new chairman of the House Committee on Public Buildings and Grounds, noted that times were such that a "responsible architect upon favourable [sic] terms" could be found to renovate the basement and this short-term remedy was adopted.[6]

Again in 1845, the Treasury's bureau chiefs responded to yet another space survey ordered by the House Committee on Public Buildings. Part of the reason for the creation of new departments—such as the Department of the Interior—was to house bureaus with like functions together to facilitate frequent interaction.

The responsibilities of each of the Treasury Department's bureaus were outlined by Mills in his *Guide to the Capitol and National Executive Officers* (1847–48) and updated in a second guidebook of the same name in 1854.[7]

Yet, Congress did not appropriate the funds and by 1847 three local entrepreneurs erected office buildings specifically for rental to the government, two located adjacent to the President's Grounds and the third on Capitol Hill. The fireproof Corcoran Building, located at the corner of 15th Street and Pennsylvania Avenue, containing forty rooms in its five stories, was built "intending to accommodate some of the offices attached to the Treasury." The rental cost in these buildings was very high, the War and Navy departments paying $175 per month per room at the Winder Building on 17th Street on a five-year contract.[8]

Early in 1849 the House of Representatives reported on the probable cost of extensions to both the Capitol and Treasury Building. Mills submitted plans for both buildings, having already presented the first of his five designs for the Capitol Extension in 1846. Secretary of the Interior Thomas Ewing appointed Mills architect and superintendent for construction of the Patent Office wings in April 1849, only to fire him in July 1852 when he hired Thomas U. Walter as his replacement. In 1850–51 Mills and Walter were the two major competitors for the Capitol Extension, the latter's design selected.

Sometime in 1851, Mills responded to Secretary of the Treasury Thomas Corwin's request for information about extending the Treasury Building.[9] The architect proposed that the State Department occupy a new north wing, while Treasury bureaus expand into a new five-story south wing. (fig. III-2) This proposed extension would bring the State Department wing to the intersection of 15th Street and New York Avenue. Thus, the north portico would be visible at the end of that avenue to complement the south portico's view along Pennsylvania Avenue.[10]

III-2 In 1851 Mills planned to extend the spine and house the State Department in the North Wing.

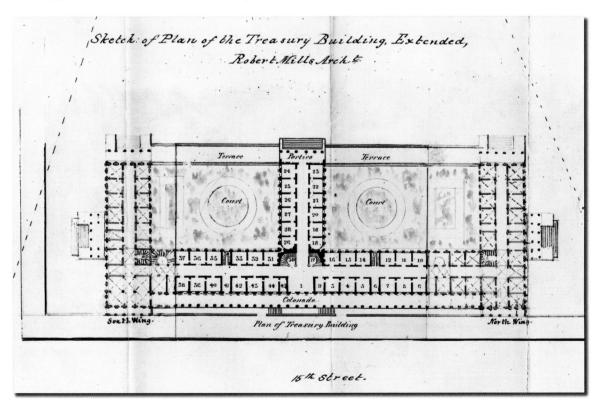

Congress must have viewed Mills's estimate of $630,000 as woefully inadequate when it considered the expenses of earlier government buildings. Mills misjudged the changing mood of Congress after the Gold Rush, when the nation's wealth suddenly increased dramatically. While the professional and political machinations surrounding the selection of the Capitol Extension's design can be followed in manuscript and published government records, as well as the local press, no corresponding documents record the epic struggle between Mills and Walter for the Treasury Extension. Mills's letter and drawing sent to Corwin in 1851 were not his final attempt to secure that job, but they are the end of the paper trail. His supporters in both the executive and legislative branches were Democrats and Walter's success as architect of the Capitol Extension, coupled with support from fellow Whigs, effectively shunted Mills aside as Walter became the public architect in the eyes of Congress. Printed government documents that included executive depart-

ment reports and the debates of Congress were so widely disseminated that Walter was soon accepted nationally as the government's principal architect.

"[T]heir Fancies to Run Riot:" The Treasury Extension's Evolving Design, 1852–1856

Choosing Walter's master plan for completing the Treasury Building was one part of an ongoing evolutionary process that involved four major American architects with varied conceptions of what constitutes great architecture as well as differing attitudes about Washington's cityscape. Mills's proposed extensions were the starting point. An 1840 engraving based on one of his lost drawings shows he planned to continue a modified version of the east colonnade for the walls

III-3 Mills wanted to extend the regular rhythm of the long 15th Street colonnade to his wings.

THE NEW TREASURY BUILDING

Robt Mills. *Arch.^t*

T R E A S U R Y

of his wings. (fig. III-3) Ionic columns on the facade of Mills's wings seem to be engaged, or attached to the walls directly behind them. Mills planned on maintaining a constant rhythm around the entire building to simulate the effect of a continuous, or peripteral, colonnade. He intended a shallow south portico to keep open the vista between the Capitol and President's House. Moreover, he enclosed its entrance steps between walls that continued the horizontal lines and treatment of the east wing's rusticated basement walls. In 1848 Mills published the plan of the existing Treasury Building in his *Guide to the Capitol and National Executive Offices,* the outlines of his proposed wings corresponding to the 1840 lithograph. Because Mills's scheme for completing the building was reproduced in several guidebooks during the 1840s, the public accepted his version, which presupposed that 15th Street would be graded to be nearly level.

Mills's 1851 sketch plan to extend the Treasury pushed the north and south porticoes slightly forward to have double rows of columns and decreased their widths to increase space for offices. At the same time, he moved the six

III-4 Ideally 15th Street's future level grade would diminish the basement's uneven height.

columns of the east facade's north and south pavilions forward to align with the stairs leading to the 15th Street colonnade. A lithographic perspective of his 1851 design apparently done following another lost Mills drawing shows 15th Street graded, but not level, with the Treasury's basement, partially masked by an intricate cast iron fence. (fig. III-4) Most notably, as with his earlier extension design, Mills did not plan pediments atop his end pavilions, but continued the cornice's horizontal line, breaking it only at the wings' entrance porticoes. Mills's strategy was to pattern the Treasury's east facade on the east front of the Louvre, one of several instances where he designed an Americanized version of a great European work of architecture. (see fig. II-13)

Many factors led to Mills's professional decline in the early 1850s. Neither his aesthetic tastes nor his politics were shared by many in power, and Walter's drafting skills far surpassed those of Mills. The Philadelphian's stunningly beautiful watercolors depicted visions of grand public buildings for a confident age. Walter (fig. III-5) worked all day and into the evening on Saturday February 7, 1852, "at designs for [the] new departments," that is, to provide for the State Department in the Treasury Building and for a new building to house the War and Navy departments on the west side of the President's Grounds. On the sixteenth, after visiting the Treasury Building, he worked later that day on his drawings for the multi-departmental building. By March 1 his diary entries change, recording that he "worked at plans of Pub. Buildings on Pres. Sq." In mid-August Walter made plans specifically for the "Treasury and State Departments," completing five drawings on August 28, a site plan, a plan of the main story, and three elevations of the east, west, and north fronts.[11]

Three of Walter's drawings for the Treasury Extension survive, the first a site plan signed and dated 1852 that he apparently made because his inscription notes that it "exhibit[ed] designs for new State, War, & Navy Departments." (fig. III-6) For this building he planned to replicate the Treasury's east colonnade along 17th Street and bring the building to its adjacent sidewalk similar to the Treasury Building's 15th Street siting. In contrast to Mills's 1845 and 1851 designs for an E-shaped building to complement his 15th Street colonnade, Walter created a quadrangle with four monumental facades that allowed for a continuous central corridor to connect all four wings. Three massive porticoes had back rows of columns recessed into the body of the building to form outdoor vestibules that opened directly onto central corridors in each wing. Walter replicated this design for his Treasury Extension plan, his source the Propylaea (entrance gate) to the Athenian Acropolis. (fig. III-7) Walter's second surviving drawing (fig. III-8)—unsigned and undated—had its origin in his 1852 designs but is linked to a similar architectural drawing he made for the State, War, and Navy Building two

III-5 Thomas U. Walter, architect of the 1852 master plan for the executive department offices.

years later. (fig. III-9) In theory, the facades could be cut out and attached to the edges of the plan to form a rudimentary three-dimensional model to aid clients in understanding the relationships between exterior forms and interior spaces.

At the beginning of January 1854, Walter sent the Senate Committee on Public Buildings a Treasury Building design "so as to embrace accommodations for the Dept of State" with much larger rooms. By using his modern system of vaulting with iron girders alternating with shallow brick arches, the rooms would require no heavy corner supports and "a skylight may be made in each of the upper rooms, which would render them the most desirable rooms in the building" for draftsmen and clerks who "require a constant and strong light." A bill was reported to authorize both Walter's Treasury Extension (to include rooms for the State Department) and his plan for a new War, Navy, and Interior Department Building west of the President's House. Neither building was to exceed 470 feet in length and 270 feet in

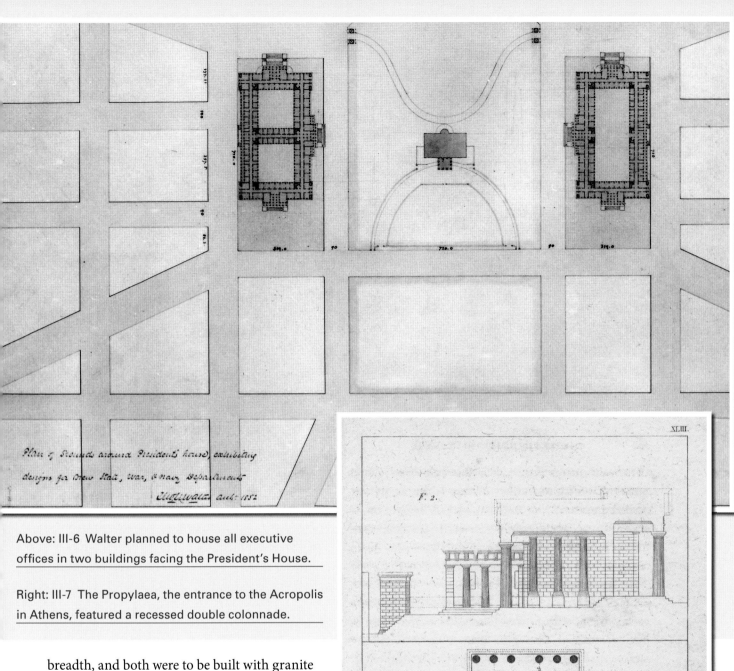

Plan of Grounds around President's house, exhibiting designs for New State, War, & Navy Departments Thos U Walter Arch. 1852

Above: III-6 Walter planned to house all executive offices in two buildings facing the President's House.

Right: III-7 The Propylaea, the entrance to the Acropolis in Athens, featured a recessed double colonnade.

breadth, and both were to be built with granite foundations and marble facades. No alterations to the existing Treasury were allowed except the "present line of columns on 15th street shall be finished by constructing a recessed portico with a pediment at each end." Walter's plan with its octastyle (eight-columned) central porticoes, and recessed ones for the end pavilions, was described but "the details … shall be subject to the approval and direction" of the president. The bill called for an appropriation of $600,000 to be used to begin either or both buildings, which might be built consecutively or simultaneously, but "if only one be constructed at a time, the building designed for the

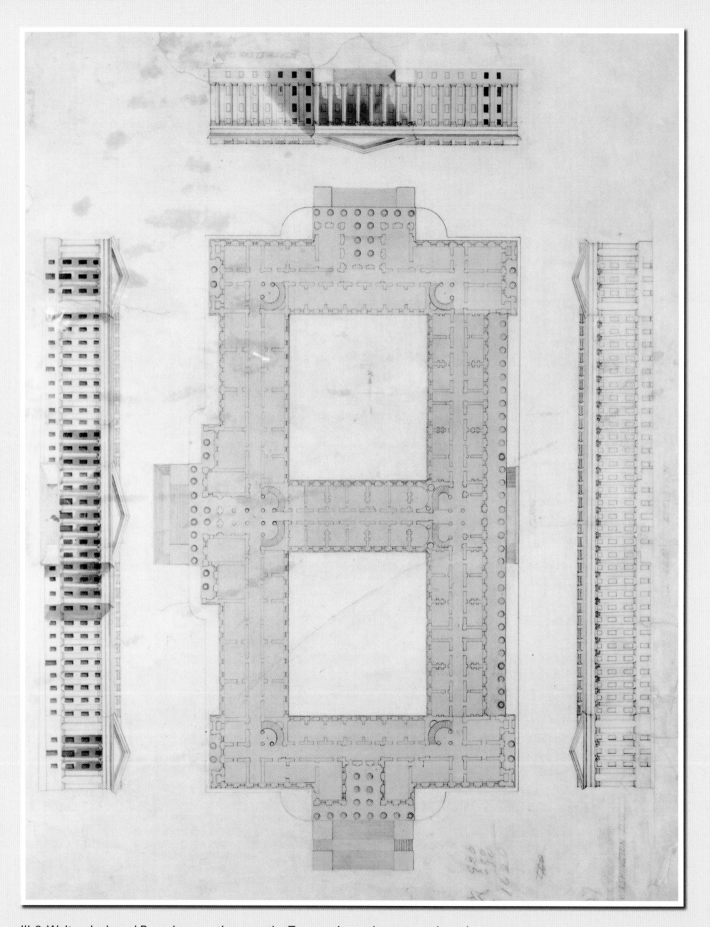

III-8 Walter designed Propylaea porticoes as the Treasury's south, west, and north entrances.

Fortress of Finance: The United States Treasury Building

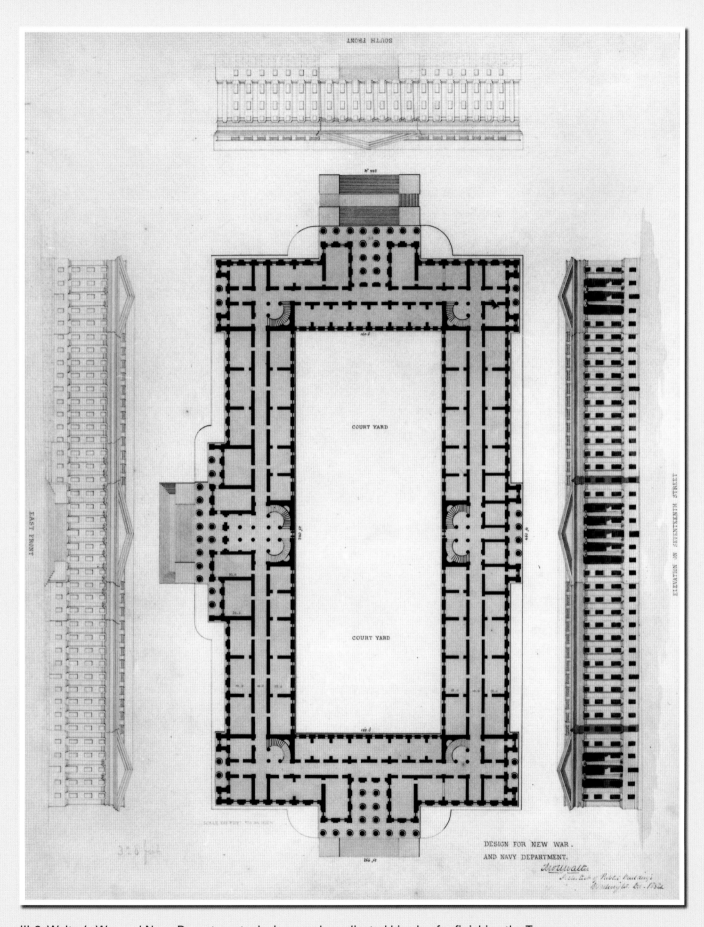

III-9 Walter's War and Navy Departments design nearly replicated his plan for finishing the Treasury.

State and Treasury Departments shall be first completed."[12]

In his 1854 Treasury Extension design, Walter planned corner pavilions as Mills had done, but articulated their walls with double pilasters framing two columns (columns *in antis*), the whole topped by a pediment on their long sides only. Ground-level entrances facing 15th Street and the President's Grounds opened onto a central corridor; on the main level a door from the corridor led to balconies screened by the *in antis* columns. Walter's was a more orthodox neoclassical solution than Mills's for finishing the building's corners, therefore more acceptable to a wider audience. Moreover, Walter's north and south porticoes were more massive than Mills had planned, with eight rather than six columns, and Walter planned his southern staircase to have two flights divided by a platform with narrow, perpendicular staircases attached to the central ones.

Judging from Mills's 1851 drawing, the additional depth of Walter's portico and stairs would still have maintained the Capitol/President's House sightlines along Pennsylvania Avenue. On March 3, 1855, Congress appropriated $300,000 to begin Walter's revisions to Mills's basic design. Although Walter's perspective watercolor sent to President Pierce two days later has not been located, W.G. Metzerott included a probable engraved version of it in his booklet *Our National Buildings! Views of Washington, D.C.* (fig. III-10) For more than a decade, Mills consistently saw the Treasury Building completed as an E-shape; by 1845, he hoped it would be replicated by the War and Navy Building on the west side of the President's House. (see fig. II-8) He was ever attentive to preserving the house's bucolic setting as the triple prongs of his wings allowed the landscape to expand around them while providing a solid wall along the street perimeters to protect the privacy of the President's grounds. Walter's proposed quadrangular buildings flanking the President's

House created three distinct precincts, each with its own definable grounds, a more urbanistic response to the executive complex, especially after roadways were built separating the three imposing buildings. The mood of urban and industrial progress, to match the new awareness of the country's vast extent and natural abundance, outweighed romantic views of Washington as a city in a garden.

All of the congressmen agreed that an extension to the Treasury and a new State Department Building would be necessary in the near future, but Ohioan Salmon P. Chase argued that, considering the current expense of the Capitol and Patent Office Extensions, only the Treasury Extension should be started immediately. Two days after the debate, the Senate passed the bill to erect both of Walter's buildings, but the House referred the bill to their Committee on Public Buildings where it was not considered until the next session. On March 3, 1855, the House appropriated $300,000 for the Treasury Extension but made no provision for the State Department.[13]

While this public debate at the national level was underway, Walter and his colleague at the Capitol Extension, Montgomery Meigs of the Army Corps of Engineers, were vying behind the scenes for the assignment of supervising the Treasury Extension's construction. The other contenders were New Englander Ammi B. Young and corps officer Alexander H. Bowman, who since 1852 had been the architect and engineer, respectively, for the Treasury Department's Bureau of Construction. From Washington, they directed the design and construction of all the government's civil buildings—customs houses, courthouses, post offices, marine hospitals, and assay offices. Meigs, drawing upon a long career in government service, predicted that Young and Bowman would be chosen to oversee the Treasury Extension, but Walter, after several meetings with President Pierce and various cabinet members, believed that he

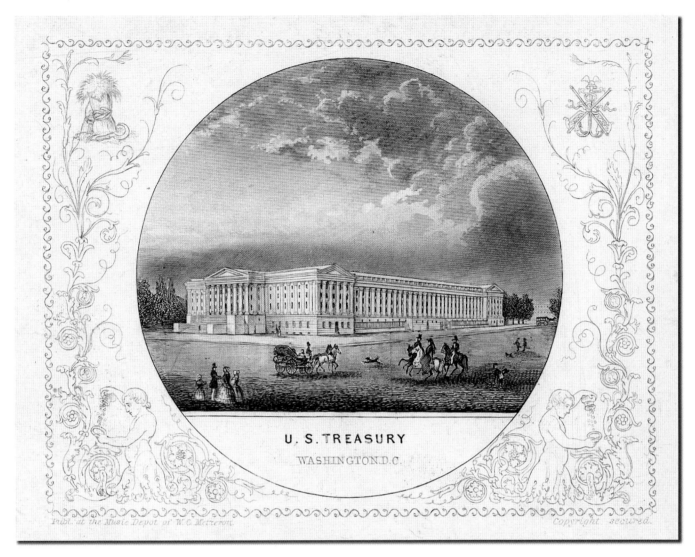

U. S. TREASURY

WASHINGTON. D. C.

III-10 An 1855 perspective view was probably based on Walter's lost watercolor approved that year.

would be selected to carry out his design. On March 3, 1855, Mills died at his home on Capitol Hill; his obituary in the *Washington Union* noted that the 73-year-old architect thought he had been promised the superintendence of both the Treasury and Post Office Extensions, "but learned a few days since that they were to be placed under the supervision of Capt. Bowman and Capt. Meigs, of the engineers corps. The disappointment was too much for him. He became deranged and died." Two days later, Walter sent his now-lost perspective drawing for the Treasury Extension (signed by the chairmen of the House and Senate Committees on Public Buildings and Grounds) to the president along with an invoice for $1,000 for his design drawings.[14]

In early April Secretary of the Treasury James Guthrie[15] consulted Young about the relative cost of a totally new four-story plus basement building versus Walter's addition to the Treasury. Young replied that a new building with about the same amount of space would be less expensive to build.[16] The following day, Walter met with Pierce and "agreed to build the Treasury according to the plan, commencing with the south wing."[17] Two weeks later, Walter wrote the Capitol's marble contractor.

I am afraid the Treasury is gone—the Secy. insists on building it himself, that, is put it under Bowman and make Young the Architect, and it is understood by all concerned, that this will be the arrangements, but no really official action has yet been had on it; they will probably wait until Capt. Bowman returns; he is at New Orleans and will not be back for a month … It is not, however, impossible for things to take another turn before Bowman gets back.[18]

On May 2 Guthrie asked President Pierce for authority to oversee the Treasury Extension's superintendence. The same day the *Evening Star* "learn[ed] that the president has determined to have this work commenced as soon as the preliminaries can be properly arranged, and has devolved on the Secretary of the Treasury its general management." Walter wrote a friend, "No movement yet made in reference to the Treasury but rumor says it is going into the hands of Bowman and Young—if it does the work will fly next winter."[19]

"Science and Art:" The Bureau of Construction

Significant mechanical and technological advances born or evolved during the previous half-century coincided with the maturation of America's 150-year experiment with classical architecture to complete the Treasury Building. This collaboration of science and art was fostered by the government for the mass production of quality federal buildings. The Army Corps of Engineers—always commissioned from among West Point's top graduates—was at the forefront of examining European developments in the industrial revolution. It devised variants that considered available American materials and factories as well as transportation routes to move materials to widely dispersed government sites. Moreover, the corps's expertise in large-scale project management—acquired while building canals, roads, and fortifications and managing major waterways—taught Army engineers how to work effectively within the federal bureaucracy. As part of the War Department but responsive to congressional mandates aimed at developing the nation's infrastructure, the corps had honed its procedures by the middle of the nineteenth century. In 1852, when Bowman was put in charge of the Treasury Department's new Bureau of Construction, the government accelerated its evolving practice of assigning military officers the superintendence of its civil buildings.

Beginning with Washington hiring L'Enfant in 1791 and Jefferson selecting Latrobe in 1803, the government routinely sought out the country's best architectural talent to design and supervise the construction of federal buildings. Ammi B. Young's appointment as the architect for the Bureau of Construction's buildings reversed for the first time on federal architectural projects the line of authority with the architect answering to an engineer. His design and superintendence of the Boston Custom House was apparently one of the few of the great federal buildings of the 1830s and '40s to be carried out with total honesty. Other important factors were Young's mastery of building in granite and his knowledge of the New England granite business, which he helped develop from its infancy to a major industry.

Customs duties were among the government's main sources of revenue and by 1853 twenty-three customs houses were in use. Four years later, the Bureau of Construction could boast that forty-one customs houses had been built since 1850. Before 1852, with the exception of Robert Mills's New England customs houses, most of the responsibilities fell to local architects and superintendents hired by the department. "But there was no system of keeping or rendering accounts at the respective works, nor of keeping the same in the department" complained Secretary Guthrie in December 1853.

He particularly noted several abuses when too much power was left to local supervision of government contracts, including selling them to other vendors. Such practices opened the way for uncontrollable use of shoddy materials and substandard workmanship. Guthrie alerted Congress of the steps he had taken to institute a proper centralized bureaucratic structure to supervise and monitor such a vast building program.[20]

With a view to a more efficient management, application was made to the Secretary of War for a scientific and practical engineer to be placed in charge of the construction of these buildings and Bowman was assigned that duty. "General regulations for the conduct of the business have been adopted and sent to those in charge of the respective works, and a bureau of construction organized for the supervision of the whole … The compensation paid to Captain Bowman has been fixed at $8 per day, less his pay as captain, with his travelling [sic] expenses whilst inspecting the works; and the architect has also been retained, to aid the department in his particular line … [I]t is expected that greater dispatch, and an improvement in the work and materials, will result from the new arrangements."[21]

Guthrie's thirty-eight regulations were comprehensive, ranging from centralized control of site selection to requiring that all paperwork generated locally be sent to Washington where it underwent a rigorous system of checks and balances. The regulations were all directed at defining the powers and responsibilities of both the officers in charge in Washington and the local superintendents. The ultimate aim was to ensure that frauds against the government were difficult, if not impossible, while guaranteeing quality building materials and construction. These regulations, compiled by Bowman and Young, were based on the corps's high standards of accountability and the Treasury Department's experience with long-distance oversight

of earlier buildings. About seventy government buildings were built during the 1850s and '60s, contracts that made millionaires of quarry owners as well as iron founders. These government commissions were possibly the single greatest contribution towards the nation's industrialization in the middle of the nineteenth century.[22]

"A Scientific and Practical Engineer:" Alexander Hamilton Bowman (1803–1865)

Captain Alexander Hamilton Bowman, who graduated from West Point in 1825, brought to the Bureau of Construction more than a quarter century's experience as a seasoned corps officer involved in designing and building varied public works. (fig. III-11) Beginning in 1826, Bowman oversaw the improvement of harbors and rivers and designed the defenses of Charleston harbor including the construction of Fort Sumter. For the two years prior to his appointment in 1852 as the engineer in charge of the Bureau of Construction, Bowman taught practical military engineering at West Point where he returned at the end of his eight-year assignment in Washington.[23]

III-11 George Eichbaum's portrait of Lt. Col. Alexander H. Bowman, a captain when he served in Washington.

Bowman's education in civil engineering at the military academy was the best available in the country in the 1820s and his subsequent varied experience prepared him to manage large-scale building projects. This included writing proposals and specifications, evaluating bids, examining building materials, directing a diverse workforce, calculating when materials were needed at various stages in the building process and ensuring they arrived on schedule. The Army held all corps officers to a very high degree of accountability; it was their reputation for honesty and disinterestedness that convinced Congress to place Bowman in charge of the Bureau of Construction and to name Meigs as the Capitol Extension's engineer a year later. When Bowman was charged with oversight of the Treasury Extension in 1855, he was already managing several government buildings in all parts of the country that required frequent inspection trips. Running the Treasury Extension's day-to-day operations thus fell to his assistants, Alfred B. Claxton (1855–57), Major Edmund French (1856–59), and Spencer M. Clark (1860–68). French graduated seventh in West Point's 1828 class and Clark was a civilian who had been the bureau's chief clerk since August 1856. As the government's disbursing agent, Bowman signed off on all engineering and financial matters because he was legally liable for the decisions, actions, and errors of his subordinates.

"Granite Ribbed from Basement to Roof:"[24] Ammi Burnham Young (1798–1874)

On September 29, 1852, President Millard Fillmore appointed Ammi Burnham Young (fig. III-12) as the Treasury Department's architect based on his expertise as a designer and builder of granite structures and his experience working for the government. Rectangular granite slabs quarried in horizontal layers had been used during the eighteenth century for the foundations of numerous New England buildings and began to be used for entire structures there early in

the nineteenth century. The walls of Young's Vermont State House (1834–41) were built from granite quarried in Barre and dragged more than twelve miles to Montpelier; the shafts of its six Doric columns, each composed of six, six-foot-long drums, each six feet in diameter, were set in place without derricks. This impressive undertaking helped Young win the competition for the Boston Custom House, built of Quincy, Massachusetts, granite. Its construction techniques exemplified what came to be known as the "Boston Granite Style." Granite blocks placed on end, with the rock's strata running vertically, or even diagonally (rather than horizontally), were stronger and allowed for increasing the ratio of windows to walls, thus solving the dark interiors which had been a major drawback of using granite for public buildings. Aesthetically, the Boston Granite Style's severe architecture developed partly from the structural dictates of building with large granite slabs so hard they were "hammered" (rather than carved) to achieve finished effects. Moreover,

III-12 C. Roger's 1845 portrait of Ammi B. Young, architect of the south wing.

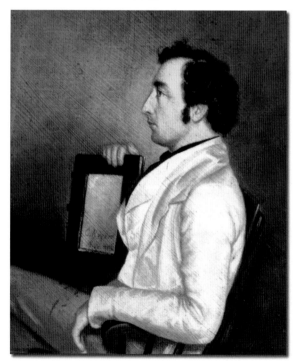

the Boston aesthetic reflected a New England taste for simplicity, dignity, and strength that seems to have comported well with the government's image of itself during the great building campaigns of the 1850s–60s. Granite also was much less expensive than marble, quarries of which were being opened about the same time, because they often were accessible to shipment via water and because there was not as much waste through breakage.[25]

When all of Washington was preparing to be under siege during the summer of 1861, the public buildings were hastily fortified. One newspaperman commented:

> If any of them is calculated to withstand the shock of war, certainly the Treasury building is that one, and the cannon with "their bowels full of wrath" might "spit out their iron indignation 'gainst [sic] its walls" with but little effect. We speak of the southern extension. The immense granite pilasters weighing from 50 to 60 tons each—four feet through of solid stone—bound together by other gigantic blocks and slabs worthy to figure at Karnak or Edfou, are fitted together so closely that the building could not be more substantial if cut out of a solid rock.[26]

Security, stability, and permanence were important factors. Yet, the Treasury Building was not so much a fortress as an office building that needed to house hundreds of employees comfortably. Young felt confident enough in his abilities to heat and ventilate stone buildings—the subject of much discussion in building the Boston Custom House—to write President Fillmore in 1850, offering to make the President's House much more comfortable. Young's considerable experience as a competent builder of his own well-planned, fireproof, and handsome designs combined with his political allegiances

gained for him the much coveted position as the government's principal architect.[27]

Bowman and Young had identified multiple sources of supply for both stock and commissioned goods during the Bureau of Construction's formative years and followed closely evolving industries and technologies. Mass production of cast and rolled iron made it possible to build the Treasury Extension relatively inexpensively and quite rapidly. Steam engines probably turned the lathes that cut the Treasury Extension's monolithic columns. Steam power drove the ships carrying them and thousands of granite blocks from a coastal Maine island to a Washington wharf, and steam engines powered the derricks that raised iron beams and granite blocks alike into place. Two nineteenth-century inventions—lithography and photography—were married together by the 1850s to produce multiple copies of architectural drawings used by the bureau to solicit bids, by its chosen contractors to fabricate precision parts, and by its foremen charged with assembling the buildings. Dated photographs recorded the progress of the Treasury Building's construction, but also kept all interested officials abreast of progress on the complex building site where as many as six hundred skilled workmen and common laborers were employed.

The Treasury Extension's design process did not end with presidential and congressional approval of Walter's design. During the spring of 1855, Bowman and Young, anticipating their appointments as its engineer and architect, began preparing for their largest project. Young's earliest known drawings reveal that he planned three major revisions to Walter's design. A drawing of the two end walls indicates that he initially planned six square Doric piers to replace Walter's two central Ionic columns framed by piers, although this change was not carried out. (fig. III-13) Moreover, Young's piers had greater depth than those Walter proposed resulting in a better transition to the thicker

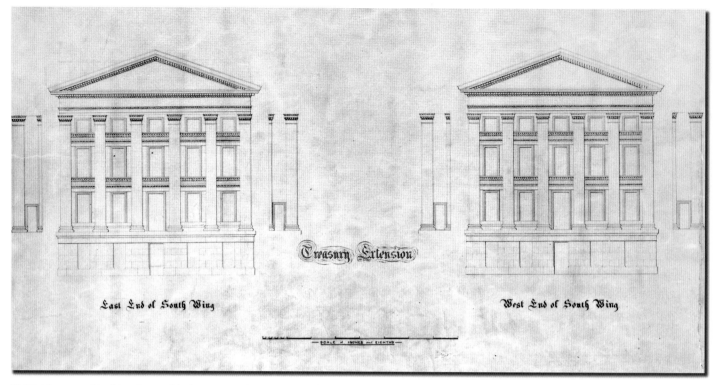

Treasury Extension

East End of South Wing   West End of South Wing

SCALE 4 INCHES and EIGHTHS

III-13 Young added horizontal belt courses between stories to build in the Boston Granite Style.

pilasters Young planned for the south walls. Lastly, Young introduced wide, ornamented belt courses between the stories. He made these changes because of the way he proposed knitting the granite building blocks together. Walter's walls revealed a refined use of the classical language of architecture, the verticality and balance of his window-to-wall ratios continuing the rhythm of Mills's east facade. Young's facades were boldly innovative, a dynamic balance of horizontals and verticals—a stated rather than implied grid—that downplayed rather than visually supported the east colonnade's verticality.

In his 1856 annual report, Bowman recorded the reasons for the changes to the design "authorized by Congress." Walter's design was,

contained upon two sheets of drawings, consisting of a general plan of the entrance story, and three elevations upon one sheet, with a perspective view from the southwest upon the other. They contained few or no details and but few admeasurements, while the elevations and perspective view were at variance with each other in several particulars, so that in the execution of the work very much was left to the judgment of the superintendent.[28]

Bowman emphasized that the variations on Walter's drawings "seemed to fully warrant any deviation from the details of the building that utility, good taste, or necessity required."[29]

In 1856 Anna Ella Carroll wrote of her distaste of Young's changes in her avowedly political tract *A Review of Pierce's Administration.*

Mr. Walter's plan has been changed by the superintendent and architect having the extension in charge. They have allowed their fancies to run riot, and all their dreams of "palace halls" are being realized at the expense of the American people … The plain front originally designed, and the economical plan proposed, under Mr. Fillmore's administration … have been totally abandoned, and a front of Italian "gingerbread-work" substituted instead of Mr. Walter's design. The elaborate and costly style substituted is of no consequence to Mr. Pierce; but the people will be greater dupes than we take them to be, if they tacitly submit to the robbery of *their* treasury for the purpose of pampering the pets of the executive.[30]

In May 1856 the House Committee on Public Buildings compared Walter's and Young's designs, apparently satisfied with what they learned at that time, but later investigations solicited more critical appraisals. The Irish-born and -trained architect Charles B. Clusky, who came to Washington in 1848 from Savannah and did some work for the Bureau of Construction on the Treasury Extension, was dismissive of Young's design.

> The approved plan [Walter's] was in strict conformity with the architecture of the original; the colonnade then erected fronting on Fifteenth street, whilst the south and west fronts, … and the portico "in antis," … which connects with the south end of the colonnade are not. Many of the distinguishing characteristic features of the style being altered and others, somewhat grotesque, introduced or substituted, none of which are admissible where a proper appreciation of the best models and correct taste prevails.[31]

Clusky further complained that Young had introduced *entasis*—bulging in the mid-points of columns so they appear to be vertical—in the south wing columns (fig. III-14), while Mills's had been tapered, wider at the bottom and narrower at the top, although old photographs do not seem to support this assertion. Clusky particularly disliked Young's belt courses:

> [T]he spaces between the antae [pilasters], which are plain in the original [Walter's drawings], are crowded with a medley of moldings in every shape, the separation between the several stories being marked throughout with heavy cornices, the jambs of the windows being moulded [*sic*] to excess, and the material part of the moulding [*sic*] of the base of the antae continued around the entire building, thus giving the composition a confused appearance, and destroying the effect which the repose of plain surface between the antae would have given to the whole, by throwing out prominently the principle features, the columns, the antae, and the entablature, had the original plan of the building been adhered to.[32]

Clusky disputed that the Boston Granite Style of construction with pilasters, window frames and jambs, and transoms "all in one piece, placed on their ends" made for stronger construction. (fig. III-15) "It does not; on the contrary, it would be more permanent and better construction were it of heavy ashlar properly bonded, as in the case with the Capitol, Patent Office, and Post Office." All of these extensions were designed by Walter, who during the 1838 investigation of the east wing had criticized Mills's construction techniques. In Walter's view, Mills as well as Young wrongly deviated from America's European-derived building practices.[33]

Carroll's and Clusky's critiques of Young's design were both to some extent self-serving; other critics were impressed with the massive presence of the south wing, particularly noting the size (thirty-two feet tall) and weight (75,000 pounds each) of the monolithic columns and pilasters (up to 100,000 pounds each). Washington columnist George Alfred Townsend astutely observed in 1870 that the "Grecian Ionic order of architecture has been adopted, but it has been treated in many respects as a Roman order, being mounted on a podium or basement, crowned with an elegant balustrade."[34]

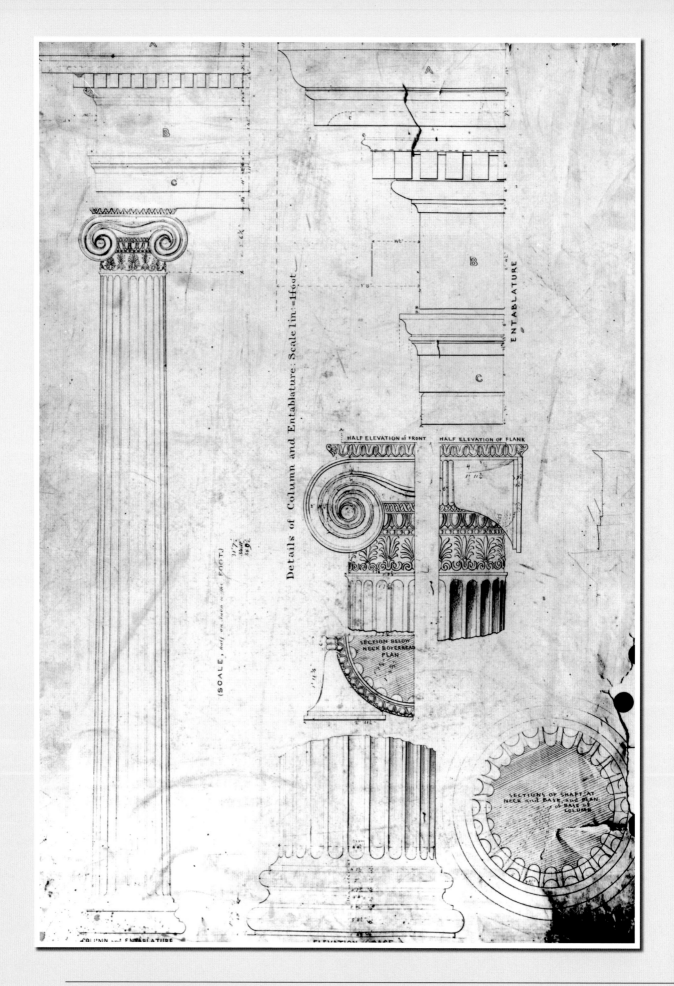

Details of Column and Entablature: Scale 1in.=1foot

HALF ELEVATION of FRONT   HALF ELEVATION OF FLANK

SECTION BELOW NECK & OVERHEAD PLAN

SECTIONS OF SHAFT AT NECK and BASE and PLAN of BASE of COLUMN

III-15 Monolithic pilasters set in place in 1858 replaced walls as the building's vertical armature.

No one remarked that the south wing's width—a result of Young's spacious offices and particularly wide corridors—pushed its portico forward to obscure the view of the President's House from the Capitol and vice versa. It is probable that Young intentionally altered the vista along Pennsylvania Avenue because Walter's Capitol dome changed the equation of the symbolic balance of power represented by the reciprocal sightlines between the two buildings. The Capitol's previous domes were on a scale comparable with the south portico of the President's House, but Walter's 287-foot-high dome dwarfed Hoban's semi-circular portico, now much too modest visually to carry the

executive branch's comparable symbolic weight. Young's massive eight-columned south portico, while not as powerful as the Capitol dome, did assert the executive branch's authority better than the south portico of the President's House. (figs. III-16 & III-17)

Walt Whitman described his perception of the relationship between the recently completed dome and portico when viewed along Pennsylvania Avenue as he witnessed Lincoln's second inaugural parade in March 1865.

[T]he wide Avenue, its vista very fine, down at one end closed by the capitol, with milky bulging dome, and the Maternal Figure over all, (with the sword by her side and the

Opposite page: III-14 Young's South Wing Ionic columns were to be monoliths, single massive pieces of granite.

III-16 The view of the President's House along Pennsylvania Avenue during the 1840s.

III-17 The majestic south wing's portico responded to the Capitol's contemporary cast iron dome.

Fortress of Finance: The United States Treasury Building

sun glittering on her helmeted head;) at the other, the western end, the pillared front of the Treasury Building, looking south; altogether quite a refreshing spot and hour, and plenty of architectural show with life and magnetism also.[35]

"Skillful Artist & Clever Expert:" Photographer Lewis E. Walker (1824–1880)

Apparently, the first use of printing techniques in America to produce multiple copies of architectural drawings—a great savings over having draftsmen make copies—was Robert Mills's lithographed sets of two alternate marine hospital designs (1837) to be sent to local superintendents. Photography soon served the same purpose. Although the Treasury Extension's assistant engineer, Major Edmund French, wrote Meigs in January 1855 that he had just received a "Photographic Apparatus and would like to try its power and accuracy," it is not known how he applied his new device to his work. A year later, Meigs wrote Secretary of War Jefferson Davis asking for approval to buy photographic equipment and materials for use at the Capitol Extension. "We have a large number of some hundreds of working and other drawings, many of which are upon too large a scale to be conveniently preserved or referred to and the reduction of which by hand would be tedious and expensive, as we pay our draftsmen from $3 to $4 per day." In mid-May 1856, Meigs hired a draftsman to make "reduction in photography of our drawings" and, by the middle of December, Bowman inquired how much the equipment and the "services of a competent operator" would cost. When Meigs replied that he paid his "photographic draughtsman" $5 per day, he also sent Bowman samples of photographic reproductions of drawings but

noted that they were "not so clear and clean as in lithographic prints."[36]

Late in 1856 or early in 1857, French ordered for use on the Treasury Extension a camera, chemicals, and sheets of French plate glass for four sizes of negatives from the New York photographer Edward Anthony, who continued to advise him on processes and to suggest instruction books. (Anthony took many of the early stereographs of Washington scenes, including several of the Treasury Building.) In February 1857 French asked Anthony to recommend a "Photographic Operator, one who has had experience taking Views and Copying Engravings or drawings and who is a Draughtsman would be preferred so that he would at times make the working or other drawings." Anthony advised French to train a draftsman to be a photographer but, by the middle of April, one of Anthony's employees, Lewis E. Walker, wanted more information about the job. Apparently, French decided that the Treasury Extension needed a full-time architectural photographer, for on May 7 French offered Walker $5 per day to begin in two weeks. Walker was the Treasury's official photographer until his death in 1880 when his friend Timothy O'Sullivan, famous as the first photographer of the Grand Canyon, replaced him.[37]

Walker proved to be a very valuable member of the Treasury Extension's staff. He not only copied and reduced hundreds of working drawings, considerably shortening the time between design and production of parts, but "also cop[ied] letters of instruction on Department business, hundreds of which are dispatched weekly." Walker is best remembered for his beautifully finished photographic views that recorded the Treasury Building's construction progress, copies of which were presented to other government agencies as well as diplomats. (fig. III-18) By late 1857 Young routinely ordered not just photographs of drawings but one hundred sets of lithographs

III-18 On September 16, 1861, Lewis Walker photographed raising the last west portico column.

photographically reduced in size for iron and stonework drawings to ensure that every bidder received the same visual information and could be held accountable for what they produced. Moreover, if one supplier failed them, others had the same information to duplicate parts as needed. By late 1858 Bowman boasted to a correspondent in Paris (to whom he sent six photographs) that his "very skillful artist & clever expert" had devised a simple method to make color photographs. Bowman included instructions on Walker's technique, noting that a similar discovery had just been made in England "and kept a secret, with the view of levying a contribution of Fifty thousand dollars from Photographers for a knowledge of the process." Six months later, Bowman noted that

Walker's color process duplicated that discovered concurrently in Europe and sent specimens of Walker's work to Paris, presumably some in color, although no examples of these images are known to survive. Bowman, who had earlier sent sets of the Bureau of Construction's *Plans of Public Buildings* (1856) abroad to libraries and intellectual societies, wished to demonstrate to Europeans America's rising ascendancy in the arts and sciences under his purview and the American government's willingness to share freely its scientific discoveries. In return, he received dozens of the latest publications relating to many aspects of international progress in engineering and architecture.[38]

Walker also made more typical photographs, recording distinguished visitors and ceremonies at various events including the launching of a ship at the Navy Yard in May 1860. In June 1860 his request for a leave of absence to join an expedition to Labrador was turned down because the department could not do without his services for forty or fifty days. On July 11, 1861, Secretary Chase wrote Abraham Lincoln reiterating his verbal request that the president sit for a portrait by Walker. "Your countenance must do its part towards making our Treasury notes current," argued Chase. During the Civil War, Walker's services were often loaned to the War Department to make photographic copies of maps. While traveling north in the fall of 1862, Walker wrote the department. "I cannot find anything new in the Photographic line in New York; but find that Anthony & O'Neil are using a process for preparing Albumenized paper (& considering it a great secret) that I have been using for a considerable time." Although he seems to have not aspired to be an art or topographical photographer, Walker's mastery of the science of photography seems to have been second to none. In 1867 the bureau's measurer, Bartholomew Oertly, designed a "photographer's office" for Walker. (fig. III-19) It was built on the grounds south of the Treasury, probably to isolate the noxious smell of the chemicals Walker routinely used. Dozens of portraits of unidentified people—many surely Treasury employees—taken in this studio, attest to its varied usage. In 1901 the charming wood Stick-Style building was renovated to serve as the office and garden shed of the landscape architect in charge of the President's Grounds.[39]

The Swiss-born Oertly (c. 1821–1878) was one of several European-trained architects (he graduated from the University of Heidelberg) hired by the Bureau of Construction as draftsmen in 1855. By 1861 Oertly was working primarily on the Treasury Extension as its computer in charge of calculating the amounts and prices of all of its materials and evaluating all proposals. Because Oertly countersigned every payment issued by the bureau, his knowledge of the construction history of the south and

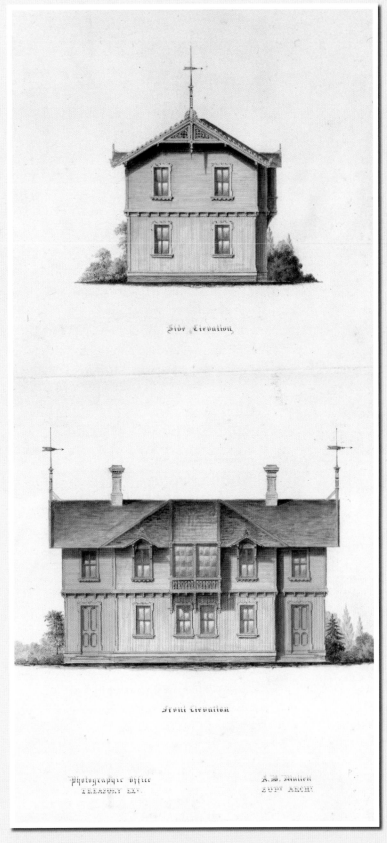

III-19 The photography studio, built south of the building, isolated noxious chemical odors.

west wings was comprehensive. In July 1866 Mullett recommended that Oertly be formally appointed the assistant supervising architect as he had "practically fulfilled all the duties" of the position "for some time past." In his letter of resignation in April 1867, Oertly noted: "My motives for leaving the service of the Department, though imperative, are purely private." Mullett prevailed upon him to remain by promising him an annual raise of twenty percent but the funds were slow in being paid and in 1868 Oertly accepted a position as assistant engineer for the District of Columbia. While working on the Treasury Building, Oertly's efficiency was matched by his trustworthiness, and his responsibilities increased until he was appointed acting supervising architect in 1865 to be a steadying influence during a volatile period in the Treasury Building's history.[40]

"Great Animation Prevails:" Building the South Wing's Granite Envelope

The protracted political maneuvering throughout the spring of 1855 to choose the architect of the Treasury Extension was hurting the city's artisans and workmen who had been waiting for work since the appropriation was made in early March. On May 2 President Pierce left the decision of superintendence in Secretary Guthrie's hands; by the end of June, the *Evening Star* repeated a cynical allegation "that the president had determined to refuse to execute the law under which this work is to be constructed purely for the intense gratification he will enjoy in starving native born mechanics." Young spent the intervening two months making working drawings, for on June 26, Bowman solicited bids for stone in newspapers as far south as Richmond and as far north as Albany, but mainly in New England. His unusually lengthy call for bids was for both granite and marble and he included a table

detailing the dimensions for different parts of the building.[41]

For example, marble columns might be made up of four or five drums while granite ones were bid on the basis of two or three drums of equal length. Each bidder was required to submit a sample cube, four of its sides to be "hammered" with different finishes (designated as numbers one through four), the Boston Custom House serving as the model for these surfaces. By the 1870s, eleven gradations of hammered or "dressed" stone had been standardized, number one being the coarsest with one cut per inch and number eleven having a smooth surface. Bidders for the Treasury Extension's stonework were required to submit bonds and all prices were to be calculated on stones "wrought, fitted, and delivered in a proper state to be put into the building." By mid-July 1855, Secretary Guthrie ordered one hundred lithographic copies of a "Sheet of drawings of the details of Stone Work for the Treasury Department Extension" to be sent to the bidders. No copy is known to survive.[42]

"Yesterday afternoon, at 3 o'clock, a large number of workmen commenced breaking ground on the southern side of the Treasury building, of the addition thereto, authorized by the last Congress," reported the *Evening Star* on July 17. The excavation was not completed until late October. On August 25 Guthrie signed a contract to provide granite for the foundation from quarries in Port Deposit, Maryland, near Baltimore, and broken stone from Little Falls Quarry on the Potomac for the concrete parts of the foundations. This contract, like all those made for materials for the Treasury Extension, required the contractor to deliver the stone to the building site and included stringent forfeitures should the schedule not be met. Every Treasury Extension contract also closed with the stipulation: "It is further agreed & understood that no member of Congress, or other person whose name is not at this time disclosed, shall be entitled to any interest in this contract." While the site was being prepared, Bowman and Young began collecting experienced superintendents. The excitement of playing a part in a major new project was conveyed in newsprint. "It is a subject of congratulation among our fellow-citizens to witness the rapidity with which the foundations for this important edifice is going up—all around it great animation prevails."[43]

Eighteen bidders responded to the proposal for stone, about half offering both granite and marble. As it took some time for Oertly to evaluate all the bids, Bowman did not report to Secretary Guthrie until the beginning of October. Based on its lower cost, beauty, and durability, he recommended granite, "having the shafts of each column and the caps of each buttress be in a single piece." Bowman disqualified several bidders who had failed to comply with all of the proposal's numerous parts, while noting that Beals & Dixon of New York and Dix Island, Maine, had answered all the criteria and was the lowest bidder. "The style of cutting proposed by them is at least equal to any other—the Stock is more beautiful and equal in durability to any proposed as the price is undoubtedly reasonable." The *Evening Star* noted that, in addition to beauty and economy, Beals & Dixon granite was chosen because "it will assimilate more nearly with the existing structure," the east wing's brown sandstone colonnade and walls having been painted to imitate granite by 1851.[44]

The contract with Beals & Dixon laid out in detail the costs for each size and shape of stone delivered ready to be set in the walls. The cost of each of the monoliths, including "struck, freight and workmanship," differed according to its hammering shown on their sample, which seemingly was reversed from the standard adopted later in the century: columns hammered #1 would cost $2,700; #2 would be $2,450; and, #3, $2,200. Because Beals & Dixon

was contracting to provide all the granite (except the foundations) for the south wing, the bond they had to post was high, $50,000. The proposals published in newspapers stated the successful bidder would be the contractor for the granite to complete the entire extension and that proviso was included in the October 10, 1855, contract with the Maine quarry owners. Another stipulation was standard for all Bureau of Construction contracts. If the contractor failed to meet his obligations, the Treasury Department undertook to complete the work at the contractor's expense rather than re-advertising the work. During a lengthy correspondence in late autumn, Bowman sent detailed stonework drawings and "bills of particulars." In response, Beals & Dixon queried Bowman about details and found many discrepancies that needed to be resolved before producing precision parts for a complex three-dimensional puzzle.[45]

Because the granite contract with Beals & Dixon stipulated that each stone was to arrive in a finished state, a visiting New York newspaperman noted that "this imposing work has gone on almost without the sound of a hammer." Almost surely this provision of the contract was partly to ensure relative quiet for the Treasury Department's employees who continued to work in the east wing while the south and west wing walls rose between 1856 and 1859. Yet, by 1858 Beals & Dixon set up sheds, manned by their own stoneworkers, on the Treasury grounds after many finished stones had been damaged in shipping. As soon as each wing was habitable, busy Treasury offices were moved into new quarters, but the south wing was not fully occupied until 1863, delayed because of the outbreak of the Civil War in 1861.[46]

Little is known of Vermonter Horace Beals (1811–?), reputedly a millionaire who in 1850 acquired Dix Island, Maine, in payment of a debt. (fig. III-20) He was not an absentee owner, but instead was in charge of quarry-

III-20 The wharf at Dix Island, Maine, with a barque built specifically to ship heavy granite blocks.

ing operations on the eighty-acre stone island at the entrance of Penobscot Bay. He opened the quarry in 1851, fifteen years after the first Maine quarries began to be worked. Dix Island granite, categorized as pinkish buff in color and medium to coarse in texture, became very popular, especially for government buildings, its beauty and consistent markings often praised. A town of 150 buildings sprang up on the island and experienced quarrymen from Ireland, Scotland, and Italy were landed directly at its wharfs. Five large boarding houses—two named the "Shamrock" and the "Aberdeen"—housed a thousand workers. The workforce of nearly 1,500 men was also served by a theater that seated several hundred people. Beals's partner Courtlandt Palmer Dixon (1817–83), the son of a member of Congress from Rhode Island, began his career working in his uncle's New York hardware store. It was Dixon's political connections and lobbying efforts that led to a number of government contracts for the Dix Island Granite Company, the Treasury

Extension being its first large commission. Dixon may have been introduced to the granite business by his father-in-law, Ephraim Williams of Stonington, Connecticut, after whom the company's barque, the *Ephraim Williams,* was named. It was built in 1857 specifically to transport the Treasury Extension's thirty-two-foot-tall columns and pilasters.[47]

More is known about the transport and landing of the Treasury's granite than about how it was quarried and worked, the early history of the Dix Island Granite Company being lost. *Harper's* reported:

> The large blocks of granite taken from that quarry have a beauty, compactness, and uniformity nowhere else equaled in the world. So steep and sheer are the sides of the island that vessels drawing thirty feet of water come in direct contact with it, and the large masses of rock are quarried out and swung aboard without intermediate hauling. Vessels of peculiar construction and of great strength are made for the special purpose of shipping the immense pilasters, columns, and other large stones to Washington. The absence of all necessity for land carriage renders this stone cheaper than that from Quincy [Massachusetts] and other places much nearer the Seat of Government than Dix Island.[48]

Bowman worked with Washington entrepreneurs Morgan & Rhinehart in 1856 to rebuild the wharf at the foot of 21st Street in Foggy Bottom. (fig. III-21) In late August 1857 Young reported to Dixon that a series of

III-21 Granite was off-loaded at the 21st Street dock and stored south of the President's Grounds.

low tides caused the *Ephraim Williams* to run aground, which required removing two-thirds of the stone from the holds. Bowman convinced Mayor William B. Magruder to deepen the Potomac River's north channel, arguing that the wharf was also being used to off-load materials for the Washington Aqueduct. When Dixon bought the wharf in 1858, he had five ships transporting granite to the Treasury's building site. The government took possession of the wharf during the Civil War, but it reverted to Dixon in 1865 and he used it to off-load all the granite for the entire Treasury Extension until the building was finished.[49]

Although bids for the stone were not due until August 27, 1855, Young began to immediately secure the services of Seth W. Barton (1800–61), a master rigger from New England, who had been his "chief Derrick hoisting Man" at the Boston Custom House. Barton spent a few days in Washington in late August, when it was decided he would need to build three derricks. He proceeded to Boston to buy and ship the necessary iron parts. The ready availability of iron parts like gears of various sizes and iron rope made by Roebling Brothers necessary to operate the derricks reveals how quickly these newly manufactured items were put to use by the government. The Bureau of Construction was a major client for these materials, particularly Roebling's rope, because they were replaced frequently to insure the safety of building sites.[50]

Either then or when Barton returned to Boston in mid-September to buy parts to build three steam engines (to power the derricks), the rigger learned that the two derricks he had built for the Boston Custom House were for sale. The Treasury Department bought them and they were installed immediately to lay the foundations of the south, west, and north wings. They also served as models for new and improved derricks built following Barton's instructions. These derricks were not designed on paper by a West Point-trained engineer, but rather evolved in the hands of a self-taught engineer and were modified by him as their varied uses dictated. "I believe them to be the best Derricks in use when properly made," opined Young who sent photographs of them to an inquiring engineer at West Point. He added: "I do not now know of any one who constructs them, or where drawings of them could be obtained." Young was protecting Barton's interests because a drawing made under his aegis and dated 1857 details their construction.[51] (fig. III-22)

On a single day in September 1856, Meigs reported that the Capitol's steam-driven derrick lifted sixty-five blocks of stone while dismantling Charles Bulfinch's 1823 dome, "dropped them all into wagons with drays and hauled them away to the yard," a collision between new and old building technologies, which was a commonplace occurrence. Although military colleagues were out to best the architects with whom they worked and vice versa, the competition between Meigs and Bowman was also fierce as they put additions on Washington's major public buildings. Meigs moaned: "Berry and Mohen say that they cannot set the stone [at the Post Office] for less than 18 cents per cubic foot. Bowman says that he set the other day [at the Treasury] 410 feet with his boom derricks for $13, which is about 3 cents per cubic foot. I find by a careful account of Provost and Winter's work for 3 days upon the north wing of the Capitol that they set about 300 cubic feet in the 3 days at a height of about 57 feet and that it cost in wages 14 ½ cents per cubic foot." The difference in cost per cubic foot in lifting stone at the Treasury and the buildings Meigs supervised was because Young used larger building blocks.[52]

Barton was one of a new breed of American mechanics whose skills as a practical engineer

Opposite page: III-22 Seth Barton designed and built several derricks to hoist heavy loads of granite and iron.

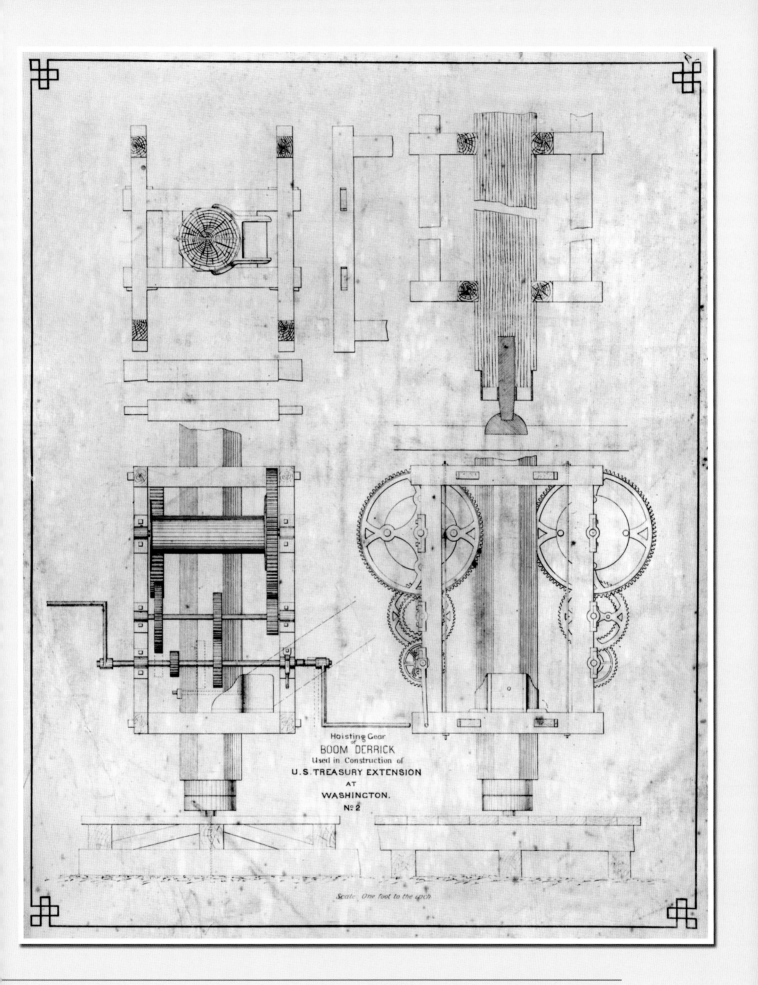

Hoisting Gear
of
BOOM DERRICK
Used in Construction of
U.S. TREASURY EXTENSION
AT
WASHINGTON.
Nº 2

Scale, One foot to the inch

made it possible for the Treasury Extension to be built as quickly and efficiently as it was. By the beginning of the 1857 building season, there were six "large Derricks able to lift Stones of from 15 to 18 tons" and additional riggers were needed. "Now I want a man who could take charge of the Engine, Derricks and Machinery and arrange the gearing to do the maxm [*sic*] amt of work [and] to arrange and set up the machinery … A practical working man who could make the derricks move as they did at High Bridge and who is a good workman & mechanic is the kind wanted," wrote Bowman's assistant in 1857 when he needed an additional rigger.[53] The exciting spectacle of raising the massive monoliths was photographed by Lewis Walker and described in 1857 and again in 1858. (fig. III-23)

Crowds of persons are to be seen every day, eager spectators of the gigantic operations going on about the south front—an inclined plane of sixteen feet elevation and some one hundred and thirty-six feet in length, has been erected to be used for drawing up the granite pilasters, which are to form the facing between windows of the second and third stories; by this arrangement of heavy stones, which are lifted from the wagons to the planes by means of purchase screws worked by hand, are drawn up to the required position on the basement wall in the space of four minutes by steam process.

III-23 Raising the first monolithic pilaster in 1857 drew a large crowd of awed spectators.

This process, done by hand labor, would require something like two days to each pilaster.[54]

Once each column was positioned on the inclined plane, "they were grappled by the iron jaws of monster steam derricks and lifted as if by magic into upright positions, where they are likely to remain for a thousand centuries." By June 1860 there were thirteen derricks of different sizes being used to build the Treasury Extension and a crane at the 21st Street wharf. Barton served as the superintendent of riggers until he became the inspector of materials shortly before his death in November 1861.[55]

Bowman was optimistic about the rapid construction of the granite work when he wrote his annual report at the end of the 1855 building season, predicting that Beals & Dixon had "already commenced the work, with a very large force; and, from facilities possessed by their quarry for furnishing blocks of any required dimensions, I feel great hopes that they will be able to fulfill their contract at a much earlier day than the one stipulated," October 1, 1857. Many mishaps with the supply and quality of granite occurred during 1856: delays in shipping because of bad weather; Young's lengthening of pilasters by seven inches in November after six were already cut; and hammering by the contractors that fell below the requisite quality. To these were added significant amounts of time setting up the derricks and their steam engines and then dismantling and moving them as required.[56]

All were minor problems compared to the congressional investigation of contracts for materials held in April. No factual basis could be found for the suspicion among many of the original bidders that Young had colluded with Beals & Dixon. In his reply to the House Committee on Public Buildings and Grounds, Secretary Guthrie pointed out that Beals & Dixon was the only bidder who specifically quoted prices and surface hammering for each shape of stone

under consideration. Young may have advised them to be absolutely explicit in their proposal. For example, their bid included the costs of monoliths and those composed of three or more drums—each bid stipulating three distinct surface treatments at differing prices—the monoliths costing about $1,000 more than those with multiple drums. None of the other bids, sealed and opened at the same time in the presence of witnesses, was as complete in every detail.[57]

Bowman reported the Treasury Building's progress at the end of September 1856. "The cellar and area walls were completed, the arches turned for the floor of the basement, and the ashlar of the basement completed to the belt course, inclusive, except a small space left out for introducing some heavy columns." During 1856 Beals & Dixon delivered far more granite than Bowman's workforce was able to handle. Their contract was extended on the first of January 1857 as they began preparations to cut the monolithic pilasters and columns out of the quarry bed. On March 25 Young sent them the "tracing of the Scroll of the capital" as the model for the volutes that were shallower than those used on the east front's Ionic capitals because the granite was much denser than sandstone and more difficult to work. At the end of July, eight pilasters sitting at the wharf were ready to be hoisted into place, delivered by Beals & Dixon's barque which hauled 450 tons of granite on that inaugural trip. The first pilaster was hoisted up to the second story on August 21, the *Evening Star* reporting that it weighed twenty-eight tons and was thirty-two feet, five inches high. The second pilaster was not raised until September 7. A Walker photograph, taken in March 1858, illustrates the written record, showing pilasters on the west end of the south facade set in place atop the basement story. (fig. III-24) The "walls" consisting solely of window frames and belt courses were quickly placed between the pilasters, apparently a less spectacular but more delicate operation.[58]

III-24 The Boston Granite Style interlocked pilasters, belt courses, and window surrounds.

III-25 By December 1858 the south wing was enclosed and some offices occupied.

The *Evening Star* summed up 1857's progress on October 12.

The south front, in its progress, presents some new features daily. The long heavy pilasters are being set at a rate of from two to three per week; the labor of preparing each of these gigantic blocks of granite for hoisting generally occupies the greatest part of two days, and is the most dangerous part of the business, each rope and block requiring to be watched with the closest scrutiny, and with great regard to the proper capacity of sustaining the immense weight of the stones. Some ten of the pilasters are set, and the intervening spaces built up as fast as the hoisting process is continued.[59]

The centerpiece of the Walter-Young south wing exterior was its central portico, conceived as a major ceremonial entrance leading to the department's most important offices. The long approach through the elaborate iron gateway, then up two levels of stairs divided by a broad plaza, prepared visitors for the majestic experience of entering the Treasury Building through eight columns and a lofty vestibule. As a processional route it vied with the Capitol's. Young revised the portico's details while the main block was under construction as he and Bowman calculated the weight and forces exerted by the massive granite pieces used to build its perimeter walls. By the end of 1857, most of the pilasters on the walls behind the portico had been "set and secured." The quarry charged an additional $450 each to carve the vestibule's columns with entasis, or bulging centers. Other design changes included dividing the vestibule's ceiling into nine separate coffers supported by six columns; initially Young planned a granite ceiling, but it was changed to cast-iron in 1858. Finer grade hammering to create "highly finished moulded [sic] stone" was ordered to give subtle definition to pilasters, columns, window frames, and walls within the vestibule.[60]

Once above ground, pieces of the granite puzzle were rapidly being lifted into place and the contractors were getting paid—but trouble was on the horizon. Work commenced in the early spring of 1858 but came to an abrupt halt on May 1 when Bowman let many workmen go because the wing's appropriation was nearly exhausted. "A limited number of hands have been retained on the south wing, and the progress of that portion of the building towards completion has been, considering all the drawbacks, very fair. Only one course of stone cornice on the southwest section remains to be laid, and the wing will be ready for roofing," reported the *Evening Star* on June 14 as part of its campaign to support Washington's working men. Work began again on July 1, 1858, under a $50,000 appropriation to finish just the south wing. Letters sent to Beals & Dixon telling them to halt work on both quarrying and dressing stone for other parts of the building went unanswered, apparently as they were consulting with their lawyers about their protections under their contract. Even after work began in July under a new $50,000 appropriation, Beals & Dixon was warned to supply only granite for the south wing.[61]

By the end of the 1858 building season, Bowman was able to report that all the floors of the south wing had been arched as the building rose in horizontal layers. Moreover, because the south half of the west wing needed to connect seamlessly with the west end of the south wing, portions of its exterior walls had to be built concurrently. Fifty-one pilasters and columns had been raised on both wings. The south's entablature was complete except for its pediment and the pediments on the east and west ends of the south wing were finished. (fig. III-25) With the exception of the columns for the south portico, all the granite for that wing was at the site, as well as most of the granite to complete the exterior of the west wing. Carrying both the south and west wings to completion according to this method, however, was threatened by

III-26 The south wing's portico and staircase were nearly finished by March 15, 1860.

congressional concerns about the cost of such a massive undertaking.[62]

On December 30, 1858, Bowman briefed Secretary of the Treasury Howell Cobb in preparation for replying to the House Ways and Means Committee's query concerning the final cost of finishing the south wing and merely stabilizing the west and north wings in an unfinished state.[63] Bowman advised against agreeing to the committee's strategy, which he estimated would cost approximately $700,000. He noted that, since approximately $381,000 remained in the current appropriation, Congress would only have to find another $300,000. His principal argument was that if the large amount of materials on hand—both granite and iron—were left exposed for an appreciable amount of time they would deteriorate; the cost of putting them under cover, he opined, would be "extravagant." Moreover, the contractors, especially

Beals & Dixon, would have to be compensated to the full extent of their contracts to avoid the government paying damages. Lastly, Bowman considered that curtailing the Treasury Building by completing just the south wing would be treating the workmen "harshly." If they were forced to leave Washington to seek employment elsewhere, Bowman would need to retrain a new crew when future congressional appropriations allowed work to resume. He particularly noted that training each skilled group to work in harmony with the others, about 400 men working efficiently in different locations within the building, had taken time. As a result, there had been no deaths and only one serious injury in the first three years, remarkable considering the size of the building site where so many men were constantly moving heavy loads of material.[64]

The 35th Congress decided to appropriate $50,000 to secure the materials on hand, leaving Bowman with approximately half a million dollars to complete the south wing. However, he was barred from proceeding until the Senate reported on a second investigation concerning cost overruns. A resolution passed on February 8, 1859, asked for a detailed accounting of what had been spent and an estimate of future granite costs as well as an explanation of why these aggregate costs "so far exceeds the estimated amount placed against the names of the successful bidders." Bowman disingenuously blamed Walter's drawings which, he noted, were "totally devoid of details" for accurate estimates, although he knew full well, as did members of Congress, that Young had drawn up detailed bills of particulars. These specifications were based on preliminary stonework drawings made by his draftsmen and were sent to every bidder who requested them. More convincing was Bowman's argument that the project was simply so massive and complicated that it was inevitable that they were learning as they went along.[65]

In late November 1859, when the building's construction was winding down at the close of the building season, the "exterior flight of granite steps at the entrance to the south portico … [was] gradually approaching completion. (fig. III-26) The process of laying each step is one of much care and nicety." Young probably was prompted to create an elaborate Italian marble "mosaic pavement" for the vestibule's floor to increase the space's ceremonial importance by reinforcing its connection to the main hallway. On May 28, 1860, Henry Parry, a New York importer of foreign stones, was awarded the contract to provide the materials and workmen to professionally lay the simple pattern of light-colored large octagons connected by smaller, dark squares. In contrast, the centerpiece's complex eight-pointed star and its framing elements were composed of multicolored marbles, including green verde antique, which was unavailable in this country.[66] (fig. III-27)

III-27 Multicolored domestic stones and imported marbles created the portico's pavement pattern.

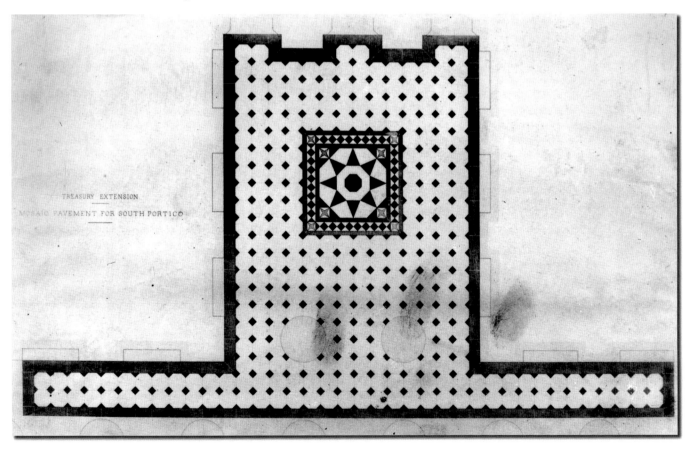

TREASURY EXTENSION

MOSAIC PAVEMENT FOR SOUTH PORTICO

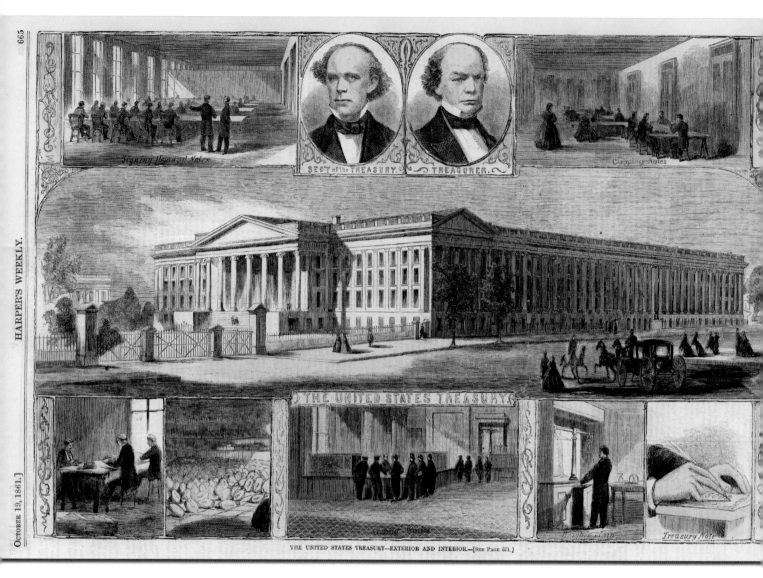

THE UNITED STATES TREASURY—EXTERIOR AND INTERIOR.—[See Page 671.]

III-28 The Civil War made the public avid for news about the Treasury Department and its building.

On March 1, 1859, the House reduced the appropriations to $50,000—just enough, according to Bowman's estimates, to complete the south wing. From the balance on hand of a quarter of a million dollars, $90,000 had to be paid to Beals & Dixon. In addition, Congress would be liable for the full amount of the contracts because Beals & Dixon had hired 1,200 men exclusively for the Treasury Building contract and had built three vessels "utterly useless for aught else" than transporting the Treasury's Buildings particularly large molding blocks, pilasters, and columns. Bowman practically begged Congress to appropriate the necessary funds to complete the entire extension in his

1859 annual report, citing malicious damage by vandals to finely wrought blocks intended for the west wing.[67]

Every bureau of the Treasury Department was tested and strengthened during the Civil War. Not only did the south wing play a critical role in protecting the President's Square, many of the workmen who built it were temporarily employed in erecting fortifications around the city. Passage of legislation to print currency in the Treasury Building meant modifications to the south wing's architecture and alterations to the west wing while it was under construction. Because these and other aspects of the multiple roles the south wing played during the war are integral to the history of the west wing's development, they are discussed in chapter four. (fig. III-28)

"Fraudulently Drawn from the Treasury:" The French Fraud

"The advent of the Chief of Police in the Treasury Department yesterday … naturally created not a little stir in the building … [and] there was the widest field of conjecture until the actual facts came out," reported the *Evening Star* on August 20, 1859. The Bureau of Construction's seemingly thorough system of accountability was breached, despite the fact that written orders for materials were checked for quality and completeness as they arrived, and both deliverymen and vendors were given receipts. Some clerks were assigned to keep copies of all correspondence, while others recorded every stage of each financial transaction.

The fraud was discovered when a Philadelphia contractor unknown to Bowman presented him with a bill for $1,200 for materials about which he knew nothing. "Suspicion [led] at once to French, who was immediately confronted with his superiors, in the Solicitor's office and called upon to explain, which he could not do, and appeared a great deal confused. He was shown his books and requested to explain why entries had not been made of the articles charged, and his manner at once betrayed him." Attempts to mitigate this damning public account soon appeared in the *Washington Star.* Invoked as signs of his innocence were French's "good family" background (his brother was a former minister at Epiphany Episcopal Church within sight of the Treasury Building), his solid social standing (diplomat and resident of Lafayette Square, Benjamin Ogle Tayloe, posted his bond), and his substantial annual salary of $3,000.[68]

Bowman's initial investigation led him to believe that $5,000 was missing. After French's arrest, he directed the tedious process of a thorough audit of the Treasury Building's accounts that included contacting every contractor and asking them to examine their own books.[69] By September 5 the department was able to determine that six local businesses had signed duplicate vouchers totaling $9,716.28 after being told by French that the first ones had been destroyed. The *Evening Star* reported on October 4:

> Too much cannot be said in commendation of the promptness with which those of our Washington mechanics, contractors for furnishing the materials used in the construction of the Treasury Extension, &c., came forward and volunteered to stand between Major Bowman and the Government in any loss that might be sustained in reference to Major French's defalcation, considering themselves morally responsible, from their negligence in signing vouchers twice over, under the impression that these first signed had been destroyed.[70]

However, Oertly, who claimed that French "was exercising almost exclusive control over the work" later explained the apparent good-heartedness of the contractors.

> They were no loosers [*sic*] by the operations and it was on this account that Majr. Bowman, accusing them of collusion (and I think in some cases by threats) got them to sign bonds, shielding him[self], the responsible Disbursing Agt. against loss, and to refund money. He also got a deed of trust on the property of Majr. French.[71]

In November 1860, however, Bowman claimed that as soon as several contractors "learned the improper use of the duplicate sets of Vouchers … [they] promptly gave bonds, to indemnify the U.S. for the amount fraudulently drawn from the Treasury." Bowman's possible coercion of the contractors can be explained because "it [was] decided by an Attorney

General, that after a fraudulent voucher has been allowed by the accounting officer in an account with the Disbursing Agent it cannot be re-examined, and that … redress is on the Agent alone, not upon the Government."[72] When the contractors Morris Tasker & Co. baulked at Bowman's suggestion that they post a bond, a percentage of which would be subtracted monthly as other contractors had agreed to, Bowman wrote them in great agitation.

> [Y]our signing and sending a second set of vouchers amounting to $1,522.22 *assisted* Major French to defraud *me* not the Government out of that amount … If you had withdrawn the first Voucher before you gave # two covering the same items (as I think you will admit you ought to have done) no fraud could have grown out of that transaction.[73]

Early in April 1860 French's team of Washington and New York lawyers requested a complete accounting "stated by a competent person" of all the monies he was accused of embezzling. French's first court date of July 5 was recessed for two days because he was ill; his doctor was present when he died at 1:30 a.m. on July 7 and verified that he had suffered for several weeks from what appears to have been cancer of the liver. His attorneys had ready several depositions attesting to French's upright character, but the "Court ordered the clerk to record the honorable acquittal of Mr. French by death, but refused to permit the depositions … holding that the court could not consistently take any action on or make any order tending to any expression of opinion with regard to the charges against the deceased."[74]

At the end of March 1860 Bowman tendered his resignation as a member of the Light House Board to President James Buchanan citing the "present state" of his health. A week later, he thanked Treasury Secretary Cobb for his "kind and voluntary offer of a leave of absence, for the purpose of recruiting my health." He recommended that chief clerk Spencer Clark be appointed "acting engineer in charge" and that Young be appointed "Acting Superintendent of the Treasury Extension." By early May Bowman had returned to his family home in Wilkes Barre, Pennsylvania, having taken a formal leave of absence; his miseries were compounded when his eldest daughter died there of scarlet fever four months later. He tried to recover some of the money from French's estate but, since French was considered legally innocent, he had no recourse. Bowman did not return to his post at the Treasury Extension; rather, at the beginning of March 1861, he began a three-year tenure as superintendent of the U.S. Military Academy at West Point. He died at Wilkes Barre on November 14, 1865.[75]

After the "French fraud"—as Bowman dubbed it—was uncovered, Beals & Dixon waited patiently to be reimbursed, not pushing their claims until December 1862, when they found that two of their payments totaling $4,705.76 had not been credited. Secretary of the Treasury Salmon P. Chase ordered an investigation that uncovered a second fault in the Bureau of Construction's accounting systems that involved forged checks. In March 1863 Beals & Dixon pointed out to Chase that they supplied the government with more than one million dollars worth of granite and the government's claim that the disbursing agent rather than the government was responsible was "too monstrous to be sustained by the Secretary after he is advised of the facts." On October 12 the contractors acknowledged receiving repayment of the total amount due them. In the end, French (and perhaps others) defrauded the Treasury Extension (or Bowman) of almost $20,000.[76]

"Spacious and Airy Saloons:" Decorating the South Wing

Walter's plan for the Treasury Extension called for not just larger rooms than Mills had designed for the east wing, but connected most of them to their neighbors. Mills had planned only a few suites of rooms. Young carried out Walter's internal organization because it had probably been bureau heads who suggested suites would allow for more efficient departmental operations. (fig. III-29) Various aspects of the south wing's rooms were commented on favorably at the time. *Harper's New Monthly Magazine* noted:

"Instead of the narrow cell-like apartments, with one or at most two windows, into which the public departments in Washington are subdivided, the Treasury Extension will present the health-promoting novelty of spacious and airy saloons [*sic*], capable of accommodating the clerical force of a bureau." The central corridors as well were more spacious than those in the east wing and Bowman and Young exploited advances in glass technology to light them. Along the center lines of the hallways they inserted thick rectangular glass panels into the

III-29 Compare the width of corridors and size of suites of rooms between the east and south wings.

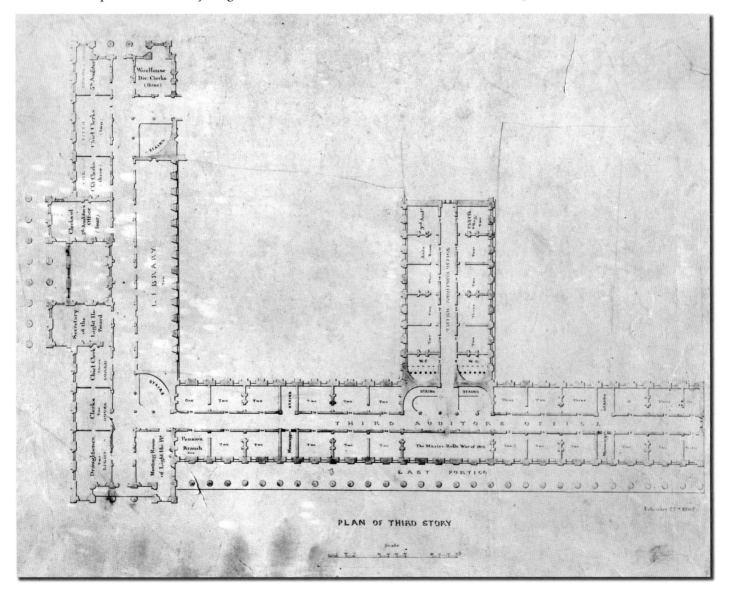

PLAN OF THIRD STORY

floors to allow light admitted through skylights on the roofs to filter down three levels.[77]

Elegant décor matched the increased size and better lighting of all the south wing's spaces in sharp contrast to the east wing's modest and chaste ones. The new interiors were decorated using three methods that drew upon both ancient techniques and modern technology. Gas chandeliers married the new source for lighting interiors with the ancient art of bronze casting. The ancient practice of painting walls with fresco (dry pigments applied to wet plaster) and its variant, dry fresco (wax-impregnated encaustic paint on dry plaster), gained great popularity in mid-nineteenth century America. Architectural parts that would have been made of wood (occasionally stone) in earlier American buildings—door frames, entablatures, balusters, and newel posts—were now cast in iron, their ornamental surfaces integral with their structural function. Two artists were primarily responsible for the south wing's interior appearance and the symbolic meaning of its painted and three-dimensional ornament. One was a prominent, native Washingtonian—designer J. Goldsborough Bruff—and the other a little-known émigré painter, Hubert Schutter.

"A Very Designing Man:" J. Goldsborough Bruff (1804–1889)

Joseph Goldsborough Bruff was born in 1804 in one of the "Six Buildings" on Pennsylvania Avenue, seven blocks northwest of the Treasury Building where much of his surviving work as a decorative sculptor remains an integral part of its structure. (fig. III-30) While a young man, Bruff began a "veritable museum," a collection of paintings, manuscripts, archeological and natural artifacts from around the world, and hundreds of curious items that simply struck his fancy. The breadth of his collections and their historical importance were recorded in a lengthy and admiring newspaper article, written when

III-30 J. Goldsborough Bruff worked as a government draftsman and designer for 61 years.

Bruff was on his deathbed in 1889. His collection ranged from a piece of the elm tree under which Penn signed the treaty with the Indians to "hand-shackles and a dark lantern, found in the hold of the Confederate ram *Stonewall*, which had been used in the slave trade." Bruff's autographed letters included one from President John Quincy Adams and another from writer John Howard Payne, author of *Home Sweet Home*, "who was a warm friend of Mr. Bruff's." Bruff was the curator of his museum as well as its collector, labeling each artifact and recording its history. A few made their way to the Smithsonian Institution but most were scattered, their present whereabouts unknown. The most interesting parts of his collection for the Treasury Building's history were his Indian objects.[78]

Bruff worked for the government as a draftsman, cartographer, and designer for about sixty-one years, his experiences broader and more unorthodox than the majority of his contemporaries. A year after the death in 1816 of his father Thomas—a physician, dentist, and inventor—Bruff shipped as a cabin boy and is known to have visited Britain and the Netherlands. In 1820 Bruff was admitted to the U.S. Military Academy at West Point, but either resigned or was dismissed two years later because he allegedly engaged in a duel. His mother having died in 1821, Bruff again set out to see the watery world, visiting the West Indies and South American countries before he settled in Norfolk, Virginia, in 1827. There he was employed as a draftsman at the Gosport Navy Yard where, the following year, he wrote and illustrated a manuscript he hoped to have published, "Heraldry, with Explanations and Rules Illustrated by Drawings & Examples." This document, along with other scattered drawings and notes Bruff made until at least October 1845, are now part of the Treasury Department's collections. Together, Bruff's manuscript, drawings, and miscellaneous notes demonstrate his extensive knowledge of the theory and history of emblematic and symbolic languages, which was crucial to his approach to designing the Treasury Building's decorative sculpture.

After a decade at the Gosport Navy Yard, Bruff worked for nearly two years as a draftsman at Fortress Monroe, Virginia, before transferring his allegiance from the Navy to the Army in early 1838. While a draftsman for the Bureau of Topographical Engineers in Washington, Bruff "made duplicate drawings of all of Fremont's reports, maps, plates, &c. for the two houses of Congress—it revived the Spirit of adventure so long dormant," he wrote, and at the age of 45 he set out for the California Gold Rush.[79]

A life of eager adventure in many of the most romantic regions of the globe … in search of whatever might enrich a portfolio [of drawings] with the bold, the beautiful, and strange; or a cabinet [of curiosities] with real realities rare and precious in science, from the shells of the shore to the minerals of the mountains—had by no means quenched a desire, long cherished, to cross my native continent, from the Atlantic to the Pacific, from its first sunrise to its last sundown.[80]

After a few months of miscellaneous government work upon his return to Washington, on September 14, 1853, Bruff was appointed a draftsman in the Office of the Supervising Architect, a position he held until July 1, 1869, when he transferred to the Register's Office. In 1876 Bruff returned to the Supervising Architect's office where he remained for the rest of his career. Interiors in the south, west, and north wings of the Treasury Building contain important examples of his imaginative and emblematic designs. Regrettably, all the objects he designed that could be removed—chandeliers, iron fences, and two outdoor fountains—have been destroyed.

Two of Bruff's miscellaneous designs for public and private commissions relate to his work at the Treasury Building. In 1847 two of his lithographs were published in Robert Mayo's *Synopsis of the Commercial and Revenue System of the United States as Developed by Instructions and Decisions of the Treasury Department for the Administration of the Revenue Laws.* Each synthesized the allegorical with the real, a hallmark of Bruff's approach to designs he considered particularly and appropriately American. In 1856 Bruff designed the cover used for at least sixty sets of lithographed plans for government buildings—customs houses, court houses, post offices, and marine hospitals—erected by the Bureau of Construction throughout the country during the 1850s and '60s. (fig. III-31) These compact yet detailed lithographs were made to solicit bids for materials and to aid contractors, but were also sent to libraries as records of the government's concerted building campaign. The contemporary perception that art was the flower of civilization and science its fruit was embodied in Bruff's design for these covers. The end of a room drawn in cross section on Bruff's cover is filled with an Italianate style altar, probably intended to portray an American altar of liberty because the keystone of its arch is surmounted by the national motto

E Pluribus Unum and a splayed eagle derived from the Great Seal. The walls of the room are decorated with ornaments Young used in his government buildings, and Bowman's structural system is depicted, supporting the roof with shallow brick arches springing from I-beams. The implements lying on the altar relate to the Treasury Department's varied functions as well as those of other departments located in the buildings being constructed by the Treasury Department. The trident relates to customs and it, along with the caduceus, also refer to marine hospitals. The scales, gavel, and sword of justice

III-31 Bruff's title page of lithographed plans for federal buildings erected in the 1850s and '60s.

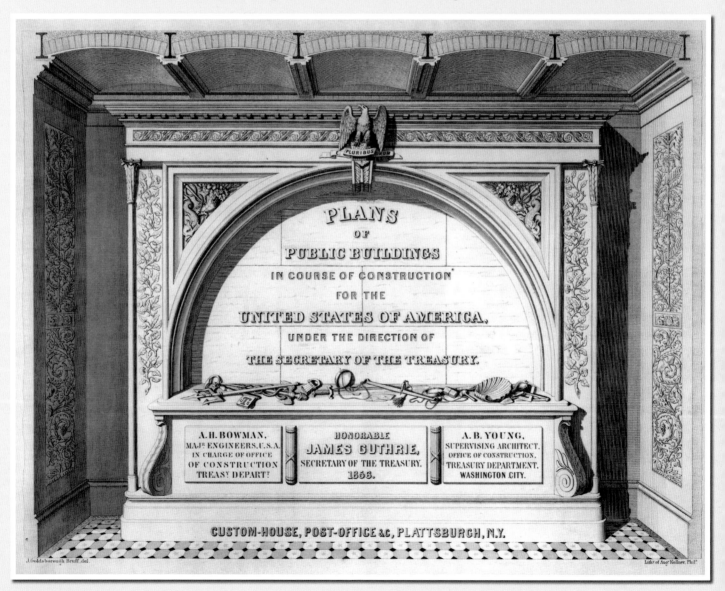

Fortress of Finance: The United States Treasury Building

symbolize the federal courts, letters, the Post Office Department (but also the federal bureaucracy), and the drafting instruments, the Office of the Supervising Architect itself.

Peace and Prosperity: The South Wing's Chandeliers

Both the content and the nature of the Capitol Extension's art programs were touchstones for the Treasury Extension's architectural and decorative sculpture as well as its murals. At the end of December 1854, the Italian émigré fresco painter Constantino Brumidi chose the Roman emperor Cincinnatus being called back to public service from retirement at his farm in the House Committee on Agriculture room. This patriotic theme resonated with Americans because George Washington and other Revolutionary War officers called themselves the American Cincinnati. Brumidi clothed Cincinnatus in ancient garb but his painting at the opposite end of the room, the "Calling of Putnam from the Plow to the Revolution," clothed the Massachusetts farmer in American eighteenth-century dress. Beginning in 1856, Brumidi designed his murals in the Pompeian style that relied heavily on mythological and allegorical figures to depict American historical events.[81]

The Washington Art Association was founded in 1856, partially in response to the style of Brumidi's frescoes, Bruff being one of its active members. In the introduction to its second exhibit held in 1858, the association's president, sculptor, and physician Horatio Stone, explained some of the reasons for its founding. "We cannot justly consider the arts and sciences separately and independently of each other … It is most lamentable that … the art decorations of the public works are … in charge of engineers instead of artists. The time has come for a more expanded exertion of the genius of the nation upon works of national art … in painting and in enduring marble." [82]

The Washington Art Association's attitude about realism in public art was a widely held popular American view. In March 1858 Bruff was one of seven Washington delegates who attended a national convention of artists convened to lobby Congress to found a "national school of art" comparable to France's Ecole des Beaux-Arts. (America's first graduate of the Parisian school, Richard Morris Hunt, spent a few months in 1855 working on the Capitol Extension.) Bruff was the secretary of the association whose lectures repeatedly explored the theme of the progress of the arts in different civilizations in order to encourage artists to represent American history within a historically realistic context. When Congress chartered the National Gallery and School of Art in 1860, Bruff was elected to the board of trustees and named its recording secretary. While these aesthetic issues were being debated, he designed the Treasury Building's architectural and decorative sculpture and its fresco artists began to paint its rooms.[83]

Major French decided that the Treasury Building's gas fixtures would be works of art rather than merely utilitarian sources of artificial light. In April 1857 Bruff wrote French that the "gas fixture cont'r call'd tother [sic] day, to see me, having someway learnt my ability as a very designing man. He said you told him you thought those fixtures should be appropriately and characteristically ornamented … Now I would like much to design 2 or 4 Brackets & 1 or 2 chandeliers in proper form for the occasion." Over the next two years, Bruff designed three elaborately symbolic chandeliers and eight ornate brackets for the Treasury Building's important public areas and the offices of senior employees. Initially, Bruff's lighting fixtures were intended for future Bureau of Construction buildings but eventually were made exclusively for the Treasury Building's south wing.

Bruff also designed eleven utilitarian chandeliers to light most of the building's corridors, offices, and workrooms, but only two of these seem to have been manufactured.[84]

Within three months of writing French, Bruff designed at least one chandelier, an allegory of the fate of distinct Indian tribes whom European settlers encountered in the course of exploring and settling many regions of the country. (fig. III-32) Atop its three branches were Indians sitting in similar poses facing pine tree-stump "campfires," differentiated by clothing, hair treatment, and implements. A quiver of arrows is slung across the shoulder of a hunter who holds his bow (on the lower left) while a rifle rests against the shoulder of the Indian on the upper left. The Indian on the right, seated on a bison skin, smokes a peace pipe. Acanthus and other leafy decorations on the chandelier's main stem and the scroll brackets supporting the Indians are resolutely European in origin. This separation of figural and decorative elements—even the subtle suggestion of the Indians being supported by Europeans—was Bruff's way of expressing the different traditions and separate coexistence of the nation's native inhabitants and Euro-Americans.

The emblems for the flat panels between the branches are further keys to understanding the meaning of these chandeliers. America's armorial shield of stars and stripes flanked by flags represents the federal government while the Treasury Department's key superimposed on a caduceus (the attribute of Mercury, the god of commerce) in the second panel denotes their intertwined roles in the nation's economic well-being. In the third panel, a quill pen lies across an engrossed treaty covered by an olive branch (the traditional symbol of peace), emblematic of the government's policy during the previous quarter century of signing peace treaties with Indians and settling them on reservations.

Bruff almost surely designed this pacified-Indians chandelier in response to Thomas

Crawford's 1856 "Dying Chief Contemplating the Progress of Civilization" for the Capitol's north wing pediment. Only a generic feather headdress identified Crawford's nude male as a Native American; his pose was adopted from the famous Roman sculpture, the "Dying Gaul." Bruff, on the other hand, dressed each of his Indians in clothing authentic to their specific tribes, information that he could have known from his own travels and collections or by visiting the War Department's collection of Indian portraits and artifacts. Another authentic ethnographic source he would have known was George Catlin's *Letters and Notes on the Manners, Customs, and Conditions of the North American Indians* (1857, second edition), which included an engraving of a seated Indian with a discarded quiver of arrows and a rifle resting on his shoulder among its dozens of images of Indians from various tribes. Bruff's overt message in his 1857 chandelier was the progressive stages of civilization American Indians underwent after contact with Europeans—arrows to rifles to peace pipes. His covert meaning, like Crawford's and Catlin's, was an elegiac commentary on their plight in the face of the westward expansion Bruff witnessed firsthand during the Gold Rush.

In November 1859 Bowman sent Bruff's drawings for two chandeliers and eight wall brackets to the Philadelphia gas fixture manufacturers, Cornelius & Baker, alerting them that "in making your estimate [calculate] that there may be a large amount required." Within four days, Cornelius & Baker prepared estimates. The most expensive chandelier would cost $61.50 while the least costly bracket was $6. Bruff's 1857 chandelier drawing of pacified Indians was identified as "No. 2" in the 1859 set of drawings, while "No. 1," Indians hunting

Opposite page: III-32 Bruff's pacified Indians chandelier compared their lives before and after westward expansion.

Fortress of Finance: The United States Treasury Building

CHANDELIER
for the
TREASURY BUILDING.
Designed and drawn by
J. Goldsborough Bruff
July 1857

deer and buffalo, was for a four-branch chandelier probably designed at the same time as the pacified-Indians chandelier. (fig. III-33) Conceptually the hunters chandelier preceded the pacified Indians chandelier because it depicted Plains Indians engaging in traditional activities of their culture before contact with Europeans. On the top left, a bowman on foot shoots a stag while the more pictorially developed image below shows an Indian on a rearing horse using a spear to attack a bison. All that can be discerned of the upper right image is a figure on horseback shooting a rifle; however, the detailed image below clearly shows a horseman with a bow closing on a bison. Wild indigenous animals, including panthers, grizzly bears, wild cats, and wolves, were contained above the scrolls supporting the branches.[85]

The central stem of Bruff's hunting-Indians chandelier was "the great fir tree of California"—a redwood—rising from a teepee or "Indian lodge," as they were identified in an 1860 description after a pair of the chandeliers was installed in the Bureau of Construction's office. Four decorative base panels contain an eagle poised for flight framed by a band decorated with stars. (The eagle, chosen to represent Congress in 1784, signified power in both European and Native American cultures.) The state seals seem to be below these panels and the lowest part is decorated with a number of caducei, Mercury's staff intertwined with snakes. The 1860 description noted a variation in the manufactured chandelier from Bruff's initial drawing: "there is a terminal of elk horns and sculls." These elements were apparently borrowed from Bruff's third chandelier design, "No. 23" (fig. III-34), that may have lent elements to his "No. 26," for which many chandeliers were ordered but neither drawing nor description located.[86]

Following his standard practice, in January 1860 Bowman sent photographs of Bruff's ten designs to "gas fitters" in several cities along with a circular asking for bids to manufacture them in bronze. "The designs being the property of the Government, they must not be copied, or produced except under its order, and you will therefore return these copies with your Bid," the circular stated. In response to one inquiry, Bowman elaborated that bids could be "both in real Bronze & in Brass with a coating of Bronze." As to the number wanted, "it is impossible to say, but there will be a large number wanted as the building is 4 stories high and 873 feet long, and 267 feet wide." The firm of Cornelius & Baker, the lowest bidder by about 15 percent, was awarded the contract on April 15 and asked to make samples of each kind so that the "style of work may be criticized, and, if found satisfactory, retained as standards." In July Cornelius & Baker put their "strong force of artists, modelers & chasers" to work on translating Bruff's drawings into models. Although "the preparation of these new patterns involved a large amount of work which could be done only by our best & most skillful hands," the firm was able to produce these custom designs for about the same price as standard fixtures being sold at their Chestnut Street store.[87]

In August 1860 acting engineer Spencer Clark critiqued Cornelius & Baker's sample of the hunters' chandelier soon after it was hung in the Bureau of Construction's office.

> The large Chandelier does not look so well in place as it did in your workroom. It is too crowded, looks huddled in a mass. Upon comparison with the drawings this effect appears to be produced by an enlargement of the figures, without a corresponding enlargement of the spread.
>
> It may be relieved by bronzing (*not* gilding) the ribs or groins of the Indian Lodge

Opposite page: III-33 Bruff's hunting Indians chandelier drew on scenes he witnessed during the Gold Rush.

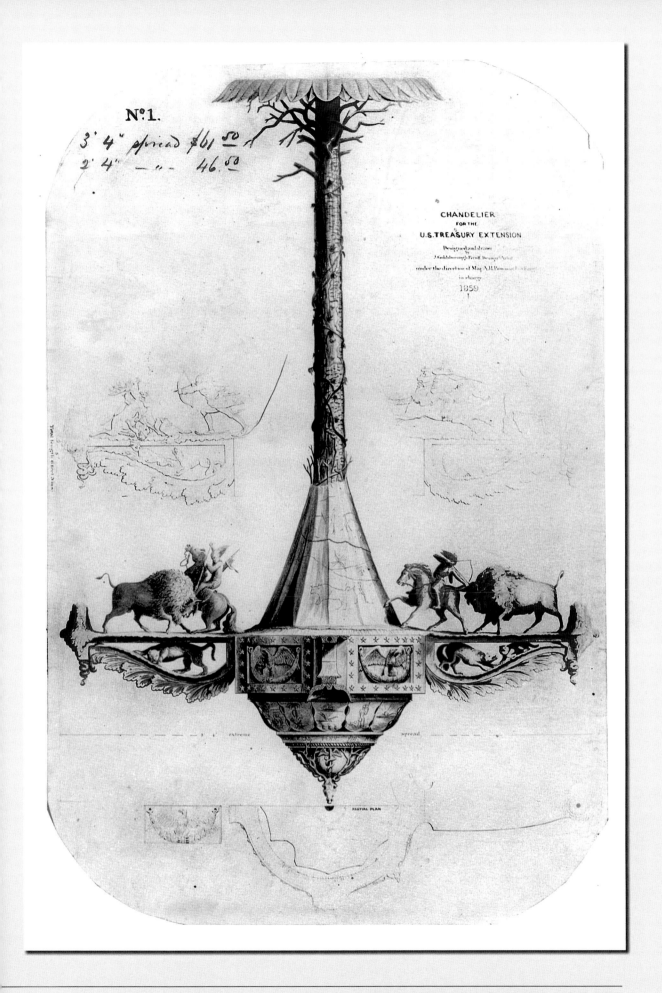

in the centre [sic] which would lighten it up a little.

The edge of the shields containing the coats of arms should have been made with a gilt brass to relieve them. This may now be measureably [sic] affected by gilding the bell or interior, which would throw the shields out with some relief.

The vine on the central piece (or shaft) would look better not to be gilt, but either dark bronze, or same color, as the lodge. When these changes are made, please send one as sample, to be used in Attorney General's Office, and Extension. (He is moving in today.)[88]

In his first two chandelier designs, Bruff chose to contrast the vigorous life of hunters on their own lands with their passive poses as reservation Indians, a poignant commentary on freedom versus captivity. More than thirty of each of these chandeliers were installed in south wing offices and halls between 1859 and 1862. The buffalo hunt came in three sizes: four feet four inches; three feet, four inches; and two feet, four inches, in horizontal spread, while the seated-Indians chandelier was only produced in the two smaller sizes. The relatively small scale of the figures on these chandeliers and the height at which they were hung (in rooms ranging from thirteen feet, five inches to fourteen feet, eight inches high) would have made their details difficult to see. They were probably curiosities to most people rather than potentially volatile political statements critical of the government's Indian policies. Bruff's chandeliers were hung only in the south wing—someone in authority did not like them as works of art or for their political content.

Some of Bruff's designs for eight wall brackets related to his chandeliers while others explored entirely different aspects of contemporary American life. His design number three (fig. III-35) would have been appropriate in the same room as his hunting-Indians chandelier, or its ante-rooms, because a horseman chases a wounded bison towards the gas jet. In fact, only three of these designs are documented as having been ordered. One was for the chief clerk's room, and on the same day that order was placed the smallest size of the hunters' chandelier also was ordered for the same room. A second model had to be made for the Indian and bison bracket, as Clark was not happy with the first. "The horse has lost all his spirit, and looks more like the toy horse of the shops than a live animal; and the Buffalo's badly poised on two legs, (instead of 3 as in the original,) [and] looks more like an insane rat than a Buffalo." In December Cornelius & Baker wrote that "it is difficult in so small a model to give all the life and spirit we can in a large one" when they sent a new model. Bruff's number five bracket repeated the alert Indian of the elk chandelier; three are known to have been ordered, one for the secretary's office on July 17, 1861. On the same day, one of the fifty-two-inch-wide hunters' chandelier was ordered for the secretary's office as well as one of bracket "No. 6," an eagle with an olive branch (fig. III-36) for his walls and two for his private clerk's office. Nearly a month later (on August 13), three of the pacified-Indians chandeliers were added to the secretary's office.[89]

From the erratic distribution of the chandeliers and brackets, it would seem that the occupants of offices were allowed to select their fixtures, but it was not always the case. In November 1861, when a shipment from Cornelius & Baker did not match what was ordered, Clark complained, "you give to the Clerk as large a Chandelier as I do his Chief."[90] In December Clark ordered a unique fixture for Chase's office, eight months after his

Opposite page: III-34 Bruff's drawing for a third chandelier records further Indian dress and customs.

III-35 Many of Bruff's gas brackets depicting Indians were meant to complement his chandeliers.

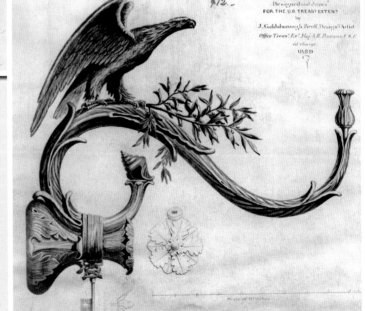

III-36 On July 17, 1861, an eagle and olive branch bracket was ordered for Secretary Chase's office.

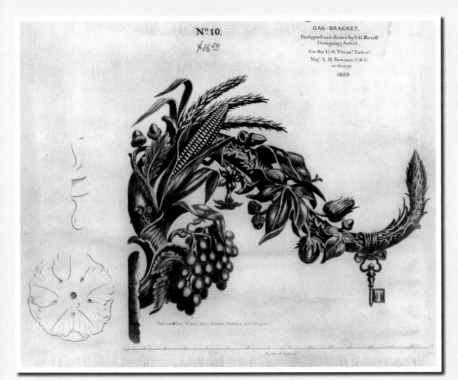

III-37 The Treasury Department held the "key" to unlocking America's abundant natural bounty.

appointment and two months after he moved to his southeast corner suite of rooms.

> Please make for the Secretary's Office a Pillar light with Goddard burner, of a more elaborate pattern than these hitherto ordered. There is not time for any modeling, and there will be only *one* wanted of the pattern. Please make up a tasty one from the Treasury pattern, selecting a handsome shade for it and send it with 9 feet of Tubing.
>
> He desires the tubing to be of a kind in use at the President's House, which appears to be moved with thread in red, white and blue. The article is new to me but you will probably recognize it by this description.[91]

Three of Bruff's bracket fixtures featured America's agricultural and natural bounty. The most elaborate was number ten (fig. III-37), its S-curve weighed down with a cluster of grapes, an ear of corn, sheaves of wheat, a pine branch, a tobacco leaf and flowers, acorns, and cotton plants. It was not particularly popular—only a few were ordered and the only known destination for one of these brackets was a revenue

clerk's office. The Treasury key hanging from its branch served as the knob to turn the fixture on and off but also functioned allegorically to denote that the Treasury Department's functions enabled the unlocking of the country's natural bounty. The notion of forming the fixture's "key"—the proper terminology in gas fixtures for the control knob—in the form of a Treasury key was a visual pun typical of Bruff. Cornelius & Baker suggested changing the "key" to one stamped with their name normally used on all their fixtures. Bracket "No. 4" (see fig. III-35) decorated with corn, wheat, and grapes was the most popular of the natural-bounty type, with forty-nine hung on the walls of offices associated with seven bureaus, including the assistant secretary's room and the solicitor's suite of offices. Eleven were ordered for "Mr. Attlee's" room in late November 1861. S. York Atlee was the Treasury Department's librarian. His long room was located on the third floor overlooking the courtyard.[92]

Bruff's "No. 7," a lavishly clothed woman's arm holding a Roman oil lamp, was atypical of his Treasury gas fixtures, initially seeming out of place within the context of the other lighting

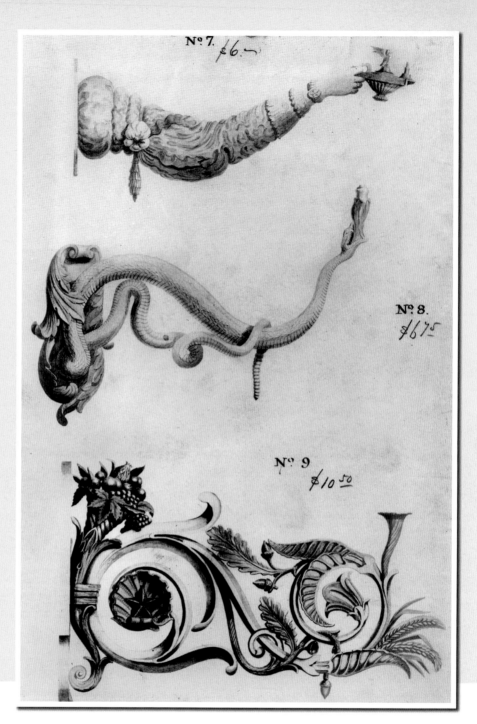

No 7. $6.—

No 8.
$6 75

No 9
$10 50

III-38 Bruff's rattlesnake recalled
Benjamin Franklin's cut-snake
emblem of union made in 1754.

fixtures. (fig. III-38) It may have commemorated the Treasury Department's hiring of the federal government's first female clerk, Jennie Douglas, who apparently roomed with the Bruff family in February 1861. At least thirteen bracket number sevens were hung in the south wing, including the secretary's office and the library. Bruff's simplest design for a branch fixture featured an American rattlesnake, a reference to Benjamin Franklin's cut-snake device, the first American symbol created in 1754 to urge political union among the colonies. Bruff's uncoiled snake is whole—but poised to strike—to signify the continued union of the states at precisely the time when this union was most threatened since the Revolution.[93]

It is unknown when Bruff's chandeliers and wall brackets were removed, but they were probably destroyed within a few years of their manufacture. No fragments and only one photograph of them in place survives. (fig. III-39)

III-39 Only one photograph of Bruff's chandeliers in the Treasury Building is known to survive.

Bruff's Cast-iron Architectural Sculpture

America's first cast-iron room was Thomas U. Walter's Library of Congress, installed in the Capitol in 1853. All of its seemingly solid (but actually hollow) parts, fusing art and structure, were bolted together into an intricate three-dimensional structure. When Bowman and Young exploited this fireproof marriage of interior ornament and structural architecture for the south wing's cast-iron elements, they had available several founders ready to compete for the work. As importantly, Bruff was eager to coordinate unique designs for the Treasury Extension's interior column capitals, the entablatures carried above them, and the balusters, railings, and candelabra framing the staircases as well as other minor decorative elements. In 1857 and 1858 Bruff prepared design drawings to be congruent with his contemporary chandelier and gas bracket designs. He later redesigned some of the same elements for the west and north wings, changing details to express different allegorical meanings. Moreover, his three different entablature designs for the south, west, and north wings were a subtle way for employees and visitors to quickly orient themselves within the building.

The drawing of Bruff's original 1857 design for the Treasury Extension's unique American capital is lost. Its details were altered, Bruff claimed, by the sculptor who translated the drawing into the wood model to be used by the iron founders. An indignant Bruff wrote Major French in October.

> The Model of a Capital sent on to me is not the one I designed in any particular, but on the other hand is an inappropriate and tame production. The most prominent object is the Baboon's head (perhaps a type of the designer thereof). If it were a lion's head it then would be a good national symbol of the British Treasury. The graceful volutes over water leaves at the angles of my design are not attempted in this. Instead of oak leaves and acorns producing shadow and effect—in the model sent are small leaves, close together, and totally without character. And besides throwing out the Symbolic tablets from the Abacus to introduce the nondescript head, the model-man has also changed the members of the abacus. I disclaim it entirely, as an abortion, if intended to be a model of my design, and if not it is as poor a capital as I ever saw.[94]

The capital illustrated in "Architecture in Washington," published in *Harper's Weekly* two years later, was the design adopted and seems to combine elements of Bruff's original and altered versions. (figs. III-40 & III-41) Within the outline of a Roman Corinthian capital, Bruff substituted eagles for the traditional furled acanthus leaves beneath the volutes, inserting between them the Treasury Department's emblem, a hand grasping a key with the letter T in its bit.[95]

Bruff's design of c. 1857 for the south wing's entablature included a Roman frieze, its continuous arabesque interspersed with fruit, flowers, and grains to express the rich abundance of America's natural bounty, the whole emblematic of the Treasury Department's role in fostering America's prosperity. (fig. III-42) The upper of the two moldings in the architrave above this frieze were rightly understood by *Harper's* author as a "laudable and successful attempt to nationalize the interior embellishments." Bruff replaced the classical egg and dart moldings with "an acorn and Indian arrowhead, and while the transformation is too slight to alter the general effect, the symbols to the close observer are more satisfactory because more significant." Moreover, for the stylized leaf motif in the lower frieze, Bruff chose oak leaves over acanthus. Arrowheads related the frieze ornaments to Bruff's chandelier designs while

AMERICAN CAPITAL IN THE INTERIOR OF TREASURY DEPARTMENT.

Left: III-40 Bruff's American capital combined American eagles with classical Ionic volutes.

Below: III-41 A hand grasps the Treasury's emblematic key in a capital in a west wing corridor.

III-42 Peace and prosperity were Bruff's themes in his 1857 frieze of the fruits of American plants.

-ONE OF THE 12 SECTIONS OF SCROLL ORNAMENT.

Above: III-43 On the eve of the Civil War, Bruff chose national symbols of union, stars, and arrows for a frieze.

Right: III-44 Oak branches and acorns—symbols of long life—for balusters promoted the union's permanence.

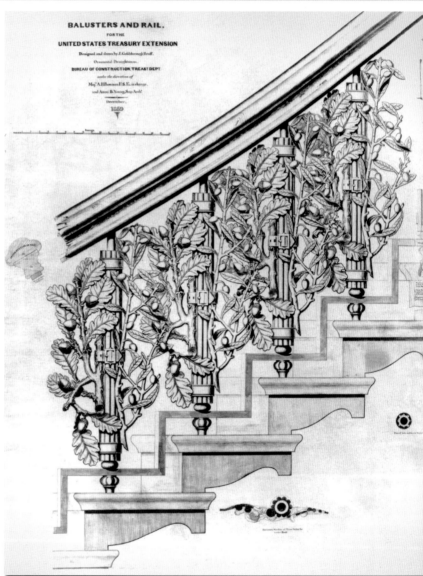

acorns and oak leaves symbolized prosperity and long life.[96]

A full-scale Bruff drawing dated October 18, 1859, "Enrichment of the Frieze and Cornice of an Entablature to a Stair-well in the U.S. Treasury Extension," reflected a dramatic change in the message to be conveyed by the Treasury Department's symbolic ornaments. (fig. III-43) Its scroll frieze incorporated stars from the American flag and thirteen arrows from the Great Seal of the United States, two of the most readily recognized symbols of national union dating from the Revolutionary era. That same day—October 18—abolitionist John Brown and the surviving armed insurrectionists who attempted to capture the federal armory in Harper's Ferry, West Virginia, were arrested. Brown's extreme protest against the legality of slavery in the United States threatened the very survival of the union of the states under the Constitution—the basis of the federal government, in Bruff's view.

Bruff's richly sculptural design for the Treasury Extension's staircase railings, balusters, and candelabra, dated March 1860, continued to explore how America's earliest symbols could be modernized to respond to new threats to national union. (figs. III-44 & III-45) His

III-45 Bruff's capitals, friezes, and balustrades are unique to the Treasury Building.

INVERTED PLAN
of the ORNAMENTATION of the ANGLE
in STAIR-WELL CORNICE of
U.S TREASURY EXTENSION

III-46 Bruff added tobacco leaves to traditional oak, olive, laurel, and acanthus leaves to link the new world with the old.

balusters were based on the fasces, the bundle of rods tied together with a leather thong that Roman lictors carried over their left shoulders when they preceded Senators through the streets of Rome. Fasces were symbols of union because the combined rods could not be broken and were commonly used to decorate the early Republic's public buildings, including the Capitol. By reviving their use for the Treasury Building on the eve of the Civil War, Bruff affirmed the continuing validity of the Revolution's primary goal, the union of the states. In binding the Treasury Extension's candelabra's fasces (atop the newel posts) with bands of stars adopted from the flag—the most commonly understood symbol of the union of the states—Bruff emphasized the continuing validity of that union. In binding its

baluster fasces together with a contemporary buckled belt, Bruff reinvigorated America's emblematic legacy.

Open ornamental screens composed of olive and oak branches, each bearing its respective fruit, framed the staircase balusters. Olive branches were the symbol of peace on the Great Seal, in contrast to the arrows of war. Bruff used not arrows but rather oak branches, emblematic of prosperity and long life—the fruits of peace which could be assured by saving the Union. He repeated his oak-and-olive-branches motif in wreaths decorating the corner triangular segments of ceilings in the stairwells. (fig. III-46) The wreaths were framed by alternating acanthus and tobacco leaves, Bruff's linkage of the new world with the old.

Inventive intermingling of ancient, early American, and contemporary imagery to convey the reality of the nation's origins, development, and challenges were at the crux of Bruff's thinking. Bruff's stair railings and balusters form a permanent decorative screen silhouetted against the light-colored granite walls. Originally, their flickering shadows cascaded down four levels of circular stairs, lit by the skylights in the domes above them. At eye level, their tactile qualities drew innumerable hands that polished highlights on the bronze. Many of the olives and acorns were snapped off by souvenir hunters.[97]

"Every Description of Ornamental Painting:" Fresco Artist Hubert Schutter (1826–1904)

The wet and dry fresco techniques brought to America by artists fleeing political unrest or simply seeking new opportunities were the same as those used by European artists since antiquity. German decorative painters who settled in Washington after the 1848 revolutions in Europe decorated the Treasury Extension's walls and ceilings as well as those of many Washington churches, theaters, halls, and private homes. The most important of the south wing's fresco painters was the German-born and educated artist Hubert Schutter who emigrated to America at age twenty-five and immediately settled in Washington.[98]

At the end of December 1857, the South Wing's "basement story rooms are being finished, most of them are all ready for the fresco painters, and some of them are now being beautifully decorated in *al fresco*, by Schutter & Co." The following July, a reporter described Schutter's paintings in one of the rooms in the basement, now considered the first story. "The ceilings and wall of this are handsomely frescoed, the panels of the latter being ornamented with representations of growing maize and vines," while most of the other rooms and the hall "have yet to be painted and frescoed." During the next few years, Schutter and various

partners ornamented many south wing rooms and corridors, painting the ceilings in "watercolor," that is in the wet fresco technique, and their walls in the more durable encaustic paint that contained wax on dry, or cured, walls.[99]

Schutter's most important work was done for the suite of two rooms on the second (now third) floor in the south wing's southeast corner. His April 17, 1861, proposal left the room's actual color in the hands of the acting superintendent as well as the decision of whether to use encaustic paint for the ceilings as well as the walls (Major Franklin chose encaustic). "Understanding that said room [the smaller, corner one] is intended for the occupation of the Hon: Secretary, we calculated on ornamenting ceiling as well as sidewalls in elegant style, hence the comparatively higher charge; should it please you however to make any reduction whatsoever, we can limit our designs accordingly, which will be subjected to the approval of the Superintendent."[100]

Secretary Chase was the first secretary of the treasury to occupy this room, moving there in October 1861 and remaining until his resignation on July 1, 1864. It is likely that he was consulted about its decoration, as he routinely made minor decisions about the Treasury Extension's construction. The "Chase Suite" again served as the secretary's office between 1897 and 1910, when it was photographed by Frances Benjamin Johnston. Parts of the decorative and allegorical paintings on the walls and ceilings survived until they were painted over in 1910. In August 1973, while the ceiling was being scraped in preparation for repainting, Schutter's two allegorical figures, *Treasury* (as abundance with a cornucopia) and *Justice*, were revealed as were the Treasury Department's seals in each corner. (fig. III-47)

Extensive official records on the south wing's construction and ornamentation contain scant information on Schutter's decorative motifs or his allegorical content. One exception

Fortress of Finance: The United States Treasury Building

was a July 1861 letter Spencer Clark addressed to Senator Joseph Lane asking if he could furnish an image of the Kansas state seal because he wished to incorporate it "in the ornamentation of the principal room of the Treasury Extension." Five days earlier, the Confederacy won the first battle of Bull Run and the next day Congress passed a resolution stating that the Civil War was being fought "to preserve the Union." On August 5, at the instigation of Secretary Chase, Congress created the Bureau of Internal Revenue to finance what Lincoln and his cabinet now realized was more than a state of insurrection, but a full-blown war. On the same day, the government extended the term of service for Union volunteers from three months to two years.[101]

Between mid-July and mid-August 1861, Schutter decorated Chase's office walls to reflect the nation's bounty, and the imminent threat to it—disunion of the states. His design recalls one of America's early symbols of national union that had particular meaning for the Treasury Department, Benjamin Franklin's 1777 "union chain" designed for the Continental Congress's first currency. Each of the chain's thirteen links contained the initials of a state but later versions of the device, including a carpet woven for Congress Hall in Philadelphia, placed state seals in the center of each link. A description of Schutter's lost frescoes that made a scathing allegorical commentary on the Confederacy, linked them to the union chain device.

> The walls and ceilings of the Secretary's room are beautifully frescoed. Each panel is relieved by an apparent moulding [sic] of heavy scroll work, which forms medallions for the devices of the seals of each of the thirty-four States and of the Treasury Department. The tops of these scrolls are festooned with grapes [the traditional sym-

bol of fertility and sacrifice] of the different varieties grown in this country, and the lower portions are painted with accurate imitations of the various staples and other products of the State whose devices are copied in neutral tint upon the medallions.

> Only the products of our own country are used for ornamentation. On the panels devoted to the Seceding States a symbol of their present attitude is introduced in the shape of a venomous snake peculiar to the State.[102]

A splendidly ornate mirror made by Samson Cariss & Company of Baltimore that symbolically represented the national sacrifices of the Civil War and the hoped-for triumph of the Union was designed for Chase's office to complement Schutter's frescoes (or vice versa). (fig. III-48)

> The plate of more than usual thickness, is of the best French glass, and gives a most brilliant reflection of every object placed before it; but the frame is the most attractive, on account of its proportion, its peculiar design, and the elaborately carved gilded work. It measures 7 ½ feet in width and 9 in heighth, [sic] and the top is slightly arched. Upon the lower corners are carved representations of cannon, pointing inward with balls, ammunition, and other appendages, whilst near the center are large United States shields, illuminated with stars. In the center of the lower part is a large key, surrounded with other emblems, indicative of the important branch of the service for which the mirror is designed. The sides of the frame are circular, and around them are entwined gold bands of the richest pattern, the enclosed spaces, diamond form, being filled with carved work, finished in pure white. The frame is surmounted by a large eagle with extended wings, whilst

　Fortress of Finance: The United States Treasury Building

its talons grasp a shield, across which is a bundle of arrows. Extending from each side of the main figure are clusters of fruit, all of American growth, including the orange, pomegranate, pear, grapes, and the apple; also, bunches of the cotton plant and other agricultural products, all of which are richly gilded.[103]

Bruff may well have provided the inspiration for Schutter's paintings and the actual drawings for Chase's mirror because he determined more than a year earlier that the allegorical meaning of the Treasury Extension's decorations would be peace and prosperity. The finishing touches were put on Chase's office during the fall of 1861. At the secretary's request, Clark wrote New York decorators in October seeking "two plaster Busts to place in niches in his office. He would prefer (if possible to obtain them Busts of some of the former Secretaries of the Treasury) but, if these are not to be had, then get those of some suitable and proper character."[104]

"Quite Plain but of Fine Proportions:" The South Terrace

The bold scale of the Treasury Building's south wing required not only a fitting approach to the new formal entrance of the building, but also modifications of the established grounds of the adjacent President's House. One of Young's first requests in 1855 was for an existing detailed plan of the President's Grounds. When it was decided in 1848 to enclose the grounds south of the President's House, Washington's mayor petitioned Congress to continue E Street south of the grounds between 15th and 17th streets as a public street. Three years later, extensive grading of the area

began to prepare the grounds for planting Andrew Jackson Downing's picturesque garden design, work that was completed by August 1854 when the driveway south of the President's House was opened to the public. To accommodate the Treasury Extension's construction, the south side of this road had to be closed temporarily to store granite and to build sheds for stoneworkers to finish some of the more delicate pieces. By 1857 Bowman had to encroach further on the President's Grounds by moving both the greenhouse and stables to accommodate the derricks ranged along the west front.[105]

When Downing made his plan in 1851, he supposed that Robert Mills's E-shaped Treasury Building would be completed. (fig. III-49) He planned an elaborate Roman triumphal arch on Pennsylvania Avenue as the ceremonial entrance to the President's Grounds. The road split into three carriageways immediately south of the Treasury Building with no intervening open space between Mills's shallow portico and the northernmost driveway. Subsequently it was decided to open E Street as the sole east-west public street between Downing's Ellipse and the fenced President's Grounds and to shift the entrance to the grounds south of the center of Pennsylvania Avenue. This allowed room for a substantial terrace and flanking gardens on the Treasury Building's south side, the whole fenced as a proper setting to frame Young's much admired south portico.

On March 25, 1859, Young requested a personal interview with Secretary Cobb to call his "attention to several important facts connected with the changes proposed to be made, from the original design, in the Buttresses and Steps of the south Portico … before [his] final approval of that change." Young was concerned about the relative costs of his own design compared to those of Bowman and Walter's. (fig. III-50) Walter's original idea was to have two wide flights of steps facing south with narrow flanking steps descending to the east and west from

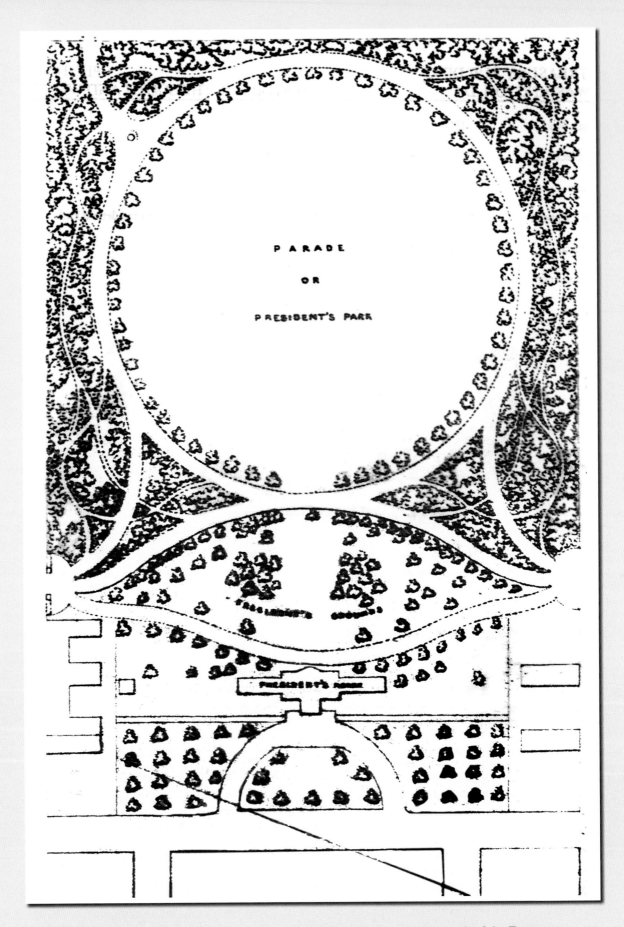

III-49 On this 1851 landscape plan visitors entered the President's grounds south of the Treasury.

Fortress of Finance: The United States Treasury Building

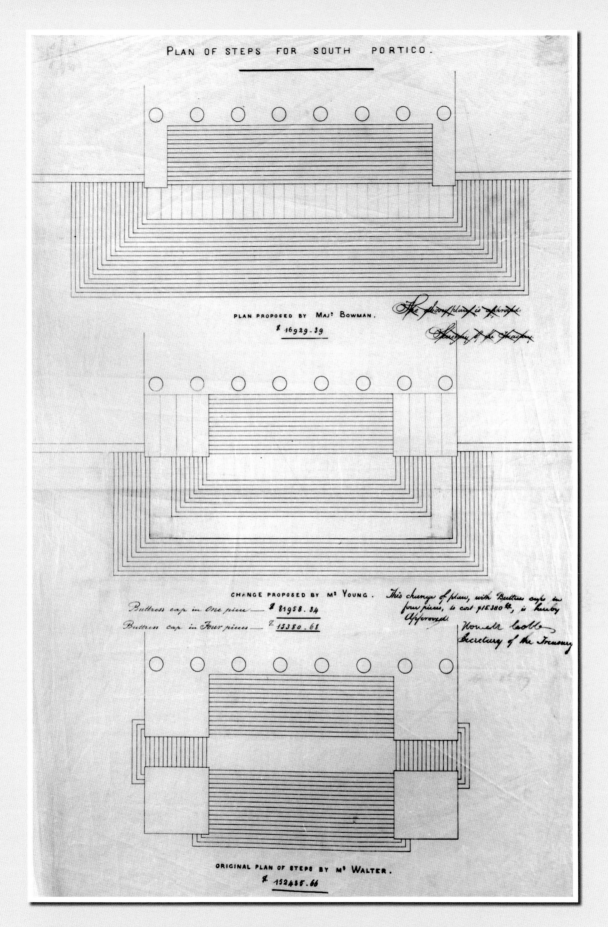

PLAN OF STEPS FOR SOUTH PORTICO.

PLAN PROPOSED BY MAJ. BOWMAN.
$ 16929.39

CHANGE PROPOSED BY M. YOUNG.
Buttress cap in One piece — $ 81958.34
Buttress cap in Four pieces — $ 13380.68

ORIGINAL PLAN OF STEPS BY M. WALTER.
$ 152435.66

III-50 Alternate designs for the staircase leading to the south portico differed widely in cost.

the plaza connecting the two main staircases. Because he planned massive buttressing piers, two columns wide on both sides of the flanking stairs, the estimated cost of Walter's staircase was $152,455.66.[106]

Young and Bowman each designed less expensive staircases, with the architect retaining Walter's wide piers but limiting them to the sides of the top of three flights of stairs. Moreover, he designed the two lower flights in the shape of the letter C to permit easy access from three sides. This arrangement provided a visually solid base for his portico, similar to Walter's staircases that lead to the new House and Senate wings at the Capitol. The estimator calculated the cost of Young's entrance at $81,958.34, a considerable savings over Walter's design, but still a very significant amount of money. Bowman responded with narrow side buttresses that retained Walter's two main flights but wrapped the lower one around the sides as Young proposed. Bowman planned two steep rises of steps that provided an even wider visual base for the portico than Young's proposal, estimated at $16,919.29.

The apparent outcome of Young's meeting with Cobb was to substitute pier caps made of four pieces of granite, rather than one truly massive slab of granite, that reduced the cost of his design to $15,380.68. Less than two weeks later, Young wrote Beals enclosing an unofficial bill of particulars so quarrying could begin. Young repeated his suggestion of a few days earlier that they change their normal working arrangement by having rough stones delivered to Washington and "hammering them here at your sheds, as the patterns &c could better be fitted here on the ground and give less trouble than to hammer them at the Island."[107]

In the spring of 1857 President Buchanan balked at the increasing encroachment of the Treasury's construction site on the President's Grounds and initially refused to let Bowman move the President's stable located immediately

west of the south wing. Thereafter, Buchanan closely monitored the Treasury Building's landscaping and on September 8, 1860, approved conditionally Young's plan for correlating the fences, gates, and drive with existing paths and roads leading to the President's House and gardens. Working out the details of these designs fell to Bruff who planned multiple granite gateposts at three entrance points connected by cast iron fences of elaborate and distinctive patterns.[108]

Three carriage and two pedestrian gates were built on 15th Street, their granite posts graduated in size as were the heights of the iron pickets. Bruff's drawings for the gates and pickets done on a large scale demonstrate his mastery of structural principles as well as his characteristic inventiveness. (fig. III-51) He planned each of the gates to combine upright cast-iron pickets with a wheel of six radiating spokes made of rolled wrought iron. In the center of the wheel for the main grouping of gates on 15th Street, he inserted the union shield, his initial design having floriated edges at odds with the mechanistic appearance of the structural pieces. Bruff also initially planned to replace the traditional stars in the top third of the shield with the initials "US," another of his symbolic affirmations of national union.

The emblems on Bruff's final design closely followed traditional renditions of the Union shield, signifying that these gates led to the President's Grounds as well as the Treasury Building. (fig. III-52) An eagle was the final central motif for the central gate while union shields decorated the two sides gates, both elements derived from the Great Seal of the United States. When the gates began to be set in place in August 1861, they were particularly admired, the *Evening Star* noting that no garden enclosure in the city surpassed them in beauty. (figs. III-53 & III-54) Surprisingly, the *Star* considered "the railing quite plain, but of fine proportions." Bruff's designs for the finials of

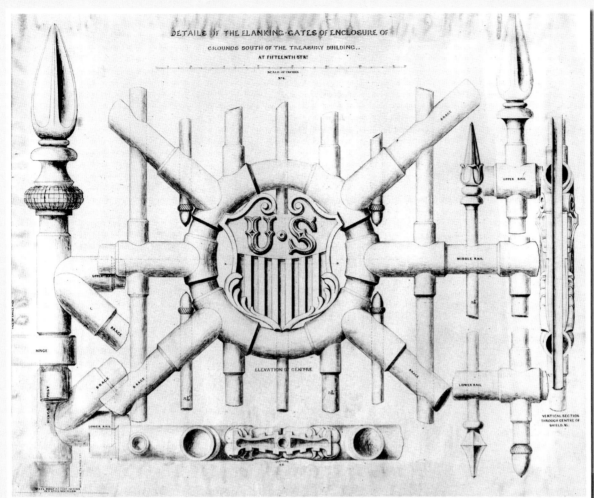

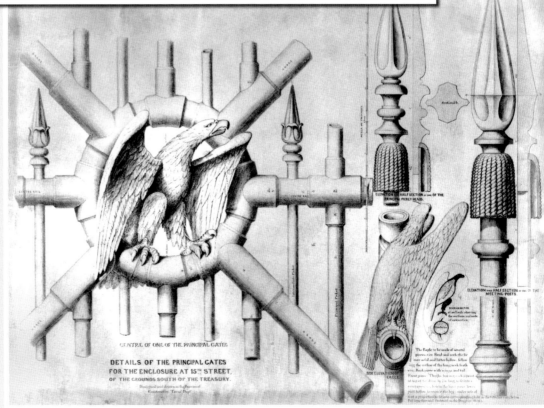

Above: Ill-51 Bruff's Union Shield variant for the Treasury's gates included "US" to affirm national union.

Right: Ill-52 An alert, watchful eagle guarded the Treasury's main south gate, a typical Bruff visual pun.

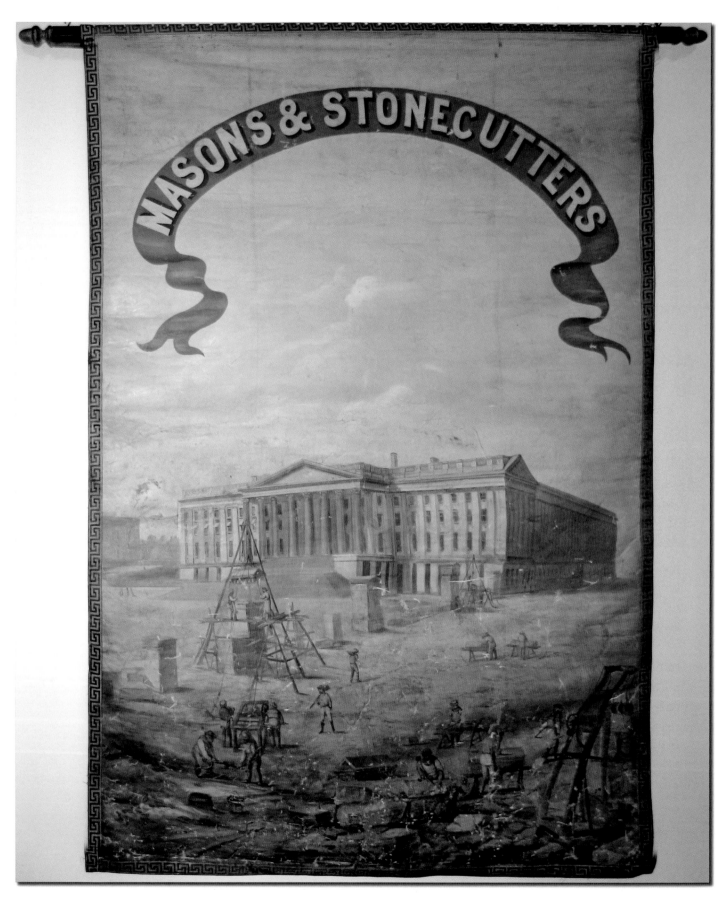

III-53 A Masonic banner showing the south gate construction celebrated the Treasury's workmen.

the rails and pickets of these posts seem to have been his personal translations of Latrobe's corn, tobacco, and magnolia orders designed for the Capitol earlier in the century.[109]

Young's site plan called for a service road from 15th Street that went under the south portico where coal storage vaults simultaneously supported the terrace and stairs. In 1866 the architect of the north wing, A.B. Mullett, replaced Young's lawns with formal garden parterres planted with bushes and flowers. Three years later, Mullett closed the service road because he found its large square openings unsightly, particularly when the Treasury Building was viewed from the southwest, the prospect from the President's Grounds. He also redesigned the stairs, removing those sections that extended beyond the piers and enclosed them with new balustrades—an extensive stair-

III-54 The south wing has been the Treasury Building's most recognizable facade since 1860.

case that significantly increased the processional experience of entering the south portico. Although Mullett had just completed the north portico to be the Treasury Building's official entrance, he recognized that the south wing presented its most striking view and benefited from the measured approach he created for it.

"Financial Honor:" The Alexander Hamilton Statue

On January 11, 1908, the 151st anniversary of Alexander Hamilton's birth, Secretary of the Treasury George B. Cortelyou announced to the Hamilton Club in Brooklyn, New York, "that it had been proposed

Fortress of Finance: The United States Treasury Building

to form an organization known as the Alexander Hamilton Memorial Association, with headquarters in Washington, for the purpose of erecting a statue of Hamilton in the nation's capital." At a trustees meeting held a month later at the Willard Hotel, Associate Supreme Court Justice John M. Harlan was chosen president. In January 1909, Congress agreed to allow on the south wing's plaza a standing figure raised on a base, appropriating $10,000 for preparation of the site and pedestal, the remaining $90,000 of its projected costs to be raised by the association privately. Contributions accumulated slowly until 1911, when the Senate passed a bill providing a $100,000 public appropriation; however, it was defeated in the House of Representatives. That same year, the newly formed Commission of Fine Arts agreed with the choice of the site for the Hamilton statue, further suggesting that a plaster model of the selected design be erected to judge the appropriate scale and composition of the statue and base together.[110]

By 1917 the association had raised about $7,000 towards the statue's cost when "an intense admirer of Hamilton," a woman from New York, who wished to remain anonymous, selected the sculptor and donated the statue to the nation. Sculptor and descendent of two prominent families, Gertrude Vanderbilt Whitney, was thought to be that woman. She apparently selected James Earle Fraser (who designed the Buffalo nickel for the U.S. Mint) as the sculptor. Fraser's 9-foot, 6-inch bronze Hamilton, clothed in unusually elaborate and realistic eighteenth-century dress, stands erect carrying his hat, possibly originally "a parchment" as described by the *Washington Post*, in his right hand, a cloak draped over his left arm.

When the statue arrived in Washington in 1923, the *Washington Post's* art critic, Dr. Gertrude Richardson Brigham, remarked that Fraser's masterful modeling of Hamilton's face revealed a "poetic, imaginative, romantic personage" rather than a dull financier; to modern viewers, his alert, serious expression speaks of farsightedness as well.[111] (fig. III-55)

Henry Bacon, the architect of the Lincoln Memorial, was selected as the designer of the base and planned a series of low stepped platforms leading to the tall pedestal that together are the same height as Fraser's figure. Bacon chose pink Stony Creek, Connecticut, granite for the plinth, its four corners marked by bound fasces that echoed Bruff's extensive use of the Roman symbol of union within the south wing. Bacon hung garlands of olive leaves between the fasces, their curves complementing Fraser's richly detailed costume. The inscription quotes Daniel Webster's assessment of Hamilton. "He smote the rock of the national resources and abundant streams of revenue gushed forth. He touched the dead corpse of the public credit and it sprang upon its feet." President Warren G. Harding gave the address at the statue's dedication on May 17, 1923, before dignitaries that included Secretary of the Treasury Andrew Mellon as well as several former secretaries.

> Washington riveted the confidence of the new possessors of independence, Jefferson was the foremost advocate of democracy, Franklin was the philosopher in the making of the Constitution, but Hamilton had the conception of a Federal government, upon which plan the American people have builded [sic] to their own satisfaction and, to no small degree of world astonishment. When his plan was adopted he became the master builder, and the integrity of the nation's financial honor is his monument for the ages.[112] 🔑

Opposite page: III-55 James Earle Fraser's sculptural masterpiece was his Alexander Hamilton, dedicated in 1923.

Endnotes, Chapter Three

1 "Expected Discharge in the Treasury," *Washington Post,* February 9, 1882, 2.

2 John Milligan and others to Congress, Petition, June 16, 1840, and Keim to Lincoln, June 29, 1840, both in HR 26A-G17.1, entry 19, RG 233, NAB. Mills to unknown recipient, December 1841, 3014/5, entry 6, RG 42; NAB.

3 Forward's eighteen-month tenure began on September 13, 1841.

4 House Committee on Public Expenditures, *Treasury Building,* 27th Cong., 2d sess., 1842, H. Rep. 549, 2.

5 Ibid., 5. Commissioner of Public Buildings, *Letter from the Commissioner of Public Buildings,* 27th Cong., 2d sess., 1842, H. Rep. 195, 1–7.

6 Forward to Boardman, June 20, 1842, HR 27A-D17.1, entry 19, RG 233, NAB. *House Journal,* 27th Cong., 2d sess., June 21, 1842, 1001-2.

7 Washington Topham, "The Winder Building," *RCHS* 37–8 (1937): 169–172.

8 House Committee on Public Buildings, *National Edifices at Washington,* 28th Cong., 2d sess., 1845, H. Rep. 185, 2–3. W. B. Bryan, "The Sessford Annals," *RCHS* 11 (1908): 336.

9 Corwin was appointed July 23, 1850.

10 Mills to Corwin, n.d., box 1422, entry 26, RG 121, NACP.

11 T.U. Walter, Diaries, February 7 to August 24, 1852, Thomas Ustick Walter Papers, Diaries, Philadelphia Athenaeum, Philadelphia, PA (hereafter cited as Walter's Diaries, Philadelphia Athenaeum).

12 Walter to Bayard, January 10, 1854, in undated newspaper clipping found among Walter's Correspondence, box 14, Philadelphia Athenaeum. *Congressional Globe,* 33rd Cong., 1st sess., February 21, 1854, 202; ibid., March 3, 1854, 556.

13 *Congressional Globe,* 33rd Cong., 1st sess., July 12, 1854, 1701–2.

14 "Death of an Architect," *Washington Union,* March 4, 1855, 2. Walter's Diaries, March 5, 1855, Philadelphia Athenaeum.

15 Guthrie was appointed on March 7, 1853.

16 Young to Guthrie, April 11, 1855, reel 1, entry 7, RG 121, NACP.

17 Walter's Diaries, April 12, 1855, Philadelphia Athenaeum. Walter's report to President Pierce has not been found.

18 Walter to John Rice, April 26, 1855, Walter's Letterbooks, Philadelphia Athenaeum.

19 Guthrie to Pierce, May 2, 1855, entry 3, RG 56, NACP. "The Construction of the Extension of the Treasury Building," *Evening Star,* May 2, 1855, 3. Walter to Rice, May 2, 1855, Walter's Letterbooks, Philadelphia Athenaeum.

20 Clark to Cobb, June 23, 1857, reel 2, entry 7, RG 121, NACP.

21 Secretary of the Treasury, *Report on the State of the Finances,* 33rd Cong., 1st sess., 1853, S. Ex. Doc. 2, 19.

22 Ibid., 278–84. Secretary of the Treasury, *Letter of the Secretary of Treasury, Wrought Iron Beams,* 33rd Cong., 2d sess., 1855, S. Ex. Doc. 54, 1–10.

23 "Alexander Hamilton Bowman," *National Cyclopaedia* (New York: James T. White & Co., 1907), 5:522–3.

24 "The Treasury Extension," *Evening Star,* June 19, 1858, 2.

25 Daniel Robbins, *The Vermont State House* (Burlington, Vermont: Vermont Council on the Arts, 1980), 20–7. Margaret Nash De Laittre, "Ammi Burnham Young and the Construction of the Boston Custom House" (master's thesis, University of Virginia, 1979).

26 "The Treasury Extension," *Evening Star,* August 22, 1861, 3. The reporter quoted Shakespeare, *King John,* 2.1.217–9, in his description of cannon fire.

27 Young to Fillmore, May 19, May 30, June 6, and August 9, 1851; reel 1, entry 7, RG 121, NACP.

28 Secretary of the Treasury, *Report on the State of the Finances,* 34th Cong., 3d sess., 1856, H. Ex. Doc. 2, 570.

29 Ibid.

30 Anna Ella Carroll, *A Review of Pierce's Administration* (Boston: J. French & Company, 1856), 122–3.

31 *Expenditures on Public Buildings,* 37th Cong., 2d sess., 1862, H. Rep. 137, 35.

32 Ibid., 36.

33 Ibid., 36-7.

34 George Alfred Townsend, *The New World Compared With the Old* (Hartford: S.M. Betts & Co., 1870), 383.

35 "Washington," *New York Times,* March 12, 1865, 5.

36 French to Meigs, January 29, 1855, vol. 1, entry 13, RG 121, NACP. Wendy Wolff, *Capitol Builder: The Shorthand Journals of Montgomery C. Meigs, 1853–1859, 1861* (Washington: Government Printing Office, 2001), 362; 396; 403. Bowman to Meigs, December 11, 1856, entry 15, RG 121, NACP. Meigs to Bowman, December 15, 1856, box 1424, entry 26, RG 121, NACP.

37 "Purchase of E. Anthony," n.d., box 1424, entry 26, RG 121, NACP. Anthony to French, January 17, 1857; Anthony to French, February 9, 1857; Walker to French, May 9, 1857; all box 1427, entry 26, RG 121, NACP.

38 "The Treasury Building," *Evening Star,* July, 28, 1858, 3. Bowman to Vattamare, November 30, 1858; and May 24, 1859; both reel 3, entry 7, RG 121, NACP.

39 Spencer M. Clark to F. Buchanan, May 13, 1860; Clark to Walker, June 20, 1860; both reel 4, entry 7, RG 121, NACP. Chase to Lincoln, July 11, 1861, General Correspondence, series 1, Abraham Lincoln Papers, Manuscript Division, Library of Congress. Walker to Clark, September 26, 1862, box 1439, entry 26, RG 121, NACP. "Plants for the Parks," *Washington Post,* April 6, 1901, 3.

40 "Bartholomew Oertly," Notable Employees, RG 56, entry 213, box 3. "From Life to Instant Death," *Washington Post,* October 17, 1878, 4.

41 "The Extension of the Treasury Building," *Evening Star,* June 25, 1855, 3. "Proposals," *Evening Star,* June 26, 1855, 4.

42 "Proposals," *Evening Star,* June 26, 1855, 3. Guthrie to unknown recipient, July 14, 1855, entry 13, RG 121, NACP.

43 "Extension of the Treasury," *Evening Star,* July 17, 1855, 3. Secretary of the Treasury, *State of the Finances,* 34th Cong., 1st sess., 1856, S. Ex. Doc. 2. Contract between James Guthrie and D. O'Neill, August 25, 1855, box 1422, entry 26, RG 121, NACP. "Appointments on the Treasury Extension," *Evening Star,* September 19, 1855, 3. "The Extension of the Treasury Building," *Evening Star,* October 31, 1855, 3.

44 Oertly, "Synopsis of Bids," August 27, 1855, box 1422, entry 26, RG 121, NACP. Bowman to Guthrie, October 5, 1855, reel 1, entry 7, RG 121, NACP. "Awarded," *Evening Star,* October 9, 1855, 3.

45 Bowman to Beals & Dixon, October 10, 1855, box 1422, entry 26, RG 121, NACP. Beals & Dixon to Guthrie, October 10, 1855, box 1422, entry 26, RG 121, NACP.

46 Oertly, "Account," May 19, 1858, box 1430, entry 26, RG 121, NACP.

47 Norman Drinkwater, Jr., "The Stone Age of Dix Island," *Downeast Magazine,* 10 (September, 1963), 43–7. "Courtlandt Palmer Dixon," obituary, *New York Times,* June 6, 1883, 4.

48 "Washington in 1859," *Harper's New Monthly Magazine,* 65 (December 1859): 11.

49 Bowman to Dixon, August 26, 1856, vol. 1, entry 13, RG 121, NACP. Bowman to W. B. Magruder, July 29, November 30, 1857, reel 2, entry 7, RG 121, NACP. Young to Dixon, August 14; 26, 1856, reel 1, entry 7, RG 121, NACP. "Improved and Improving," *Evening Star,* August 1, 1859, 3. "Verdict for the Dix Company," *Washington Post,* May 29, 1894, 4.

50 Young to H. W. Benham, July 7, 1855, reel 3, entry 7, RG 121, NACP. Barton to Young, July 20, 1855, box 1422, entry 26, RG 121, NACP. Guthrie to Barton, August 6, 1855, box 1422, entry 26, RG 121, NACP.

51 Barton to Young, September 17, 1855, box 1422, entry 26, RG 121, NACP. Young to Benham, July 16, 1859, reel 3, entry 7, RG 121, NACP.

52 Meigs, *Diaries,* 434, 428, September 4, 1856.

53 French to Horatio Allen, March 11, 1857, entry 13, RG 121, NACP. "The Treasury Extension," *Evening Star,* June 19, 1858, 3.

54 "Treasury Extension," *Evening Star,* October 29, 1857, 3.

55 "The Treasury Extension, *Evening Star,* June 19, 1858, 3.

56 Secretary of the Treasury, *Report on the Finances,* 34th Cong., 1st sess., 1856, S. Ex. Doc. 2, 232–3.

57 Secretary of the Treasury, *Treasury Extension—Contracts for Materials,* 34th Cong., 1st sess., 1856, H. Ex. Doc. 96, 1–14.

58 Secretary of the Treasury, *Report on the Finances,* 34th Cong., 3d sess., 1856, H. Ex. Doc. 2, 569. Beals & Dixon, Contract Extension, January 1, 1857, box 1438, entry 26, RG 121, NACP. Young to Dixon, March 25, 1857, reel 2, entry 7, RG 121, NACP. Bowman to Beals & Dixon, July 28, 1857, entry 13, RG 121, NACP. "Treasury Extension, *Evening Star,* August 15, 1857, 3. "Today the First of the Long Pillars," *Evening Star,* August 21, 1857, 3.

59 "Treasury Extension," *Evening Star,* October 12, 1857, 3.

60 "Treasury Extension," *Evening Star,* December 26, 1857, 3. Clark to Oertly, July 4, 1858, reel 4, entry 7, RG 121, NACP. "Notes to Increase of Quantities," February 18, 1859, box 1430, entry 26, RG 121, NACP.

61 Secretary of the Treasury, *Report on the State of the Finances,* 35th Cong., 1st sess., 1857, S. Doc. 1, 121. Young to Beals, January 20, 1858, reel 4, entry 7, RG 121, NACP. "Treasury Extension," *Evening Star,* June 14, 1858, 3; June 19, 1858, 3. French to Beals & Dixon, May 20, June 25, and September 10, 1858; all vol. 1, entry 13, RG 121, NACP.

62 Secretary of the Treasury, *Report on the State of the Finances,* 35th Cong., 2d sess., 1857, S. Ex. Doc. 2, 111.

63 Cobb was appointed March 7, 1857.

64 Bowman to Cobb, December 20, 1858, reel 3, entry 7, RG 121, NACP.

65 Secretary of the Treasury, *Granite for the South Wing of the Treasury,* 35th Cong., 2d sess., 1859, S. Ex. Doc. 41, 2–3.

66 "Treasury Department," *Evening Star,* November 23, 1859, 2. Clark to Perry, May 17, 1860, reel 4, entry 7, RG 121, NACP.

67 "The Work on the Treasury Extension," *Evening Star,* March 12, 1859, 2. Secretary of the Treasury, *State of the Finances,* 36th Cong., 1st sess., 1860, S. Ex. Doc. 3, 120–2.

68 "An Embezzlement," *Evening Star,* August 20, 1859, 2. "The Alleged Defalcation," *Evening Star,* August 24, 1859, 3. "Further Concerning the Recent Defalcation," *Evening Star,* August 25, 1859, 2.

69   Several letters from Bowman to contractors are in vol. 1, entry 13, RG 121, NACP. "Statement of Amounts Receipted," September 5, 1859, box 1432, entry 26, RG 121, NACP. Beals & Dixon to Chase, March 24, 1863, box 1435, entry 26, RG 121, NACP.

70   "Washington Mechanics and Manufacturers," *Evening Star,* October 4, 1859, 3.

71   Oertly, "Recital of Facts," April 4, 1863, box 1435, entry 26, RG 121, NACP.

72   Bowman to H. H. Lambell, November 9, 1860 and Dixon to Chase, March 24, 1863, both box 1435, entry 26, RG 121, NACP.

73   Bowman to Tasker, n.d., (just before December 8, 1859), vol. 1, entry 13, RG 121, NACP.

74   Joseph H. Bradley to Secretary Cobb, April 3, 1860, box 1435, entry 26, RG 121, NACP. "Death of Edmund French," *Evening Star,* July 7, 1860, 2. "Criminal Court," *Evening Star,* July 7, 1860, 3.

75   Bowman to James Buchanan, March 28, 1860 and Bowman to Cobb, April 4 and 10, 1860; all reel 3, entry 7, RG 121, NACP. Bowman telegram to Clark, June 1860 and Bowman to Clark, September 5, 1860, both box 1435, entry 26, RG 121, NACP. "Died," *National Intelligencer,* November 13, 1865, 2.

76   Chase was appointed on March 7, 1861. Oertly, "Recital of Facts," April 14, 1863; Beals & Dixon to Chase, March 24, 1863; Beals & Dixon to Edward Jordan, October 12, 1863, all box 1435, entry 26, RG 121, NACP.

77   "Washington in 1859," *Harper's New Monthly Magazine,* 115:20 (December 1859), 11.

78   "An Old Resident Dying," *Washington Post,* April 8, 1889, 2.

79   Ibid. Joseph Goldsborough Bruff, *Gold Rush,* Georgia Willis Read and Ruth Gaines, eds. (New York: Columbia University Press, 1944), vol. 1, xxx.

80   Ibid, xxvi.

81   Barbara Wolanin, *Constantino Brumidi, Artist of the Capitol* (Washington: Government Printing Office, 1998), passim.

82   "Lectures on Art," *Washington Union,* January 6, 1858, 2.

83   "National Convention of Artists," *Evening Star,* March 22, 1858, 3. "National Art Convention," *Evening Star,* March 23, 1858, 3. "Washington Art Association," December 29, 1858, 3. "The National Gallery and School of Art," *Evening Star,* October 5, 1860, 2.

84   Bruff to French, April 25, 1857, box 1427, entry 26, RG 121, NACP.

85   Bowman to Cornelius & Baker, November 14, 1859, vol. 1, entry 13, RG 121, NACP.

86   Pamela Scott, "Power, Civic Virtue, Wisdom, Liberty, and the Constitution: Early American Symbols and the United States Capitol," Donald R. Kennon, ed., *A Republic for the Ages. The United States Capitol and the Political Culture of the Early Republic* (Charlottesville: University Press of Virginia, 1999), 412–23. "Beautiful American Works of Art, *Evening Star,* September 3, 1860, 2.

87   Bowman to several gas fitters, January 24, 1860; Bowman to unknown recipient, February 3, 1860; Bowman to Cornelius & Baker, April 15, 1860; all reel 3, entry 7, RG 121, NACP. Cornelius & Baker to Bowman, November 18, 1859, box 1431, entry 26, RG 121, NACP. Cornelius & Baker to Bowman, July 16; August 18, 1860, box 1434, entry 26, RG 121, NACP.

88   Clark to Cornelius & Baker, August 5, 1860, reel 4, entry 7, RG 121, NACP.

89   Cornelius & Baker, Invoice, July 17, 1861, box 1436, entry 26; Clark to Cornelius & Baker, November 4, 1861, entry 13; Cornelius & Baker to Clark, December 18, 1861, box 1437, entry 26; Clark to Cornelius & Baker, August 13, 1861, NARA, RG 121, vol. 1, entry 13; all RG 121, NACP.

90   Clark to Cornelius & Baker, November 22, 1861, vol. 1, entry 13, RG 121, NACP.

91   Clark to Cornelius & Baker, December 4, 1861, entry 13, RG 121, NACP.

92   Cornelius & Baker to Clark, August 18, 1860. box 1434, entry 26, RG 121, NACP.

93   Bruff, March 13, 1861, Manuscript Diary, February 15, 1861 to April 26, 1861, J. Goldsborough Bruff Papers, MS381, Historical Society of Washington, D.C., (hereafter Bruff's Diary).

94   Bruff to French, October 17, 1857, box 1427, entry 26, RG 121, NACP.

95   "Washington in 1859," *Harper's,* passim.

96   Ibid, 11.

97   Bruff, "Specifications for Balusters and Rails for East and West Stairways, South Wing," April 16, 1860, box 1439, entry 26; Clark to Hayward & Bartlett, and others, April 16, 1860, reel 3, entry 7; Clark to Van Cleve, May 7, 1860, reel 4, entry 7; Wood & Perot to Clark, November 20, 1862, box 1439, entry 26; all RG 121, NACP.

98   "Fresco Work at St. Peter's" *Evening Star,* August 28, 1854, 2.

99   "Treasury Extension," *Evening Star,* December 26, 1857, 2. "The Treasury Building," *Evening Star,* July 28, 1858, p. 2. Schutter & Company proposals, July 5, 1861 and August 3, 1861, box 1423, entry 26, RG 121, NACP.

100   Schutter to Franklin, April 17, 1861, box 1423, entry 26, RG 121, NACP.

101   Clark to Lane, July 26, 1861, entry 13, RG 121, NACP.

102 "The Treasury Extension," *Evening Star,* August 22, 1861, 2.

103 Ibid.

104 Clark to unknown recipient, October 4, 1861, box 1439; A. T. Stewart & Co. to Clark, November 16, 1861, box 1437: both entry 26, RG 121, NACP.

105 W. W. Seaton, "Resolution," May 13, 1848, HR-30A-G17.1, RG 233, NAB. Bowman to Meigs, October 26, 1858, reel 3, entry 7; Jno. B. Turton, Proposal, February 27, 1867, box 1424, entry 26; Bowman to John B. Blake, March 23, 1857, entry 15; all RG 121, NACP.

106 Young to Cobb, March 25, 1859, reel 3, entry 7, RG 121, NACP.

107 Young to Horace Beals, April 8, 1869, reel 3, entry 7; Bowman to Beals & Dixon, April 12, 1859, entry 13; Oertly, draft "Mem of answer to House committee," February 1862, reel 5, entry 7; all RG 121, NACP.

108 Bowman to John B. Blake, March 23, 1857, entry 15, RG 121, NACP. "The New Enclosure at the Treasury Extension," *Evening Star,* August 13, 1861, 2.

109 Ibid.

110 "Genius and Patriot," *Washington Post,* January 12, 1908, 1. Commission of Fine Arts, *Eighth Report* (Washington: Government Printing Office, 1908), 84.

111 Gertrude Richardson Brigham, "Impressive New Monument to Alexander Hamilton," *Washington Post,* March 11, 1923, 89. Sculptor Bruce Moore, a student of Fraser, revealed Whitney's philanthropy to art historian Dr. Michael Richman.

112 "Text of President's Speech," *Washington Post,* May 18, 1923, 2.

"The Combination of a Palace and a Manufactory:" The West Wing, 1857–1865

Chapter Four

"Various Sources:" The Long Prelude

Construction of the Treasury Building's west wing began in 1857 with the peaceful laying of its foundations concurrently with those on the south and ended by 1865 in the tumultuous aftermath of the Civil War.[1] (fig. IV-1) The basement story was so well built by Bowman and Young that it was chosen in April 1861 to shelter President Abraham Lincoln and his cabinet in the event of an attack on Washington. When the Treasury Building's construction was halted at the outbreak of the war, its stonemasons, bricklayers, and carpenters were among the principal workmen drafted to build fortifications to protect the city. In 1860 more than fifteen hundred federal employees worked in Washington, the majority working for the Treasury Department. Five years later, about seven thousand government workers crowded the executive office buildings, rented commercial office buildings, and converted homes and stores throughout the downtown area. At the same time the outbreak of the Civil War was delaying completion of the Treasury's west wing, the dramatic expansion of the federal bureaucracy was pushing it forward, and construction resumed during the spring of 1862.[2]

Two of the west wing's important architectural developments—the installation of rooms to serve as vaults for the Comptroller and U.S. Treasurer and the redesign of its attics to house the National Note Bureau (predecessor of the Bureau of Printing and Engraving)—were a direct result of the Treasury Department's proactive response to the war. So was the hiring of women and girls for clerical positions in both

these offices. A significant architectural feature, the elegant suite of offices planned to be the Secretary of the Treasury's permanent office overlooking the President's House, suddenly became President Andrew Johnson's office for six weeks following Lincoln's assassination. The architects collectively responsible for the wing's design—Thomas U. Walter, Ammi B. Young, Isaiah Rogers, and Alfred B. Mullett—never expected it to serve as an army barracks, bank, factory, and presidential office at all, let alone concurrently.

Late in December of 1857, as the unusually long building season was coming to an end, the *Evening Star* noted that "the concreting of the basement walls is laid, and a good portion of the area and basement walls are laid; and the stone necessary to complete the basement story of the entire wing will be ready for setting on the opening of the [building season] next spring." (fig. IV-2) Bowman and Young had tested their logistical systems for building the extension's immensely heavy walls on the south wing before moving around the southwest corner. By the end of the 1858 building season, Bowman enumerated the cost and weight of all the permanent materials that had been put in place in the south and west wings, the work on the latter consisting of finishing its basement story. "Moreover, a large portion of granite and other materials for the west wing have been delivered, and will be used as soon as the other work is brought up to receive them." The bureau's procurement systems were also operating smoothly. "The various sources from which materials are received, granite quarries, brick yards, furnaces, rolling mills, etc., are now so thoroughly organized and equipped that materials can be procured as rapidly as they can be

IV-I Deep excavations for the west wing impeded access to the State Office's south and west entrances.

used." A laborer had suffered a broken leg when the section of embankment he was excavating for the west wing collapsed in August 1857, but Bowman could boast that "no serious accidents of any kind" had occurred during 1858.[3]

On March 1, 1859, Congress reduced the appropriation for the Treasury Extension from the requested $350,000 to $50,000, the result of an investigation into the cost of granite used in the south wing. Secretary Cobb ordered work on the west wing suspended. Bowman argued in his fall 1859 report that, if Congress appropriated money during the winter, instead of waiting several months for the general appropri-

ations, "the whole work can be finished easily in two years. Almost the entire [sic] of the granite for the west wing is quarried, cut, and delivered, and encumbers the adjacent ground."[4]

The workmen let go in the spring of 1859 were not rehired in 1860, even though additional monies were appropriated, because Cobb determined these new resources were to be used on repairing construction faults in the south wing. In mid-April 1860 Cobb appointed Young acting superintendent to replace Bowman, his 1860 report unusually critical of Bowman, citing several examples when the engineer had overridden Young's objections to inferior materials and a dubious construction technique in laying slates on the south wing's roof. No additional labor force was hired in 1861. As for

IV-2 The west wing's basement was finished in late December 1857, the wing completed in 1865.

the small band of skilled workmen who were retained in 1859, they were busy building forts on both sides of the Potomac River during the spring and summer of 1861 and completing the south wing by the end of the year.[5]

"Apprehension of Danger:"[6] The Treasury Building during the Civil War

The Civil War transformed Washington from a large, sprawling town into a major city. The war also transformed the Treasury Department from a stronghold of southern sympathizers into a leading force in

winning the war under the direction of Salmon P. Chase. A Republican Party elected on an anti-slavery platform would have created a volatile situation even if the capital was located farther north, but its location between Maryland and Virginia meant that Washingtonians felt particularly threatened. Howell Cobb from Georgia, who had been appointed Secretary of the Treasury in the spring of 1857, "urged his state's immediate secession after Lincoln's victory and then quit in early December" 1860.[7] Massachusetts Congressman Henry Dawes remembered that, by late December:

The public mind at Washington had become greatly excited by the belief that a conspiracy had been formed to seize the Capitol and Treasury, to get possession

COOKING AND EATING ARRANGEMENTS IN THE COURT-YARD OF THE TREASURY BUILDING, WASHINGTON, D. C.—Sketched by our Special Artist.—[See Page 33

IV-3 Fear of a Confederate attack led to the Treasury Building being chosen as the city's final citadel.

of the archives of the government, and to prevent the counting of the electoral vote and the election of Lincoln; thereby creating chaos and anarchy, out of which might come the establishment of the Confederacy as the government *de facto* in the very halls of the national Capitol. Treason was known to be plotting to that end in the Cabinet itself.[8]

Thus, defending Washington was a priority even before Lincoln took office. On New Year's Day 1861, commander of the armies General Winfield Scott appointed his former aide, Charles P. Stone, as the city's inspector general. Stone's vivid recollections of his preparations to defend Washington during the first few months of 1861 include several accounts of the Treas-

ury Building's importance in the effort. Stone organized forty local militia units, including ones "formed by masons, carpenters, painters and other craftsmen," and then vetted them for southern sympathizers.[9] (fig. IV-3) At the same time, he was planning three central defensive positions at key locations in the city, at City Hall Square (today's Judiciary Square), the Capitol, and the,

Executive Square, including the President's House, the War, Navy, State and Treasury Departments, in each of which … I placed a force every night after dusk. The citadel of this center is the Treasury building. The basement has been barricaded very strongly by Capt. Franklin, of the Engineers, who remains there at night and takes charge of the force. The front of the Treasury building is well flanked by the State Department building and fifty riflemen are nightly there on duty. In case of attack, [troops stationed on the city's north side will] fall back and finally take refuge in the Treasury building, where they will be joined by the detachments guarding the river front when the attack shall have become so marked and serious that only the center can be held. In the Treasury building are stored two thousand barrels of flour, and perhaps the best water in the city is to be found there.[10]

General Scott refined Stone's plan.

All else must be abandoned, if necessary, to occupy, strongly and effectively, the Executive Square, with the idea of finally holding only the Treasury building, and, perhaps, the State Department building, properly connected. The seals of the several departments of the Governments must, this night, be deposited in the vaults of the Treasury. They must not be captured and used to deceive and create uncertainty among public servants distant from the Capital. And, should it come to the defense of the Treasury building as a citadel, then the President and all the members of his Cabinet must take up their quarters with us in that building! They shall not be permitted to desert the Capital![11]

In early February the Treasury Department allotted the War Department the southeast corner room on the third floor (now the fourth floor) of the south wing "as a dormitory for the guard to the building." On Meigs's recommendation, Captain William B. Franklin, his assistant engineer on the Capitol Extension, was named as Bowman's replacement as superintendent of the Treasury Extension. The Treasury Department's ornamental designer,

J. Goldsborough Bruff, described the scene near the building on Lincoln's first-term inauguration day: "A most extraordinary event in the history of the Republic. Immense assemblage— the avenue massed with vehicles and human beings;—dust, uniforms, sabers and bayonets. A section of Artillery, unlimbered—in battery position, with charged pieces, and matches burning opposite the Treasy building. Guards, ridettes, spies, and detectives, in all directions."[12]

Using the Treasury building as part of the city's defenses was separate from defending the department's integrity. Register L.E. Chittenden recalled in his memoirs that Secretary Chase (who took office on March 7, 1861) "would like to have [the bureau heads'] views concerning the defence [sic] of the Treasury, if an attack should be made upon it." U.S. Treasurer and former Mexican War General, Francis E. Spinner, was the first to speak.

"I am for defending the Treasury," he said; "but first I would put it into a condition to be defended. The building needs cleaning out. I prefer to take my secession clear, unadulterated, from the outside. We should know whom we can depend upon. The doubtful and uncertain should be excluded from the building. I do not wish to have men around me who require watching."[13]

While Chase was devising how the department could guarantee the loyalty of its employees, actually fortifying the building began in mid-April. (fig. IV-4)

Moveable barricades were being constructed for the protection of the lower story of the Treasury Department. The material used is four inch plank. Sand bag barricades—the best in the world—have been prepared to be used on the steps of the Department porticos should that be

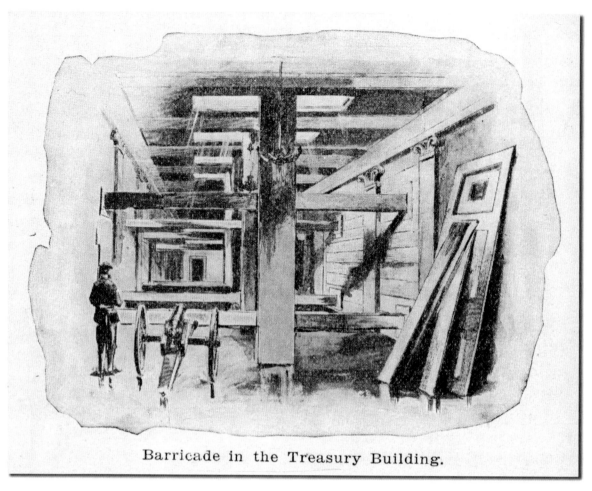

Barricade in the Treasury Building.

IV-4 Treasury's basement was barricaded and guards slept in the southeast corner of the top floor.

necessary. At least five hundred troops of regulars and volunteers bivouac there nightly now, so stationed as that they can defend it against a storming party of thousands, the building being well nigh a thorough fortification in its strength of construction."[14]

The Treasury Department paid $737 for barricading the building from April 20 through June 2, but a $400 voucher in May for building bakery ovens was charged to the War Department's subsistence office. (After a central bakery was built, Chase ordered the bakery removed from the building at the end of April 1862.) On June 5, 1861, Chase agreed that his department would provide Army engineers rudimentary furniture for three rooms on the first (now second) and second (now third) floors in the south wing—writing desks, tables on trestles,

cane-seated chairs, shelves, and a wardrobe for papers. In mid-August Young ordered "composition locks, hinges, and handles for Ammunition Magazine Doors" from a Boston supplier. Presumably, the magazines were located in the unfinished west wing's cellars rather than those under the occupied south wing in case they blew up. In 1863 and again in 1865, the Treasury Department sought reimbursement from the War Department for $40,000 it spent during the spring of 1861 "for work on Fortifications surrounding Washington."[15]

Throughout the spring of 1861, the *Evening Star* reported the names of military and civil government employees who resigned their positions. The Treasury Department lost many men, particularly after the *Star* reported that native-born Virginians would never be allowed to return to the state if they chose to remain with the Union. On July 16, 1861, assistant secretary

BATTERY RODGERS

George Harrington ordered that all employees in the Bureau of Construction be required to take an oath of allegiance. On August 24 Young reported that all except the chief clerk Spencer M. Clark (who was away from Washington on a special duty) had taken the oath. John O'Brien, who had transferred from the secretary's to Young's office, asked for time to "consult with his mother" while Mr. Clements, himself loyal to the Union, had three brothers who had joined the Confederacy and would not like to "take up arms, unless necessary."[16]

On August 6, 1861, the formality of a written oath was required of all Treasury employees when Washington's city authorities required all residents to sign an oath of allegiance or leave the city and forfeit their property. Treason was serious business. By the end of August 1862, the *Evening Star* reported on executions of Washingtonians who signed the oath of allegiance

IV-5 In 1861 Treasury workmen oversaw construction of all the forts and batteries protecting the city.

and later spoke publicly against the government. Some people leveled charges of Southern sympathies against rivals, and Young assured Chase that proper testimonials had been obtained from his employees accused of disloyalty. In mid-October 1861 Clark reported to Harrington on the status of five questionable Treasury workmen. Clark asked that two men—"both unusually competent"—be allowed extra time to "present evidence of their loyalty." About the carpenter Edward H. Dougherty, Clark wrote that he knew him to be entirely loyal.[17] (fig. IV-5)

From the first commencement of our troubles in April last, he has labored in season and out of season, by day and night, without extra pay, to do any thing required of him for our defense. He has had in charge the woodwork of every fortification, redoubt, or breastwork that has been built in and around the city, and the building of every block House and Stockade—his line of duty extending from below Fort Washington to above the Chain Bridge, on both sides of the river, where he has deservedly won the entire confidence of the War Department. He is also Master Carpenter in this Building, and has had the entire confidence of every one connected with this office, new and heretofore. If he is not loyal, no man is. I respectfully ask, in his case also, time for him to submit proof of his loyalty.[18]

Clark's intervention and Dougherty's proof were evidently successful. On the first of January 1863, Dougherty was appointed Assistant Superintendent of the Treasury Extension, his time divided between work under Rogers and Clark in the National Note Bureau.[19]

Some competent workmen who were loyal to the Union did lose their jobs at the Treasury because of petty jealousies and professional intrigues. Just before Christmas in 1862, E[dward] Krouse was let go after working for seven years as a bricklayer on the Treasury Extension. Krouse, like the carpenter Dougherty, used his experience in a local militia and building Washington's fortifications to prove his loyalty. "In that gloomy hour when Washington was threatened, my Company offered their services and was accepted by the Gov. We were the first to cross the Potomac at the Falls Bridge, we planted the first Flag in Va and we captured the first prisoners taken in the War. I then serve[d] six months on the defences [sic] of Washington … Men are retained who never stretched a uniform on their backs or know no more the decissons [sic] of a battle than does a spinster."[20]

THE QUARTERS OF THE FIFTH MASSACHUSETTS REGIMENT, AND THE SECOND U. S. CAVALRY,

"Armed and Supplied with Ammunition:" The Treasury Guard

Harrington issued a circular in mid-April 1861 ordering all department employees to make their way to either the Treasury or Corcoran Building in the event of a night attack and "report to Capt. Shiras or Capt. Franklin, who will see that they are supplied with arms and ammunition." A week earlier District volunteers were mustered north of the War Department, "the first citizen troops called into the service of the United States to oppose secession." Soon volunteer regiments from northern states began arriving daily. When Colonel Samuel C. Lawrence's Fifth Massachusetts Regiment arrived in Washington, it set up camp near the southwest corner of the Treasury Building.[21] (fig. IV-6)

On September 2, 1862, three days after the Union defeat at the Second Battle of Bull Run, Lincoln directed that "all the clerks and employees of the Civil Departments, and all employees on the public buildings will be immediately organized into Companies under the direction of Brigr. General Wadsworth, and will be armed and supplied with ammunition for the defense of the Capital." Confederate General Robert E. Lee led a force across the Potomac from September 4 to 7, and a week later General Stonewall Jackson captured the federal arsenal at Harper's Ferry, West Virginia, but no attack was then mounted on Washington itself.[22]

In late June 1864 Confederate General Jubal A. Early began an offensive in the Shenandoah Valley by consolidating infantry divisions. On July 5 he crossed the Potomac River from Virginia into Maryland and four days later routed Union troops at the battle of Monocacy, southeast of Frederick. About noon on July 11, Early, commanding a force of about 15,000 men, arrived at Silver Spring, Maryland. These troops were within striking distance of Fort Stevens on the 7th Street Road

IV-6 Union troops were quartered southwest of the Treasury Building from early 1861 until 1865.

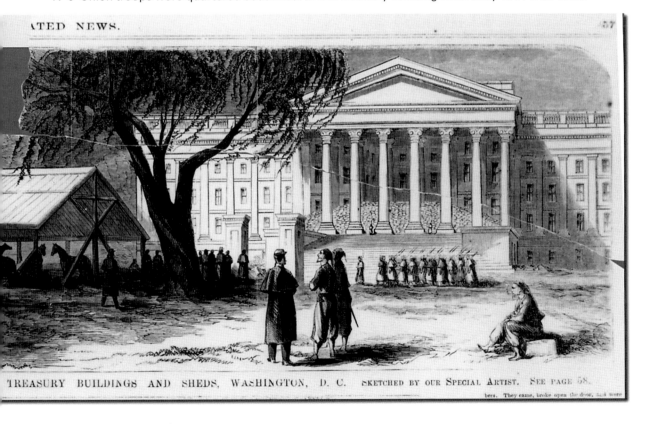

ATED NEWS.   57

TREASURY BUILDINGS AND SHEDS, WASHINGTON, D. C.   SKETCHED BY OUR SPECIAL ARTIST. SEE PAGE 58.

TREASURY GUARD.

IV-7 A satire of the Treasury Guard, composed of more than 900 employees, preparing for battle.

(now Georgia Avenue), one of the ring of sixty-eight forts and batteries protecting the city. Lincoln was present at the fort on the eleventh and the next day witnessed a skirmish, the only instance in American history when a President was under fire while in office. When news of the skirmish reached Washington, the Treasury Guard was ordered into action on July 13, but never left the city because, during the night of the twelfth, Early retreated across the Potomac. The Treasury Guard preparing for battle was one of Francis Colburn Adams's targets in his *Siege of Washington,* an 1867 satire on the war's military blunders in the guise of a children's book.[23] (fig. IV-7)

Although the immediate danger had passed, on July 15 the Treasury Department complied with the War Department's request that its clerks and workmen suspend work at 3:00 p.m.

(instead of 4:00) to allow for an hour of military drilling. Names of members of the "Fessenden Guards" (so-called for Treasury Secretary William P. Fessenden, newly appointed by Lincoln on July 5) who were absent from drill were collected. Isaiah Rogers, who was named Supervising Architect of the Treasury Building in June 1863, accounted for those men directly under his control who missed drills. A physician deemed draftsman Eugene Bonnet "old & infirm," draftsman William Steinmetz was excused because of the "loss of leg," while Judson York, the department's roving inspector of construction, was ill. Because Rogers considered the services of his chief clerk Samuel F. Carr and "computer" Bartholomew Oertly (who calculated the costs submitted by all vendors) indispensable, they were exempt. Photographer Lewis Walker, busy making multiple photographic copies of drawings of gunboats for the Navy, maps of coasts and battlefields for the Corps of Engineers, and guns and arsenals for the Ordnance Bureau, was excused from drills. Fifty-nine-year-old Bruff claimed to be infirm, having suffered disabilities when his companions abandoned him in the Sierra Madre Mountains en route to California.[24]

By August 15 even those whose work required attendance at their desks until 4:00 were formed into a company of the Treasury Guard under the direction of Treasurer Spinner, drilling in the halls on Tuesday and Friday evenings at 7:30. A week later, Rogers estimated a 150-foot-square wood building "for an Armory, and purposes of drilling troops" would cost $30,000. The day Admiral David Farragut captured Mobile—August 23, 1864—the Treasury Guard made its first public appearance in a dress parade on the Ellipse, designed in 1851 for just such occasions. "They were fully uniformed, and numbered over 900 muskets," before a "furious rain storm" prevented their intended parade through the city. "In the ranks were Assistant-Secretaries Harrington and Field, Gen. Spinner, and other prominent gentlemen."[25]

That same day Harrington reduced drilling to Saturday afternoons and prohibited "all cleaning of muskets, or other military duty" during office hours. By mid-December when Harrington reduced drills to the last Saturday of the month, the Union's victory seemed assured. The musicians among the Treasury Guard gave a concert at Ford's Theater, the tickets "being taken very rapidly, and by the most fashionable portion of the community;" the Fourth Auditor begged for the room "now used for the storage of Guns;" and soon the Saturday drills were history. In September 1865 Hugh McCulloch (Secretary of the Treasury since March 9) asked Secretary of War Edwin Stanton to disband the guard which he did via a special order on October 16, 1865.[26]

"Utmost Dispatch:" The West Wing's Construction Resumes

"It is expected that such progress will shortly be decided in relation to the work upon the west wing of the Treasury Extension, that you could be employed to advantage," Young wrote a rigger working for the Milton (Massachusetts) Railroad at the end of December 1861. During January 1862, 167 workmen ranging from six stonecutters to seventy carpenters began the building season carrying out minor repairs to the south and west wings while sixty-six laborers continued to fortify the building. The critical need for additional office space was the driving force. The department's "vast increase of business" meant moving more bureaus into rented space, or completing the west wing. "The demand for Stores and dwellings in the vicinity of our principal thoroughfares, growing out of the great increase of business in this City (contingent upon the war) has absorbed every desirable locality," Clark wrote Chase in mid-February 1862. Buildings not fireproof were unacceptable, Clark noted, as he strongly urged Chase to seek congressional appropriations to finish the building.[27]

Only "151 hands" were employed around the construction site in February and the number fell to 126 the following month. In late March 1862 Chase drafted a letter to an unknown congressional committee member (enclosing Clark's February letter) outlining the department's "absolute need of more room," particularly for the "duties growing out of the issue of Treasury Notes." Congress passed the National Currency Act in July 1861, authorizing the government's first issue of paper money, "greenbacks," reluctantly proposed by Chase to shore up the nation's finances. Although these notes were printed in sheets of four by private companies in New York and Philadelphia, they were shipped to the Treasury Building, individually signed and separated by Treasury

IV-8 After the 1861 National Currency Act passed Congress, the push was on to complete the west wing.

clerks located in different rooms, all under close supervision. These operations required secure spaces within the building to process notes valued at $250 million.[28]

"I know of no speedier or more economical way to obtain the desideratum than to complete the Treasury Extension, which is now partially advanced, and much of the paid for material for its completion scattered about the streets adjacent to the Treasury, exposed to severe injury," Chase informed the congressional committee. Oertly compiled an estimate of $400,000 to complete both remaining wings and Harrington wrote Clark that Chase "desires the utmost dispatch in the execution of the west wing." In anticipation of an imminent appropriation, the riggers and stone masons began raising pilasters and had two portico columns in place and another ready to lift when Walker photographed them on April 23.[29] (fig. IV-8)

On May 15, five days after Chase ordered utmost dispatch, Young sent Beals & Dixon

the authorization to fill an order for pilasters that had been in limbo for more than a year, as well as a list of all the remaining granite needed to complete the west wing. A week later the New York Times reported that "most of the granite columns which have encumbered Pennsylvania-avenue, in front of the White House, for several years past, have been raised to their proper position. It is said that the work will be prosecuted without interruption until the extension is completed, the room being much needed for the increased business of the Treasury Department." Walker's photograph taken the following day showed that work had progressed to the middle of the portico's vestibule. Another made on June 7 demonstrated that the columns were free-standing once they were set in place and surrounded by their bases. (fig. IV-9) Raising the columns was accomplished by a relatively small, experienced, and well-coordinated work force. Four stonemasons worked with two riggers in April (out of 148

IV-9 The 1862 congressional investigation stimulated Young to quickly build the west wing's portico.

IV-10 By July 9 the west wing's wall armature was standing and the lower window frames inserted.

men on the site) and five stonemasons were employed in May out of 199 workmen. Work continued at breakneck speed during June (while Young was increasingly under assault from a congressional investigation) and, by July 9, all the pilasters on the long west front were in place and secured.[30] (fig. IV-10)

"It Is Alleged That Immense Frauds:" Isaiah Rogers Replaces Young

Political intrigue almost ended Young's career with the Bureau of Construction at the outset of Lincoln's turbulent administration. Within six weeks of taking office, while he was still feeling his way around the bureaucracy, Lincoln received a letter from a New York architect applying for Young's job. "I am told there is an office in your department called 'the Supervising Architect of the Treasury Department, connected with the Bureau of Construction,' which is now held by a man of the name of Young, and wanted by a gentleman by the name of Christopher Adams," Lincoln wrote Chase. "Ought Mr. Young to be removed, and if yea, ought Mr. Adams to be appointed? Mr. Adams is magnificently recommended. What say you?" In fact, Adams also wrote Chase in mid-April, 1861, but Chase took no known action, possibly because Adams (about whose career nothing is now known) was not qualified to take on the job's complex responsibilities. Lincoln's inquiry was anything but exceptional. "During his four years and one month of presidential appointive-powers, Lincoln, according to later estimates rather carefully based, removed 1,457 out of a possible 1,639 officials." Young's politics and alleged support of Vice President John C. Breckinridge, a Democrat running in the 1860 election, should have been enough to depose him early in Lincoln's administration. His key position overseeing fortification of the Treasury Building, building forts, and completing the west wing as expeditiously as possible, apparently protected his employment, at least temporarily.[31]

In mid-December 1861 the House Committee on Expenditures on Public Buildings began investigating cost overruns at the Capitol and Treasury Extensions. The *New York Times* reported that "it is alleged that immense frauds have been practiced upon the Government in the construction" of both buildings. The specific inquiries centered on whether original designs were being carried out, contracts fulfilled, the high costs of materials, "and also whether the officers of the Bureau of Construction are, in the judgment of this committee, qualified to discharge the duties thereof and whether they have done so or not." No equivalent pointed reference was made concerning the Architect of the Capitol's office; arguably its design underwent greater changes (and higher cost overruns) than those at the Treasury Extension.[32]

Young's professional rivals, colleagues, and former employees were called as witnesses, the questions asked directed towards eliciting answers that blamed Young for high granite and furniture costs and structural faults that led to costly repairs. For example, when Young first testified on February 24, 1862, he was questioned closely about his relationship with Beals & Dixon and how contracts were advertised. Clark and Oertly were questioned about specific costs on both the Treasury Extension and Charleston Custom House but said nothing particularly damaging about Young.[33]

On May 30 engineer T.A. Curtis, who was hired by Young as a clerk in the Bureau of Construction in November 1857, testified about the south wing's roof, replaced because the way its slates were originally laid led to massive leaks. Curtis also testified about an experimental heating system in which "hot air, which was to come up from below through a perforation made in an iron baseboard runing [sic] round the rooms and passages" had to be replaced by hot water radiators. When Curtis (who left the bureau in April 1861) was asked "who is responsible for such failures and blunders as the roof and heating apparatus," he replied, "the supervising architect." The preceding year Young had reported to Chase that Bowman's construction of the south wing's roof was faulty, a report that exists only in manuscript form because no annual report relating to the Treasury Building was printed in 1861.

In July 1862 the House committee reported on its investigation. "There is extravagance in the expenditure of the public moneys in constructing public buildings" was the first finding, but the committee concentrated its ire on the marble columns used on the Charleston Customs House rather than the Treasury Extension's construction. The committee's second conclusion was "that the buildings thus constructed, however strong and imposing to the inexperienced eye, lack the thoroughness and abiding strength that should characterize such structures." This astonishing statement—considering that the Treasury's fortress-like construction led to its selection as the government's last stronghold in case of a prolonged siege—reveals the influence of Thomas U. Walter. Moreover, the visual evidence of its stability—wisely recorded in Walker's photographs—was available to any visitor to the Treasury Extension's construction site.[34]

The committee's complaint against Young's structural system seems to echo Walter's opinions.

> We are aware that the tall antae or pilasters which stud the building; the slabs of granite between the antae, set endwise, extending from the sill-course to the caps; and the wall face between the antaes or pilasters at the angles of the building—with two exceptions made by setting a slab of granite endwise of the same length as the antae, (36 feet 6 inches)—have an imposing effect, and it may be difficult to make a superficial observer understand how such vast masses of granite can make the building insecure; but the system of putting in these large stones for the benefit of the contractor, or for any other motive, is a fatal mistake.[35]

A lengthy technical explanation argued that large exterior pieces of granite simply could not be attached to internal brickwork. This echoed Walter's claim during his 1838 congressional testimony when he predicted the inevitable collapse of the east facade.[36]

The committee's examples of "correct" constructional methods were three Walter buildings—Girard College and his extensions to the Patent Office and General Post Office—and Isaiah Rogers's New York Merchant's Exchange. Moreover, although the committee on expenditures had set out to investigate both the Architect of the Capitol and the Supervising Architect of the Treasury, it noted that they did not have "time to go into the cost of the Capitol Extension [designed and being supervised by Walter]. The work on the Treasury Extension is illy [sic] done, insecure, and unsubstantial. The original designs [by Walter] are not being carried out, but are varied from in many particulars, which largely increase the cost to the government and lessen the value of the building."[37]

The committee determined that both Young and Clark were unqualified, as well as culpable of abuses, and recommended that both be removed. Young was officially fired two weeks after the report was made public. Clark, who, without any known training as an engineer, was named acting engineer after Bowman left, went on to head up the National Note Bureau (although he also lacked known manufacturing experience). He later served as the Treasury Extension's disbursing officer, successfully surviving an even more virulent 1864 congressional investigation.

Ten days after Curtis's testimony, Chase wrote Isaiah Rogers inquiring if he would accept the position as "Supervising Architect of the Treasury Department." (fig. IV-11) Like Young, fellow New Englander Rogers was trained to design and build with granite, his much-acclaimed hotels in Boston, New York, and Cincinnati appreciated by a diverse

IV-11 Isaiah Rogers replaced Young as Supervising Architect of the Treasury in mid-June 1862.

in the *New York Times* credited Congressman William Wall (R-NY) with protesting against the "architectural horror rising before the eyes of the nation" and uncovering the fact "that the men who contrived and superintended the work were not architects, or engineers, or otherwise professionally prepared for their office; that parts were put together without any regard to permanency or security." Eight days later Chase wrote Rogers appointing him "Engineer in charge of the Bureau of Construction." The following day Chase sent Young a terse note. "It is proposed for the present at least, to devolve the duties of Supervising Architect on the engineer in charge of the Construction Bureau. Your services therefore are no longer required."[39]

Young tried to hang onto his job as the "Assistant Superintendent of the Treasury Extension," but Chase soon made it clear he was no longer working for the department. Nearly a year later, Chase appointed Rogers "Supervising Architect of the Treasury Building" at $3,000 per annum and revoked his earlier appointment as head of the Bureau of Construction.[40] The *New York Times* crowed:

> The appointment of Isaiah Rogers, of Cincinnati, as Chief of the Bureau of Construction, and Supervising Architect of the Treasury Extension, is warmly commended. Mr. Rogers is one of the most accomplished architects in the country. The Merchants' Exchange, New-York; Tremont House, Boston; Burnett House, Cincinnati, and other public buildings, were built from his designs. The important appointment now given him by the Government is the first practical result of the recent thorough *expose* of the mismanagement in the Bureau of Construction, made under Mr. Wall's resolution in the House.[41]

When Rogers's appointment appeared in Cincinnati newspapers, two prominent local

clientele, while his New York Merchants' Exchange and New York Customs House were used by a smaller audience. Ohioan Chase probably learned about Rogers through contacts in Cincinnati, where Rogers had been living and working since 1848. His credentials for finishing the Treasury Building probably surpassed those of most contenders for Young's job. Although Rogers professed to be very surprised at the job offer, he lost no time accepting the position.[38]

What actually transpired between Chase and Young after Curtis's damning congressional testimony is unknown, but the architect lost no time calling in his supporters. Vermont newspaperman E.P. Walton, hearing the "rumor of an attempt to procure the removal" of Young, wrote Chase that he knew of "no man who more thoroughly minds his own business, or who is more sensitive when he supposes any body is interfering or marring his own." But for Young, such lobbying was too little, too late. An article citizens immediately wrote Chase. Militia Colonel F.J. Mayer (who became Cincinnati's postmaster in 1864) was astonished at the announcement. "I deem it my duty to intrude on your valuable time and warn you that [Rogers] needs close watching to prevent *friendly understandings* between him and Contractors." Enoch T. Carson, Cincinnati's Surveyor of Customs and a prominent Mason, was of the same opinion. He named three local contractors whom he predicted "would start immediately for Washington City," as they had formed a ring with Rogers to obtain contracts throughout Ohio. Carson even went so far as to exclaim: "woe to the State, County, or *nation* that gets into their clutches." How ironic that Rogers should be accused of the same abuse of position in Ohio of which Young was suspected in Washington, and how disgruntled Chase must have been to receive these warnings from men who would have had first-hand knowledge of Rogers's Ohio career. In fact, in the fall of 1862 Rogers ordered copper for the Treasury's roof from one of his Cincinnati associates, H.F. Handy & Company.[42]

Rogers signed the oath of allegiance on July 23, 1862, and began work five days later. He wrote no annual report for 1862, claiming the "records of this office were so imperfect and confused that it was utterly impossible for me to procure the necessary information in time." Rogers instituted a new system of record-keeping, enabling government officers to know immediately the amounts of unexpended appropriations for each building. He soon determined that the corrugated iron roofs Young and Bowman specified for their buildings leaked so seriously they all needed to be replaced. The south wing's roof was among the first Rogers rebuilt while he was redesigning the west wing's roof to be waterproof. He soon revised his design to accommodate the National Note Bureau, engineering the iron roof girders to support the anticipated weight of the new bureau's printing presses. Interior pragmatic

concerns began to subtly affect the west wing's exterior appearance.[43]

Six months after his own appointment, Rogers appointed as his assistant architect Alfred B. Mullett, who would play a major role in the building's completion. Mullett came to the Office of the Supervising Architect with both Secretary Chase and Rogers as his patrons. Born in England and brought to Ohio as a child, he completed courses in mathematics at the Ohio Farmer's College in 1854. He joined Rogers's Cincinnati firm in 1856 and was made a partner two years later. Mullett left the firm in 1860 and at the age of 26 embarked on an autumn tour of England, Belgium, France, and Germany. This trip was apparently Mullett's only first-hand experience of European architecture as an adult.[44]

Mullett came to Washington as part of Chase's entourage from Cincinnati and was "appointed a temporary Clerk in the Office of the Secretary of the Treasury under the Act authorizing the issue of Treasury Notes, approved 17th December 1860, at a compensation at the rate of Twelve hundred dollars per annum," less than a month after Chase's appointment. Mullett's temporary position was renewed on October 21, but "annulled" three weeks later. In June 1862 he withdrew his resignation from Chase's office after meeting with Cincinnatian Victor Smith. "I am led to take an entirely different view of my position here, and especially of my duty to yourself," Mullett wrote Chase.[45]

One interpretation of Mullett's avowal is that both men were biding their time until Rogers found a position for his former partner. In January 1863 Rogers appointed Mullett a clerk in the bureau. The young architect rose quickly, named Spencer Clark's replacement as chief clerk on April 23 and "First Assistant Superintendent for [the] Treasury Extension" on May 13. Chase's patronage surely reinforced the prior association of Mullett and Rogers. On June 3 Rogers appointed Mullett "'Chief of the

Office of Construction' and 'Superintendent of the Treasury Extension' during my absence from the Office at any future time." A week later both Rogers and Chase wrote the young architect that Rogers was appointing Mullett "Assistant Supervising Architect of the Treasury Building" at his current rate of pay, $2,000 per annum. Chase's letter reaffirmed the appointment and revoked all earlier ones.[46] Mullett was frequently away from Washington on extended inspection trips to the bureau's few buildings still under construction in northern and western states. When in Washington he took an active part in the Treasury Building's progress and the bureau's administration.

"Sure Ould Abe Is a Laboring Man:" The Workmen Strike

Washington in early 1863 was experiencing the economic effects, both good and bad, of being the center of the Civil War. Businesses for the past year were profitable and for the first time hotels were full when Congress was not in session. Concurrently, prices for goods and services began to rise above the means of the working classes. Early in March Rogers reported to Chase the carpenters' request for an increase in their wages to match the $2 per day paid those employed privately in the city. While Rogers conceded "there seems to be much truth in their remark that everything in the way of living is very high in prices," he also pointed out that many privately employed carpenters were unable to find work. "I do not consider that persons should expect to make much more than a living, and that not of the most luxurious nature, until a change, for the better … takes place in our National affairs." Yet, by the autumn, Rogers advertised for twenty carpenters. "To good workmen, the highest wages will be given & steady work," after his own actions ignited a strike.[47]

Rogers was a stern taskmaster. On January 27, 1863, he circulated among the workmen a list of seven rules and regulations to govern both the mechanical trades and laborers on the site. The workday began at 7:30 and ended at 5:30, the dinner hour set between noon and 1:00. No workman could leave before the bell was rung (unless he had the permission of his foreman) and no smoking was permitted on the site. Failure to comply with the regulations led to immediate dismissal. Ten months later when he was feeling pushed to complete the wing, Rogers changed the hours from 6:45 a.m. to 5:45 p.m., angering the workmen who on October 12 went on strike to work from one hour after sunrise until sunset, the traditional winter workday in the building trades. They voted on a resolution thanking the stonecutters (who worked a different schedule) for supporting them and another condemning the bricklayers who did not strike. The laborers also pledged to stop work immediately if any leader among them was later fired, all strategies associated with organized labor later in the century. A committee met with Rogers who agreed to rescind his new rule. "Mr. Rogers had, however, decided that they were to lose the time while they had been engaged in this meeting, and in this all parties acquiesced."[48] (fig. IV-12)

The longer workday and the probable haste of the workmen soon led to tragedy. During the evening of October 20, after the clerical force had left the building, master rigger Lucius A.R. Teasdale was lifting a printing press to the attic story when the tackle broke. The 5.5-ton press hit the scaffolding, Teasdale and a laborer fell to the ground and, though seriously injured, they survived. A laborer manning the crank on the derrick platform fell thirty feet and was killed instantly. This incident led to overtime pay, with Rogers writing the foremen on October 31. "You are hereby notified that on and after the 2d of November, the pay of the workmen on the Treasury Extension will be made according to the rates heretofore paid. All work performed each day after hours, will be allowed and paid for at the usual compensation for such over work."[49]

Either Rogers or Chase ordered Mullett to look into the wages and hours among Washington's private employers and elsewhere in the country. Mullett recommended that a ten-hour day be instituted, while informing workmen that the "highest rates paid in private establishments be considered the standard by which the prices of labor will be governed." He also noted it was "well known that private employment, is much harder, than Government work."[50]

On November 3 a committee of workmen met with Chase, while the strikers met at Washington's Temperance Hall to consider Mullett's recommendations. Chase thought their grievances could be addressed without a strike. "The committee told Secretary Chase that they could not take the word of the man over them, (Mr. Rogers) because he had heretofore violated his word solemnly given." Chase promised a written response by the end of the day. "Secretary Chase was a man and a gentleman, and one in whom the whole country placed confidence, and why should not we?" queried the committee's secretary.[51]

The strike and its implications became national news on November 4.

> The strike of Treasury extension carpenters, masons, and laborers has infected the compositors and bookbinders in the Government Printing Office. This menaced strike is based partly on the monstrous prices of food, fuel and rents in Washington, and principally on what is alleged to be the little work and big pay of the Department clerks. Secretary Chase has not decided what to do in the case of the workmen on the Treasury extension who struck yesterday.[52]

IV-12 Although the Masonic order served as a "union" for builders, it did not regulate hours and wages.

The *New York Times* predicted on November 5: "It is probable that to-morrow over one thousand men will march to the White House and ask the President to enable them to meet the awful cost of living here by leaving their wages for the Winter what they have been receiving during the Summer. This informal resolution of the crowd scattered through the Treasury Grounds got its sanction and finish from an Irishman in nine words—'Sure Ould [*sic*] Abe is a laboring man like ourselves.'"[53] (fig. IV-13)

When Chase met with the workmen's committee on November 6, he "deprecated the strike as he would any other attempt to coerce the Department to adopt any rule by dictation." He rescinded the half-hour dinner rule, urged them to return to work under Rogers's original

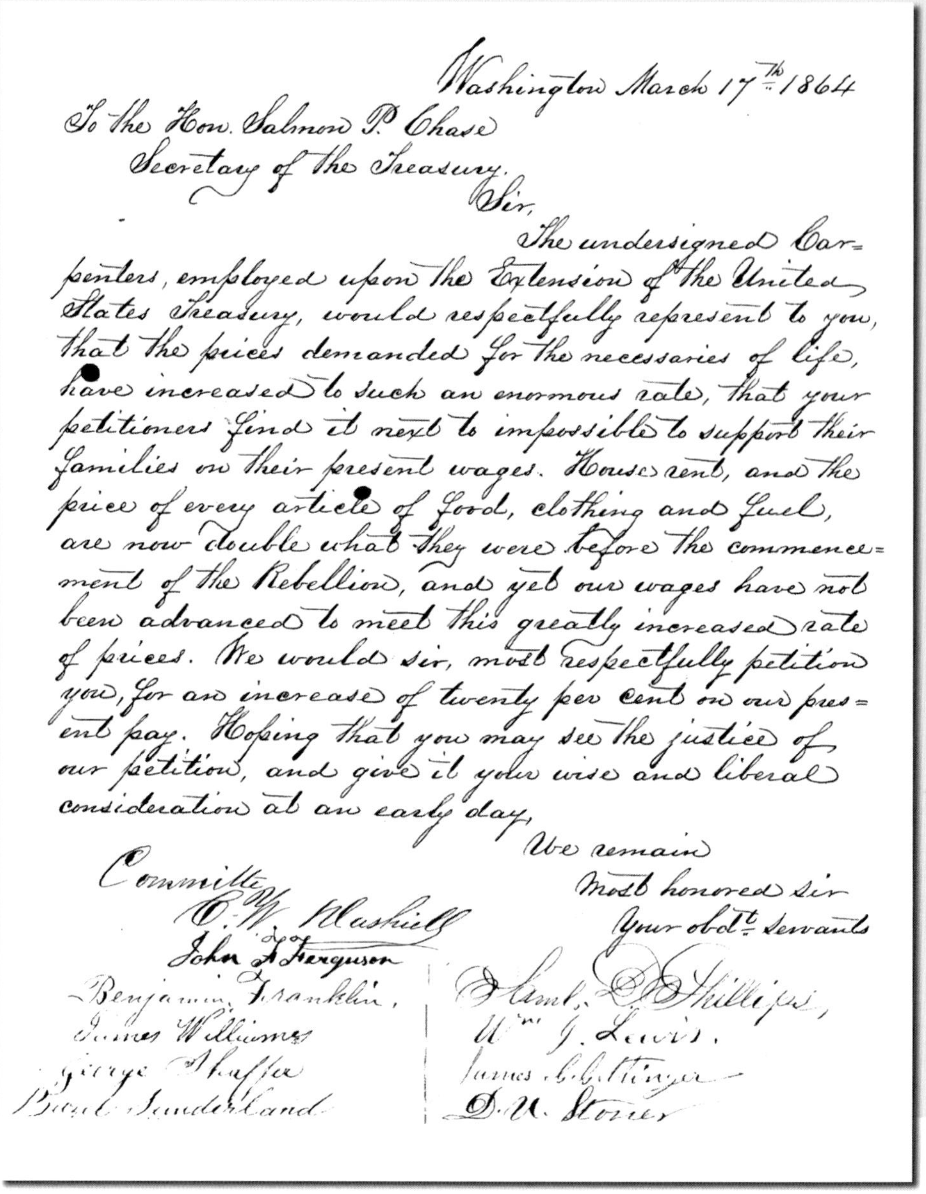

Washington March 17th 1864

To the Hon. Salmon P. Chase
Secretary of the Treasury.
Sir,

The undersigned Carpenters, employed upon the Extension of the United States Treasury, would respectfully represent to you, that the prices demanded for the necessaries of life, have increased to such an enormous rate, that your petitioners find it next to impossible to support their families on their present wages. House rent, and the price of every article of food, clothing and fuel, are now double what they were before the commencement of the Rebellion, and yet our wages have not been advanced to meet this greatly increased rate of prices. We would sir, most respectfully petition you, for an increase of twenty per cent on our present pay. Hoping that you may see the justice of our petition, and give it your wise and liberal consideration at an early day,

We remain
Most honored sir
Your obdt. Servants

Committee
C. W. Mashull
John A. Ferguson

Benjamin Franklin
James Williams
George Shaffer
Benj. Sunderland

Saml. D. Phillips,
Wm. G. Lewis.
James C. Ottinger
D. N. Stover

IV-13 Inflation during the Civil War led to economic hardships for the Treasury's mechanics.

order "so as not to interfere with the progress of the work." Chase needed more time to consider the length of their workday in relation to other federal departments. Many at the meeting felt Chase had not truly addressed their concerns. Rumors, of course, were legion. Rogers had gone north to find workmen to replace them; no, he had gone to New Orleans; and, facetiously, the 63-year-old architect "had gone to answer a draft notice." About three-quarters of the meeting's attendees voted to go back to work from 7:00 to 5:00, taking an hour for their mid-day meal.[54] On November 19 Rogers wrote each of the foremen. "From this date until further order by direction of the Secretary of the Treasury, the hours of work will be from one hour after Sunrise, to Sun-set, with one hour for Dinner. The bells will be rung accordingly." Rogers's half-hour dinner break had been defeated.[55]

Chase's "Damned Old Paper Mill:"[56] The National Note Bureau

On July 17, 1861, Congress authorized the Treasury Department to issue as much as $250 million in paper money to facilitate the government's financial transactions because the Civil War impeded the shipment of gold and "was carried on chiefly by the use of treasury notes as a circulating medium."

In mid-August Young ordered a safe six feet high by four feet, six inches wide but only two feet, two inches deep for the use of the "Treasury Note business," part of his preparations for accommodating this high-security operation. The implications for the building of the National Note Bureau could not have been anticipated, as the law required the Treasury Department only to provide authorizing signatures on notes printed by New York banknote companies. Notes were shipped to the Treasury Building in sheets of four, separated, trimmed, and "signed," each step done by separate groups of clerks as insurance against theft and fraud. By the end of November a workday for the forty "signing" clerks (each paid $1,200 per annum) was three thousand signatures, the number established by Chase. Five men who managed to sign four thousand notes per day were accordingly given raises because the "work on which they are engaged is very confusing and laborious."[57]

In addition to being very costly, signatures by multiple hands on the paper currency facilitated forgeries. Acting Engineer Clark suggested substituting mechanical signatures, a step that quickly led to printing currency and bonds in the Treasury Building on a unique paper manufactured in the basement. (fig. IV-14) In February 1862 Clark was working on designs for a cutting machine to replace laborious hand cutting by scissors. He consulted with a Philadelphia engineer about how to automate the counting and cutting processes.[58]

> Each machine now requires two girls (four in all) and their best days work has been 6000 sheets; (while two more have been required as relays, for motive power.) Four of the best cutters by hand (girls without male help) can cut 6000 sheets; if paid by the piece, they will cut more than 6000.[59]

Clark was trying to work out how to make delivery automatic (even considering using steam power), to have sheets fall on tables when exiting the machines and equipping them with counters to register the number of sheets processed.

In April 1862 Clark outlined for Chase an entire printing program based on mass production, men and women operating machines in separate rooms laid out as an assembly line. Because minimizing collusion between those with access to the paper and those involved in each stage of printing was integral to Clark's thinking, many processes had to be segregated. Moreover, there were unpleasant, even hazardous, aspects to several of them—noisy, vibrating machines and noxious odors—that might affect not only other Treasury employees but also those at the adjacent State Department Building. Every mechanical step that Clark devised had corresponding security and architectural implications. Parts of the printing operations spread incrementally from the basement to the attic and several rooms in the building's northwest corner.

Chase decided to try Clark's proposal to print fractional currency (small paper substitutes for coins less than one dollar in value) and one- and two-dollar Treasury notes in the building. "This order is not issued as a permanency," he cautioned Clark in August. "It is my intention to give the experiment of machinery a full and fair trial, and this order is issued for that purpose." The first machinery was soon installed in the southwest corner of the south wing's basement and a week later Clark, one male assistant, and four female "operatives" began printing money. By November 7, when Clark had a clear idea of the steps in the process, he was planning to equip rooms in the west wing's basement (now the first floor) and cellar (now designated the basement) with a dumbwaiter to lift paper manufactured there to the plate-printing room in the attic (now the fifth floor). He proposed separate drying, trimming, separating, and packing rooms, suggesting the drying lofts be cast-iron rooms.

IV-14 Unique paper used to print "greenbacks" was manufactured in the west wing's basement.

Large windows lighting these workspaces overlooked the courtyards, and Clark worked with the architects who did not want factory windows marring the building's architectural beauty.[60]

As soon as Chase was satisfied with Clark's trial run, the push was on to finish the west wing as quickly as possible. Attic stories were the first priority and Rogers adapted his designs accordingly. The west wing's attic was built as normal construction progressed, followed quickly by alterations to those in the other wings, the east attic rooms completed last. Rogers redesigned the rooms on the east half of the west wing to have twelve-foot ceilings with tall windows overlooking the courtyard. Roof ventilators along each roof's sloping side were probably not visible from the streets or President's Grounds.[61] (fig. IV-15)

Chase pushed the Bureau of Construction to complete the attic rooms quickly. At the end of September 1863, Mullett reported to Chase as to exactly when orders were received and filled for drying racks, furniture, "Granite platforms for the ink Mills," and gas fittings. The following day Chase urged Mullett to "complete the room designated as the Laboratory within six weeks, as you propose. If it be at all possible, let it be completed within a month."[62] Chase continued to urge Mullett to concentrate on the Note Bureau's needs. On October 8, 1863, the secretary tersely wrote:

I enclose a letter of this date from S.M. Clark, Esq., Chief 1st Division, National Currency Bureau, calling my attention to the fact that a partition requested by him to be erected in the basement floor, on Sept. 11th, is not yet completed.

Please examine into and report the cause of the delay at once.[63]

Mullett reported back:

Mr. Borland, Master Carpenter, informs me that he received verbal orders from Mr. Rogers to complete it at the earliest possible moment, and that it has been pressed on rapidly as the means at our disposal will permit, nearly every available workman being engaged in work for the Note Bureau.[64]

Rogers had earlier warned Chase, apparently not for the first time, that "in spite of all precautions, the deflection in the Beams under the north press room has perceptibly increased." Dr. Stuart Gwynn, with the note bureau, suggested hanging a one-hundred-ton counterweight from the cornice in the west wing's north courtyard to offset the weight of the machines. This alarmed Rogers, who felt it his "duty to protest against subjecting the Cornice to any such unprecedented test." Although Rogers felt the cornice might sustain the weight during a test, "I do assert that the experiment would be a hazardous one, even for a short time: and as a permanent burden, would certainly injure the building, and be liable at any moment to cause a serious accident."[65]

When a fatal accident occurred soon after, it led not only to payment of overtime wages, but also to changes in the lifting mechanism. Early in the evening of October 20, a five-and-a-half-ton hydraulic press being lifted into the attic fell

IV-15 Multiple operations associated with printing currency were done in the attic, hence the roof ventilators.

twenty feet when its tackle broke, killing one man and injuring two or three others.[66] The following day Rogers proposed:

> I would respectfully suggest that the entire Apparatus be removed farther into the Building, so as to bring the whole bearing of the weight permanently on the wall, and in order that the Rope be made to pass through, instead of down the outside of the Cornice.
>
> This may be done by simply raising the machine about two feet higher in a horizontal position. If this be satisfactory and I can see no objection to it there would be no mutilation of the Granite, as is the case with the present arrangement.
>
> We would, moreover, feel secure from casualties likely to occur from the insufficient support for the weight.[67]

Getting the National Note Bureau up and running drove the west wing's completion but at costs beyond the original estimates and appropriations. At the beginning of May 1864, when the alterations to accommodate the note bureau were almost complete, Harrington (who now called it the "engraving and printing division") called for an accounting. The Bureau of Construction had created five rooms in the attic covering 33,027 ½ square feet for $50,529 exclusive of the alterations to the roof, Rogers reported, but Harrington was not satisfied. Rogers subsequently reported that the total cost of alterations to the building, including attic stories in all three wings, was $154,246, of which $21,612 was spent renovating the offices for the Third Auditor on the third story (now the fourth) of the east wing. Its groined ceilings were removed to make a level floor for the entire attic story. The cost of ironwork had increased by sixty-one percent and that of brickwork by more than one hundred percent, salaries for bricklayers rising from $2.50 to $4 per day, all attributable to the war. Moreover, "the desire to give to the Note

Bureau large rooms unobstructed by columns required strong, and costly iron Roof-trusses, and accordingly increased the cost heavily."[68]

Harrington was gathering this information because yet another congressional investigation was underway. On June 16, 1864, the Senate Committee on Finance was instructed to investigate printing of all kinds in the Treasury Building, a revival of complaints of the bank note engraving companies that had instigated the 1862 investigation. The committee's lengthy report concluded that Clark was unfit to superintend the "Money Printing Bureau." Yet, Clark survived and in November reported that two hundred thirty-seven men and two hundred eighty-eight women operated three hundred twenty-four machines under his direction.[69]

Secretary Fessenden curtailed public visits to the attic printing rooms in September 1865 because forgers in the guise of tourists had gleaned information. A privileged Washington journalist was granted a tour of the operations in the basement two years later. There, a recently installed Fourdrinier machine printed fractional currency and the department's paper and envelopes.[70]

"Some Light and Ventilation:" The West Wing's Attic Vestibule

When Rogers redesigned the west wing's attic, ventilating the long rectangular space was as crucial as lighting it and calculating the stresses caused by the weight of its machines. Tall windows facing the courtyard brought in east and south light, but also unwelcome heat. When ventilators along the roof's western ridge were inadequate to counteract the heat and fumes, the architect designed a double dome within a fifty-five-foot square to cover the central double stairway. (fig. IV-16) The inner dome was attached to rafters that roofed the square projection rising above the roofline and was topped by an

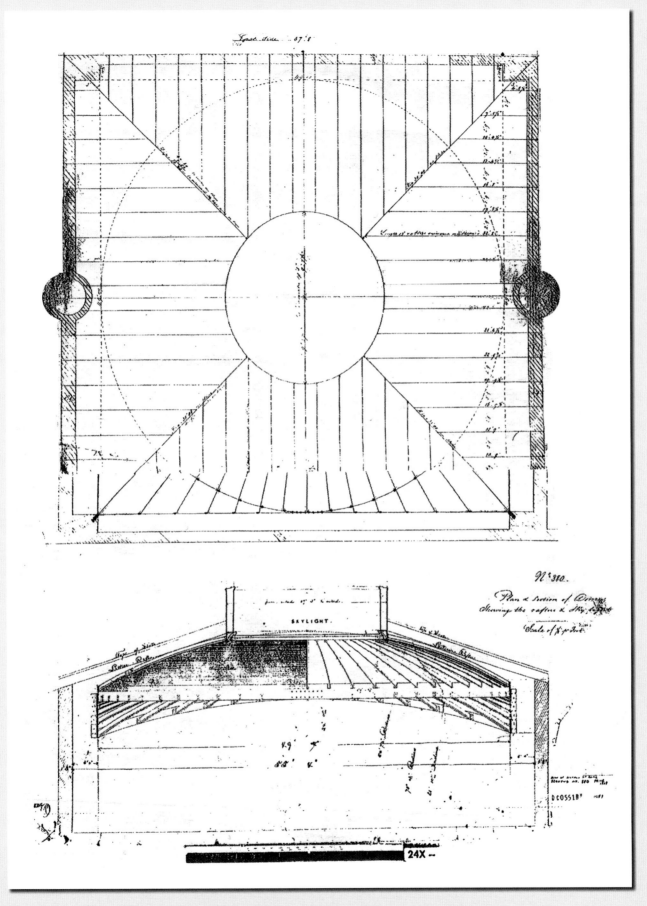

IV-16 Rogers installed a turret over the west central stairway to help ventilate the attic story.

exceptionally wide—seventeen-foot, three-inch—clerestory monitor, a form of cupola. Although apparently (or ostensibly) erected as part of the building's defenses, when the monitor's windows were open, heat trapped at the top of the central staircase could escape.

Mullett, consistently dismissive of Rogers's talents and expertise from the time of his appointment in 1863, was particularly vicious in his criticism of the west wing's turret in his 1868 report after he became supervising architect.

> I desire to call attention to the unsightly protuberance over the west front, generally supposed to be a shot-proof turret on the "monitor" principle erected for the defense of the building, but which was supposed by its designer to be a sky-light. Efforts have been made to use it for that purpose since its completion, though without much success. I recommend its removal and the erection of a sky-light to the main stairway, that will give some light and ventilation to the building without disfiguring the exterior.[71]

Mullett removed Rogers's turret in 1869, the critical first step of major structural and aesthetic alterations to the attic's vestibule preliminary to improving its ventilation. His timing coincided with a major shift in American architectural principles and tastes away from English-dominated movements—of which the Treasury Building's Greek Revival architecture was an outstanding national example—towards the acceptance of France's Second Empire architecture, the revival of its own Renaissance and Baroque traditions. Mullett became one of America's leading Second Empire style architects, and the Treasury Building contains an initial example of his stylistic development.

Significant local and national architectural events stimulated Mullett's emerging French approach to architectural design. In 1859 James

Renwick designed the Corcoran Museum of Art, two short blocks from the Treasury Building, as a miniature version of the Louvre. In April 1866 Quartermaster General Meigs prophesized that "at some future time Congress will doubtless make provision for the erection of a building on 17th Street and Pennsylvania Avenue in style and construction to correspond in some degree with the Treasury Building." Meigs's participation in obtaining a design for the War Department included promoting English public buildings designed in the Second Empire style. Between 1867 and 1871, Mullett was instrumented in the design of two key American Second Empire buildings, the controversial New York Court House and Post Office and the State, War, and Navy Building (currently the Eisenhower Executive Office Building), both eventually built following his designs.

Mullett's frequent interaction with the émigré interior designers and furniture makers Auguste Pottier and William P. Stymus probably helped develop his taste for elegant French designs. In general, Mullett's extensive travel to major American cities would have alerted him to a greater variety of new architectural approaches. The New York Post Office controversy, in particular, strengthened Mullett's turn towards Second Empire for buildings designed by the Office of the Supervising Architect. Five New York architects, including Richard Morris Hunt, all with previous experience with French architecture, won the competition sponsored by the city government. Because it was a federal building, their design was sent to Mullett's office, and served as the primary aesthetic stimulus for a series of important government buildings done by the supervising architect's office under Mullett's direction.[72]

Mullett brought this change in America's intellectual and aesthetic landscape to the Treasury Building in 1869, two years before he began the State, War, and Navy Building. On March 3 Congress appropriated $8,500 "for

IV-17 In 1869 Mullett replaced Rogers's turret with triple skylights set in an ovoid coffered dome.

completing main stairway, west wing."[73] In May 1869 Mullett finalized his design by replacing Rogers's square with a hippodrome-shaped dome that spanned the width of the double central staircase. (fig. IV-17) Unlike Rogers's utilitarian dome, the plaster inner surfaces of Mullett's were decorated with hexagonal coffers. (The whole dome was restored in 2006.) Triple skylights in the dome's center, each with glass set within the center and between radiating spokes of iron wheels, were probably suggested by contemporary French domes that pioneered an ahistorical approach to the use of iron in contemporary buildings. Mullett may well have been familiar with earlier or contemporary American domes inspired by these French buildings, but many structures of this era have been destroyed without being documented. Whatever his inspiration, Mullett's notable Second Empire design for the State, War, and Navy Building was preceded in Washington by his domed attic vestibule in the Treasury's west wing.

"Mysterious Conglomeration of Metal, Mortar, and Stone:" The Treasury's Vaults

The National Note Bureau required four secure storage rooms larger than the safes found in many Treasury offices. In April 1856 Secretary Guthrie assured Congress that all thirty-five of the Bureau of Construction's buildings were equipped with burglar and fireproof vaults, the term vault used generally in the department's correspondence to denote a large safe as well as a secured room. By December 1857 Bowman was constructing a vault for the use of the Treasurer in the south wing, but its specific details are not known. Many south-wing offices had safes made to the department's specifications, but there was only one walk-in vault. At the end of April 1862, Clark ordered two custom strong boxes twenty-four inches by thirteen-and-a-half inches by thirteen-and-a-half inches "for the transmission of Treasury Notes to distant points," to test the workmanship of the G.R. Jackson Company in New York. "As soon as you decide on the method of construction," Clark wrote the company, "please send me a piece a few inches square … that I may experiment upon it … and [determine] what the uniform character of the Box will be." At the same time, he ordered fireproof file cases from the Architectural Iron Works in New York for the Sub-Treasury there. "The file cases will not be *counterparts* of those in the Treasury, but *similar* in style and design. They will be of different *height* from those in use here, and some will have passage ways through them, which these have not."[74]

In January 1862 Clark took the lead in researching and acquiring safes and vaults for the Treasury Building and the bureau's other buildings. After examining the vaults at the Sub-Treasury in New York, he commented that "no private Banker, or individual, would attempt a business of one tenth of the magnitude [of the Treasury's], with such accommodations for a single day." In early March he ordered improved vaults for the Sub-Treasury and the Philadelphia Mint, their walls composed of alternating plates of Franklinite (the hardest of known ores) and boiler iron. On April 26 Oertly estimated the cost of three variants of a new floor-to-ceiling vault, the medium-priced one having floors and ceilings constructed of double sets of angle-iron bars with double brick walls separated by a hollow space. For a little more than an additional thousand dollars, each wall might be formed of "one piece of Granite fitted & scribed to the Granite columns, the whole enclosed by a brick wall." It is unknown if any of the three options actually replaced the south wing's existing vault; by that time the Treasurer, and other bureaus storing bonds and monies, were probably slated to move to the west wing.[75]

In April 1863 Rogers wrote an unusual advertisement for safes for west wing offices. Instead of stating that specifications and drawings made by the Bureau of Construction would be sent to competitors, he asked manufacturers to submit descriptions "accompanied by drawings showing the mode of construction, and full size sections of the material used." Rogers chose this route, "to present the claims of [each company's] own Safes," but it also prevented would-be thieves from obtaining drawings and provided Rogers with the latest technological advances in a rapidly developing industry. Before choosing a manufacturer, Chase required that each of the eight bidders submit a sample lining to be tested by a New York locksmith. Only half passed the test, those composed of alternating layers of boiler iron and hardened steel, the best manufactured by W.B. Dodds & Company of Cincinnati.[76]

Some of the safe specifications and illustrations arriving on Rogers's desk aided the architect in conceiving his own modification to vault linings via a system of rotating balls to make them impermeable to drilling. Frederic H. North of New Britain, Connecticut, for example, offset rivets in thick layers of iron and steel to prevent "a hole from being drilled into the safe by following the line of rivets." The most suggestive submission came from a New York iron founder who held patents for iron and glass skylights. In his report to Chase evaluating the proposals, Rogers noted that "sample No. 14 submitted by Geo. R. Jackson & Co. of New York is of the same construction as the new Vaults in the Sub Treasury, New York, recently completed, and is composed of cast iron balls, enclosed in combinations of wrought or cast iron, or Steel."[77]

During the summer of 1863, Rogers gave Jackson & Company the order for the Comptroller of the Currency's vault, because he "is becoming very uneasy as the accumulation of Bonds in his hands is very rapid, and his Safe room is totally inadequate." (fig. IV-18) At the beginning of September, Rogers urged Jackson to complete the vault as quickly as possible, "as should the Comptroller be pleased, his opinion

will have great weight with the National Banks." On September 17 Rogers sent Jackson a plan of his own design for the vault's decorative outer wall to be married to the internal workings.[78]

> I wish to have the Front made to extend from the antae [pilasters] to the wall, which is figured [decorated]. Only the outside lining will run past the line of the Safe. The object is to make uniformity in the Front and have the door of Vault in the centre of exterior—it will throw it out of the centre of the safe on the interior. You will see by the Ground-Plan the positions of the vault in each Story.[79]

Rogers sent additional drawings of the front of the vault as well as a full-size section drawing of the room's cornice in early October. "The sketch showing the front of [the] Vault shows the height of the underside of the Fascia [the board covering the eaves] below the

IV-18 Four walk-in vaulted rooms, including this one for the Comptroller, were installed in the west wing.

Cornice from the floor. The Panelling [*sic*] of the front to be adapted to suit the size of your Plates."[80]

Rogers later decided that the cornice and fascia would be cast in Washington where the models were located and sent Jackson revised drawings. When Jackson queried the size of the vault's room in mid-October, Rogers replied: "Let the outside be governed by the thickness of the lining. I cannot see the necessity of its being 4 1/4 inch thick if you can make it less by your Pattern & of this you, yourselves can form the best Judgement [*sic*] and act accordingly." He also took this opportunity to inquire about the progress of the Comptroller's safe. Letters crossed in the mail and on October 22 Rogers supplied Jackson with requested drawings of "ornaments for Panels of Safe. They differ somewhat from those sent by you but I hope they may suit. A detailed sketch of same will be sent you as soon as we can have it made." These drawings referred to Rogers's decoration for the outer wall for the Comptroller's vault, possibly identical to the very handsome, over-size anthemion-decorated vault wall Rogers designed for the Treasurer's office. The latter was uncovered during renovations to that room in 1985, the only survivor of four large vaults Jackson & Company and its successor firm, Geo. R. Jackson, Burnet & Company, manufactured for the Treasury Building.[81]

During the prolonged delay in manufacturing the Comptroller's vault, Rogers modified Jackson's lining system, receiving patent number 40,947 on December 15, 1863, for his improvement to "burglar-proof safes." (fig. IV-19) Rogers's claims of innovation were "having the space between [the safe's] walls provided with balls arranged in such a manner that they may turn and still be retained in proper position," the use of balls of different diameters, and a steel plate between the sheets holding the revolving balls. The following day a drawing titled "Sectional plan of iron safes," signed by Rogers, was countersigned by Jackson as "proprietor of the patent." The Jackson-Rogers system was used for the walls of three of the Treasury Department's four vaulted rooms.

In February 1864 Rogers expressed his and Chase's growing impatience when he wrote Jackson. "I must once again urge upon you the importance of completing the Four large Vaults ordered of you for this Building some Months ago." The delay was because the firm was building safes and vaults for other government buildings and simply could not find enough skilled ironworkers in the north; many had gone to war. By the end of February, Jackson sent Rogers bills of lading for four cases of balls for the bureau's workmen to insert in the door of the Comptroller's vault. On March 22 the architect sent Jackson the receipts in the amount of $13,940.95 for this vault, the first of the four to be installed.[82]

Locks for the safe and vault doors were manufactured by locksmiths who sent them to Jackson where they were carefully fitted to the doors, disassembled, then shipped directly to the Treasury Building in separate packages. New York locksmith William Bellamy was called to Washington more than once to unlock doors of the department's safes. In February 1864 he was appointed the Treasury's "Super-intendent of Locks," a part-time position divided between Washington and New York. The four Eureka locks manufactured by W.B. Dodds & Co. for the Currency vault, for example, cost $200 each, and Bellamy was the official who certified they arrived in working order.[83]

Fitting the locks to the doors was Jackson & Company's responsibility. At the end of March 1864, Mullett asked the firm to send a skilled workman immediately. "There is a deficiency in some of the fixtures for it; for instance, the screws for the plate with catches." Five days later Rogers wrote Bellamy that he had "just telegraphed you to come on at once and adjust the Lock for Currency Safe." The problem was still not solved, for in mid-April Rogers reported that the "great weight of the door, when open, has thrown the centre of the [entire vault's] Front out of plumb from 1 ½ to 2 inches. I see no other way to remedy the evil, but to get beams, 12" deep and have one placed on each side of the door, extending from the floor to the top of the safe, well secured to the lining."[84]

Five years later James Sargent of Rochester, New York, was allowed to test the Treasury's combination locks after he claimed they "could be opened with ease without injuring the locks, or attracting attention."[85] It took Sargent one hour and seven minutes to pick a Dodd's Eureka lock.

Gen. Spinner, the custodian of the funds, was notified of what had been done, and hastened to the room of Mr. Mullett, where Mr. Sargent again gave him proof of the

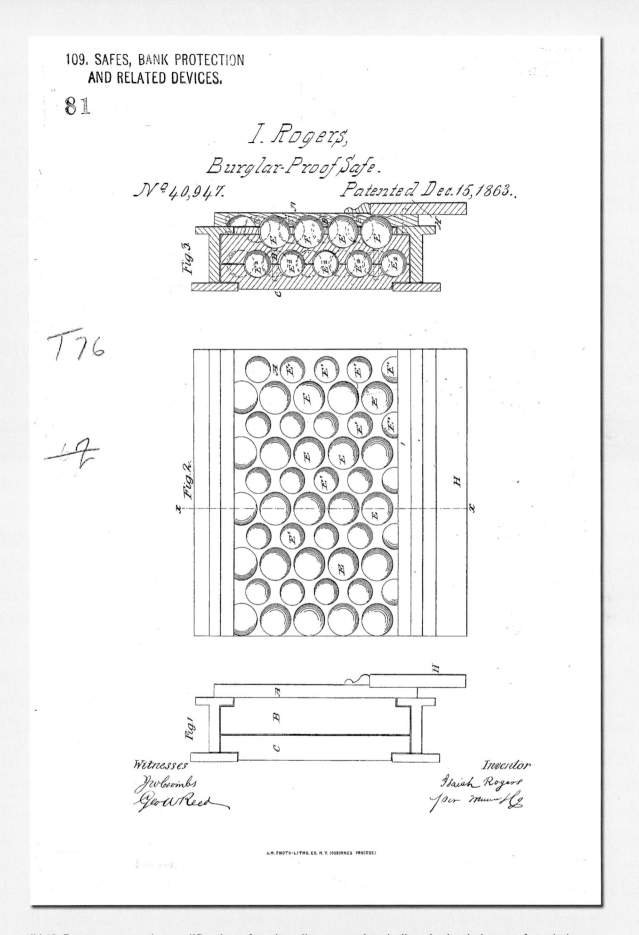

IV-19 Rogers patented a modification of vault wall construction, balls spinning in layers of steel plates.

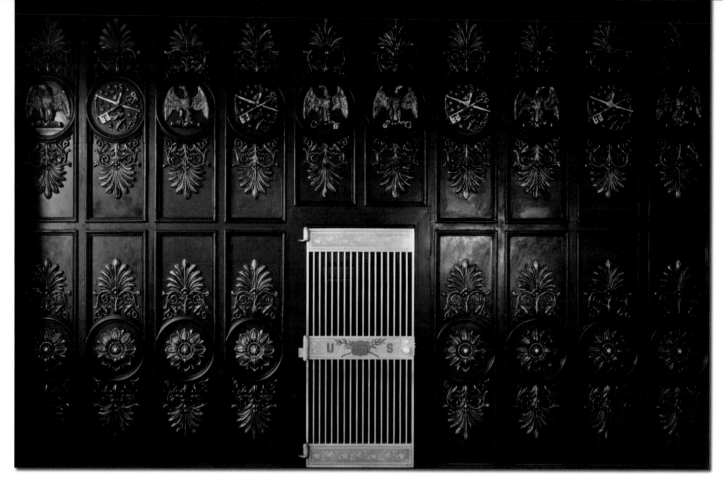

IV-20 Rogers combined Greek ornament and Treasury's symbols for the vaults' decorative exterior walls.

insecurity of the locks. It is Gen. Spinner's custom to try every door of the vaults and safes of his office after office hours, and on Saturday, after Mr. Sargent's experiments, he spent a little extra time in examining the exterior mechanism of the different parts of the safe as he passed from room to room. He will now have every lock thoroughly examined, and efforts will at once be made to secure some sort of a lock that will be burglar-proof.[86]

On March 1, 1864, Rogers advertised for "all the Fire and Burglar proof safes and Vaults required by the Treasury Department," until May 1865. Despite the delay in delivery of the Comptroller's vault, Rogers awarded George R. Jackson the contract. Jackson had formed a partnership with James J. Burnet and together they founded the Excelsior Iron Works in Brooklyn, perhaps in response to Jackson's increased government business. At the end of

May, Rogers contracted with Chase & Company of New York for less substantial vault doors only three-eighths-inch thick into which wire mesh windows were inserted; at the same time he ordered metal counter railings, all to be installed in the Treasurer's cash room where wages were paid out to government employees and the public could cash checks. (fig. IV-20) In November Rogers ordered black and white marble tiles for the floor outside the counter, apparently because foot traffic in the area was so heavy.[87]

The romance attached to the Treasury vaults was partly owing to the vast sums of money known to be deposited in the building, but also because of rumors about other kinds of treasure. In December 1870 one of Washington's most prominent newspaper women, Emily Edson Briggs, writing as "Olivia," visited the Treasury Building specifically to verify for her readers the "fabulous stories [that] have been afloat in Washington concerning the secret of the United States Treasury vaults."

It has been whispered by certain snowy-locked clerks who have been noted for years of strictest veracity that hidden away in the dust and darkness of a certain vault might be found jewels that would vie with or possibly eclipse those found in the diamond cave by Sinbad the Sailor. Hidden away in the wooden boxes, it has been said that pearls as large as pigeon's eggs have nestled, their waxen beauty undisturbed by human eyes, whilst diamonds, both great and small, have winked and blinked without awakening a shaft of feminine envy. In this same vault it has been known that parcel after parcel has reposed, whilst hands that placed them there have crumbled into dust, and the mystery connected with them has been lost to this generation forever.[88]

With the help of Treasurer Spinner and his assistants, Briggs was allowed to peek into the "mysterious conglomeration of metal, mortar and stone," as she described the Treasurer's vault. There they did indeed find jewels—pearls and diamonds—that Briggs assumed had been diplomatic gifts, as well as banknotes, counterfeit dies and currency, Confederate bonds, and a bit of the Treasury Building's own history. "Package No. 8 contained the sad relics left by a defaulting Treasury clerk in his desk. The man's name was E. French, and he was assistant disbursing clerk in the Treasury extension. After he had absconded his keys, papers, and money was [sic] safely lodged in the vault. The money consisted of $50 in gold and $2.10 in silver."[89]

By 1880 the storage of silver coins was a serious problem—$1 million in value weighed thirty tons and occupied two hundred cubic feet of space—with storage in the Treasury's

COUNTING CASH IN TREASURY VAULTS

IV-21 After the 1878 Bland Act mandated silver and gold coins, several vaults were built to store $100 million.

basements seemingly the only solution. The following year, the *Washington Post* reported that twenty men guarded a billion dollars in securities, half that amount in bonds and a half million in gold along with several millions in silver, the result of the 1878 Bland Act which mandated silver and gold coins. Six years later the supervising architect's office designed a massive twelve-foot-tall wire cage, eighty-nine feet by fifty-one feet. It was divided into sixteen cells (fourteen were actually built) placed within a steel-walled vault built under the north courtyard, capable of storing $100 million in coins. (fig. IV-21) "A dozen different men will be required to open the vault. Each will have the secret of opening one lock and no more. Besides, by the application of clockwork and electricity to the locks, there will be some of them which will open at certain hours of the day known only to the Treasurer of the United States." It took about six months to fill the vault with silver dollars, transferred from the various mints and sub-treasuries to Washington. The silver vault became an object of great curiosity, with visitors "permitted to walk around the mass of treasury, following a narrow passage which runs between the sides of the box and the steel walls of the vault."[90]

A congressionally appointed committee of experts convened in 1892 to evaluate the Jackson-Rogers-era vaults and safes found them "practically useless." The *Washington Post* paraphrased the report's conclusions. "The vaults in the big Treasury building are characterized as a disgrace to the government and of such obsolete character and inferiority of construction and minimum of security as would cause them to be rejected as unfit for use by any country bank in a backwoods town." The commission credited the Treasury's system of guards as the department's most effective protection. "Any system which keeps the deposits under the eye of any considerable number of persons is the safest possible against all but mob violence."[91]

In 1900, when the Comptroller of the Currency was in dire need of additional vault space and the Treasurer's needs were serious, Supervising Architect James Knox Taylor obtained from Congress a $40,000 appropriation to enlarge their four existing vaults. In the case of the surviving Treasurer's vault, Rogers's wall was left standing, but covered up. In less than a decade, the Treasury's accumulation of bonds, securities, gold, and silver required yet more secure storage space. A new two-story currency vault equipped with steel shelves similar to library stacks was built under the south plaza, its roof at pavement level. Its outer walls were a sandwich of two-foot thick masonry walls followed by a "mat of closely woven steel wires," its inner walls half-inch-thick steel walls. Electrical sensors would trigger alarms when any breeches to the walls or roof occurred.[92]

"Purely Grecian:" The West Facade

Thomas U. Walter designed the west facade to be the Treasury Building's major architectural statement and its ceremonial entrance because it faced the President's House. (fig. IV-22) Walter's west facade was more than an expanded version of the traditional Renaissance central and end pavilions connected by wall curtains. To mark its importance, he framed its central, eight-columned pedimented portico with colonnades to emulate the Capitol's east portico, designed by B. Henry Latrobe and Thomas Jefferson in 1806. Three years before his Treasury design, Walter designed the east porticoes for the Capitol Extension's House and Senate wings with flanking colonnades, but without pediments. (fig. IV-23) Walter's probable goal was architectural unity among the federal buildings, but according to his own tastes and interpretation of historical precedents. In addition to echoing the Capitol feature at the Treasury Building, he replicated a distinctive feature of the 1799 Treasury Office (based on the Propylaea on the Athenian Acropolis), its recessed vestibule behind the south portico. These architectural quotations suggest he synthesized distinctive elements from two of the federal government's founding buildings as an act of national historical memory.

Not unexpectedly, considering the number of architects involved, there were differences of opinion about how to execute the details of Walter's approved design. Rogers redesigned Young's revisions to Walter's west portico, and then built it with input from Clark and Mullett.

IV-22 Walter designed Treasury's west portico to be its grandest because it faced the President's House.

IV-23 Walter based Treasury's west portico on those he designed for the Capitol's House and Senate wings.

IV-24 Rogers believed Treasury's Greek Revival architecture demanded a Greek antefix cornice.

Clark recommended using the crypt beneath the portico's podium for mechanical equipment because it connected to the National Note Bureau's suite of rooms in the south and west basements. He also proposed inserting windows on the podium's north and south sides to increase the room's usefulness. Rogers designed the portico's marble floor with two-foot-square gray tiles from American quarries in Scranton, Pennsylvania, and Glens Falls, New York, to harmonize with the lighter gray granite of the portico's approaches, columns, and walls. Ornamental carver Charles Seltman made the pattern for the spread-winged eagle that decorated the portico's ceiling, probably following a drawing by Bruff. Seltman lived in Washington but was born and trained in Germany.[93]

Rogers made one significant change to Walter's much admired arrangement of the west facade, replacing the tall, Renaissance balustrade with cast-metal ornaments. (fig. IV-24) Rogers called them "acroteria," more properly antefixes, or ornamental slabs in the form of anthemia or palmettes. In classical architecture, antefixes stood along the edges of roofs to conceal the ends of roof tiles. In 1865 Rogers claimed this change was among the first Chase approved soon after he hired the architect in 1862. Rogers's acroteria represented considerable savings in time and material costs, but also remedied the defect of green stains noticeable on the south wing's granite entablature and upper walls caused by oxidized copper leaching from the gutters.[94]

At the beginning of the 1863 building season, when Rogers was concentrating on finishing the west wing's roof and portico, he solicited bids for three hundred twenty-five feet of acroteria combined with gutters made from galvanized iron. The acroteria were in place above the walls in the fall of 1863, and additional ones were ordered in 1864 in preparation for the completion of the portico's roofs. Rogers later

IV-25 The cast metal antefixes, or "acroteria" as Rogers called them, did not oxidize and stain the granite.

defended his first set of acroteria, commenting that they had survived all kinds of weather for two years and the "clean appearance of the west wing cornice (especially when compared with that of the south wing) proved the success of my plan."[95] (fig. IV-25)

In July 1865 newly appointed Assistant Secretary William E. Chandler countermanded Rogers's order to remove the south wing's granite balustrade in preparation for replacing it with acroteria to match the west front. The architect explained his aesthetic and historical rationale. "I also think that every man, who appreciates Grecian Architecture, will agree with me, that the acroteral [sic] ornamentation is more in harmony with the purely Grecian sub-structure, than the massive Roman Bal-

ustrade." Their source, probably suggested by Rogers, was the most famous Greek building with continuous anthemion roof ornaments, the Choragic Monument to Lysicrates, illustrated in James Stuart and Nicholas Revett's *Antiquities of Athens*, the bible of American Greek Revival architects.[96] (fig. IV-26)

Moreover, the palmette form of the acroteria echoes Bruff's anthemion frieze designed for the plaster cornice for the antechamber to the secretary's new office in the west wing. (fig. IV-27) Both are variants on the anthemion frieze, or necking band, of the Ionic order Mills determined would be the Treasury Building's

IV-26 Rogers's ancient authority for his acroterial cornices was the Choragic Monument of Lysicrates.

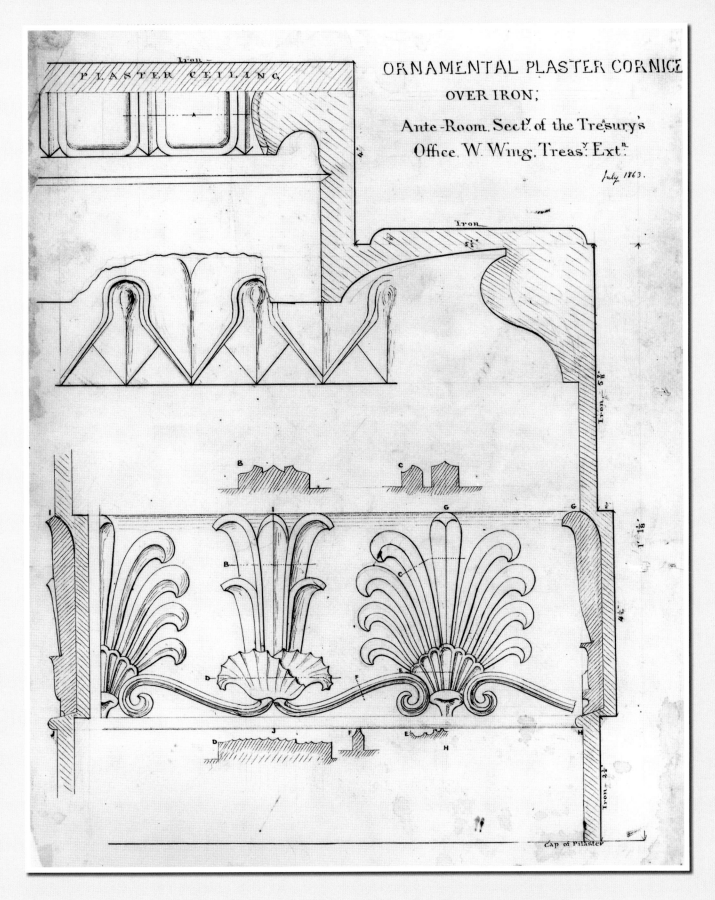

ORNAMENTAL PLASTER CORNICE
OVER IRON;

Ante-Room, Sect.y of the Treasury's
Office, W. Wing, Treas.y Ext.n

July 1863.

IV-27 Variants of Mills's palmette frieze on the east colonnade were used to decorate all four wings.

defining classical motif. While Rogers's acroteria at first seem to be an inappropriate anomaly, they were his attempt to unify the Greek Revival architectural character of all the building's wings. While Bruff freely adapted Roman and Renaissance classical ornamentation in the south wing to include American symbols under Young's superintendence, Rogers required him to be more academically rigorous by adhering to specifically Greek motifs for the west wing.

Tensions between Rogers and Mullett surfaced late in the summer of 1865 over finishing the granite approaches to the western portico. Among the portico's numerous designers must be added the men left in charge when Rogers was traveling, Oertly and Mullett, both of whom revised its designs and ordered materials accordingly. When Chandler made a particularly careful examination of the building's progress, Mullett noted "two separate lots of Granite were ordered, cut, and paid for; and that the work is now being constructed on a different plan." Rogers claimed Mullett ordered the unusable granite; Mullett countered that he supervised construction "in accordance with plans that had been previously approved, and with the preparation of which [he] was neither directly nor indirectly concerned." Mullett continued to criticize his management until Rogers was fired in September 1865.[97]

"Certain Elaborately Ornamented and Elegantly Furnished Rooms:" The Andrew Johnson Suite

Andrew Johnson succeeded President Lincoln on the morning of April 15, 1865, when the president succumbed to the bullet fired by John Wilkes Booth the night before at Ford's Theatre. Five hours after Lincoln's death, President Johnson held his first cabinet meeting in the anteroom south of Treasury Secretary McCulloch's main office. In deference to Mary Todd Lincoln, McCulloch offered this room to Johnson as his temporary office. There, during the next six weeks, the president worked to reassure the American people about the government's stability, met with hundreds of delegations representing all sections of the country, and even held a reception for foreign diplomats. Although Johnson's principal office was in the Treasury, each of the other executive departments reserved a room for his use when conducting business related to those departments. The restored rooms in the Treasury Building are now called the "Andrew Johnson Suite." (fig. IV-28)

The creation of these elaborately decorated rooms in the west wing of the Treasury Building had occurred at the height of the Civil War, reflecting perhaps both the growth of the department and rapidly changing American tastes that favored elegant public interiors befitting the importance of their occupants. Considerably larger than the secretary's previous office in the south wing, the larger suite accommodated the secretary and his immediate staff while several close-by rooms housed assistant secretaries and bureau chiefs. A minor consideration prompting the new offices may have been that the secretary's previous suite in the south wing was tainted by association—it had initially been built for Howell Cobb who joined the Confederacy. (Routinely, the President's House interiors were redecorated with every change in administration to replace old associations with new ones.) Another possibility is that the older southeast offices overlooked Pennsylvania Avenue and the Capitol; the more appropriate symbolic orientation for the secretary's office was overlooking the President's House because the Treasury Department was part of the executive branch. The three rooms in the west wing served as the secretary's suite of offices until 1875 when Secretary Benjamin Bristow moved the principal office back to the south wing, to a room (today numbered 3314) that faces south with a view across the Mall and the Potomac River.

Frank Leslie's Illustrirte Zeitung.

Erster Empfang des diplomatischen Corps durch Präsident Johnson.

IV-28 President Johnson used Secretary McCulloch's office for six weeks after Lincoln's assassination.

How openly the architects discussed considerations regarding his office with Secretary Chase is not known. The west wing's symbolic message differed from the south wing's, conveyed as much through elegant French and English-inspired furnishings as via American symbols cast into its architectural ornament. (fig. IV-29) Bruff's Indian chandeliers were replaced by a standard "new Treasury pattern," a variant of his column capitals that were based on the Great Seal's device. Some were ordered without the eagle while others, including five brackets ordered for the Internal Revenue Bureau, specifically had no olive branches. Rogers wrote Cornelius & Baker that all gas fixtures were to be "furnished only upon Requisitions from this office," apparently to enforce uniformity among the fixtures and to prevent individual bureaus acquiring furnishings without Rogers's or Mullett's knowledge.[98]

Rogers recognized Mullett's considerable talent in interior design and decoration and delegated many aspects of the west wing's finishing to the younger man. For fine furniture, Mullett favored New York and Philadelphia firms that included several émigré interior designers. Many of the building's earlier suppliers were retained, however, including Henry Parry who continued to make fireplace mantels to the department's designs. (fig. IV-30) In mid-October 1863 Rogers sent Parry a sketch of changes because it was "necessary to have the shelf of the Mantle for the secretary's room somewhat longer," possibly because the secretary's south-office mirror was to be moved to the west wing. The building's heating contractors, Hayward, Bartlett &

Above: IV-29 The "Johnson Suite," designed to be the secretary's permanent offices, was elegantly restored in 1989.

Left: IV-30 Henry Parry provided the mantel for the Johnson Suite, its symbols relating to Treasury's functions.

Company of Baltimore, furnished a special "heating apparatus for the private Rooms of the Secretary" that included a separate boiler to heat water for his bathtub.[99]

Sometime late in the summer of 1863, new players entered on front center stage—the New York decorating firm of Pottier & Stymus. They quickly became one of the country's leading interior design firms specializing in lavish furnishings for prestigious private and public clients. On September 29, on Mullett's orders, the firm sent Chase a detailed estimate for "Furniture, Curtains, Carpets, Pier Mirrors & Cornices" for his new office suite. The estimate for furnishing three rooms, the "Blue Room," immediately north of the west portico and the "Drab & Green Room" south of it and its adjoining "Chamber & Bath Room," was accompanied by a sketch. (fig. IV-31) Pottier & Stymus planned the placement of desks, chairs, sofas, bookcases, mirrors, and even a bedstead for those occasions when the secretary remained overnight in the building. The sketch's surprising revelation was Rogers's annexation of the upper story of the outdoor vestibule to create the two antechambers. The Drab and Green Room had a clear view of the east end of the President's House and gardens.[100]

Although well within the current American taste for French-inspired furnishings, the timing of Pottier & Stymus's September estimate and order could hardly have been worse in that season of labor strife. The Treasury's workmen went on strike on October 12 after Rogers lengthened their workday and shortened their dinner hour (to hasten completion of the west wing) without any corresponding rise in wages. Yet, Pottier & Stymus proposed and Rogers agreed to provide Secretary Chase with a "large Walnut Book Case Best French Plate Glass," fourteen feet in width at a cost of $750; to cover

IV-31 Pottier & Stymus's sketch plan placed their furniture in the secretary's three rooms.

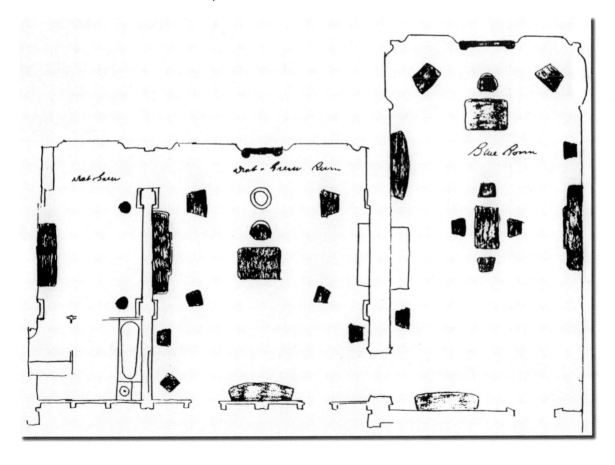

his windows with "4 sets of Blue Cloth Window Curtains Lined with silicia [sic] Interlined with Canton flannell [sic] full silk and worsted Trimmings" for $580; and to lay on his floors "115 yds Blue Star Wilton Carpet" for $404. In reality, the total expense of $5,158.44 to furnish these three rooms was not monstrous, just quite expensive. Presumably, Rogers and the department considered it a necessary expense to express the secretary's and the department's prestige. On October 16 Rogers sent Pottier & Stymus drawings of the rooms "for which carpeting has been ordered by the Hon. Secretary of the Treasury." A month later Mullett sent the decorators a revised plan "showing some variations in the size and arrangements, from the plan previously furnished" of the three rooms because they were altered while under construction.[101]

While Mullett was away during the middle of the winter, Chase visited his proposed new office rooms. His response was immediate and negative.

> I have to express my decided disapprobation of the expense you have incurred in finishing them; they are in my opinion entirely too ornate for a Public Office, and a violation of that Republican simplicity I desire you to observe in finishing and furnishing this Building. You will therefore make the necessary changes.
>
> I also disapprove of the Bath arrangements you have introduced, and you will therefore remove them.[102]

Chase's distinction between "finishing and furnishing" may be an important one; at the beginning of February 1864, Chase could only have seen Mullett's wall and ceiling treatments. The department was obliged to honor its contract with Pottier & Stymus and the furnishing work continued unabated. The furniture and carpets were shipped on February 24, but the arrival of the installation crew led by Stymus was delayed by a few days because the rooms were not ready. Mullett and Rogers were also juggling the work of other contractors providing different decorative elements for the suite. When screens—manufactured by Hayward, Bartlett to shield the bathtub's boiler from causing accidental burns—did not fit properly, Mullett required their replacement. Early in March Rogers complained the "French Looking Glass plate for the Secretary's room," arrived with its silver backing damaged and he wanted it replaced. Pottier & Stymus's final bill for $5,587.72 included more furniture than their original estimate as well as Stymus's traveling expenses. Ball, Black & Company of New York supplied some of the chandeliers of an unknown design for the secretary's suite; Rogers declined to pay $5 extra to Cornelius & Baker for gilding the eagles on their chandeliers.[103]

Assistant Secretary Field, who occupied the "Drab and Green" room, ordered particularly elaborate furnishings. Its carpet was possibly Bigelow's Brussels design number 704 in green, ordered from Alexander J. Stewart's Broadway store in early February 1863. On March 17 Mullett ordered from Pottier & Stymus "a Mahogany Sofa, for the room to be occupied by the Hon. M.B. Field, Asst. Secretary of the Treasury, to be covered with Green Reps. of such a shade as you may consider most desirable." The chairs formerly in Chase's south wing office were reupholstered for Field's use. "I have concluded to adopt your suggestion of recovering the chairs now used by the Secretary of the Treasury with Green-Reps, and having a Sofa made to correspond with them, as ordered above. You will therefore please forward Reps, Gimp, and nails sufficient to cover 12 chairs, and of the same materials as you will use on the Sofa." Mullett was initially even willing to ship the chairs to New York, but withdrew the order for the sofa, "as it is quite probable that we will not need it." In early May Field visited Pottier & Stymus's

New York showrooms and ordered his sofa "which will be put in hand & finished at once—the cost will be somewhat more than those we are making for Mr. Harrington & others, owing to the advance of Materials & Labour [sic]."[104]

In March 1864 Rogers wrote Chase that escalating furnishing costs were affecting the congressional appropriations to complete the building. "From September 28, 1861 to September 30, 1863, the expenditures for furniture, partly bought in open market, but mostly prepared by our Cabinetmakers, all of it for the Treasury Extension, and paid for out of the appropriation for the construction of the building, amounted to $58,734.15." A congressional act approved on March 14, 1864, stipulated that specific monies would be appropriated for furnishing government offices, allotting $25,000 for the Treasury building. Prior to that date, each of the Treasury's bureaus paid for its own furniture from its contingent funds, most of which was made in the department's carpenter shop. Rogers alerted Chase that between September 10, 1863 and March 14, 1864, "the expenditures for furniture have been $39,006," or more than $6,000 per month. Moreover, "there is not only no abatement in the demand for all sorts of costly furniture, but the demand is steadily increasing." Because the Treasury's $25,000 furniture allotment had been spent, construction funds were being charged and Rogers was very concerned.[105]

Chase added to this financial drain. At the end of March the secretary's offices were ready, but his occupancy was delayed. "The Secretary desires a change of carpet in his blue room, the one now down being too intensely blue to satisfy him, and wishes me to procure some patterns for his inspection." Rogers requested several samples to allow Chase a selection, but thought "a small blue figure upon some light ground" would be appropriate. Six weeks later, on June 30, Lincoln accepted Chase's resignation—the fourth he had tendered—all over control of

the department's appointments. That same day Congress passed a revision to the Internal Revenue Act, which increased taxes to pay for the war following a string of Confederate victories led by Robert E. Lee that resulted in heavy Union losses.[106]

Field recounted Chase's ambivalence about changing the location of his office.

> When speaking of Mr. Chase's Presidential aspirations, I am reminded, as Mr. Lincoln used to say, of a little story. When I first went to Washington, the Secretary occupied for his office a room on the south side of the Treasury building, with a beautiful outlook down the Potomac. Soon afterward it was proposed that he should remove to certain elaborately ornamented and elegantly furnished rooms on the west side of the building, which had been arranged for his occupation by Mr. Mullett, the architect of the Department. Mr. Chase had consented to make the change; but after the new rooms were ready he delayed removing. Several times he appointed a day to do so, but when the time came he had changed his mind. One afternoon, while he was still hesitating, I was standing with him at one of the windows of the largest of the new rooms which faced the Executive Mansion. Turning to me, he asked me to assign one sufficient reason why he should change his quarters. I told him that there was at least one obvious advantage in the exchange, that that was, if he should come to these offices, he would *always be able to keep his eye upon the White House!*[107]

Annotations on Pottier & Stymus's July 1864 invoice assigned each piece of furniture ordered to individuals or bureaus. (fig. IV-32) Field's mahogany sofa upholstered in green reps cost $110, but his "best plate mirror" mantel frame was considerably more expensive at $230.

IV-32 Pottier & Stymus identified the elegant furnishings they provided for individual Treasury officers.

While both Rogers and Mullett were away from Washington in early September, Samuel F. Carr served as the acting supervising architect. He sent Pottier & Stymus a particularly telling order for yet more furniture. "I desire to procure for the Register of the Treasury, one Mahogany arm chair, with a covered open-work back, precisely similar to the one used by Assistant Secretary Field, with the exception of *black* leather seat instead of *green* as is his." Carr closed with the plea: "Please forward it at the *earliest day possible*."[108]

While the Treasury's workmen were having difficulty housing and feeding their families, and the Civil War was at a critical juncture, there was frenzied competition among the department's bureau heads and clerks for the most impressive office furnishings. This may well reflect a response, understandable if not admirable, to the intense stresses the Treasury workforce encountered daily. During the period of the greatest escalation of furniture costs, Chase was overtly trying to wrest the Republican nomination for the 1864 election away from Lincoln. During the same months, the Union seemed destined to lose the war; if Washington were captured, the Treasury's officers and clerks would lose their jobs, perhaps their lives. Rogers and Mullett were fortunate in being able to travel annually to northern and western cities (at the government's expense) where a few government buildings were still under construction. Most Treasury employees had to stay in the overcrowded city where Washington's traditionally gracious pace of life had changed dramatically, and permanently, many judged. Moreover, they worked in a seriously overcrowded building under hundreds of watchful military and police eyes protecting not them, but their workplace and its new product—currency. Seen from this perspective, the expenditure of large amounts of public monies on furnishings may be a barometer of the department's collective mental state.

Mullett probably played some role in promoting the legislation of March 1866 which aimed to standardize furnishings throughout the Treasury's offices. By that time he acknowledged as excessive the $93,114.50 spent to furnish seventeen offices in the past two years. Additional furniture for the secretary's office totaled $18,960.60 during those two years, was followed closely by $17,025.90 for the Treasurer's office, with only the Attorney General, First Auditor, Sixth Auditor, and Commissioner of Customs, modest in their needs. Mullett explained the situation to McCulloch and suggested a remedy.

> All Requisitions for furniture have been duly honored, but at no time has this Office had any Knowledge as to the *positive necessity* for such. It is believed that for want of proper supervision of the matter by some person who could personally examine into the actual wants of the different Offices for furniture, the demands have been unnecessarily large in many instances, especially in ordering very expensive desks, &c., causing an expenditure which might have been avoided. This system has been a source of much annoyance and interruption to the regular business of this Office, requiring much additional clerical labor in recording the many requisitions and keeping proper account of the furniture supplied to the various Bureaux [*sic*].[109]

Mullett's solution was to turn all matters relating to the building's furnishings over to the building's superintendent, the officer responsible for its daily upkeep. Moreover, he decreed that the future manufacture and repair of furniture be done solely by the cabinet shop. "Among the advantages to be obtained by this arrangement, would be the power to transfer *furniture* without controversy from one Bureau to another as may be necessary: the adoption of a uniform system and style, instead of indulging the fancies of each clerk; and I believe to greatly increased economy." For whatever reason, competition among the employees to enrich their surroundings apparently ended when the war was over.[110]

"The Disgraceful Isolation of Grounds:" Landscaping the West Wing's Site

Oertly claimed the "West Front of the Treasury building is altogether one of the happiest architectural conceptions known," his rationale for a new landscape design of excellent quality facing the President's House. The site's major problem became evident in 1857 when Bowman excavated the west wing's basement and sub-basement to connect with those of the south wing. He excavated only as far westward as necessary to build the west portico's foundations. That the adjacent President's Grounds were considerably higher than the Treasury Building's established ground plane remained an unresolved quandary. Moreover, the ground level at the building's north end was about twenty feet higher than the south end.[111] (fig. IV-33)

Sometime in the spring or early summer of 1863, Rogers set up in his office "a large model of the whole building, with its approaches and grounds" to demonstrate succinctly his proposed changes to its site. A complicating factor was the military encampment in the grounds south and west of the Treasury. In April 1862 Spencer Clark asked General Decimus Wadsworth to move the two companies of Pennsylvania cavalry who were "quartered on the President's grounds immediately contiguous to the Treasury Building." Not only were their temporary barracks in the way of a private road Clark wanted to construct between the Treasury Building and the President's House, "their removal will become a sanative necessity as the warm weather approaches, for the healthfulness" of their occupants.[112]

Grading the entire area could not be realistically undertaken until all the troops were gone, a congressional appropriation secured, and a suitable design solution found. In early April 1865 Rogers drew up for Beals & Dixon a list of the granite needed for the west and north wings' area walls and their balustrade. Late in the month he sought McCulloch's instructions because there was not enough money to cover these costs without another congressional appropriation. Part of the difficult design problem was public and departmental access to the basement levels agreeable to all parties. Yet Secretary McCulloch and President Johnson jointly "expressed a desire of having the steps of, and the grounds in Front of the West Portico of this building, appropriately finished." In the very midst of this project, Rogers was dismissed in September 1865—a tale to be told in chapter five. Oertly was temporarily placed in charge of the Treasury construction. When the two large caps for its buttress piers arrived in mid-October, Oertly reported that the "whole of the Portico, steps and platform" would be completed as soon as they were set.[113]

Yet, no final landscape and areaway design had been chosen. At the end of October, Oertly explained the difficulties when he submitted his design for their completion. He considered Rogers's plan for the grounds "grand, of easy comprehension, [and] exhibiting the structure to its fullest advantage." It had not been approved when he was fired and McCulloch suspended all his designs. Oertly's solution was a modification of Rogers's design, differing only in the treatment of the areaways. Rogers specified expensive flagging for their pavement while Oertly proposed plainer, less expensive paving similar to what was being laid on some of Washington's streets. In late October McCulloch alerted Oertly that President Johnson approved his design "except that portion of it relating to the

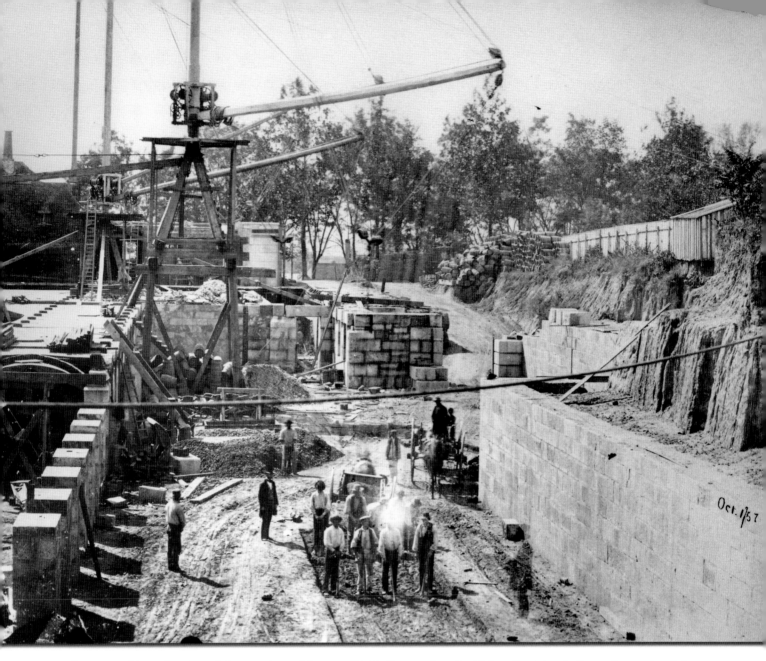

IV-33 Connecting the higher President's Grounds, on the right, to Treasury's grounds was a difficult problem.

enclosure and iron fencing of the portion with a granite Balustrade."[114]

Oertly either sold, or had torn down, several frame buildings that were impeding the progress of the road intended to connect Pennsylvania Avenue on the Treasury's south side at the intersection of 15th Street, and the north side facing Lafayette Square. This route was initially planned as a ceremonial entrance for distinguished visitors to the President's House and the Treasury Building, as well as a service road to provide access to the Treasury's basement levels. Including its brick sidewalks, the macadamized road was to be seventy feet wide, its grade "will be very gentle, say 2 feet in the hundred. It will be closed for public use, after business hours, by gates at either end, and the traffic on it will be subject to the regulations of the Department."[115]

Grading the road was well underway late in the fall of 1865. Over the winter Oertly prepared for its completion by designing the gates and advertising for North River flagging for its sidewalks. When Mullett replaced Oertly at the end of March 1866, he moved quickly to finish the landscaping and took over two parts of the project that Oertly had underway—the terraces and the fountain—and worked with Oertly on fences and gates for the north entrances and one replacing Bruff's south gates.[116]

Oertly struggled with the department's policy of enforcing "strict economy" versus the "dictates of taste" over the terrace and parterre design. He estimated Rogers's design would cost more than $15,000. In mid-April 1866 Mullett sent Beals & Dixon sketches for the coping and bases for the west parterre balustrade and those for his new design for the south terrace. Within a month, Mullett asked Architect of the Capitol Edward Clark (who succeeded Walter in 1865) to send him "marble-curb (for flour-beds [sic]) as per the accompanying sketch. There are 340 lineal feet of the same required for straight borders and 180 lineal feet for circular borders." On June 6 the *Evening Star* noted the "west front of the Treasury, recently completed, is among the finest architectural ornaments of the Capital. Sixteenth street [soon renamed 15 ½ Street, now East Executive Avenue] is being opened and graded past this front, between it and the President's grounds, and elegant little parterres of shrubs and flowers are arranged on either side of the granite steps leading to the entrance." The department took particular pride in its grounds. In 1903 it was noted that the "Treasury building is the only place in the city where the plants are set out by the employees of the building," the geraniums arriving there earlier than elsewhere.[117]

Successive fountain designs located on the edge of the President's Grounds opposite the West portico were part of the lengthy transition between Rogers and Mullett. (fig. IV-34) At the end of June 1865, Rogers sent Beals & Dixon a drawing made by Bruff of the fountain's basin, each of its twelve pieces to be hammered to number one, or rough, finish. Rough uncut granite pieces for the fountain were delivered in late October. Whether statuary or a water jet was to rise from the center of the fifty-foot-diameter fountain was yet to be decided. The following April Mullett designed a second foun-

tain, ordering from Beals & Dixon granite "cut as per patterns to be furnished by this Office." The dimensions of individual stones for both fountains were substantially the same, except Mullett ordered ten curved pieces at a total cost of $10,000. Thousands of sightseers came on June 12, 1866, to see Mullett's fountain turned on, "one of the most attractive features" of the new landscape. Three vertical jets rose from a central parachute surrounded by six revolving jets that threw water out at a forty-five degree angle.[118]

On June 20 Mullett sent McCulloch a plan showing the arrangement of the granite posts upon which the entrance gates—a replacement for one facing Pennsylvania Avenue at 15th Street and a new one overlooking Lafayette Square—would sit. He noted that the south one would "remedy the disgraceful absence of all design at present so conspicuous to all observers. I believe the interests of the Department and the appearance of the building imperatively demand the change, and would respectfully request authority to carry out the proposed arrangement." Bruff, the designer of the original gates, was still employed in the supervising architect's office, but tastes had veered away from his rather quirky and robust designs popular less than a decade earlier. Mullett revised his design for the north gate in response to a suggestion made by McCulloch.[119] (fig. IV-35)

In as much as the Entrance gates opposite 16th Street cannot be seen but from a short distance, the posts ought to be of smaller dimensions than those on 15th Street where they are exposed to view at the end of a long and magnificent vista.[120]

The new south gates were particularly noted by an *Evening Star* reporter.

Under the superintendence of the Supervising Architect of the Treasury (Mr. A.B.

IV-34 Mullett's elegant landscape linked the Treasury to the President's House visually and physically.

IV-35 McCulloch suggested to Mullett that the Treasury's north gateposts be lower than its south ones.

Mullett,) considerable improvements are being made about the Executive Mansion and grounds. The gateways at the head of the avenue (just south of the Treasury building,) have been removed to give way to a handsome group of gates—three pairs for carriages, the largest in the center, and two pairs for foot passengers. From this point on the south side of the Treasury building there will be a roadway of the best material and most approved construction, which is already being extended between the building and the Executive Mansion. It will be flanked by flag footways, which are bordered by grass plats and flower beds. The outlet is directly opposite Madison (or 15 ½ street,) where massive gates of granite and iron, of the same style, are being placed.[121]

The construction of the Treasury Building not only continued, it accelerated through some of the most challenging years in the history of the United States and of its capital city. Just as the completion of the Capitol dome is often seen as emblematic of the Union's victory, the completion of the west wing of the Treasury Building reflected the increase in size and functions of the federal bureaucracy that both emerged from, and helped to win, the war. ⚷

1 Secretary of the Treasury, *Report on the State of the Finances,* 42nd Cong., 2d sess., 1871, H. Ex. Doc. 2, 404.

2 Elden E. Billings, "Social and Economic Conditions in Washington during the Civil War," *RCHS* 63-65 (1965), 198.

3 Secretary of the Treasury, *Report on the State of the Finances,* 35th Cong., 1st sess., 1857, S. Doc. 1, 120–1. "Treasury Extension," *Evening Star,* August 15, 1857, 3; October 12, 1857, 3; October 29, 1857, 3; December 26, 1857, 3. Secretary of the Treasury, *Report on the State of the Finances,* 35th Cong., 2d sess., 1858, S. Ex. Doc. 2, 110–2.

4 Secretary of the Treasury, *Report in Answer to a Resolution of the Senate,* 35th Cong., 2d sess., 1859, S. Ex. Doc. 41, 1–10. Secretary of the Treasury, *Report on the State of the Finances,"* 36th Cong., 1st sess., 1859, S. Ex. Doc. 3, 122.

5 Young to Cobb, September 30, 1860; Young to Chase, September 30, 1861; both box 2437, entry 26, RG 121, NACP.

6 [John Nicolay] to unknown recipient, April 19, 1861, in Helen Nicolay, *Our Capital on the Potomac* (New York: Century Company, 1924), 363.

7 Ernest B. Furgurson, *Freedom Rising, Washington in the Civil War* (New York: Alfred A. Knopf, 2004), 8; 25. Cobb's two immediate successors served just under three months before Lincoln appointed Chase.

8 Furgurson, *Freedom Rising,* 26.

9 Ibid., 33.

10 Charles P. Stone, "The Capital in Danger," *Washington Post,* June 8, 1884, 6.

11 Ibid.

12 Clark to Capt. Morris S. Miller, February 7, 1861, reel 4, entry 7, RG 121, NACP. Wolff, *Capitol Builder,* 773. Charles P. Stone, "Washington in March and April, 1861," *Magazine of American History,* 14 (July–December 1885): 11. Bruff's Diary, passim.

13 L. E. Chittenden, *Recollections of President Lincoln and His Administration* (New York: Harper & Brothers, 1891), 112.

14 "The Treasury Department," *Evening Star,* April 22, 1861, 2.

15 "Barricading Building," April, 1862, box 1437, entry 26, RG 121, NACP. Chief of Engineers, [list of furniture], June 5, 1861, box 1438, entry 26, RG 121, NACP. Young to E. Robinson & Co., August 15, 1861, vol. 1, entry 13, RG 121, NACP. "Draft of Expenditures," n.d., box 1437, entry 26, RG 121, NACP. Mullett to Chase, November 16, 1863, reel 7; Rogers to [illegible] War Department, April 12, 1865, reel 8; both entry 7, RG 121, NACP.

16 "The Purpose of Concentrating Troops Here," *Evening Star,* April 23, 1861, 2. "Resignations," *Evening Star,* July 31, 1861, 2. Clark to Harrington, July 18; August 1, 1861, reel 5, entry 7, RG 121, NACP. Young to Chase, August 24, 1861, vol. 1, entry 13, RG 121, NACP.

17 Young to foremen, August 26, 1861, vol. 1, entry 13, RG 121, NACP. "Sent to the Old Capitol Prison," and "Rebel Prisoners," *Evening Star,* August 28, 1862, 2. Young to Chase, September 1, 1863, reel 7; Clark to Harrington, October 13, 1861, reel 5; both entry 7, RG 121, NACP.

18 Clark to Harrington, October 13, 1861, reel 5, entry 7, RG 121, NACP.

19 Rogers to Dougherty, January 1, 1863, vol. 2, entry 13, RG 121, NACP.

20 Krouse to Clark, December 26, 1862, box 1439, entry 26, RG 121, NACP.

21 Harrington to Heads of Bureaus, April 16, 1861, Letters Sent Relating to Treasury Department Administration, entry 30 (hereafter cited as entry 30), RG 56, NACP. Marcus Benjamin, "The Military Situation in Washington in 1861," in Benjamin, ed., *Washington During War Time,* 17; 23.

22 Assistant Adjutant General to Commissioner of Public Buildings, September 2, 1862, entry 1, RG 42, NAB. James S. Wadsworth, "Circular," September 3, 1862, box 1439, entry 26, RG 121, NACP.

23 Mark M. Boatner III, *The Civil War Dictionary,* (New York: David McKay Company, 1988), 255–6. Harrington, Order, July 12, 1864, entry 30, RG 56, NACP.

24 Harrington to N. Sargent, June 15, 1864, entry 30, RG 56, NACP. Rogers to Harrington, August 10, 1864; Rogers to M.B. Field, August 10, 1864; both reel 8, entry 7, RG 121, NACP.

25 Field to bureau chiefs, August 15, 1864, entry 30, RG 56, NACP. Rogers, "Estimate of Cost," August 20, 1864, reel 8, entry 7, RG 121, NACP. "The Treasury Clerks Regiment," *Evening Star,* August 24, 1864, 3. "News from Washington," *New York Times,* August 23, 1864, 1.

26 Harrington to Second Auditor, August 23, 1864, entry 30, RG 56, NACP. "Treasury Regiment," *Evening Star,* December 16, 1864, 3.

27 Young to West, December 30, 1861; April 21, 1862, vol 2, entry 13; Monthly Report, February 1, 1862, box 1439, entry 26; Clark to Chase, February 10, 1862, reel 5, entry 7; all RG 121, NACP.

28 Chase to unknown recipient, March 29, 1862, box 1441, entry 26, RG 121, NACP.

29 Chase to unknown recipient, March 29, 1862, box 1441; Oertly, Estimate, April 23, 1862, box 1439; Harrington to Clark, May 10, 1862, box 1441; all entry 26, RG 121, NACP.

30 Beals & Dixon to Clark, June 3, 1861, box 1438; Young to Beals & Dixon, May 15, 1862, box 1441; both entry 26, RG 121, NACP. "News from Washington," *New York Times,* May 22, 1862, 5. Monthly Report, July 1, 1862, box 1441; Monthly Report, June 1, 1862, box 1439; both entry 26, RG 121, NACP.

31 Carl Sandburg, *Abraham Lincoln, The War Years* (Boston: Charles Scribners Sons, 1950) 4: 105. Mark Nely claims 1,195 of 1,520 presidential officers were removed, www.mrlincolnandfriends.org, 30; Lincoln to Chase, May 8, 1861, www.mrlincolnandfriends. org; (accessed January 13, 2008). William Morris Davis et al to Chase, July 15, 1861, box 1437, entry 26, RG 121, NACP.

32 "News from Washington," *New York Times,* February 13, 1862, 8. House Committee on Expenditures on Public Buildings, *Expenditures on Public Buildings,* 37th Cong., 2d sess., 1862, H. Rep. 137, 1.

33 "News from Washington," *New York Times,* February 13, 1862, 8.

34 *Expenditures,* 1862, 1. "Expenditures on Public Buildings," *New York Times,* July 15, 1862, 2.

35 *Expenditures,* 1862, 6.

36 Ibid., 30–2.

37 Ibid., 8.

38 Chase to Rogers, June 10, 1862, "Isaiah Rogers," entry 213, RG 56, NACP.

39 Chase to Rogers, July 23, 1862, entry 213, "Isaiah Roger," RG 56; Walton to Chase, June 28, 1862, "Ammi B. Young," entry 213, RG 56; both NACP. "The Treasury Extension," *New York Times,* July 15, 1862, 5. Chase to Young, July 24, 1862, "Ammi B. Young," entry 213, RG 56, NACP.

40 Chase to Rogers, June 10 (two letters), July 23, and July 24, 1862, "Isaiah Rogers," entry 213, RG 56; both NACP.

41 "Our Special Washington Dispatches," *New York Times,* July 27, 1862, 4.

42 Mayer and Carson to Chase, July 24, 1862, reel 20, Salmon P. Chase Papers, Manuscript Division, LC (hereafter cited as Chase Papers). Rogers to Handy, n.d., vol. 2, entry 13, RG 121, NACP.

43 Secretary of the Treasury, *Report on the State of the Finances,"* 38th Cong., 1st sess., 1863, H. Ex. Doc., 3. 136.

44 D. Mullett Smith, *A.B. Mullett: His Relevance in American Architecture and Historic Preservation* (Washington, D. C.: Mullett-Smith Press, 1990), 100.

45 Chase to Mullett, October 21, 1861, "Letters Sent Relating to Appointments, Removals, and Other Personnel Matters," vol. 1, entry 31, RG 56, NACP. Mullett to Chase, June 14, 1862, reel 21, Chase Papers.

46 Smith, *A.B. Mullett,* 101–2.

47 Billings, "Washington," 193. Rogers to Chase, March 7, 1863, reel 5; Rogers, Advertisement, n.d., reel 6, both entry 7, RG 121, NACP.

48 "A Strike at the Treasury Extension," *Evening Star,* October 12, 1863, 3.

49 "Fatal Casualty at the Treasury Department," *National Intelligencer,* October 22, 1863, 2. "The Treasury Extension Strike," *Evening Star,* November 5, 1863, 1.

50 Mullett to Chase, November 2, 1863, reel 7, entry 7, RG 121, NACP.

51 "The Strike at the Treasury Extension," *Evening Star,* November 3, 1863, 3; and November 4, 1863, 3.

52 "News from Washington," *New York Times,* November 4, 1863, 4.

53 "The Treasury Extension Strike," *Evening Star,* November 5, 1863, 3. "News from Washington," *New York Times,* November 5, 1863, 4.

54 "The Adjourned Meeting of the Strikers at the Treasury Extension," *Evening Star,* November 7, 1863, 3.

55 Rogers to foremen, November 19, 1863, reel 7, entry 7, RG 121, NACP.

56 Tyler Dennett, ed., *Lincoln and the Civil War and the Diaries and Letters of John Hay* (New York: Dodd, Mead & Company, 1939), 99.

57 John Jay Knox, *United States Notes* (New York: Charles Scribner's Son, 1884), 84. Young to North, August 19, 1861, reel 5, entry 7, RG 121, NACP. Jesse Stiller, "Bureau of Engraving and Printing," in Kurian, *A Historical Guide,* 200. C. M. Walker to G. Rodman, November 26, 1861, Office Files of the Appointments Division, box 1, entry 207, RG 56, NACP.

58 Clark to Howard, February 6 and 18, 1862, reel 5, entry 7, RG 121, NACP.

59 Clark to Howard, April 13, 1862, reel 5, entry 7, RG 121, NACP.

60 Treasury Department, *History of the Bureau of Engraving and Printing, 1862–1962* (Washington: Government Printing Office, 1962), 3, 5. S.M. Clark, *First Division, National Currency Bureau* (Washington: Government Printing Office, 1864), 104–9.

61 Rogers to Cornelius & Baker, June 19, 1863, reel 6, entry 7, RG 121, NACP.

62 Mullett to Chase, September 29, 1863, reel 6, entry 7, RG 121, NACP. Chase to Mullett, September 30, 1863, box 1447, entry 26, RG 121, NACP. Mullett to Chase, October 2, 1863, reel 6, entry 7, RG 121, NACP.

63 Chase to Mullett, October 8, 1863, box 1444, entry 26, RG 121, NACP.

64 Mullett to Chase, October 8, 1863, reel 6, box 1447, entry 26, RG 121, NACP.

65 "The New Treasury Building," *National Intelligencer,* October 31, 1863, 3. Rogers to Chase, October 9, 1863, reel 6, entry 7, RG 121, NACP.

66 "Fatal Accident at the Treasury Department," *Evening Star,* October 21, 1863, 3.

67 Rogers to Chase, October 21, 1863, reel 6, entry 7, RG 121, NACP.

68 Rogers to Dougherty, January 1, 1863, vol. 2, entry 13; Rogers to Harrington, May 30, 1864, reel 7, entry 7; both RG 121, NACP.

69 House Select Committee, *Treasury Department,* 38th Cong., 1st sess., 1864, H. Rep. 140. "Investigation into the Affairs of the Treasury Department," *Evening Star,* July 1, 1864, 1.

70 "A Ramble Through the Treasury Vaults," *Evening Star,* July 1, 1867, 1.

71 Secretary of the Treasury, *Report on the State of the Finances,* 40th Cong., 2d sess., 1868, H. Ex. Doc. 2, 184.

72 "Bureau of Construction Employees," March 13, 1861, vol. 4, entry 6, RG 121, NACP.

73 *Congressional Globe,* 40th Cong., 3d sess., March 3, 1869, 314.

74 Guthrie to L.D. Campbell, April 3, 1856, reel 2; Bowman to W. Medill, December 14, 1857, reel 2; Young to Frederick H. North, August 31, 1861, reel 5; Clark to G.R. Jackson Company, April 29, 1862, reel 5; Clark to W.F. Nisbet, April 28, 1862, reel 5; all entry 7, RG 121, NACP.

75 Clark to Chase, January 23, 1862, reel 5, entry 7; Clark to James Pollock, March 8, 1862, box 1439, entry 26; Clark to F. H. North, April 11, 1862, reel 5, entry 7; Oertly, Estimate, April 26, 1862, box 1439, entry 26; Clark to Chase, January 23, 1862, reel 5, entry 7; all RG 121, NACP.

76 "Proposals Will Be Received," *Evening Star,* April 13, 1863, 3. Rogers to Harrington, May 11, 1863, reel 5; Rogers to Bellamy, May, 12, 1863, reel 6; Rogers to Chase, June 26, 1863, reel 6; Chase to Dodds, August 13, 1863, reel 7; all entry 7, RG 121, NACP.

77 North to Rogers, May 7, 1862, box 1444, entry 26; Mullett to Chase, August 18, 1863, reel 7, entry 7, Rogers to Chase, June 26, 1863, reel 6; all RG 121, NACP.

78 Rogers to Jackson, September 2, 1863, reel 7, entry 7, RG 121, NACP.

79 Rogers to Jackson, September 17, 1863, reel 7, entry 7, RG 121, NACP.

80 Rogers to Jackson, October 3, 1863, reel 6, entry 7, RG 121, NACP.

81 Rogers to Jackson, October 19 and 22, 1863, reel 6, entry 7, RG 121, NACP.

82 Rogers to Jackson, February 8, 1864, reel 7, entry 7; Jackson to Rogers, February 27, 1864, box 1448, entry 26; Rogers to Jackson–Burnet, March 22, 1864, reel 7, entry 7; all RG 121, NACP.

83 Rogers to Chase, February 12 and 26, 1864, reel 7, entry 7;. Rogers to Chase, February 29, 1864, box 1449, entry 26; both RG 121, NACP.

84 Mullett to Jackson-Burnet, March 30, 1864; Rogers to Bellamy, April 4, 1864; Rogers to Jackson, April 15, 1864; all reel 7, entry 7, RG 121, NACP.

85 Rogers to Jackson-Burnet, April 21, 1864, reel 7; Rogers to Bellamy, April 21, 1864, reel 7; Rogers to Bellamy, several letters between July 22 and Sept. 22, 1864, reel 8; all entry 7, RG 121, NACP.

86 "Experiment Lock Picking at the Treasury Department," *Evening Star,* August 23, 1869, 4.

87 Rogers, Proposal, March 4, 1864; Rogers to Jackson, May 7 and 8, 1864; both reel 7, entry 7, RG 121, NACP. Smith, Gray & Company Building Designation Report, 4, www.nyc.gov/html/lpc/downloads/pdf/reports/smith_gray_bldg.pdf - 2005-08-03 (accessed January 13, 2008). Rogers to Chase, May 25, 1864, reel 7, entry 7; Chase to Rogers, May 26, 1864, box 1449, entry 26; Rogers to Chase, May 28 and 30, 1864, reel 7, entry 7; Rogers to Parry, November 5, 1864, reel 7, entry 7; all RG 121, NACP.

88 Emily Edson Briggs, *The Olivia Letters* (New York: Neale Publishing Company, 1906), 223.

89 Ibid., 225, 228.

90 "The Storing of Silver Coin," *Washington Post,* November 13, 1880, 3. "The Better Guarding of the Treasury," *Washington Post,* May 14, 1881, 4. "A Great Money Vault," *Washington Post,* June 4, 1887, 1. "Filling the Silver Vault," *Washington Post,* August 28, 1888, 2. "Silver Dollars Ten Feet Deep," *Washington Post,* August 30, 1888, 6. "New Treasury Vaults," *Washington Post,* September 16, 1900, 28.

91 "All the Vaults Insecure," *Washington Post,* April 13,1892, 1. "Treasury Vaults Unsafe," *Washington Post,* January 29, 1894, 6.

92 "Bureaus Plead for Room," *Washington Post,* January 22, 1900, 4. "New Vaults for Treasury," *Washington Post,* August 29, 1900, 9. "The Last Word in Vaults Now Protects $300,000,000 in Fifteenth Street," *Washington Post,* June 27, 1909, SM2.

93 Clark to Rogers, September 11, 1863, box 1447, entry 26; List of Proposals, September 19, 1863, reel 6, entry 7; Seltman, Invoice, January 7, 1863, box 1446, entry 26; all RG 121, NACP.

94 Rogers to Chandler, July 14, 1865, reel 9, entry 7, RG 121, NACP.

95 Proposal, April 11, 1863, reel 5, entry 7; Synopsis of Bids, May 6, 1863, box 1443, entry 26; Contract, May 30, 1863, box 1434, entry 26; Rogers to Moorhead, June 16, 1863, reel 6, entry 7; Rogers to Moorhead, June 9, 1864, reel 7, entry 7; Rogers to Chandler, July 14, 1865, reel 9, entry 7; all RG 121, NACP.

96 Rogers to Chandler, July 14, 1865, reel 9, entry 7; Seltman, Invoice, April 27, 1863, box 1447, entry 26; Seltman, Invoice, August 4, 1864, box 1449, entry 26; all RG 121, NACP.

97 Mullett to Chandler, August 4, 1865, box 1452, entry 26, RG 121, NACP.

98 Cornelius & Baker, invoice, September 16, 1863, box 1444; Cornelius & Baker, invoice, June 13, 1863, box 1443; both entry 26, RG 121, NACP. Rogers to Cornelius & Baker, March 24, 1864; Rogers to Cornelius & Baker, July 27, 1863; both reel 7, entry 7, RG 121, NACP.

99 Mullett to Rogers, June 11, 1863, reel 6, entry 7, RG 121, NACP. Perry to Mullett, July 9, 1863, copy in Curator's Files, Treasury Department. Rogers to Perry, October 16, 1863, reel 6, entry 7; Hayward, Bartlett to Rogers, October 14, 1863, box 1443, entry 26; both RG 121, NACP.

100 Pottier & Stymus, Estimate, September 29, 1863, box 1447, entry 26, RG 121, NACP.

101 Ibid. Rogers to Pottier & Stymus, October 16, 1863, reel 6; Mullett to Pottier & Stymus, November 14, 1863, reel 7; both entry 7, RG 121, NACP.

102 Chase to Mullett, February 1, 1864, box 1448, entry 26, RG 121, NACP.

103 Pottier & Stymus to B. Field, February 23, 1863, box 1448, entry 26; Mullett to Pottier & Stymus, February 25, 1863, reel 7, entry 7; Mullett to Hayward, Bartlett, February 23, 1863, reel 7, entry 7; Rogers to Noel, Sauvel & Antoine, March 3, 1864, reel 7, entry 7; Pottier Stymus, Invoice, March 10, 1863, box 1448, entry 26; Ball, Black to Mullett, February 12; 18; 27 and March 9, 1864, box 1448, entry 26; Rogers to Cornelius & Baker, May 27, 1864, reel 7, entry 7; all RG 121, NACP.

104 Pottier & Stymus to Mullett, March 8; 11, 1864, box 1448, entry 26; Clark to Alexander J. Stewart, February 7, 1863, vol. 2, entry 13; Mullett to Pottier & Stymus, March 17, 1864, entry 7; Mullett to Pottier & Stymus, March 29, 1864, reel 7, entry 7; Pottier & Stymus to Rogers, May 9, 1864, box 1449, entry 26; all RG 121, NACP.

105 Rogers to Chase, March 21, 1864, reel 7, entry 7, RG 121, NACP.

106 Mullett to Chase, March 31, 1864; Rogers to Pottier & Stymus, April 14, 1864, reel 7, entry 7, RG 121, NACP.

107 Maunsell B. Field, *Personal Recollections, Memories of Many Men and Some Women* (New York: Harper & Brothers, 1874), 281.

108 Pottier & Stymus, Invoice, July 9, 1864, box 1449, entry 26; Carr to Pottier & Stymus, September 2, 1864, reel 8, entry 7; both RG 121, NACP.

109 Mullett to McCulloch, March 17, 1866, reel 9, entry 7, RG 121, NACP.

110 Ibid.

111 Oertly to McCulloch, October 21, 1865, reel 9; Mullett to French, May 8, 1866, reel 10; both entry 7, RG 121, NACP.

112 Clark to Wadsworth, April 26, 1862, reel 5, entry 7, RG 121, NACP.

113 Rogers to Beals & Dixon, April 5, 1865, reel 8, entry 7, RG 121; Rogers to McCulloch, April 29, 1865, reel 8, entry 7, RG 121; Chandler to Oertly, August 5, 1865, 191–2, entry 30, RG 56; Rogers to McCulloch, July 8, 1865, reel 9, entry 7, RG 121; all NACP.

114 Oertly to McCulloch, October 21, 1865, reel 9, entry 7, RG 121; McCulloch to Oertly, October 24, 1865, 212, entry 30, RG 56; both NACP.

115 Oertly to McCulloch, October 27, 1865, reel 9, entry 7, RG 121, NACP.

116 Oertly to Robert Wood & Co., January 25, 1866, reel 9; Mullett, "Proposals" [stone]; "Proposal for North River Flagging," March 27, 1866, reel 9; Mullett to Acker, April 18, 1866, reel 10; all entry 7, RG 121, NACP.

117 Oertly to McCulloch, October 21, 1865, reel 9; Mullett to Beals & Dixon, April 17, 1866, reel 10; Mullett to Clark, May 15, 1866, reel 10; all entry 7, RG 121, NACP. "Improvements," *Evening Star,* June 6, 1866, 3. "Flora for the Parks," *Washington Post,* April 29, 1903, 8.

118 Rogers to Beals & Dixon, June 27, 1865, NARA, RG 121, entry 7, reel 9. Chandler to Rogers, September 23, 1865, NARA, RG 56, entry 30, 204. Oertly to McCulloch, October 21, 1865, NARA, RG 121, entry 7, reel 9. "Improvement of the Public Grounds" *National Republican,* June 13, 1866, 3. "The Treasury Fountain" *Evening Star,* June 12, 1866, 3. Mullett to Duvall, April 3. 1866, reel 9; Mullett to Duvall , June 8, 1866, reel 10; Mullett to Ellis, June 18, 1866, reel 10; all entry 7, RG 121, NACP.

119 Mullett to McCulloch, June 20, 1866, reel 10; Mullett to Hayward & Bartlett, June 29, 1866, reel 10; Mullett to McCulloch, August 1, 1866, reel 11; all entry 7, RG 121, NACP.

120 Mullett to McCulloch, August 1, 1866, reel 11, entry 7, RG 121, NACP.

121 "Improvements of the Grounds About the Executive Department," *Evening Star,* September 10, 1866, 3.

"Numerous and Beautiful Reception Rooms:" The North Wing, 1867–1869

Chapter Five

"Anxious to Commence Work:" Preparations

In the spring of 1863, architect Isaiah Rogers proposed changes to the north wing's design in order to "restore the purity" of the Treasury Building. His suggested alterations were part of his campaign to impose rigorous Greek aesthetic principles on a building begun in 1836 at the height of that revival of ancient classicism but being completed a quarter century later during the early Victorian era's revival of Renaissance and Baroque architecture. On October 1, 1864, Secretary of the Treasury William P. Fessenden advised Secretary of State William Seward that the north wing's construction was postponed until the following year. Congress then set aside $10,000 for the rental of temporary quarters for the State Department and at the same time appropriated $500,000 for the north wing's construction. Commencement of the north wing was delayed until 1866 because the State Department had secured neither an appropriation for a new building nor temporary accommodations, although it was obvious the Treasury Department needed its site to finish the building.[1]

"The architect of the Treasury Building, anxious to commence work by the demolition of the old State Department edifice, has since the adjournment of Congress been diligently engaged in seeking a place for that Department," reported the *Evening Star*. Since there was no nearby rental property available that was both fireproof and large enough for the State Department, Rogers built an additional story on the Winder Building at the corner of Seventeenth Street and New York Avenue for Treasury offices. He also remodeled the Riggs Building at the intersection of 15th and G streets to meet the needs of the Internal Revenue Bureau. Having thus freed up considerable space within the Treasury Building by moving out some of its own divisions, he then renovated the east wing to accommodate some of the State Department's employees by adding an attic story and turning its basement storage rooms into offices. The accommodations were hardly ideal and the State Department apparently found them totally unacceptable for they rented the Orphan's Asylum.[2]

Soon after taking possession of "old State" on November 19, 1866, the Supervising Architect's office, now under Alfred B. Mullett, began its razing, which lasted until January 1867. (fig. V-1) Just over two years later, by early April 1869, the Internal Revenue Bureau had moved into its new quarters in the north wing's second and third (now third and forth) floors. The entrance level was reserved for the Treasurer's office and the basement for storage of the Register's records. In just over two years, Mullett built the north wing to acclaim from Congress for his efficiency and from the public for its beauty, a remarkable achievement given the lengthy and troubled design and building history of the earlier wings.

Among the factors contributing to the north wing's rapid construction was its long gestation, allowing Rogers to stockpile granite, beginning in the early 1860s, and providing the draftsmen with ample time to refine the details of this, the smallest wing. The record also indicates that the rapid construction was not without conflict, as contractors and the Treasury's work force bore the brunt of Mullett's heavy-handed tactics in meeting his ambitious schedule.[3]

V-1 Lewis Walker photographed the State Office's site just before excavation began for the north wing.

"Disgraceful Management:" Mullett Replaces Rogers

Since the west pavilion of the north wing was the incomplete northwest pavilion of the west wing, Rogers used the north's appropriation during the fall and winter of 1864 to concentrate his work force on completing its interiors, finishing the work by the end of January 1865. His relationship with his workmen had never been good and in February he complained to Fessenden that the 177 skilled workmen still employed on the Treasury were slacking off and that the half million dollar appropriation "is now being diminished at the rate of about \$35,000 per month, and yet no legitimate work upon the Extension is being done, aside from the earth excavations."[4]

On March 1, 1865, Rogers distributed new rules and regulations relating to the much-reduced work force. Ten-hour days were to be the standard and anyone working up to two hours more per day would be paid per hour according to their daily rate; an additional twenty-five cents per hour would be paid for work beyond twelve-hour days. All workmen needed the permission of their foreman to leave the site and the watchmen were especially charged with making sure that building materials did not stray as well as checking that the workmen did not evade the rules. Actual starting and stopping times were not specified, but Rogers noted that either a bell or the steam whistle would be sounded five minutes prior to the allotted hours, followed by roll calls by the foremen. Rogers was evasive about wages. "The prices to be paid by the day or hour as the case may be, will be regulated by the usual prices paid for similar work elsewhere; special regard being, also, had to the skillfulness of the workman." He concluded by carefully explaining the rationale for the rules to his shrunken work force.[5]

> By these *Rules and Regulations* it is not desired or intended to infringe in any way upon the right of the workman; but they are adopted only to ensure a certain means of having a proper and adequate amount of service rendered to the Government in return for the liberal wages paid its employees, and it is expected that every one employed will manifest a right spirit in faithfully carrying out these Regulations at all times during their employment on the work, and should an employee have at any time any cause for complaint or grievance, the chief of this Office will take pleasure in hearing his complaint and remedying the difficulties if possible.[6]

Compared to Rogers's other communications with the workmen, his message was probably intended to be conciliatory. It also marked the normal beginning time of Washington's building season. Nine days later Hugh McCulloch was appointed Secretary of the Treasury. He did not immediately authorize the start of the north wing, and early in June Rogers, feeling increasingly insecure about his position as the government's architect, urged the secretary to consider the losses to the government if construction of the north wing should be abandoned. McCulloch's response was testy.

"I will merely observe that after full examination of the subject, it was deemed impossible to furnish accommodations for the State Department, if the Building now occupied by it was removed, without seriously deranging the public business."[7]

Rogers believed that the north wing could be built within eighteen months because most of the materials needed were on hand, but deteriorating. The same situation had been faced when construction was halted on the west wing three years earlier. Moreover, as Captain Bowman had also argued, key workmen would have to be discharged if the wing was not begun soon. "The most efficient of this force, these first class mechanics who acquired a thorough acquaintance with the work on one of the most remarkable & modern buildings will get scattered," Rogers remarked in early June 1865, "and on a future resumption, it will take some time before an equally efficient force shall have been organized." Rogers also argued—perhaps too forcefully—that resuming construction would save the government thousands of dollars in rents, noting that he had spent months figuring out where to house the State Department in the Treasury Building, partly by moving some Treasury offices and the Attorney General into rented quarters. Rogers concluded his case to McCulloch: "if it is inexpedient now to remove the old State Department, the same inexpedience will exist for a series of years, and that the losses [by paying high rents] will be greatly increased by a suspension of long duration." In January 1869 the *Evening Star* published a list of the five buildings occupied by part or all of five bureaus and the annual rents paid for them amounted to $28,900. Rogers's primary concern was salvaging his job; McCulloch's priority was the efficient operation of his complex department in the context of the needs of the other executive departments.[8]

Another factor may have clouded McCulloch's eagerness to push for Rogers to

V-2 A.B. Mullett left his distinctive stamp on Treasury's landscape, structure, interiors, and furnishings.

complete the building. Since the fall of 1864, Rogers and his assistant Mullett had been on bad terms; the solution was to dispatch the younger man on extended site visits. (fig. V-2) Mullett left for San Francisco in January 1865 to oversee construction of his design for the U.S. Mint, not returning to Washington until June. The antagonism between the two men upon his return was so disruptive to the architect's office that on June 19 Assistant Secretary Chandler recommended that Mullett be given assignments outside the Treasury building and be answerable directly to McCulloch. The tenor of Mullett's attacks on Rogers suggests that they were not just professional disagreements but rather were calculated to challenge Rogers's authority and even his position. For example, on August 3 Mullett wrote McCulloch "on the subject of the disgraceful management of affairs on the Treasury Ex.," although his knowledge of the

construction's progress was secondhand because he had been away from Washington even after his return from California on June 13.[9]

A second letter addressed to Chandler the next day, in response to Rogers's rebuttal of Mullett's charges, reveals that Mullett accused Rogers of redesigning the approaches to the west portico's staircase after the granite for the first design had already been delivered, thus incurring a double expenditure for materials. Mullett cited the building's official records and referred Chandler to Oertly, who had been named acting assistant supervising architect while Mullett was away from the office. Mullett's three-page screed brims with charges and countercharges of malfeasance and incompetence. He appears to have embarked on a conscious campaign to drive Rogers from his job. In September Mullett ordered a second estimate for the Louisville Custom House that was $20,000 lower than the one Rogers had already accepted. This episode apparently led to Rogers's resignation on September 20.[10]

The exact circumstances behind Rogers's stepping down are not clear, but one inside account was provided a few years later by an ousted cabinetmaker. C.H. Manning, who had been released from work at the Treasury in 1865, recalled in 1869 that his colleague C.W. Dashiell (who remained employed in the Treasury cabinet shop) "informed us that being at work in the room of Sect. McCulloch, he heard Mr. Rogers say to the Sect. that he could not get along with his ast. [sic] A.B. Mullett, & would not, & should not immediately dismiss him. We represented the case to Senator Wilson who immediately waited on the Sect. (to whom he had also represented the affair) and got him to discharge Mr. Rogers, and put Mr. Mullett in his place." Manning's target in 1869 was master cabinetmaker George J. Suter, whom Manning complained dismissed "soldiers & good union men" in 1865. At that time the workmen had appealed to Massachusetts Senator Henry

Wilson who gave them a letter addressed to Rogers. "He would not read it nor listen to our complaints, but treated us soldiers with great haute[u]r."[11]

While Manning's four-year-old, second-hand recollection is somewhat confusing, the strife between Rogers and Mullett, and antipathy of some of the workmen for Rogers, is crystal clear. Whatever the final steps that culminated in Rogers's resignation, it was not Mullett but rather Oertly who was named acting supervising architect. On September 30, 1865, Oertly wrote the foremen and others, including the photographer Lewis E. Walker. "The appropriation for the Treasury Extension being exhausted, the Hon. Secretary of the Treasury has directed a total suspension of the work and the discharge of the entire force of employees, at the close of this day." The *New York Times* reported that "in some of the shops bosses were immediately appointed, with instructions to employ but a limited number of hands. This course has been adopted that the work may go steadily on until Congress shall make such an appropriation as will warrant the employment of a full force." Early in December, in anticipation that Congress might fund completion of the north wing if designated for the use of the State Department, Oertly sent McCulloch drawings for its interiors to be forwarded to Secretary of State Seward for examination and comment by State Department officers. Oertly took a markedly different (and more humane) tack than some of his predecessors in arguing for the continuation of work. "I would also humbly suggest that the Government ought to give as much work as possible, (consistent with the laws), to the labouring [*sic*] classes of this city, during the coming winter, which portends to be one of great suffering to those classes."[12]

Mullett was not officially appointed Supervising Architect of the Treasury until June 1, 1866, but he had shared responsibility with Oertly for the running of the office since the previous fall. By June nearly $150,000 was on hand to complete the north wing for the sole use of the Treasury Department in addition to an anticipated new half million dollar congressional appropriation. The department's growing Comptroller and Internal Revenue bureaus, as well as its bureaus in rented quarters, logically required centralization into the Treasury Building to maximize the department's efficiency. At the beginning of May, Mullett reported to McCulloch that he and a State Department official were unsuccessful in finding a fire-proof building that served all of that department's ceremonial and practical needs. Two days later, former Treasury Secretary Fessenden and now a senator from Maine, used his new position to address the deadlock, presenting a joint resolution asking the Senate and House Committees on Public Buildings to look into the matter. Fessenden was one among several members of Congress in the early summer of 1866 who began discussing moving the State Department into the President's House once a suitable location for a new executive mansion in Washington's suburbs was identified. During the same summer, the War Department began its campaign for a new building. The space needs of the State, War, and Navy departments finally converged early in 1870 with Mullett chosen as the architect of a massive building to house all three departments on the west side of the President's House corresponding to the Treasury Building's size and location on its east side.[13]

Demolition of the State Department building was completed in January 1867, followed by the lengthy, delicate, and dangerous task of excavating the north wing's foundations and basements and making its subsurface connection to the east wing. In early May a *New York Times* report succinctly described the challenges. (fig. V-3)

A few days since, while the workmen were engaged in excavating for the foundation of

V-3 An 18-foot difference in the depths of their foundations hampered attaching the north to the east wing.

the north wing of the Treasury extension, the earth caved in on them from the direction of the Fifteenth-street front, and they have been laboring constantly both day and night since then laying the foundation and strengthening the base supports of the main building, which it was feared would give way. Strong iron braces were placed between the colonnades at the north end, and an immense sleeper was put up with iron bands across its entire length. The work was continued to-day, and the danger has been evaded. The foundation of the main building is laid only three feet under the ground, while that of the north wing extension, now in course of erection, will extend eighteen feet further down into the earth.[14]

"Giving More Importance to the North Portico:" Designing the North Wing

Site conditions played a critical role in the north wing's design. Each of its architects reacted differently to the extent of land between its front and Pennsylvania Avenue. Because the east wing was not centered on the long rectangle between Pennsylvania and New York Avenues, the north wing's front was parallel with the building line on the south side of G Street, leaving a deep forecourt in front of the 1500 block of Pennsylvania Avenue. In Robert Mills's rudimentary sketch of 1852 suggesting that the Treasury Building be completed as an E-shaped building, he proposed extending the east wing northward, increasing its length by about one-fifth. (see fig. III-2) His primary goal was to bring the building's north portico into the same relationship to New York Avenue as the south portico would have with Pennsylvania Avenue, and aligning its northeast portico with the center of G Street, NW.

No Mills elevation drawing for the north wing from the 1850s is known. All of the schemes done by the three architects directly involved in its actual design and construction are difficult to assess. In his 1854 master plan, Walter proposed that the north wing's three principal stories to be raised on a high, exposed basement, carrying the east wing's podium around the corner to meet the west wing's above-ground basement level. (see fig. III-8) With construction of the west wing's double basements and wide areaway, connecting the east and west wings via the north wing became a major problem exacerbated by the entire site's varied grade levels and differing depths of

foundations. Moreover, in the mid-1860s both Rogers and Mullett were faced with how to solve this problem under bureaucratic and architectural conditions that were much-changed since the time of Walter's master plan—namely, the department's greatly increased workforce and the need for access to the National Note Bureau's basement printing plant.

Two elevation drawings and some plans done during the early 1860s show different solutions to the north wing's site problem as well as alternate designs for its facade. Because most were neither signed nor dated and because related textual documents are either incomplete or contradictory, one can only speculate about their authorship, dating, and relationships among one another. The elevations were either drawn by different draftsmen in 1863 or at different times but are attributed to Rogers because cast-iron antefixes (or acroteria as Rogers called them when he introduced them in the west wing) are depicted along the cornice line rather than a stone balustrade. The first elevation signed by J. Goldsborough Bruff and titled "North Front, United States Treasury Extension," probably accompanied Rogers's letter to Secretary Chase dated April 13, 1863. (fig. V-4) Rogers asked Chase to "authorize the omission

V-4 Proposals to put the State Department in the north wing led to its distinctive Greek Revival facade.

on the North Wing of the Treasury Extension of the expensive, and unsightly, moulding [sic] of the windows and between the Pilasters of the South Wing, and West Front of the Building" which were not present on Walter's master plan approved by Congress and contradictory to Greek architectural principles. The savings would be considerable and Rogers was about to place large orders for granite.[15]

Bruff's elevation depicts walls articulated by pilasters and tall, narrow windows, their attenuation made possible by eliminating Young's wide belt courses and window surrounds integral to his system of building in granite. If this facade had been carried out, one practical result would have been better lit north-facing offices. A difficulty arises in dating this drawing because the inscription in the elevation's entablature reads, "Department of State," which could link it to Oertly's December 1865 project to house that department in the north wing. This elevation drawing might instead represent some unknown, earlier (c. 1863) suggestion to locate the State Department in the north wing. Yet again, it might be a copy of Rogers's 1863 drawing prepared for Chase to which the inscription (and perhaps pedimental sculpture) was added or the inscription may have been added later to the actual 1863 drawing. Whatever the explanation, the Rogers/Oertly north elevation drawing was for a larger, updated stone version of the original 1818 State Department Building. It also embodied Rogers's conservative attempt to reverse the historical evolution of the Treasury Building's design initiated by Young in the south wing.

An unsigned site plan dated November 1865 (during Oertly's tenure as acting supervising architect) seems to be a companion drawing to this north elevation. (fig. V-5) The elevation shows the portico entrance at grade level with basement stories masked from the street by sunken areaways flanking the steps. The north areaways on the plan are slightly wider than

on the west and separated by the portico and stairs. At grade level there is a green buffer zone, a wide garden border for shrubs and flowers flanking a paved area immediately in front of the stairs. A carriageway linking 15th Street to 15 ½ Street (now East Executive Avenue) occupies the third zone, apparently for access to the State Department's principal entrance if this plan is, as it seems to be, associated with Oertly's State Department design. (The Treasury Department's vehicular entrance was at its west portico.) A circular fountain is located in the center of the fourth east-west zone running parallel to the avenue. All four zones were carefully modulated to diminish visually the real distance between the building's north facade and Pennsylvania Avenue at the same time they provided a modest landscape setting at grade level.

The second elevation drawing for the north facade may be contemporary with Rogers's Grecian design (because acroteria stand atop the cornice), given to Chase so he could judge not only alternate facade treatments but also entirely different approaches to the site. (fig. V-6) It depicts three stories above two basement levels, one above grade and one below, which retain Young's interlocking wall structure, thus conforming in appearance and siting with the south and west wings. The author increased the height of the upper basement to be a full story rather than the three-quarter story Walter planned in order to conform to the west wing's horizontal lines. He also retained the south and west wings' massive interlocking horizontal belt courses and window frames to ensure the harmonious relationship among the extension's three fronts. The staircase leading to the portico—higher, deeper, and narrower than on Walter's 1854 master plan—was supported by a tall vaulted room similar to the one under the south steps; a currency vault was eventually built in this secure area. This second north elevation drawing might have been designed by Oertly because it could also correspond to the November 1865

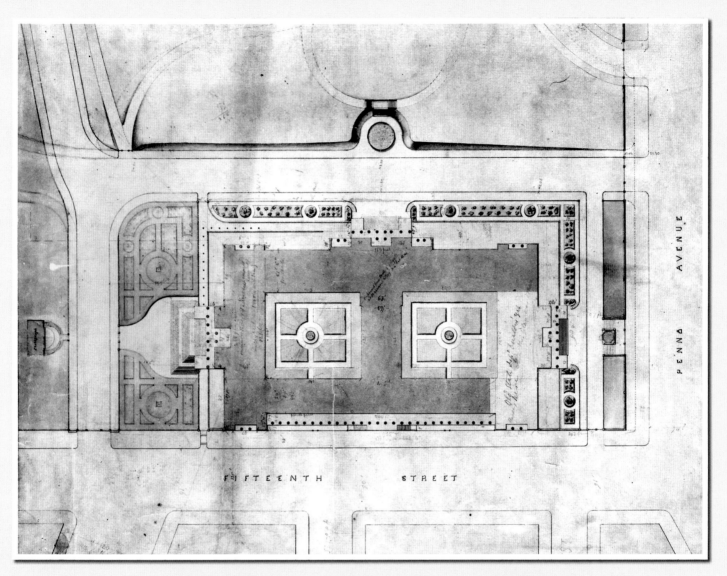

V-5 The Treasury, on axis with the President's House, was misaligned with nearby streets and avenues.

V-6 Rogers proposed two basement levels for the north wing as well as his signature acroterial cornice.

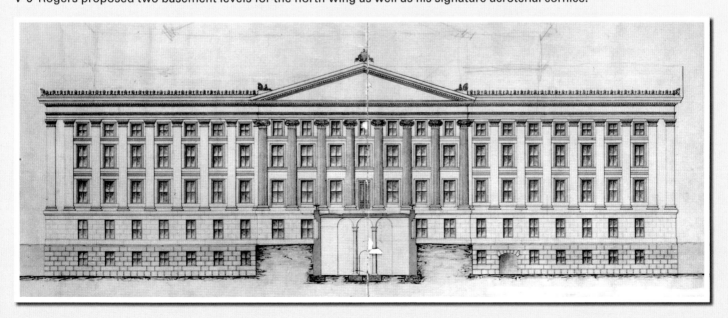

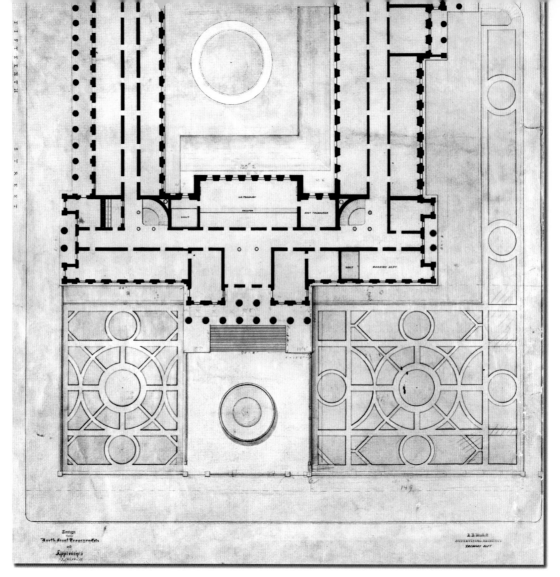

V-7 Mullett chose to distinguish the north wing via his landscape designs for its deep forecourt.

plan; it cannot be attributable to Mullett because of the acroteria which he despised.

These difficulties assigning proper credit for preliminary north wing designs arise because not all the drawings are signed and dated, because written documents are incomplete (and may never have existed), and simply because of the fluid nature of staffing the supervising architect's office during the Civil War years. No elevation design drawing of the north wing attributable to Mullett survives, but in the actual construction beginning in 1867 he followed the west wing's formula, substituting granite balusters for its cast iron acroteria as well as replacing other sham or insubstantial materials with more permanent ones. Mullett

left his distinctive stamp on the north wing through its landscape setting and its interior.

The November 1865 landscape plan for the north wing was the first step towards Mullett's complex three-dimensional connection of the north wing to Pennsylvania Avenue, an evolution traceable through a series of increasingly formal plans that sought to provide a distinct, landscaped precinct around the entire Treasury Building. In February 1867 Mullett was struggling with the major landscape problem inherent in the building's site—the east colonnade's proximity to 15th Street's sidewalk resulting in the building's asymmetrical placement within its meager grounds. (fig. V-7) He had gathered data about grading 15th Street from the city engineer and commissioner of public buildings, and wrote McCulloch urging him to recommend to Congress the grade he and these other

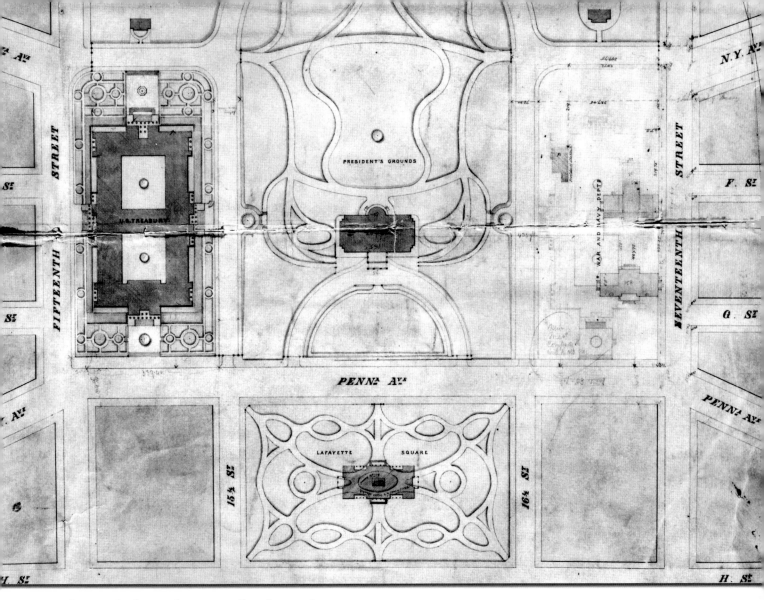

V-8 Mullett hoped to narrow 15th Street in order to have symmetrical parterres in his north garden courts.

authorities had agreed upon. Mullett designed sunken courtyard gardens flanking the north's central plaza as complex Baroque-inspired *parterres*. Their pattern, composed of circles set within squares or rectangles traversed by diagonals, drew upon the same seventeenth-century French vocabulary that Peter Charles L'Enfant used to design Washington's plan. These garden beds were unequal in size because the west areaway and flower border were wider than was possible on the east side flanking 15th Street.[16]

In the fall of 1868, after the exterior of the Treasury Building was completed, Mullett proposed pushing three blocks of 15th Street eastwards by condemning sixty-one feet of the private property facing the Treasury between Pennsylvania and New York avenues. (fig. V-8) This scheme solved three vexing problems:

rebuilding the east front to conform in style and materials with those of the extensions; annexing land along 15th Street equal to that along 15 ½ Street for landscape zones to frame the building; and, opening the vista of the north front from New York Avenue. Five years earlier Rogers had also suggested widening 15th Street to update the east front. Both these attempts, as well as another in 1876, failed because of their cost.[17]

Mullett's final 1870 landscape design for the Treasury Building was as much architectural as horticultural, using granite walls, paving, and balustrades while providing a green setting both to soften the hard-edged character of the architecture and to make a modest landscape transition to the President's Grounds and Lafayette Square. His simplified pattern of circular flower beds and fountains occupying central zones grew out of the Supervising Architect's office's search for the best solution for the north wing's forecourt. (fig. V-9) In contrast to Oertly's elevation design, Mullett's basement was well lit, overlooking expansive courtyard gardens. He had partially sunk the central plaza leading down from the street and then up to the portico and placed a substantial fountain at its center. His three enclosures were surrounded by solid, rusticated walls, or bordered by semi-open balustrades, or outlined by largely transparent fences, thus turning Oertly's restrained landscape experience into a far more dynamic one. Mullett's three-dimensional approach to

the north wing resulted from his solution to a pragmatic problem—the Treasury Department's urgent need for as much office, storage, and printing space within the building as possible—combined with his aesthetic desire to make his wing as important as the other three, each of which had its own distinctive advantage.

Every north-facing portico is at an architectural disadvantage because it is so seldom directly lit by sunlight to emphasize its sculptural qualities. When Mullett authored the annual report of 1863 (as acting supervising architect), he noted considering "giving more importance to the north portico by increasing the dimensions of the same." Neither its width of eight columns nor its height spanning three stories dictated by Walter's master plan could be changed, but the north portico's appearance could be rendered monumental via its approaches. Mullett applied new European

V-9 Treasury's formal parterres for flowers and shrubs contrasted with the informal President's Grounds.

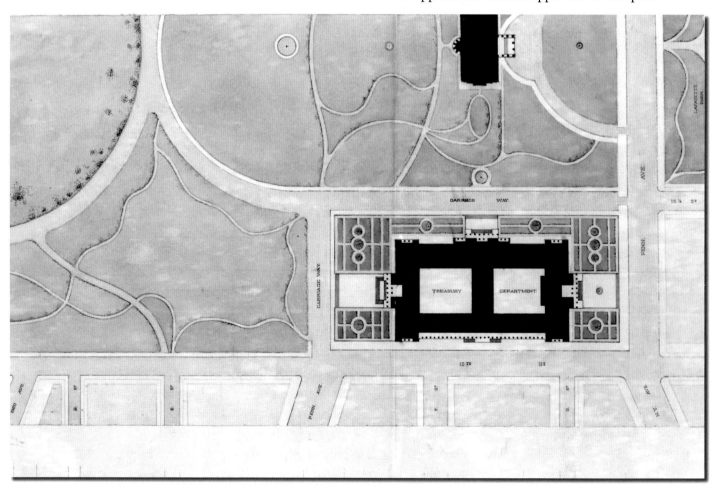

Fortress of Finance: The United States Treasury Building

V-10 Dynamic multi-level sunken garden courts and plaza reveal emerging French design influence.

architectural trends gaining popularity in America to introduce the vitality inherent in balancing simple with intricate, open with closed, and light with dark at one of the most prominent intersections in the city. (fig. V-10) As he finalized the Treasury Building's landscape, Mullett was beginning to design the New York Court House and Post Office and the State, War, and Navy Building, both major exemplars of French Second Empire design.[18]

While Mullett and his well-trained staff in the Office of the Supervising Architect focused on the large design issues of the north front, they also paid attention to how the details of texture and color of materials enhanced its effect of monumental permanence. In contrast to painted cast iron used for the west wing, Mullett stipulated granite for the north portico's flat coffered ceiling; iron window frames were complemented by iron lintels rather than stucco ones employed on the west. Henry Parry of New York supplied the portico's tile for $2,185. "The body of the tile to be of hard gray marble equal in quality to that on the west portico of the building; the stars and white tile of small portico to be of best white veined Italian and the centres [sic] of stars of best American or Belgian black," Mullett reaffirmed when he accepted Parry's proposal in July 1868. In late spring of 1867, Mullett corresponded with Robert Wood & Company, Philadelphia manufacturers of ornamental ironwork. He inquired about design modifications to a four-light candelabra with a three-foot spread, suggesting that its four globes be placed closer together. This candelabra was to stand on a small base at the west entrance; a year later Mullett ordered two additional candelabra of the same design for the same price of $125 each for the north entrance. At the same time, he hired Henri Lovie to finish them in "Berlin bronze" (iron coated with linseed oil and bronze powder fired in a kiln) at an additional expense of $25 each.[19]

"The Strikers Use No Force:" Workmen Strike, 1866–1868

While the north wing's design was still in flux, two long-standing concurrent problems—a strike and a lawsuit—threatened to delay the wing's rapid completion. Mullett's first response to labor unrest during his watch as supervising architect began the day before his official appointment. He consulted McCulloch at the end of May 1866 about a petition from the Treasury's mechanics who asked that Saturday's workday stop at 4:00. Although Mullett felt it was a good idea he had "serious doubts as to the propriety of [the] Government establishing new rules," believing that his office should be guided by customary practice in the private sector. After inquiring about common practice around the city, Mullett reported to McCulloch that only the Government Printing Office stopped work at 4:00 on Saturdays; workmen at a local iron foundry who finished at the same hour made the time up by a shortened dinner hour. When the Treasury's painters asked for a raise in mid-May 1866, Mullett pointed out that he was having a difficult time justifying the employment of so many men on the extension, promising that when work began again in earnest, he would revisit their request. Mullett apparently did not begin building up his workforce until the State Department building was being dismantled during the winter of 1866–1867. By the beginning of February 1867, he claimed it was "already larger than I can work to advantage and the prospects are that it must be materially reduced." By May 21, when shoring up the deep excavation was nearly complete, a total of 347 men were employed at the building site.[20]

Mullett certainly recognized the value of maintaining good relations with the workforce under his command, perhaps mindful of the disruption surrounding the west wing's autumn 1863 strike, but also perhaps the fruit of his long experience of overseeing the progress of many of the supervising architect's buildings. On April 10, 1867, he increased the wages of several of the key master workmen retroactively to the first of the month, expressing to each his gratification of their interest in the resumption of construction and his recognition that their workloads would now increase. He offered master mason M. Lyddan $5.50 per day, noting that he had decided not to appoint a master brick mason, but rather to combine the two positions with an additional payment to Lyddan of fifty cents per day "to continue only during such time as I may consider your duties sufficiently onerous to warrant it." Mullett was poising his workforce for an ambitious building campaign. "I trust energy will not flag and that the work will be completed within the time contemplated by me," he wrote all the foremen.[21]

A month later Mullett's strategy was tested. A committee of two men representing Washington's stone and granite cutters' associations petitioned President Andrew Johnson to curtail Saturday work hours for all the skilled workmen on the Treasury Extension, claiming the practice had been common in the city for the past year. "A large number of [the Treasury's] mechanics feeling agrieved [sic] at what they conceived to be the injustice of the Government, *in this particular,* have suspended their labour [sic] in order that their just demand might be complied with. We understand that they have all been discharged unless they comply with the requirements of the Architect." Johnson immediately directed McCulloch to comply with the request unless it was specifically forbidden by law and requested an "early report."[22]

In his five-page report to McCulloch, Mullett first noted that neither of the petitioners was employed on the Treasury and that their claim of the near universality of the Saturday hours was untrue. He recounted a May 14 meeting with a committee of the Treasury's granite cutters who claimed the association required

TREASURY DEPARTMENT,

FEBRUARY 2, 1867.

SIR: The Secretary of the Treasury directs that, from and after this date, the office hours of the several Bureaus of this Department shall be from 9 o'clock A. M. to 4 P. M., all the employees to report punctually at the morning hour and remain diligently employed till the afternoon hour.

Arriving after nine and leaving before four, absence from the office or inattention to duty during office hours, will be considered sufficient grounds for dismissal, and no employee so removed will be reinstated in any office of this Department.

No person designated to a clerkship in this Department will be allowed to enter upon the discharge of the duties of the office until he shall have been examined, appointed, and taken the oath of office and allegiance prescribed by the act of July 2, 1862.

Heads of Bureaus are requested to report immediately to the Secretary all vacancies, from any cause, occurring in their offices.

The Secretary has been much annoyed by applications for appointment founded on statements made by clerks and others that there were vacancies to be filled, and designating those vacancies. He therefore gives notice that it is not a part of the duty of clerks or others in the Department to give either information or advice on such points. All vacancies are reported to the Assistant Secretary, and will be filled by the Secretary as he may determine. He will regard any further interference of this sort as sufficient cause for dismissal.

Requests for promotion of clerks in the Department from gentlemen outside of it, who cannot be informed as to the relative duties and merits and other circumstances which should control action in such matters, may, if annoyingly pressed upon the Department, injure instead of benefitting those who obtain them; and the Secretary will not be likely to be influenced by requests of this kind.

Leave of absence will not be given except in case of absolute necessity; and such leave, for a period greater than one month in any fiscal year, will be granted, if at all, without pay.

When absence is caused by sickness, a certificate of the attending physician must be furnished, showing the nature of the disease, the daily attendance, and the amount and extent of the debility or disability caused by such sickness, with the date when first called in and that when the attendance ceased.

Every application for leave of absence should state the number of days the applicant has been absent from duty during the year previous, also the date of appointment in the Department.

Heads of Bureaus will hereafter submit to the Secretary, on the 1st of each month, a statement containing the names and official titles of such employees of their offices as have been absent from their duties during the previous month, together with reasons for such absence.

The Heads of Bureaus are charged with the faithful execution of these orders. All delinquencies in attending at the morning hour and continuing diligently employed till the afternoon hour, will be reported daily to the Head of the proper Bureau, who will make report of the same to the Secretary, unless satisfied that such absence was absolutely necessary; and any failure by the persons charged with the duty to make such report will be considered sufficient cause for reduction or removal.

The Heads of the respective Bureaus will take measures to make this order known to all their subordinates.

H. McCULLOCH,
Secretary of the Treasury.

V-11 In 1867 the Treasury's clerks worked 7-hour days while its mechanics averaged 10 hours.

all its members to abide by the Saturday hours; moreover, they assured Mullett that they would not join a strike in support of granite cutters employed elsewhere in the city. "You can imagine my surprise in learning the next morning that all of the granite cutters employed on the Treasury Extension, *save one,* had struck work in spite of their promises." Mullett claimed that most of the granite cutters had returned to work "and so far from any difficulty existing between myself and the mechanics employed on the Treasury Extension (as alleged by these men,) there is to the best of my knowledge nothing but the most kindly feelings between myself and the employees. The unprecedented dispatch with which the work is progressing is sufficient evidence of this fact." Moreover, the hours of labor for the Treasury's workmen were the same as on all other government work in Washington, he claimed, and when the norm changed he would abide by it.[23]

Mullett does not seem to have considered, at least at the outset, a possible connection between labor issues affecting the government's clerical force with the unrest among the city's building trades. (fig. V-11) At the end of November 1866, several delegates representing clerks in the government's civil service offices—

including three from the Treasury Department—met to discuss a general increase in their wages. They adjourned after agreeing that each "should exercise their own discretion in the amount of increase asked," while Congress began considering a uniform raise in government salaries. A joint resolution passed the House on February 11, 1867, to raise the pay of a wide range of the government's clerks—permanent and temporary, male and female—by 20 percent for one year beginning on the thirtieth of June. The resolution repealed the earlier raise the Treasury's clerks had secured for themselves. Excluded from the increase were those civil servants with annual salaries of more than $3,500. Everything about the resolution proclaimed it as compensation for having remained loyal during the war and suffered the privations of living in Washington without salary increases during a period of great inflation.[24]

Yet, many of the Treasury Department's clerks were unable to benefit from the increase in pay, for early in June 1867 McCulloch announced a general reduction in employees. The workload in several bureaus, notably the Second and Third Auditors offices and the Engraving and Printing Office (the former Note Bureau), had decreased sharply after the war. The majority of the printing office's clerks were women. As early as November 1866, the continued employment of the department's 700 female clerks, whose wages were less than their male counterparts, was very much in question. McCulloch considered dismissing them all "on account of the trouble and annoyance that members of Congress and others give by their importunities for positions for their female friends," was the *Evening Star's* assessment.[25]

Although many chroniclers acknowledged that a few of the Treasury's female clerks had jobs requiring little work arranged for them by powerful male patrons, most were perfectly proper women of all ages in need of employment who were making valuable contributions to the department's daily operations. When strong opposition forestalled McCulloch from targeting the women clerks alone, substandard performance was substituted as the criteria for dismissals beginning in June 1867. "Those retained will be the most efficient and faithful clerks, without any regard to classification or salaries," claimed an *Evening Star* reporter. Reductions in force continued throughout the summer and autumn.[26]

There is evidence that the clerks' success—won through negotiation by a unified body—influenced the unionization of Washington's skilled building trades. Workmen around the country were forming labor unions in the 1860s—Washington was behind the times. The clerks' compensation bill of February 28, 1867, which included even the lamplighters employed by the Office of Public Buildings and Grounds, did not include any workmen erecting the government's public buildings. At the beginning of February, McCulloch had set the Treasury clerks' daily office hours from 9:00 to 4:00 while the ten-hour day remained the rule on building sites. The inequity was not missed by the building trades. At a general meeting of working men in the city in mid-June, a Mr. Eeron "wanted to know if this was a free country. Had clerks the right to regulate the hours of labor, when their hours on the street were more than at work." The forces that prompted the Stone and Granite Cutters' Unions to seek shortened Saturday hours on the Treasury Extension in May spread to the Bricklayers Union by early June. On the eleventh, its recording secretary informed McCulloch that after Saturday, June 15, "members of this union will work but eight hours on Saturdays. We respectfully ask your approval of the same for the bricklayers working at the Treasury Dept."[27]

Washington's private employers agreed to the change and the secretary of the navy reduced the hours at the Navy Yard because he was obliged by law to conform to the hours established by private contractors. Mullett refused on the grounds that "there was a law of Congress fixing ten hours as a day's work." He offered higher wages but the bricklayers held fast to their pledge to the union; it was not wages but the principle involved of one eight-hour day per week at the end of five ten-hour days. (fig. V-12) When negotiations broke down on Friday, June 14, Mullett immediately sent telegrams to government agents in Baltimore, Annapolis, and Philadelphia, hoping to replace the north wing's eighteen bricklayers by Monday morning. On Tuesday, after those arriving from Annapolis on Monday refused to work once they encountered the strikers gathered at the corner of 15th and F streets, Mullett expanded his net to Richmond and Norfolk. Mullett applied to the city police to disperse the strikers but they were not breaking any laws. "The strikers use no force, and do not obstruct the sidewalks, but take seats on the curbstones and watch the building."[28] On Wednesday June 19 the *Star* noted:

> Yesterday, application was made at the Freedman's Bureau for colored hands, and it is said this morning that an agent has gone to Richmond to engage colored bricklayers. Should colored masons be employed it is stated that the white laborers employed on the building will strike.
>
> The committee [of the Treasury's bricklayers] have received a telegram from the First President of the National Bricklayer's Union, stating that he has informed the unions of 40 of the principal cities of the strike here.[29]

The *National Intelligencer* summed up the week's events on Thursday, noting that Mullett's intransigence was because "he would be under the same obligation to extend a like favor to all the mechanics and laborers under his control." That evening a meeting of the Workingmen's

THE STRIKE AT THE TREASURY. — This morning, one of the superintendents of the work on the Treasury Extension applied to Major Richards, at police headquarters, for a detail of men to disperse a crowd of bricklayers (now on a strike) who congregate on the corner opposite the building, and deter men who have come to Washington to work on the building from going to work. The strikers use no force, and do not obstruct the sidewalks, but take seats on the curbstones and watch the building. The superintendent says that men who are not connected with the association of bricklayers have arrived from Annapolis and from Fredericksburg, but are apparently afraid to go to work. Major Richards informed the applicant that unless the crowd referred to was disorderly, obstructed the street, or violated some law, he had no power to disperse them, but authorized him to tell the newly arrived mechanics that if they wished to go to work they might be sure of protection, which would be given if it required the entire force.

The workmen on the Extension have demanded that on Saturday they may cease their labors at 4 o'clock p. m., and that it shall be accounted a day. This has been refused because the Government has recognized 10 hours as a day for the laborers and mechanics. Upon this refusal the workmen ceased their toil, and the Superintendent of the workmen was obliged to look for other workmen.

V-12 In June 1867 Mullett defeated the Treasury's bricklayers who struck to stop work at 4:00 on Saturdays.

Assembly was held in the council chamber at City Hall. A Mr. Robinson "said the supervising architect of the Treasury was certainly a bare-faced liar, a villain, and a coward," recounting his many missteps of the previous week. A Mr. Harrison tellingly linked the 1867 clerks' bonus with the strikers' goals. "[H]e did not like to see in that building (the Treasury) some thieves, and perchance some prostitutes, who could go to hear the marine band; he did not like to see that class of persons enjoy the music while honest workmen were at work." (Frauds perpetrated by Treasury clerks were often in the news and some of the Treasury's female clerks were popularly believed to be the mistresses of members of Congress.) Others quoted Mullett's statements to the effect that the architect believed the "same rules and regulations should apply at the Treasury as in private shops. He afterwards made other statements contradictory to them," and "he said if such rules were in force on other works he would accede to them. Such rules were in force at the Patent Office and elsewhere."[30]

Mullett continued to contact government agents seeking bricklayers from increasingly distant cities as most of those who arrived the first week either found work elsewhere or went home upon learning of the circumstances prompting the strike. By June 24 the *Star* reported four bricklayers were working on the north wing, while the *New York Times* noted the next day that the "work is getting somewhat behind hand, as no new employees in place of those who quit work have been engaged." On June 26 the *National Republican* reported on the meeting of the Journeymen Bricklayers' Association attended by two hundred of its members. "A proposition was received from Mr. Mullett, offering members of the association $5 per day for five days and $6 for Saturday if they resume work; each day to consist of ten hours; and also to appoint a foreman over the bricklaying department from their association."[31]

Although this offer represented a raise of $4 per week, the bricklayers declined, arguing they were striking because of a principle. On the following day Mullett appointed Robert Clarkson master brick mason at $6.00 per day; eight imported bricklayers increased the total to fourteen, Mullett paying the first class ones $5.50 per day and the remainder $5.00, the eighteen strikers having been paid $4.50 per day for six-day weeks. With enough bricklayers now on the site, Mullett declared the strike at an end and on June 28 the *Star* reported "the work is progressing finely. There are now twenty-seven bricklayers at work." In 1866 Mullett had adroitly avoided two similar strikes of the stone cutters and masons and in 1867 succeeded in thwarting the bricklayers' aims but at the cost of about twenty percent increase in salaries for their

more numerous successors. The beginning of the north wing's construction was caught in the middle of major labor changes in the country, with the government's laboring classes hoping to gain some small part of the benefits its office workers routinely enjoyed.[32]

Mullett faced another strike nine months later, one that revealed his changing justifications, strategy, and tactics. When Washington's union of plaster workers went on strike in April 1868 for $5 per day, Ohio Republican Congressman Samuel F. Cary took up their cause, urging Mullett to employ them on the Treasury Building. After investigating that daily wages being paid by most of the city's private contractors were lower than $5.00, the architect claimed he did not feel authorized to increase their wages because "the law requires me to follow custom and not to make it." On April 14 Mullett wrote Cary that he would "willingly pay the sum demanded as soon as the rates are established outside." Mullett moreover advised Cary that the "whole difficulty can be avoided by the passage of a resolution exempting government from the operations of strikes."[33]

Three days later, on April 17, 1868, Mullett wrote the superintendent of the Appraiser's Stores in Philadelphia.

> Can you send me two or three good stucco-workers at once? The plasterers here are on a strike for $5.00 a day and are endeavoring to coerce me to yield to their terms. I propose therefore to beat them at their own game. You will readily see that I want *men*, not cowards or slaves, and if you can find me a few of the right metal I think I can teach these gentlemen a lesson. We are offering $4.00 per diem, which is the highest rate paid here.[34]

Mullett wrote Congressman Cary again on May 8, reiterating why he could not pay the plasterers union wages, noting that, if forced, he would import workmen—"such a course will be much against my wishes and will only be adopted as a *dernier resort*," he averred, although he had already started down that road—unless the "mechanics here exempt this building from their rules." He urged Cary to use his influence with the workmen to accept the terms offered, "believing that such a course would be the most advantageous to all concerned." He closed with a dire threat, perhaps in excess of his authority. "If I am unable to obtain workmen in time I shall close work for this season." Washington's newspapers covered the plasterers' strike in general; there was no coverage of how it affected the Treasury Building. At the end of May, after learning that "the majority of trades in this city have adopted the rule of stopping work at 4 o'clock P.M. on Saturdays," Mullett ordered that all of the Treasury Building's workmen be let off at that hour. A month later Congress enacted a law establishing eight hours as a day's work on all government building sites, the result of union agitation nationally for the past several years.[35]

An interesting sidelight of these important labor issues is another source for the term "redneck." On June 20, 1867, at the height of the bricklayers' strike, the *Evening Star* noted that the "stone masons and other workmen are still on the building, and are pushing forward their work, but the brick work is of course on a standstill, and the few 'red necks,' as the bricklayers are jokingly called, is remarked by passers-by." Etymologists trace the term redneck in America either to the sun burnt necks of seventeenth-century Virginia field workers or to eighteenth-century Scots-Irish Presbyterian immigrants who wore red bandanas. The *Evening Star's* usage of the phrase "red necks" seems to refer to an identifiable mark of the bricklayer's trade, the mixture of brick dust and sweat that accumulated on their necks. Stone-cutters worked in sheds on building sites, but the stone masons who raised the walls side by side with

the brick masons are not known to have been distinguished by any comparable nickname. Moreover, Walker's photographs show all the workmen on the site wearing broad-brimmed hats that shaded their necks as well as their faces. Judging from their demeanor during the 1867 strike, the Treasury's bricklayers belonged to a proud class of independent laborers who held strong opinions and stood by their principles, characteristics sometimes associated with working class people who presently call themselves, or are pegged as, rednecks.[36]

"The Cost of Granite Is Labor:" Granite Contract Disputes

Beals & Dixon's threatened legal action in 1865–68 against the government had its origins in the Treasury Department's halting of the delivery of granite in 1859 and again in 1863 and with irregularities with the order and supply of granite for the north wing in 1862–63. Normally, the Treasury's architects ordered granite to be delivered in stages timed to coincide with successive phases of construction, thus minimizing the time it occupied limited storage areas near the building. Yet, between May 15, 1862, and April 22, 1863, Beals & Dixon delivered $134,195 worth of granite for the north wing while the west wing was still the major focus of construction. Although Fort Sumter had been fired on in April 1862, the north wing's granite continued to be ordered because the congressional appropriation for it was not depleted and the department's contract with Beals & Dixon was still in force. Rogers (and the quarry owners) may well have wanted to stockpile Dix Island granite in case the war's progress (or outcome) halted its shipment from Maine. If the Treasury Building was left unfinished, it might later be completed with an inferior or mismatching material.[37]

In September 1863 Beals & Dixon complained that they had not been paid in full for the granite delivered in 1862–63, arguing that they should be paid the fifteen percent routinely withheld until the completion of the contract because the Treasury Department had unilaterally halted orders before the contract could be fulfilled. Rogers's investigation revealed that "Beals & Dixon have delivered and executed work over and above any orders received to the amount of $18,728." An acting computer (while Oertly was out of town) had erroneously certified vouchers (which Rogers had inadvertently countersigned) for incoming shipments without checking for the corresponding original written orders, Rogers claimed. Although he had "given positive orders that no work should be estimated for by the Computer, which had not

been previously ordered," it was almost inevitable that the rushed and stressful environment of the supervising architect's office during the war's early months would result in some lapses of routine. Other possible explanations are that Rogers was incapable of directing the Supervising Architect's complex operations or that internal saboteurs exploited the war's chaos to depose him. One solution was to pay for the unordered materials out of the withheld funds but Rogers recommended that "no payment be made for the unauthorized work."[38]

In April 1864, after learning that Congress had authorized new monies for the completion of the Treasury Building, Beals & Dixon "respectfully ask[ed] that the necessary orders may be given which will enable us to go on with our Contract." (fig. V-13) On May 5 Rogers placed an order for granite for the north wing,

V-13 Mullett supported Beals & Dixon in their contract dispute over the rising cost of quarrying granite.

Fortress of Finance: The United States Treasury Building

"drawings for which formerly were furnished to you." However, during the intervening months Rogers had made some design alterations and so alerted the quarry that a few new drawings would be forthcoming. Six weeks later Beals & Dixon tried to renegotiate the terms of their contract directly with Secretary Chase, arguing that when the department, without prior notice, cut off its orders they lost not just the remainder of the contract but a percentage of those costs preparing the quarry for maximum productivity the department had obliged them to make. At the time of the 1859 work stoppage Beals & Dixon considered the Treasury was in "violation of the Contract, but we obeyed the Department order, discharged our hands, sold our Vessel, and Teams, and dismantled our works." "The cost of Granite is labor," they noted, and in the intervening years, Beals & Dixon's cost of labor had risen from $1.12 ½ to $2.50 per day per workman. "As it is the Department's act alone" the quarry owners opined, "which brings our deliveries at a different period of cost, to our great disadvantage and loss every way, we think the Secretary will perceive that it is oppressive to compel us to make deliveries at the old rates." Chase determined that only Congress could decide on the matter.[39]

More than two years later Attorney General James Sneed found that the government was not liable. He particularly considered the contract's caveat that the granite be delivered "at the same prices and within a reasonable time," but did not address its provision "that any departure from these conditions or changes increasing or lessening the cost of the material and any and all differences growing out of this contract shall be adjusted by the superintendent of the work upon pro rata principles, and the decision of the Superintendent shall be final between the parties."[40]

Sneed skirted around the Civil War, never actually mentioning it, possibly because any decision based on its impact on the government might have led to many other war-related claims. Beals & Dixon maintained that the second halt in shipping their granite was caused by the war and constituted an unreasonable delay and, therefore, their prices under the 1857 contract revision should be revised. They agreed to abide temporarily by Sneed's decision, "but we can, by no means accept it as a final arbitrament [sic] of the matter—on the contrary we shall seek by all proper means to obtain our equitable and lawful rights." In late September 1866, Mullett approved Beals & Dixon's application to be paid a little less than $16,000 in retained funds—a fraction of the contested amount—because the firm was "undoubtedly suffering under great pecuniary embarrassments arising from their contract, which the Department under the decision of the Attorney General has no power to remove."[41]

Perhaps in response to political pressure, in January 1867 Assistant Secretary Chandler invited Beals & Dixon to outline once again the history of their contract with the Treasury Department. The quarrymen believed that Sneed's decision was "contrary to the opinion & practice of the Treasury Department, but also contrary to the opinions and practice of the Attorney General's office in other cases," as well as founded on incomplete evidence. Two weeks later Beals & Dixon sent McCulloch a one-page précis listing five periods of granite delivery between October 1862 and January 1867; the amounts they were paid for each (totaling $192,873); and the amounts withheld (totaling $229,331). Considering that their contract prescribed an initial payment of eighty-five percent for the Treasury's granite, there apparently was a pattern of serious irregularities, all originating during Rogers's tenure as supervising architect. No written evidence has been found indicating that these problems were recognized at the time but they may have been the real reason he was fired.[42]

At the beginning of February, MuCulloch wrote now-Attorney General Henry Stanbery asking his opinion about Sneed's ruling and ordered an in-house investigation of the granite accounts. Mullett concluded that $199,253 was "legally and justly due the contractors" which he recommended be paid them "upon their signing a receipt in full of all demands for work or claims arising" from their contract "or any violation of the same." Beals & Dixon waited until December 1867 when they had fulfilled most of the north wing's granite orders before once again laying their case before McCulloch, claiming "peculiar and grievous hardship and injustice." They concluded their discussion about the one-sidedness of benefits under government contracts with the observation that the "government cannot afford to deal more unjustly or unfairly than an individual by its faithful employees, servants or citizens." Once again McCulloch turned to Mullett, who noted that "the Solicitor of the Treasury after a careful examination of the case approved the legality of the present claim. Its justice has never to my knowledge been disputed."[43]

At the beginning of January 1868, McCulloch forwarded to Thaddeus Stevens, chairman of the House Committee on Appropriations, several documents relating to the claim, concluding that "after a careful examination of the case I am of the opinion that it merits the early consideration of Congress." Stevens turned it over to the Committee on Claims where it was shepherded by William B. Washburn, a Massachusetts Republican, who had the supporting documents printed. The handwritten draft of Resolution 217 allowed the contractors "such additional prices for material delivered after May first, eighteen hundred and sixty-one, as they may be justly entitled to under the provisions of their supplementary contract, dated January first, eighteen hundred and fifty-seven, the same to be adjusted by the proper officer and in the manner named in the Contract." The phrase "paid … out of the contingent

fund of the Treasury" was crossed out in the original.[44]

On February 28, the joint resolution was read twice and,

> *Ordered*, That it be engrossed [printed] and read a third time. Being engrossed, it was accordingly read the third time and passed.
>
> Mr. Washburn moved that the vote last taken be reconsidered, and also moved that the motion to reconsider be laid on the table; which latter motion was agreed to.

By moving to reconsider the vote and then causing the motion to reconsider to be tabled, Washburn was employing a parliamentary procedure to cement the outcome of the vote so that the issue could not be brought up again, debated, and possibly defeated. Congress had finally righted an egregious wrong. Washburn, who represented Massachusetts's 9th district that contained many quarry towns, had protected the viability of a major industry of his state and region.[45]

"At the Earliest Possible Moment:" Structural and Decorative Iron

Structural and ornamental ironwork played an important a role in the north wing's rapid construction because wider availability after the war allowed Mullett to spread the orders among several suppliers. (fig. V-14) On March 4, 1867, Mullett accepted the Phoenix Iron Company's proposal to supply iron beams and a month later was pushing them for delivery "at the *earliest possible moment*," as they were needed early in the construction process to brace the walls of the north wing's deep excavation. By early November Phoenix had shipped most of the roof girders ahead of schedule but, Mullett explained, the missing lattice girders were "key to the whole work and the rest of the frame is of very little value to me until I get them." Moreover, "as soon as the master machinist turns his back the work is at a stand still." Because of the complexity of the iron framing, Mullett asked the loan of a Phoenix employee "to help me get the roof on."[46]

Perhaps because the company was so prompt in its deliveries, Mullett was genial in his request that the remaining girders be shipped before the end of the building season. "I must implore you to hurry up the lattice girders, even if you have to work all night. The delay is killing me and all my plans. I trust you will certainly ship all of them by the end of this week." Although Mullett initially noted that his mechanics' difficulties assembling the roof girders were not the fault of Phoenix, he was reluctant to pay for the time and expenses of the men sent from Philadelphia, claiming that the "work was not properly fitted for placement" and even the company's men had to do "considerable additional fitting."[47]

When Phoenix had completed its shipment of structural iron and submitted its final invoice in the spring of 1868, Mullett found himself in the position of accepting materials for which he could not immediately pay. Ordering materials

for which he had no valid appropriation was one factor in Mullett's rapid building of the north wing; it would not have been allowed of nor sanctioned by his predecessors. In late August Mullett wrote Minnesota Senator Daniel S. Norton that he had been "compelled to anticipate the appropriation for repairs and preservation of public buildings to the amount of near $20,000, but as Congress has made such action (notwithstanding its possible necessity) a penal offence I am compelled to carry economy to penuriousness."[48]

Timely receipt of the north wing's cast iron columns, pilasters, and window and door frames was not as easy as for its purely structural pieces because they were all made to order rather than stock items. Mullett's advertisement for these "decorative" structural pieces was dated March 5, 1867, with the deadline allowing contractors two weeks to send for drawings and put together proposals. On March 14 Mullett called the attention of the New York founders Janes, Fowler, Kirkland to the announcement; their proposal was received and accepted five days later on the day bids were due. Mullett's design called for three kinds of architectural orders, full columns to cost $90 each, full pilasters (square columns) at $115 each, and "open back pilasters" (to be inset into walls) at $37.50 each. The contract stipulated delivery of the basement's pilasters and columns in less than two months (May 15), but Mullett hoped they might be available at the beginning of May along with door frames "as it is easier and cheaper to put them in while the walls are carried up than afterwards." Window frames, on the contrary, were better installed when the walls

V-14 Mullett expected to divide the north wing's iron work among many founders, but few submitted bids.

were finished. "With regard to the capitals and ornamental work, you need not deliver it unless you desire, before the roof is on the building."[49]

Mullett was anxious when he wrote the founders on May 7 because they had not yet delivered any of the basement's vertical supports; three days later he particularly asked for at least a dozen of the open-backed pilasters and door frames. (fig. V-15) "Do not fail me on this iron work as my chances of getting the building under roof this fall depend[s] in a great measure on your co-operation," he beseeched the founders. When no iron was delivered on May 15, the contract due date, Mullett adopted a threatening posture the next day. "If you cannot forward them *without any further delay*, I shall be com-

pelled to purchase them here and the extra cost will be charged to you as provided in the contract." In their reply, Kirkland promised to ship the basement pilasters and columns within a week but also queried several points not clear on the drawings or omitted altogether.[50]

Moreover, they requested the promised wood models for the capitals on the entrance story as "there is no drawing of any kind of the capital and we want the models as soon as possible." (Pattern makers at foundries used plaster or wood models provided by architects to carve wood templates for each individual piece to be cast, several being required for a capital.) Thus, quite gently, Kirkland shifted some of the burden of the delay on deficiencies in the

V-15 Stock iron I-beams were used to support ceilings, but window frames and door frames were custom made.

COUNTING WORN AND DEFACED GREENBACKS, AND DETECTING COUNTERFEITS.

This room is in the Redemption Bureau, Treasury Building.   Over One Hundred Thousand Dollars' worth of Fractional Currency alone is here daily received for redemption; out of which about $350 dollars' worth of counterfeit money is detected, stamped and returned.

Supervising Architect's office. Mullett was not inclined to be criticized, expressing his "deep regret" that delivery of the pilasters and columns were "so far delayed beyond the time stipulated" in the contract and again threatening to suspend the work and charge Kirkland with the damages. In fact, even after the order was shipped a week after the contractual due date, Mullett kept haranguing and threatening the founders.[51]

Kirkland's response was to reiterate his firm's problems translating Mullett's drawings into structurally sound ironwork. On June 1, 1867, he requested that Mullett's chief draftsman, the Prussian-born engineer William G. Steinmetz, spend a day in New York to consult about the best plan for mounting the hinges on the door frames; none of the door frames had yet been sent, a sore point with Mullett. By the middle of June, although production of the pilasters and columns for the upper stories was progressing satisfactorily, Kirkland still had not cast any door frames, as the firm awaited advice from the supervising architect's office about how they were going to be mounted.[52]

When Mullett later omitted window frames (included in the published announcement for bids) from Kirkland's original bid on March 29, 1867, he was considering framing the north wing's windows with marble. In the fall, having decided on iron, he solicited bids from other founders as well as Kirkland, which immediately objected on the grounds that they had been verbally assured in the spring they would get any future window frame contract, as they were the low bidder. Mullett disputed Kirkland's right to the window frame contract at their original bid of ten cents per pound but did award it to them, closing his letter with the exhortation that the "whole of the work must be delivered on or before January 1st 1868." Typically, Mullett inserted a sentence in published proposals that allowed him a lot of flexibility. "The Department reserves the right to accept separate portions of the various proposals, and to reject any or all of the bids, if considered for [sic] the interest of the Government to do so."[53]

Subsequently, Mullett and Oertly recalculated the weights of the individual window frames and dropped the price to seven cents per pound. "In making this decision," Mullett wrote Kirkland on November 11, "I assure you I do so with regret as it would give me great pleasure and much less trouble to award the work to you at the price you ask, but I do not feel that it would be in strict accordance with my duty to the Department." Three days later Mullett adjusted prices for the remaining door frames and all the window frames, hoping to rectify "a very grave misunderstanding" between them, but the costs were still decidedly to the Treasury's advantage. Once again Kirkland was unable to meet Mullett's ambitious deadline of January 1, 1868. On February 13 he notified the foundry that in eight days they would be in default of their contract and fifteen percent would be deducted from their final payment. In a second letter sent the same day, Mullett noted that he had repeatedly granted the firm extensions. Apparently, Kirkland met the schedule for the frames and in mid-March sent twenty boxes of "ornaments for Collums [sic]," noting that "this completes *your whole order*," grateful to have this job behind them. Mullett shot back that they had forgotten to include the screws.[54]

"Emblematic of the Dignity of the Nation:" The Cash Room

Mullett had a particular affinity for all aspects of interior design from a sensitivity to color harmonies on walls and floors, to patterns for carpets and draperies in lofty rooms and minute proportional relationships of furniture and chandeliers placed in them. Rogers recognized this talent and after he selected him as his assistant, assigned Mullett oversight of the interior design and furnishing of the buildings being erected by the Supervising

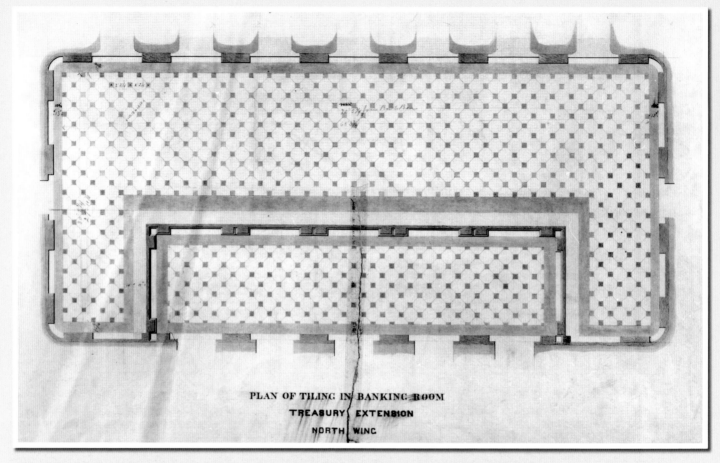

PLAN OF TILING IN BANKING ROOM
TREASURY EXTENSION
NORTH WING

V-16 The Cash Room was a banking room with clerks separated from the public via an elaborate counter.

Architect's office. Mullett quickly established contacts in firms of all kinds involved in both the manufacture and importing of fine quality goods and materials, particularly in Philadelphia and New York. In most of the government buildings he had superintended before the Treasury Extension—customs houses, courthouses, post offices—his opportunities to exercise his taste for rich but subdued opulence were limited to the rooms occupied by a few senior employees.

The Treasury Building's north wing had several rooms occupied by division heads and senior clerks who routinely met with significant figures in the national and international financial worlds who judged the status of their peers by the character and quality of the offices they could command. Neither watercolors nor photographs, and only a few descriptions, record the actual appearance of these Treasury offices as completed in 1869–1870, but correspondence

with suppliers and sometimes detailed invoices, coupled with descriptions, give some clues about the furnishing and decorating of the most important rooms. They do not, however, reflect the reality of furnishing most of the offices because desks, chairs, and book and file cases were more often made in the Treasury's own cabinet shop for which scanty records survive. Moreover, beginning in 1864 or 1865, clerks were required to submit their requests for furniture to the general superintendent of the building, rather than the Supervising Architect's office. These monthly reports for the north wing note the amounts expended on furniture alongside that spent for forage and grooming of the department's horses. The exception to this rule was the Cash Room, every aspect of which Mullett controlled. (fig. V-16 & fig. V-17)

Mullett intended from the outset that the U.S. Treasurer's Banking Room, known as the

Cash Room while it was still under construction, be the Treasury Building's crowning architectural achievement. He pointed out in his 1868 annual report that it was "the only strictly public [room] in the Treasury building," no doubt the impetus to design it to the best of his abilities and construct it of the finest and most permanent materials. His known correspondence relating to the north wing attests to his efficiency and the acerbic means

he realized it. His annual reports offered few openings for either congressional or public criticism of his designs and their cost. Mullett publicly criticized Rogers's cutting costs by using "sham" materials like iron painted to imitate stone in the west wing as he slowly maneuvered McCulloch and Congress into accepting the

V-17 Matthew Brady photographed the clerks' side of the Cash Room shortly after it was completed in 1869.

costs of the Cash Room's marble walls and floor and bronze railing and chandeliers.[55]

Mullett's intention to build the Cash Room in marble probably was in response to the Capitol Extension's stylish marble, gilded plaster, and frescoed Renaissance Revival interiors. Yet, some astute observers (including Walter) found Meigs's décor at the Capitol vulgar in its garishness. The Cash Room's harmonious and muted "tasteful" colors were in marked contrast to the Capitol Extension's vibrant ones. Mullett promoted the "purity" of the Cash Room's design as "emblematic of the dignity of the nation and the stability of its credit." Although the interiors of the President's House had been redecorated apace with changing tastes, no significant addition stood in contrast to the original building comparable to the Capitol's wings. Moreover, general access to the President's House was limited to special occasions; the Treasury Building was visited daily by a much wider range of national public officials and professional men as the department carried out the government's broad-ranging financial business. The Cash Room would not only represent the department for much of the public but the executive branch as well.[56]

In 1852–53 Walter was asked to modernize the President's House, but in 1866–67 it was Mullett who was consulted. He recommended removing the old east wing and a year later replaced it with a wide and dignified one-story Doric portico approached via a semi-circular plaza containing a fountain and a variant of an imperial staircase. (see fig. IV-34) This admirable combination of landscape and architectural solution merged the disparate levels of the President's Grounds and linked them to the Treasury's imposing west front simply and elegantly. The dispatch with which this and his other suggestions were carried out may have given Mullett some leverage with officials when urging that the Cash Room, as the executive branch's most visited public space, ought to be appropriately splendid. Vying with the opulence of the private banking houses that conducted business with the Treasury Department was probably another factor in Mullett's thinking.

In his 1874 satirical account of Mullett's dealings with Congress, the journalist and writer George Alfred Townsend described him as a,

> slender, wiry, anxious-looking gentleman, a professional architect, and possessed with a vaster ambition and a vaster field than Michel Angelo. Inigo Jones, his great prototype, was no more than a mound-builder to him, for Mr. Mullett is the absolute architectural controller of more than two hundred buildings, costing from $25,000 to nearly $7,000,000 apiece.[57]

Jones was Britain's Surveyor of Public Works (1615–1640), equivalent to the Office of the Supervising Architect of the Treasury; his introduction of Italian Renaissance architecture into England provided the decisive break with its native Elizabethan traditions. Quite possibly Townsend also recognized the interior of Jones's Banqueting House (1619–1637), located amidst London's complex of government buildings in Whitehall, as Mullett's model for the Cash Room. (fig. V-18 & V-19) As its name suggests, the Banqueting House was designed for important royal entertainments. Its two-story hall measuring 110 feet by 55 feet by 55 feet is a double cube, a shape considered in the seventeenth century to have great inherent architectural beauty. The Cash Room, at 72 feet in length, 32 feet in width, and 27.5 feet in height, is not a precise double cube but gives that impression. In fact, Mullett extended the room an additional twelve feet into the courtyard from the Treasury Extension's standard room width of twenty feet to achieve the Cash Room's satisfying proportional dimensions as well as to provide adequate space for the Treasurer's clerks on one side of its counter and their clients on the other.[58]

Above: V-18 Mullett combined seven native and imported marbles to achieve the Cash Room's muted color harmonies.

Right: V-19 Mullett's probable model for the Cash Room was Inigo Jones's Banqueting Hall in London.

The Cash Room shares other significant architectural features with the Banqueting Hall: a narrow balcony that divides it horizontally; vertical division of its long sides into seven bays; and a flat, beamed ceiling supporting its major decorative elements, three massive American chandeliers in the Cash Room and paintings on the Banqueting Hall's ceiling. Jones arranged single Ionic columns along the flanks of the Banqueting Hall's lower level (but double ones at the centers of the end walls) and Corinthian pilasters to articulate its upper walls. Mullett placed double pilasters around the perimeters of both levels of the Cash Room, pilasters so thick that they verge on being square engaged columns, to rival the three-dimensional character of the Banqueting House's free-standing circular ones. Mullett used Roman-derived Renaissance versions of Corinthian and composite orders to not only proclaim the Cash Room's architectural superiority within the Treasury Building but also perhaps to challenge architecturally another aspect of the Capitol Extension's revival of Italian Renaissance architecture, its use of the classical orders.

Walter, the architect of the Capitol Extension, and Mullett differed in their attitudes about how to design orders within the context of the histories of their buildings and the revival of classical architecture. The Romans placed the composite above the Corinthian at the top of their hierarchy of the orders, the composite's capital combining the acanthus leaves of the Corinthian with the large volutes of the Ionic. It was rarely used because it was reserved for the most important rooms or buildings. Jefferson's library room in the Corinthian rotunda at the University of Virginia, for example, is ringed with composite columns to express its supreme value to the educational community. Walter planned the new Senate as a Corinthian room, elevating its importance architecturally above that of the House chamber which was astylar, that is, decorated using none of the classical

architectural orders. Walter's use of Corinthian for the Senate reflected the ascendancy of that legislative body during the nineteenth century, a reversal of Jefferson and Latrobe's favoring of the House (Corinthian) over the Senate (Ionic) early in the Capitol's history because, they argued, the former represented the people.

In keeping with Latrobe's intellectually and visually rich tradition of inventing three American orders comparable to the Capitol's ancient Greeks ones, Walter invented an American composite order for the east vestibule leading to his Corinthian Senate chamber. (fig. V-20) He combined Latrobe's tobacco leaves, corncobs, and magnolia blossoms, placing them atop traditional European acanthus leaves to create a true "composite" capital that fused American and European traditions. Mullett, on the other hand, was very critical of the inventive variations on classicism by all of his predecessors at the Treasury Building. He denigrated Mills's colonnade as "a box of cigars escaped as they stood on end," dismissed Young's and Bruff's versions of the American order that incorporated the Treasury's seal, and scorned Rogers's acroterial cornice.[59]

Instead, for the Cash Room, Mullett adopted Roman and Renaissance orders, choosing for the upper level a Renaissance composite one (fig. V-21) and for the lower level the most elaborate Roman Corinthian, the one with central intertwined volutes between lateral ones. (fig. V-22) The latter had been invented for the Temple of Jupiter Stator in Rome, the first marble temple erected in Rome. Robert Mills drew on that model for his General Post Office; it was Washington's first marble building. The execution of the Post Office's capitals, however, was somewhat crude and the American marble of poor quality. A quarter of a century later, Mullett was able to command superb quality Italian marble to celebrate the completion of the Treasury Building with a magnificent marble room of his design. Both architects exploited

Above: V-20 The Capitol's composite order combined acanthus, tobacco, and corn leaves with a magnolia flower.

Below: V-21 Large volutes on Mullett's "correct" composite capitals decorate the Cash Room's upper story.

Right: V-22 Mullett designed traditional Renaissance Revival Corinthian columns for the Cash Room's lower story.

the Victorian era's ideal of the associative power of historical architecture to connect America's great public buildings with one of Rome's legendary ones. Moreover, Mullett may have borrowed important historical orders for the Cash Room to suggest the Treasury Department's stability within the federal government, in contrast to Congress's cyclical changes.

"A Thorough Scholar:" Bruff's Cash Room Gallery

Spacious, double-story rooms for exchanges and banks were the norm in European architecture by at least the mid-eighteenth century. Rectangular rooms modeled on the Banqueting Hall, such as London's Royal Exchange (1838–44), were one common nineteenth-century solution. The narrow galleries that divided such rooms horizontally were more than an elegant sculptural effect; they provided security personnel a commanding overview of the entire room. In Bruff's hands the Cash Room's bronze railing became a major work of decorative sculpture and during the design process its only emphatically "American" element. In early December 1867, Mullett sent photographic prints of Bruff's initial drawings for the railing to at least four foundries in Philadelphia and New York, soliciting bids for its execution. He was disappointed when he received only one proposal, a Gothic design from Robert Wood & Company of Philadelphia which he rejected.[60]

In late December Henri Lovie became involved in the railing at Mullett's suggestion. Lovie was a fellow Cincinnatian and as a painter later made watercolor renderings of the major buildings Mullett designed as supervising architect. Lovie was also a bronze sculptor and sent Wood sample balusters to show his finishing techniques. A week later Lovie sent Mullett drawings to demonstrate how to turn Bruff's design drawings into working ones comprehensible to the founders. "Whoever made the first

designs is a thorough scholar of the most severe German school and you can adhere to his judgment safely," Lovie wrote Mullett at the same time he enclosed drawings showing some minor changes because Bruff's design needed "a little more freedom in curve." Bruff combined in his initial design an anthemion frieze and running scroll motif, Greek and Roman decorative elements that tied the railing to the ornament throughout the rest of the building. (fig. V-23) He experimented with different ways of framing these free-flowing curvilinear forms, settling on the strictly geometric fretwork at the top and bottom. Mullett called Bruff's design Roman but Lovie called it Greek—the "German school" referred to a strict adherence among nineteenth-century German Greek Revival architects to ancient details rather than a free interpretation of them. "I would prefer the 'Renaissance' translation of the same scroll," Lovie advised Mullett, "for the purpose if admissible with the general architecture of the room, and of all the ornamental styles it would be the only thing admissible if the room is in purely classic style as it is in itself after all only a flowery translation of the classic." In fact, the Cash Room was a Renaissance Revival room in a Greek Revival building whose earlier interior ornament incorporated Roman elements, a synthesis recognized by Bruff in his railing design.[61] (fig. V-24)

By late February 1868 Bruff had prepared full-size working drawings that incorporated Lovie's suggestions about the three-dimensional naturalism of its elements. He eliminated the stylized anthemion flowers and leaves of his first design and developed the scroll into

Opposite page, top: V-23 Renaissance Revival palmette friezes were Mullett's first choice for the Cash Room's railing.

Bottom: V-24 Bruff added native American flora, grains, and symbols to express the dual heritage of Euro-Americans.

BRONZE RAILING

FOR

U. S. Cashiers-Room.

14 Sections 9'3½" long
6 do. 8'4" "
4 Corners ¼ circle of
10¾" radius.

Treasury Extn.
WASHINGTON D.C.

SCALE 1 INCH TO THE FOOT.

A.B.Mullett
Supervising Architect
Treasury Dept.

V-25 The Cash Room's railing allegorizes Treasury's role in all aspects of America's economic life.

horizontal arabesques still connected to traditional Renaissance models. They alternated with vertical groups composed of flora native to America that interacted with the arabesques, the whole symbolic of the dual heritage of Euro-Americans. More specifically, Bruff's Cash Room railing symbolized the Treasury Department's involvement with the country's economic life and firmly tied its content to his ornamental designs for the south and west wings. Clusters of grapes symbolizing the nation's plenty hung from the center of each arabesque while its minor tendrils terminated in cotton buds or flowers, Bruff's contribution to America's emblematic dictionary of symbols representing the country's principal economic producers, farmers and merchants. Each scroll's major stems enclosed stars that touched alternating fans composed of corn cobs supported by Mer-

cury's caduceus on one side and tobacco leaves and flowers spreading from an armorial shield of stars on the other. These were the emblems Latrobe designed for the Capitol at the beginning of the century. By 1868 their meaning was well understood and had been incorporated into the country's visual language of symbols. To supplement these new and old emblems representative of the nation's largely agrarian economy, Bruff added shells and starfish in recognition of the importance of its fishing industry. One contemporary astute observer spied that "at the corners of the balcony are overflowing baskets of peaches, apples, pears, and other American fruits," further expressions of America's bounty. The railing's overarching meaning was to represent allegorically the Treasury Department's critical role in all aspects of the nation's economic life.[62]

Mullett sent Bruff's drawings to the founders from whom he had originally solicited bids, noting that 210 lineal feet of railing were needed. Three firms responded with M.L. Curtis & Company of New York submitting the lowest bid at $25 per foot. In mid-March Mullett sent Curtis tracings for the short panels located next to the curved ones at the corners but not for the corners themselves. Mullett and Bruff had not yet solved the problem of foreshortening the vertical elements in drawn form that was necessary for the founders to make precision models in wood from which each section was cast; by early April they were successful. In July 1868 the walls had progressed to the point that Mullett was ready to install the gallery's floor, its three-foot, three-inch width supported by sixty-four cantilevered iron bars. He sent Curtis drawings for the gallery's soffit (the decorated underside of its floor) and the floor itself, asking if he wished to bid on work that had not been part of the railing contract at the same rate per pound. Curtis declined to contract for the new work at the same price but would take the job at a substantial increase. Mullett's response was that "it is contrary to the rules of this office to pay for any extra work that may be required in connection with any contract at greater rates than is paid under the original contract." Lovie was willing to do the work at $1 per pound and Mullett accepted his proposal on September 14 with a December 1 delivery date.[63]

While in Philadelphia on August 22, Mullett inspected the railing at Curtis's bronze works and pronounced himself satisfied; it was shipped the first week in September. Upon inspecting all the panels after they arrived in Washington, however, Mullett immediately found fault with them, possibly caused by shrinkage during the casting. "I regret to find that in order to save the paltry expense of different patterns for the sides and ends of the room, you have spoiled the long sections. The general finish of the railing is entirely satisfactory, but I cannot accept it until this defect is rectified." Two days later Mullett again berated Curtis for not making two patterns and closed his letter by asking if Curtis wished him to "remedy the defects at your cost or to do it yourself." Mullett accepted the work "upon agreement of Mr. Curtis to furnish additional ornaments that will remedy the difficulty." No immediate further correspondence has been found so it is uncertain what the outcome was, but Mullett had made another enemy among the skilled contractors who were busily engaged in the postwar boom in commercial and private building. More than two years later, Mullett asked Curtis to return the pattern for the railing and the founder's curt reply was that the drawings had been shipped on September 29, 1868.[64]

"Numerous and Beautiful Reception Rooms:" Ulysses S. Grant's Inaugural Ball

Washington's city authorities traditionally appointed inaugural committees to organize nineteenth-century inaugural balls; most of the volunteers on the various sub-committees were drawn from the government's clerical workers. When Grant learned on January 21 that his inauguration committee planned to meet soon to secure a venue (after the Capitol rotunda and Smithsonian's great hall were rejected), he wrote its secretary, Thomas L. Tullock. "If any choice is left to me, I would be pleased to see [the ball] dispensed with. I do not wish to disarrange any plans made by my friends in the matter of ceremonials attending the inauguration, but in this matter it will be agreeable to me if your committee should agree that the ball is unnecessary." Rather, Grant announced that he would hold "a public reception at the White House on the afternoon of his inauguration." But such a popular evening party near the end of winter—March 4—was important to Washingtonians who wished "that the excellent and time-honored usage is to be kept alive."[65]

On February 2 the *Star* announced that an enlarged committee (later revealed as bolstered by local Democrats, Grant's opposition party) had succeeded in securing the Treasury Building's north wing. It is "a place, by the way, far better adapted to the purpose than the Capitol, containing as it does, numerous and beautiful reception rooms, *en suite,* dancing accommodations for fully two hundred couples at a time, and ample and suitable quarters for dressing, refreshment rooms, etc." The Cash Room was not mentioned until February 19, after the committee had determined how the north wing's rooms were to be used. The northeast corner rooms on all floors "being about twenty-five feet wide by one hundred in length will each be devoted to dancing, as will the bank room." Four rooms on the second story (now the third) northwest of the Banking Room were reserved for President Grant, Vice President Schuyler Colfax, and their families. Ladies and gentlemen's separate cloak rooms were designated as was a barber shop; several tailors and seamstresses were on call during the evening.[66]

The *National Republican* described the Banking Room as "handsomely finished with Italian marble and the ceiling beautifully frescoed," noted that the floors of the rooms designated for dancing were bare, "but the others are carpeted with a neat small figured oak and green pattern, all the rooms being covered with the same quality and style of carpet." No other evidence of the ceiling being frescoed has been located; such a treatment would have been exactly the kind of "sham" that was anathema to Mullett. The north wing's furnishings and modern amenities provided in this first printed description of its interiors were of great interest to the curious public.

> Many of the rooms are provided with magnificent mirrors, and in each is a clock, the hands of which are moved by electricity, which is transmitted by wires from the

regulator in another part of the building, by which a uniformity of time is maintained in all the rooms in the building. The iron railing of the stairways not being ready to be put up in season for the ball, a substantial wooden one is being put up for temporary service.[67]

In fact, the Treasury's workmen built many temporary installations for the safety and comfort of the ball's attendees, their cost borne by the inaugural committee. (fig. V-26)

Washington's press excitedly informed the public that two—or rather, three—no, make that five bands were to entertain guests and that each $10 ticket would admit one gentleman and two ladies. The Treasury's east doors were thrown open to the general public at 8:00 p.m. on Thursday, March 4, with guests immediately ascending to the fourth floor (now fifth) where cloak room attendants waited to take the bulky winter wraps of six thousand party-goers. Between diners unable to reach the supper tables in the basement and departing guests leaving without their coats because they were hopelessly muddled in the crowded cloak rooms, it soon became evident that the committee had sold more tickets than the Treasury Building's allotted spaces could accommodate. Grant's inaugural ball, or reception as the *New York Times* claimed it was to be called because ex-President Johnson was not invited, became infamous for its mismanagement. Most of the attendees took it all in good humor, the dancing not ending until 5:00 a.m. on Friday morning.[68]

President Grant's popularity enticed attendees from every state and all the ambassadors and foreign ministers in the city were there. Invited guests and the diplomatic corps entered through the north portico, its columns decorated with gas jets that spelled out "PEACE." Judging from the press reports, glimpses of the nearly completed north wing were almost as much of a draw as the dignitaries, dancing, and

THE INAUGURATION RECEPTION.—Sketched by A. R. Waud.—[See Page 202.]

dining. The *National Republican* described the president's reception room as "very handsomely fitted, a real Brussels carpet of fine texture covering the floor; the furniture of rosewood and red velvet and fancy brocatelle; and the windows shrouded in handsome lace curtains." Furniture coverings and outer curtains in both the vice president's and the ladies' reception rooms—also part of the Internal Revenue Bureau's suite—were green velvet. In 1874 Mary Clemmer Ames was taken with the furnishing in these rooms after they began being used for their intended purpose. She noted they were "covered with miles of Brussels carpeting, in green and gold. Their walls are set with elegant mirrors, hung with maps and pictures. There are globes, cases filled with books, cushioned furniture—all the accompaniments of elegant

V-26   Each $10 ticket for Ulysses S. Grant's Inaugural Ball admitted one gentleman and two ladies.

apartments, and one opening into the other, forming a perfect *suite*."[69]

During Grant's inaugural ball, other rooms on the main and second floors (now second and third), many unfinished, were open for promenades, while some were reserved for invited guests. Because it was intended that Grant and Colfax would begin greeting guests in the Cash Room at 10:30, followed by dancing, a polished temporary wood floor was installed. "To the regret of the management, the gas in the principal reception room for some unknown and irremediable cause failed to burn with brilliancy sufficient to give the magnificent room anything but a hazy, twilight appearance, and as a consequence, the proposed formal reception of the President was changed," to one of the northeast rooms designated for dancing. Mullett and draftsman William Steinmetz, his chief assistant in readying the building for the event, solved the problem of the Cash Room's unfin-

ished upper walls by draping them with greenery and flags.[70] (fig. V-27)

In January 1869 Mullett hired the New York furniture manufacturers and decorators, Pottier & Stymus, to make the mahogany tellers' screen for the Cash Room's U-shaped counter to be edged with "ebony black mouldings [sic]." The firm also provided the clear plate glass windows, the whole photographed by Matthew

V-27 Red, white, and blue bunting hid the Cash Room's unfinished parts during the 1869 inaugural festivities.

Fortress of Finance: The United States Treasury Building

Brady soon after the installation was complete. (see fig. V-17) They also made the screens for the clerks' desks set perpendicular to the courtyard wall to take advantage of natural light, but the desks themselves may have been made by the Treasury's cabinetmakers.[71]

The Cash Room's three chandeliers, manufactured by M.L. Curtis & Company of New York, were suspended from the central panels in the flat iron ceiling. The large central one, purchased for $1,500, had forty-two burners on three tiers of branches. The smaller end ones initially had twenty-four burners on two tiers but were exchanged a year later for ones with thirty-six burners when they did not provide enough light. Once the counter was installed, they hung directly above its central screens illuminating the work surfaces for the Treasurer's clerks, their flickering light reflecting off the highly polished walls to make the room warm and inviting on the grayest days.[72]

The Cash Room's three chandeliers were a lighter bronze color than the "dark bronze" of those supplied for the north wing's rooms and corridors in the "Treasury pattern" by the Tucker Manufacturing Company of New York. On June 2, 1868, after the firm had sent him a sample chandelier that he installed in his office, Mullett acknowledged receiving from Tucker their "design for gas fixtures for public buildings. It comes nearer to my idea of what is required than anything that has yet been brought to my notice." In mid-July the firm sent a sample chandelier of this design but Mullett's experience of either or both of the samples led him to notify the manufacturers that their fixtures were "liable to corrosion and will in a comparatively short time become disfigured and lose their peculiar brilliance of finish."[73]

This led the company to offer a guarantee that its fixtures would "wear equal to those of any other manufacturers," at the same time they noted their goods were half the price of others on the market. Mullett immediately ordered seventy-six, six-light chandeliers of Tucker's "public building" design with a slight modification to its base. "This order is given with the understanding that this pattern of fixtures shall be sold to this Department only and for no private use, and that a guarantee bond for $2000 shall be filed in the Department." Four days later Mullett sent outline designs for smaller four-light chandeliers for the halls noting that they were only twelve feet wide. Because they were destined for the exclusive use in the Treasury Building, their seven-and-one-half-inch glass globes had a view of the building and stars etched on them. Mullett continued to order Tucker chandeliers for the north wing. By early October he sent the firm a schedule of their distribution on all five floors, seventy-six of the large chandeliers and twenty-seven small ones for hallways. In mid-September 1870 Tucker made good on his bond, providing an eight-light chandelier to replace a defective one in the "Vestibule of main entrance to Treas'y build'g." Thirty-two additional six-light chandeliers were shipped during the early fall of 1871, probably because many north-facing rooms needed additional illumination during the winter months, the work of the clerks demanding close attention to details.[74]

Mullett was directly involved in the order for some of the furniture for Treasurer Spinner's office, a suite of two rooms located in the northeast corner of the entrance floor, just a few steps from the Cash Room. (fig. V-28) Spinner's desk chair was a revolving mahogany arm chair with a cane seat, but Mullett also ordered from Pottier & Stymus comfortable stuffed furniture including a sofa, six side chairs and a single stuffed arm chair for the treasurer's frequent visitors, all at moderate cost.[75] Spinner's hospitality was legendary. (fig. V-29)

It is astonishing . . . to note the number of people, principally from the country districts, who stray into the Treasurer's room during the course of the year for the

Pottier & Stymus
Manufacturing Company.
New York Aug. 5 1870
A. B. Mullett Esq.
Dear Sir,
Yours of the 30th
ult. was duly received —
The following are the articles
ordered for Gen'l Spinner's
room — Viz
One (1) Mahog'y Revolving Armchair }
    Cane seat   *$32 —*
" (1) " Stuff'd Back Armchair $58 —
Six (6) " " @ 27 — $162 —
One (1) " Sofa $155 —
" " " Side Table Marble Top $ 68 —
" Boxing & Packing $32 —
The above prices are for leather or
in the material from the sample

V-28 The New York decorators Pottier & Stymus
provided modest furniture for Treasurer Spinner's office.

Below: V-29 Spinner's oft-visited office was across the hall from the
Cash Room, which was under his control.

purpose of shaking hands with "the man who makes that funny signature," and of looking wonderingly on to see how he makes it . . . The room is of moderate size and plainly furnished, and gives evidence that of the vast amount of money which has passed through his office, but little has been used to minister to the Treasurer's comfort. A door opens into a still smaller apartment in which the Treasurer sleeps.[76]

The chief cashier and his clerk occupied the room west of the Cash Room, its doors opening both onto it and to the main hall. The room immediately to the Cash Room's east, accessible only from behind the clerk's counter, contained the Treasurer's walk-in vault and an elevator descending to the shipping office in the basement. Three of the vault's walls had the advantage of the thickness of the room's walls for added security although it depended on alternate plates of iron and steel for its ceiling, floor, and door as well as its walls. The $11,850 contract for the vault with L.H. Miller of Baltimore was signed on July 30, 1868. It was a twelve-foot-square metal room within a granite one, ventilated via a chimney flue for the safety of the clerks and visitors. When its doors were open, the interior of its two levels were lit via a window in the granite room overlooking the courtyard. (fig. V-30) The advertisement for bids noted that the locks would be provided by the department but were to be installed by the contractor. The plans obtainable to bidders from the supervising architect's office were useless to thieves because they just showed the dimensions of the room. It took nearly a year to construct the vault, with very few modifications made to the original design except for the substitution of double doors, inner and outer, rather than a single one. Each door had two combination locks with no one knowing the combinations to all four locks. "The sides of the vault are divided into compartments, cubic in form and of con-

IN THE MONEY VAULT.

V-30 Tourists often visited the Treasury's vaults, including the two-story one adjacent to the Cash Room.

venient size, the door to each of which is numbered, so that its contents can be registered in a book, and is provided with a fastening to which a leaden seal can be affixed," *Scribner's Monthly* informed its readers in 1873. Mullett declined an elaborate ornament on the door but visitors' descriptions noted that each of the metal panels was decorated with a nation's armorial shield and the letters "U.S."[77]

Mullett did not mention the Cash Room in his 1869 annual report; in fact, his reports generally focused more on future improvements he wished to make to the Treasury Building and its grounds than on completed work. Mary Clemmer Ames helped fill the information void for the public curious about the architectural character and appearance, functions, and employees of Washington's public buildings.

> If your visit [to the Treasury Building] means "money," as it may, you pass directly through the portico to the Cash-Room, into which it opens. No other room in the world as magnificent is devoted to such a purpose . . . Exclusive of the upper cornice, the walls are built entirely of marble. Seven varieties meet and merge into each other, to the harmony of its blended hues. From the main floor it rises through two stories of the building. Thus it has upper and lower windows, between which a narrow bronze gallery runs, encircling the entire room.[78]

Ames then proceeded to recount in detail the Cash Room's seven kinds of marbles, noting their origins, colors, and placement within the room. Her critical discernment in judging the Cash Room "superb" matched her clear, lively, and informative narrative. Mullett's "vast" ambition created a tasteful, subtle, and elegant place of business where many of the executive branch's most important functions were carried out amidst beauty.

"The Services of Gallatin to His Country:" The North Plaza

Bruff probably designed the lion head fountain that stood in the center of the entrance plaza from 1869 until 1939 when it was removed for the Gallatin statue. The immensity of its scale—the main basin was thirty feet in diameter—was justly proportioned to its site. Four overflow basins projected another five feet eight inches and were fed from lion-head spouts, each about four feet in diameter. A single jet threw a tall spray up from the five-foot tall central bowl cut from a single piece of granite, while twenty-four small jets filled the basin, the whole fountain a kinetic element that further enlivened the entire corner and became a favorite subject for artists and photographers.[79] (fig. V-31)

In 1875, the *Washington Star* commented on the fountain.

> Two ladies, who fell into a polite dispute yesterday while looking at the north fountain of the Treasury and who know *The Star* to be an authority on art, have written to ask whether the sculptor has faithfully carved the heads of lions, or whether he intentionally modified the leonine phiz [*sic*] with a touch of the grotesqueness usual in gargoyles. It places us in a delicate position. We can give but one opinion, we must satisfy both parties, and we always tell the truth. These spouting beasts were good conventional lions in the beginning, but have imbibed Potomac water till they are turned into dragons.[80]

The north fountain was fed from the new aqueduct system begun by the Army Corps of Engineers in 1853, infamous for the cloudiness of the water it delivered until the filtration plant was built in the 1880s. The fountain's cost was not insignificant—Beals & Dixon was paid $35,960 for materials and labor including the lion heads, which may have gone to the National Zoo when the fountain was dismantled.[81] (fig. V-32)

V-31 Bruff's fountain welcomed visitors to the Treasury's new front door, 1500 Pennsylvania Avenue.

V-32 Grand European cityscapes inspired the north forecourt's fusion of architecture and horticulture.

In September 1868, when the Penrhyn Slate Company could not find rail transport for two carloads of tiles for the terrace, Mullett wrote directly to Cornelius Vanderbilt, president of the Hudson River Railroad, asking him to send cars to Washington County, New York. Penrhyn supplied two-inch-square, purple and green slate tiles for the area immediately around the fountain and twelve-inch-square tiles laid diagonally in a lozenge pattern for the rest of the terrace.[82]

In April 1927 a distinguished delegation visited the Treasury Building's grounds, inspecting several sites for a statue of Albert Gallatin. The Democratic Congress had just proposed to honor Jefferson's Treasury secretary with a monument at the north entrance. The group consisted of noted British architect Sir Edwin Lutyens, in Washington on business related to his design for the British Embassy on Massachusetts Avenue. He was joined by Cass Gilbert (later architect of the Supreme Court and the Treasury Annex) Louis Simon (Supervising Architect of the Treasury), Frederick L. Brooke (Lutyens's local architect), and several important federal officials, including Assistant Secretary of the Treasury Carl T. Schuneman. Six weeks later the Commission of Fine Arts approved a site on the west side of the Treasury Building, Congress subsequently appropriating $10,000 for its base on that location. Early in 1929 the Gallatin Memorial Fund Committee, composed of private citizens and chaired by New York banker Charles H. Sabin, set about raising an additional $40,000 for the statue.[83]

The funds were to be raised particularly in Pennsylvania and New York, the Swiss-born Gallatin having represented Pennsylvania in both the House and Senate before Jefferson appointed him Secretary of the Treasury in 1801. He served until 1814, the longest term of any Secretary of the Treasury. Gallatin spent his last twenty-two years in New York where he was president of the National Bank of New York and was one of the founders of New York University. By the end of October 1929, the committee had raised more than $13,000 and, despite the economic effects of Black Tuesday, the committee was able to report $15,000 in their coffers by early March 1930. At that point, the committee's vice chairman, Washingtonian Frederick P.H. Siddons, secretary of the American Security and Trust Company, took a more active role in raising funds; by mid-July the total has risen to almost $27,000; prominent bankers continued to lead the effort and by the end of 1934 the committee had reached its goal.[84]

The memorial fund committee proposed to locate the Gallatin statue next to that of Alexander Hamilton (placed on the south front's plaza in 1923), apparently mindful of expressing equality between the two most influential early secretaries of the Treasury, the Federalist Hamilton and the Democratic-Republican Gallatin. Within a year of the congressional resolution, James Earle Fraser, the Hamilton statue's sculptor, had been tentatively selected to design the Gallatin statue to ensure that the two figures would also have aesthetic equity. Fraser's sketch model, approved by the Commission of Fine Arts on December 3, 1934, was for a figure standing in a similar pose as the Hamilton, with his right hand at his side, his left on his hip, and his head turned slightly to his left. (fig. V-33) Moreover, its base would have replicated that on which the Hamilton portrait stands, designed by Henry Bacon. The major differences between the two figures was Gallatin's more informal stance, enveloping cloak, and simpler surface articulation, all of which gave the figure far greater bulk than the attenuated and elegant Hamilton. Fraser reputedly used Gilbert Stuart's portrait to model Gallatin's face.

In December 1934 the committee anticipated the statue would be finished within a year without accounting for either the design review or political processes the proposed design would have to undergo. Secretary of the Commission of Fine Arts H. Paul Caemmerer more knowledgeably stated in October 1934: "In 1927, after Congress authorized the statue, the commission recommended it be located on the west steps of the Treasury, facing the east wing of the White House. Any change in this plan will have to be approved by the commission."[85] Eighteen months later a joint congressional committee's resolution reaffirmed the site facing the White House. "While we do not intend to draw any comparison in regard to the record of these two great men, we nevertheless cannot ignore the fact that many believe that the services of Gallatin to his country will more than equal those of his great contemporary, Hamilton," concluded the resolution. The location remained unresolved until 1938. At the end of July the Commission of Fine Arts recommended that the statue be placed on the Treasury's north plaza and in November met jointly with the National Capital Planning Commission to consider that site. Sectarian politics were surely the reason for the repeated delays; if Gallatin were to overlook the White House, his site would be more prestigious than Hamilton's; if they were to share the south steps, Hamilton would lose his primacy of place as the first Secretary of the Treasury.[86]

Since bronze sculptures in particular need direct sun in order to appreciate their three-dimensional qualities from overall form to surface details, either the south or west locations would have been preferable to the one on the north. Yet, the Commission of Fine Arts continued to push the north plaza site, apparently a compromise aimed at getting the statue erected. Its success was announced in May 1939, soon after the commission approved a simple pedestal, probably designed by Albert Randolph Ross who often worked with sculptors. Placing the Gallatin in the middle of the plaza well forward of

V-33 James Earle Fraser designed the statue of Albert Gallatin to stand beside Hamilton on the south plaza.

V-34 In 1939 the north plaza site for the Gallatin was chosen, but its dedication was delayed until 1947.

the North portico assured that the statue would be under direct sun during the middle of the day, although his cloak would be highlighted while his face was shaded. Bronze was unavailable for sculpture during World War II, so no further progress was made on the ten-foot-tall statue until it was cast after the war. On October 15, 1947 Gallatin's great-granddaughter, Mrs. Louise Gallatin Gay, unveiled the figure. Secretary of the Treasury John W. Snyder addressed the audience gathered on the north portico's steps and plaza. He likened the size of the post-war national debt to the one that Gallatin faced and solved, as his tribute to the fourth Secretary of the Treasury.[87] (fig. V-34)

"Considerable Additional Space:" Conclusions

Mullett was not satisfied with the roles he played in the Treasury Building's south, west, and north extensions. In October 1873 he reported to Secretary William A. Richardson that the solution to the department's ever-increasing space needs—and the problem with poor ventilation interfering with the productivity of the clerks working in the "old building"—was to rebuild in granite the east and center wings. The architect claimed he could increase their size by one-third. Moreover, "considerable additional space can be obtained on the south front of the building, by remodeling the centre on the same plan as the north wing is completed." Mullett's final suggestion was to seek congressional appropriations for a building for the "Printing Office," as the National Note Bureau was then called. Mullett was unsuccessful in his attempts to alter the "old building," but the Bureau of Engraving and Printing Building, designed by Supervising Architect of the Treasury James G. Hill as a plain brick Victorian building congruent with its near neighbors, was located on the south side of the Mall at 14th Street within sight of the Treasury Building. By 1917 the department was asking Congress for $1.25 million to build the Treasury Annex on the north side of the 1600 block of Pennsylvania Avenue facing the Treasury's north portico. Cass Gilbert's Beaux-Arts annex, its twentieth-century neoclassicism totally in harmony with its neighbor, was the result of design parameters established by the Senate Park Commission fifteen years earlier.[88]

Planning and constructing the first two buildings to house the Treasury Department was an epic undertaking spanning more than three-quarters of a century. Thousands of people ranging from Secretaries of the Treasury to stone cutters on a remote Maine island participated in the endeavor, a few leaving identifiable marks, while the contributions of most are invisible, but not entirely unknown. America's leading architects vied to execute the Treasury Office and Treasury Building that both advanced and bedeviled the careers of Hadfield, Hoban, Mills, Young, Walter, Rogers, and Mullett. The Treasury Building stands as a reminder of their achievements coupled with the advancing technology, transportation, and trade capabilities of the growing nation. While the Capitol and the White House are more iconic, there may be no other building in Washington that more clearly embodies the growth of this country and its federal government during the middle of the nineteenth century.

1   Rogers to Chase, April 13, 1863, reel 5, entry 7, RG 121; Fessenden to Seward, October 1, 1864, vol. 2, entry 6, RG 56; both NACP. "The Treasury Building," *Evening Star*, October 6, 1864, 3.

2   "The Treasury Building," *Evening Star*, October 6, 1864, 3. Secretary of the Treasury, *Report on the State of the Finances,* 39th Cong., 1st sess., 1865, H. Ex. Doc. 3, 186.

3   "Report of the Supervising Architect of the Treasury Building," *National Republican*, November 30, 1867, 3. Secretary of the Treasury, *Report on the State of the Finances,* 40th Cong., 2d sess., 1867, H. Ex. Doc. 2, 168.

4   Rogers to Fessenden, January 24, 1865; Rogers to John Suter and Rogers to John Borland, both February 27, 1865; Rogers to Suter, February 28, 1865; Rogers to Joseph J. Lewis, April 4, 1865; all reel 8, entry 7, RG 121, NACP.

5   Rogers, "Rules and Regulations," March 1, 1865, reel 8, entry 7, RG 121, NACP.

6   Ibid.

7   Rogers to McCulloch, June 9, 1865, reel 9, entry 7, RG 121; McCulloch to Rogers, June 8, 1865, vol. 3, Bb & B Series, entry 7, RG 56; both NACP.

8   Rogers to McCulloch, June 9, 1865, reel 9, entry 7, RG 121, NACP. "Buildings Occupied by the Treasury Department," *Evening Star,* January 29, 1869, 3.

9   Antoinette J. Lee, *Architects to the Nation. The Rise and Decline of the Supervising Architect's Office* (New York: Oxford University Press, 2000), 71. Daisy M. Smith, ed., *A.B. Mullett Diaries, Etc.* (Washington: Mullett-Smith Press, 1985), 85.

10   Mullett to Chandler, August 4, 1865, box 1452, entry 26, RG 121, NACP.

11   C.H. Manning to Mullett, April 1869, box 1465, entry 26, RG 121, NACP.

12   Oertly to Walker, September 30, 1865; Oertly to Mullett, December 4, 1865; Mullett to Seward, December 6, 1865, all reel 9, entry 7, RG 121, NACP.

13   Secretary of the Treasury, *Report on the State of the Finances,* 39th Cong., 2d sess., 1867, H. Ex. Doc. 4, 193. Mullett to McCulloch, May 1, 1866, reel 10, entry 7; Seward to McCulloch, May 7, 1866, box 1456, entry 26; both RG 121, NACP. Jennifer Laurie Ossman, "Reconstructing a National Image: The State, War and Navy Building and the Politics of Federal Design, 1866–90," (PhD diss., University of Virginia, 1996), 29–57. Pamela Scott, *Capital Engineers, The U.S. Army Corps of Engineers in the Development of Washington, D.C., 1790–2004* (Alexandria, Virginia: U.S. Army Corps of Engineers, 2005), 73–4.

14   "Washington, Affairs at the National Capital," *New York Times,* May 6, 1867, 5.

15   Rogers to Chase, April 13, 1863, reel 5, entry 7, RG 121, NACP.

16   Mullett to McCulloch, February 9, 1867, box 1461, entry 26, RG 121, NACP.

17   Secretary of the Treasury, *Report on the State of the Finances,* 40th Cong., 2d sess., 1868, H. Ex. Doc., 183–7.

18   Secretary of the Treasury, *Report on the State of the Finances,* 38th Cong., 1st sess., 1863, H. Ex. Doc. 3, 138.

19   Mullett to Parry, July 9, 1868, reel 21; Mullett to Wood, May 8 and May 23, 1867, reel 19; Mullett to Wood and Mullett to Lovie, both June 6, 1868, reel 20; all entry 7, RG 121, NACP.

20   Mullett to McCulloch, May 31, 1866, box 1456, entry 26, RG 121, NACP. Mullett to McCulloch, June 6, 1866 and Mullett to George W. Parker, and others, June 5, 1866, both reel 10; Mullett to Dr. W. J. C. Duhamel, February 1, 1867, reel 12; Mullett to McCulloch, May 21, 1867, reel 14; all entry 7, RG 121, NACP.

21   Mullett to Barton, Borland, Tisdale, Vaux, and Lyddan, April 10, 1867, reel 14, entry 7, RG 121, NACP.

22   James J. Mitchell and R.A. Miller to Johnson, May 20, 1867, box 1461, entry 26, RG 121, NACP.

23   Mullett to McCulloch, May 21, 1867, reel 14, entry 7, RG 121, NACP.

24   "The Clerks Movement for Increase of Pay, *Evening Star,* December 27, 1866, 3. "Meeting of Clerks, *Evening Star,* February 11, 1867, 3. "Extra Compensation," *Evening Star,* February 12, 1867, 2. "Passage of the Clerks' Compensation Bill," *Evening Star,* February 26, 1867, 3.

25   "Government Clerks Association," *Evening Star,* March 27, 1867, 3. "Female Clerks," *Evening Star,* December 11, 1866, 3.

26   "Women in the Treasury Department," *Evening Star,* December 29, 1866, 3. "Reduction of Force in the Treasury," *Evening Star,* June 8, 1867, 3. "Reduction of Force at the Treasury," *Evening Star,* September 2, 1867, 2. "Clerks Hire in Washington," *Evening Star,* August 24, 1867, 3. "Reduction of Force at the Treasury," *Evening Star,* September 2, 1867, 3.

27   Comptroller to Mullett, March 13, 1867, box 1461, entry 26; McCulloch, printed circular, February 2, 1867, reel 12, entry 7; both RG 121, NACP. "The Treasury Strike," *Evening Star,* June 20, 1867, 3. Jacob D. Bontz to McCulloch, June 11, 1867, box 1461, entry 26, RG 121, NACP.

28   "The Strike of the Bricklayers," *Evening Star,* June 19, 1867, 3.

29   Ibid.

30   "Strike at the Treasury Extension," *Evening Star,* June 17, 1867, 3. "The Bricklayers Strike at the Treasury," *Evening Star,* June 18, 1867, 3. "The Strike of the Bricklayers." *National Intelligencer,* June 20, 1867, 2. "The Treasury Extension," *Evening Star,* June 29, 1867, 1.

31 "The Bricklayers' Strike at the Treasury," *Evening Star,* June 24, 1867, 3. "The Strike at the Treasury Building," *New York Times,* June 25, 1867, 4. "The Bricklayers—No Compromise," *National Republican,* June 26, 1867, 2. Mullett to Clarkson, June 26, 1867, reel 15, entry 7, RG 121, NACP. "Bricklayer's Union," *Evening Star,* June 26, 1867, 2.

32 "The Treasury Extension," *Evening Star,* June 28, 1867, 3.

33 Representative Samuel F. Cary to Mullett, April 9, 1868 and Statements of Thomas N. Walsh and others, April 5–8, 1867, all box 1464, entry 26; Mullett to Cary, April 14, 1868, reel 19, entry 7; all RG 121, NACP.

34 Mullett to Charles F. Close, April 17, 1868, reel 19, entry 7, RG 121, NACP.

35 Mullett to Cary, May 8, 1868 and Mullett to Capt. F.J. Myers, May 29, 1868, both reel 20, entry 7, RG 121, NACP.

36 "The Treasury Strike," *Evening Star,* June 20, 1867, 3. "Redneck," Wikipedia, http://en.wikipedia.org/wiki/Redneck, accessed January 8, 2007.

37 Rogers to Chase, September 23, 1863, reel 6, entry 7, RG 121, NACP.

38 Ibid.

39 Beals & Dixon to Chase, April 7, 1864, box 1448, entry 26; Rogers to Beals & Dixon, May 5, 1864, reel 7, entry 7; Beals & Dixon to Chase, June 17, 1864, box 1448, entry 26; all RG 121, NACP.

40 Sneed to McCulloch, July 9, 1866, box 1464, entry 26, RG 121, NACP.

41 Beals & Dixon to Mullett, August 31, 1866, box 1456, entry 26; Mullett to McCulloch, September 26, 1866, reel 11, entry 7; both RG 121, NACP.

42 Beals & Dixon to Chandler, January 15, 1867, box 1461; Beals & Dixon to McCulloch, January 28, 1867, box 1464; both in entry 26, RG 121, NACP.

43 MuCulloch to Henry Stanbery, February 1, 1867, reel 13, entry 7; Oertly to McCulloch, February 2, 1867 and Mullett to McCulloch, February 7, 1867 (draft), both box 1461, entry 26; Mullett to McCulloch, February 7, 1867 (final version), reel 13, entry 7; Stanbery to McCulloch, June 25, 1867, box 1461, entry 26; Mullett to McCulloch, December 27, 1867, box 1461, entry 26; all RG 121, NACP.

44 McCulloch to Stevens, January 3, 1868, reel 18, entry 7, RG 121, NACP. *The Case of Beals & Dixon,* (Washington: McGill & Witherow, 1868), passim. "Joint Resolution 217," February 28, 1868, HR 40A-B2, entry 19, RG 233, NAB.

45 Dr. Donald R. Kennon of the Capitol Historical Society clarified this seemingly contradictory legislative maneuver.

46 Mullett to Phoenix Iron Company, March 4 and 5, 1867, reel 13; Mullett to Phoenix Iron Company, November 13, 1867, reel 17; both entry 7, RG 121, NACP.

47 Mullett to Phoenix Iron Company, November 13 and December 17, 1867, reel 17, entry 7, RG 121, NACP.

48 Mullett to Phoenix Iron Company, April 6, 1868, reel 19, entry 7; Mullett to Senator Daniel S. Norton, August 25, 1868, reel 22; both entry 7, RG 121, NACP.

49 "Proposals for Iron Work," *New York Times,* March 13, 1867, 7. Janes, Fowler, Kirkland to Mullett, March 19, 1867, box 1461, entry 26; Mullett to Janes, Fowler, Kirkland, March 19 and 22, 1867, reel 13, entry 7; all RG 121, NACP.

50 Mullett to James Kirkland & Co., May 7, 10, and 16, 1867, reel 14, entry 7; Kirkland to Mullett, May 17, 1867, box 1461, entry 26; both RG 121, NACP.

51 Kirkland to Mullett, May 17, 1867; Mullett to Kirkland, May 17 and 23, June 7 and 14, 1867; all reel 14, entry 7, RG 121, NACP.

52 Kirkland to Mullett, June 1, 1867, box 1461, entry 26, RG 121, NACP.

53 Kirkland to Mullett, October 4, 1867, box 1461, entry 26; Mullett to Kirkland, October 20, 1867, reel 17, entry 7; both RG 121, NACP. "Proposals for Iron Work," *New York Times,* March 13, 1867, 7.

54 Mullett to Kirkland, November 4, 6, and 11, 1867, box 1461, entry 26; Mullett to Kirkland, November 14, 1867, reel 17, entry 7; Mullett to Kirkland (two letters), February 13, 1868, reel 18, entry 7; Kirkland to Mullett, March 12, 1868, box 1462, entry 26; Mullett to Kirkland, March 20, 1868, reel 19, entry 7; all RG 121, NACP.

55 Secretary of the Treasury, *Report on the Finances,* 40th Cong., 2d sess., 1868, H. Ex. Doc. 2, 183.

56 Ibid.

57 George Alfred Townsend, *Washington, Outside and Inside* (Hartford: James Betts & Co., 1874), 513.

58 "The Treasury Cash-Room," *Appleton's Journal of Literature, Science and Art,* 7 (May 1872): 551–2.

59 Townsend, *Washington,* 567.

60 Nicholas Pevsner, *A History of Building Types* (Princeton: Princeton University Press, 1979), 201–7. Mullett to Curtis, December 5, 1867; Mullett to Ball & Black, Robt P. Wood, and Cornelius & Baker, December 12, 1867; both reel 17, entry 7, RG 121, NACP.

61 Lovie to Wood, December 29, 1867, box 1464; Lovie to Mullett, January 7, 1868, box 1462; entry 26, RG 121, NACP.

62 William R. Hooper, "The Treasury Cash Room," *Appleton's Journal of Literature, Science and Art* 7 (May 18, 1872): 551.

63 Mullett to Wood, February 27, 1868, reel 18, entry 7; "Synopsis," February 26, 1868, box 1464, entry 26; Mullett to Curtis, March 11, 1868, reel 19, entry 7; Curtis to Mullett, April 2, 1868, box 1464, entry 26; Mullett to Curtis, April 4, 1868, reel 19, entry 7; Mullett to Curtis, July 10 and 27, 1868, reel 21, entry 7; all RG 121, NACP.

64 Curtis to Mullett, August 31, 1868, box 1463, entry 26; Mullett to Curtis, September 17, 1868, reel 22, entry 7; Curtis to Mullett, December 12, 1870, box 1464, entry 26; all RG 121, NACP.

65 "Gen. Grant and the Proposed Inauguration Ball," *National Republican,* January 22, 1869, 1. "The Inauguration Ball," *Evening Star,* February 2, 1969, 2.

66 "The Inauguration Ball," *Evening Star,* February 2, 1869, 2; "Inauguration," *New York Times,* March 5, 1869, 3. "The Inauguration Ball," *National Republican,* February 19, 1869, 3.

67 "Immense Crowd in Attendance," *National Republican,* March 5, 1869, 1.

68 "The Inauguration Ball," *New York Times,* March 5, 1869. 3.

69 "Immense Crowd," *National Republican,* March 5, 1869, 1. Ames, *Ten Years in Washington,* 349.

70 "Inauguration Ball," *New York Times,* March 5, 1869, 3. "Immense Crowd," *National Republican,* March 5, 1869, 1. "Inaugural Ball," *Evening Star* March 5, 1869, 1.

71 Pottier & Stymus to Mullett, January 18 and May 15, 1869, box 1465, entry 26, RG 121, NACP.

72 Thomas Fisher to Mullett, September 14, 1870, box 1464, entry 26, RG 121, NACP.

73 Mullett to Fisher, May 19 and June 2, 1868, reel 20, entry 7; Fisher to Mullett, July 14 and August 22, 1868, box 1462, entry 26; all RG 121, NACP.

74 Fisher to Mullett, June 22, 1868, box 1462, entry 26; Mullett to Fisher, August 24 and 28, 1868, reel 21, entry 7; Mullett to Tucker, October 6, 1868, reel 22, entry 7; Fisher to Mullett, September 14, 1870, box 1464, entry 26; Mullett to Tucker, September 19, 1871, reel 26, entry 7; all RG 121, NACP.

75 Pottier & Stymus to Mullett, August 5, 1870, copy in Office of the Curator, Treasury Department.

76 "An Hour Among the Greenbacks," *Scribner's Monthly,* 5 (April 1873): 658.

77 Contract with L.H. Miller, July 30, 1868, copy in the Office of the Curator, Treasury Department. "Proposals for Treasury Vault," *National Republican,* July 3, 1868, 4. Mullett to Miller, October 6, 1868, reel 22, entry 7, RG 121, NACP. "An Hour," *Scribner's,* 661. Miller to Mullett, June 9, 1869, box 1465, entry 26, RG 121, NACP. Laura M. Doolittle, "Uncle Sam's Strong Box," *Appleton's Journal,* 5 (February 25, 1871): 232. The vault presently has a single door.

78 Ames, *Ten Years,* 340–1.

79 "The North Wing of the Treasury Department," *National Republican,* April 7, 1869, 3.

80 "Treasury Fountain," *Evening Star,* April 13, 1876, 4.

81 Mullett to Beals & Dixon, May 26, 1868, reel 20, entry 7, RG 121, NACP. Zoo Seeking Mute Lions, They're Stone Deaf, Too; WP, 15.

82 Penrhyn to Mullett, September 16, 1868; Mullett to Vanderbilt, September 18, 1868; Penrhyn to Mullett, September 29, 1868; all box 1463, entry 26, RG 121, NACP.

83 "Design for Marine and Navy Memorial Still Considered," *Washington Post,* April 15, 1927, 22.

84 Emanuel Celler to Editor, May 25, 1928, in *Congressional Record,* 69 (pt. 9):9963. "Gallatin Fund Nearly at Goal," *Washington Post,* October 2, 1934, 3. Commission of Fine Arts, Minutes, May 27, 1927, Office of the Commission of Fine Arts.

85 "Gallatin Fund," *Post,* October 2, 1934.

86 "House Favors Gallatin Statue to Compete with Hamilton's," *Washington Post,* May 20, 1936, X1. Commission of Fine Arts, Minutes, July 28 and November 18, 1938, Office of the Commission of Fine Arts. "Two Groups to Study City Improvements at Session Today," *Washington Post,* November 18, 1938, X29.

87 "Treasury Fountain May Come Down for Gallatin Statue," *Washington Post,* May 10, 1939, 2. Commission of Fine Arts, Minutes, April 21, 1939, Office of Commission of Fine Arts. Sculptor Bruce Moore, a student of Fraser's, identified Ross as the architect in a conversation with Dr. Michael Richman. "Gallatin Statue to be Unveiled," *Washington Post,* October 15, 1947, 8. "Snyder Urges Cut in National Debt," *Washington Post,* October 16, 1947, B2.

88 "Washington, Increased Accommodation in the Treasury Department Recommended," *New York Times,* October 9, 1873, 5. "Asks $1,250,000 Treasury Annex," *Washington Post,* June 9, 1817, 2.

First in the Field:
A Compendium of the Bureaus, Services, Divisions, Offices, and Units of the Department of the Treasury

Appendix

Based on Research by Mark Walston

Mary Clemmer Ames, Washington correspondent for the *New York Independent,* wrote in her 1873 book *Ten Years in Washington*, "One might as well try to snatch up a city and portray it in a sitting, as even to outline the Treasury of the United States in a single chapter." This brief catalogue presents in chronological order the Treasury Department's services and responsibilities that grew with and reflected the development of the nation. Its genealogy is complex because the names, the duties, and the alignment of the various bureaus shifted over time. A few of the bureaus even predated the establishment of the department and some began under other departments before moving to the Treasury Department.

Treasury Department, established 1789

When Congress first convened in New York City in March 1789, the framework of the federal government was well-established by the Constitution, but the picture within that frame was far from clear. The first two departments created— State (first called Foreign Affairs) and War— addressed external relations and threats. The Treasury Department, instituted on September 2, 1789, was the first to focus primarily on the domestic responsibilities of government which gradually extended far beyond collecting, dispersing, and accounting for revenue.

President Washington's choice of Alexander Hamilton as the first Secretary of the Treasury set a broad vision for the department. He not only addressed the debt accrued during the Revolutionary War, but also created a monetary system and established a federal budget. Most significantly, he firmly established the Treasury Department's leading role in promoting the vitality of the national economy during his five years of service.

Office of the Treasurer, established 1789

The September 2, 1789, act establishing the Treasury Department created four major offices under the Secretary— Treasurer, Comptroller, Auditor, and Register. The Treasurer's key functions were to receive, keep, and disperse "the monies of the United States"—essentially to be the federal government's bank. Vaults and strongboxes in the Treasury Building, and later in various sub-treasuries around the country, physically held taxes and tariffs which were collected in coin. The Treasurer's Office also oversaw the production of United States currency, initially through oversight of commercial bank note companies and private printers. In 1861 the Treasurer assumed responsibility for the production of "greenbacks," the government's first standardized paper currency.

Comptroller of the Treasury, established 1789

The Comptroller was assigned the duties of oversight, examination, and supervision of the public accounts as it reviewed and certified the work of the department's auditors. The 1894 Dockery Act created the Office of the Controller of the Treasury—a more modern spelling for an unchanging responsibility. The task was again reassigned, and the old name was restored, when the Budget and Accounting Act of 1921 created the General Accounting Office (GAO), independent of the executive branch and led by a Comptroller General.

Auditor of the Treasury, established 1789

The Auditor was responsible for receiving and reviewing bills submitted to the federal government for payment and making recommendations to the Comptroller as to payment. As federal activities grew, the Auditor's office increased to six divisions, each with responsibilities for the accounts of different portions of the government.

The First Auditor's office received and adjusted the accounts of the Customs Service and made disbursements, appropriations, and expenditures on account of the civil list and under private acts of Congress. The Second Auditor's office received and adjusted all accounts relating to the pay, clothing, and recruiting of the army; as well as to armories, arsenals, and ordnance; and all accounts relating to the Indian Bureau. The Third Auditor's office adjusted all accounts for subsistence of the army; for fortifications, the military academy, military roads, and the quartermaster's department; for pensions and claims arising from military services previous to 1816; and for horses and other property lost in the military service. The Fourth Auditor's office adjusted all accounts for the service of the Navy Department. The Fifth Auditor's responsibilities for State Department accounts were expanded for many years to include supervision of lighthouses and other navigational aids. The Sixth Auditor handled all accounts related to the Post Office Department. The Budget and Accounting Act of 1921 shifted all these functions to the General Accounting Office, an independent government agency.

Register of the Treasury, established 1789

The Register was the department's record-keeper and produced various reports including those on commerce and navigation, as well as maintaining the registry of vessels of the United States. Nearly 150 clerks were employed keeping the nation's books before the Dockery Act of 1894 created the Division of Bookkeeping and Warrants to document the receipt and expenditure of public funds. The Office of the Register was folded into the Bureau of the Public Debt in 1956.

Customs Service, established 1789

On July 4, 1789, four months after ratification of the Constitution, Congress passed the Tariff Act, creating the new federal government's principal source of revenue. Within that month, Congress established the Customs Service and identified ports of entry where custom houses would be located to collect import duties. The brigantine *Persis* under Captain James Weeks entered New York harbor on August 5, 1789, and paid $774.41 on a mixed cargo from Leghorn, Italy—the first duty paid to the federal government. When Congress established the Treasury Department in September 1789, Customs was placed under its purview. Because it was the first and for many years the principal federal presence in numerous communities, the Customs Service administered many Treasury programs from military pensions to lighthouse supervision to the collection of dues for mariners' hospitals.

By 1835 the Revolutionary War debt which had threatened the very existence of the new government had been retired through duties collected by the Customs Service. Until the passage of the Federal Income Tax Act of 1913, tariffs remained the major source of federal revenue. After 1913 the Customs Service took on other responsibilities. The onset of prohibition in 1919 meant battling a liquor-fueled stream of smugglers and rum-runners crossing into the country both by land and sea. Customs attained bureau status in 1927. It was transferred to the Department of Homeland Security in 2003.

Lighthouse Establishment, established 1789

Congress's recognition of the essential role that maritime commerce played in the national economy led to federalizing several navigational functions. The ninth congressional act, signed by President Washington on August 7, 1789, required the states to relinquish all lighthouses in service or under construction to the federal government. When the Treasury Department was created less than a month later, the Lighthouse Establishment was placed under its aegis. Its operations were largely the responsibility of custom collectors and lighthouse keepers until 1820 when administration of its seventy lighthouses was centralized under the Fifth Auditor of the Treasury. This post was occupied by Stephen Pleasonton who expanded the system to 331 lighthouses and 42 lightships by the end of his service in 1852. His resistance to technological improvements, especially to installing Fresnel lenses, led to the creation of the Light-House Board in 1852. The board remained part of the Treasury Department until 1903, when the Bureau of Lighthouses constituted part of the new Department of Commerce and Labor.

Post Office, established 1789

The Post Office Department was established as a distinct federal agency in 1789 with the Postmaster General reporting to the President through the Secretary of the Treasury, although the Post Office was never formally a division of Treasury. In 1829 President Jackson made the Postmaster General part of the Cabinet, but the Post Office continued to function as an adjunct of the Treasury Department until 1872, when the Post Office Department was established as a separate executive agency.

Military Pensions, 1790

The Continental Congress promised lifelong pensions to Revolutionary War veterans debilitated by their injuries, but the responsibility for providing them was assigned to the states. In 1790 Congress assumed the obligation and assigned the administration of pensions to the Treasury Department, largely because customs collectors were the most widely dispersed network of federal officials. Little funding was forthcoming, however, and few pensions were paid. In 1806 a national system of pensions was established under the Treasury Department, but two years later the Bureau of Pensions was placed under the control of the Secretary of War. Today military pensions are a responsibility of the Department of Veterans Affairs.

Revenue Marine Service, established 1790

Soon after collectors of customs were appointed in 1789, they called for armed assistance in combating smuggling. The Revenue Marine Service was created in 1790 and was outfitted with ten cutters, predating the establishment of the Navy by eight years. Secretary of the Treasury Alexander Hamilton instructed the cutter captains that they should "always keep in mind that their countrymen are freemen, and as such, are impatient of everything that bears the least mark of a domineering spirit." He urged the captains to "endeavor to overcome difficulties, if any are experienced, by a cool and temperate perseverance in their duty—by address and moderation, rather than by vehemence or violence."

The Revenue Marine Service served alongside the Navy in many conflicts beginning with the War of 1812. During the Civil War its name was changed to the Revenue Cutter Service. In 1915 President Wilson combined the Revenue Cutter Service and the Life-Saving Service into the United States Coast Guard, destined to be an important Treasury Department bureau. During World Wars I and II the Coast Guard was transferred to the Navy Department by executive order, then transferred back to Treasury at the end of each war. The Coast Guard absorbed other maritime responsibilities of the department including the United States Lighthouse Service in 1939 and the Navigation and Steamboat Inspection Service in 1942. In 1967 the Coast Guard was transferred to the newly formed Department of Transportation.

U. S. Mint, established 1792

The U. S. Mint was in existence for a full century before it became part of the Treasury. The Mint was established by the First Coinage Act of 1792, under the jurisdiction of the Department of State. The successor Bureau of the Mint under the Treasury Department was created in 1873 as part of the restoration of specie—payment in actual gold and silver coin rather than Civil War-era "greenback" paper currency. Under the Treasury's management, talented sculptors and engravers created numismatic art such as Charles Morgan's Liberty silver dollars, produced during his forty-eight years of service beginning in 1877.

In 1984 the Bureau was renamed the United States Mint. In addition to producing as many as twenty billion coins annually by the turn of the twenty-first century, the Mint maintains the nation's $100 billion gold and silver reserve

at Fort Knox, Kentucky and other locations; produces proof and un-circulated coins, commemorative coins, and medals for collectors; and manufactures and sells bullion coins in gold, silver, and platinum.

The same act that established the Mint in 1792 also created an Assay Commission for the rigorous inspection of the purity and weight of U. S. gold and silver coins. The statute designated inspectors including the Secretary of the Treasury, the Chief Justice, the Secretary of State, the Comptroller of the Treasury, and the Attorney General. The cessation of production of gold coins in 1933 and of silver coins after 1976 led to the abolition of the Assay Commission in 1980.

Marine Hospital Service, established 1798

It may seem illogical that the National Institutes of Health and National Cancer Institute originated as agencies of the Treasury Department. However, one can trace their lineage to the Treasury's long-standing interest in the nation's economic vitality, which originally relied in large part on the health of merchant seamen. To provide for the medical care of those vital workers, the Treasury Department established the Marine Hospital Service in 1798. Twenty cents were deducted monthly from each seaman's pay to construct hospitals in port cities along the coasts and major rivers. Sailors employed by the Revenue Marine Service were included in 1799 as were Navy sailors before 1817, when the Navy began building its own hospitals.

A reform act of 1870 centralized administration of marine hospitals under a Supervising Surgeon, renamed the Surgeon General in 1902. National epidemics led in 1878 to the Marine Revenue Service being responsible for instituting quarantines, a significant broadening of its mission that expanded further in 1891 to include the medical inspection of immigrants at sites such as Ellis Island. In 1902 the bureau was renamed the Public Health and Marine Hospital Service; a decade later the name was shortened to the Public Health Service. Under its expanded mission, the service, still part of the Treasury Department, created the National Institute of Health in 1930 and the National Cancer Institute in 1932. The Public Health Service was transferred to the Federal Security Agency in 1939. Today it is part of the Department of Health and Human Services.

Coast Survey, established 1807

The Treasury Department's involvement in a wide variety of maritime matters also led it into the scientific realm. In 1807 Congress authorized a survey of the American coasts, but the Embargo of 1808 delayed funding and the survey's first superintendent, Ferdinand Hassler, a Swiss-born mathematician and scientist, was not appointed until 1811. The War of 1812 then intervened and work could not begin on the survey until 1816. Two years later Congress transferred the survey from the Treasury Department to the Navy Department. In 1832 the Coast Survey was returned to Treasury supervision; two years later the Navy regained control. By 1836 Treasury was again in charge, with Hassler resuming his duties as the Survey's superintendent. He also bore the added responsibility of Superintendent of Weights and Measures for the Treasury Department. The scope of the Coast Survey increased significantly in 1877 to include surveying the 39th Parallel to establish a vertical benchmark across the nation, which was recognized in 1878 when its name was changed to the Coast and Geodetic Survey. In 1903 the Survey became part of the new Department of Commerce and Labor.

Census Bureau, established 1810

The Constitution mandates a decennial census of the nation to apportion equitable congressional representation and taxation. Two censuses had been undertaken—in 1790 and 1800—under the direction of the Secretary of State before the responsibility was shifted to the Treasury Department in 1810 along with a requirement to expand data collection to include the nation's manufacturing output. In 1840 a census of mining and fisheries was added. In 1849 the Census Board consisting of the Secretary of State, the Attorney General, and the Postmaster General was established and a full-time secretary of the census was hired. The Bureau of the Census was assigned to the Department of the Interior in 1902 and a year later to the newly formed Department of Commerce and Labor.

General Land Office, established 1812

Managing the nation's vast public lands was among the Secretary of the Treasury's original responsibilities. When the General Land Office was established within the department in 1812, more than a billion acres were under federal ownership. The office surveyed public lands, resolved conflicting claims, and oversaw the transfers of land to private owners by sale or other means authorized by Congress. By 1837, sixty-five district land offices had been established to prepare patents and related land records for transmission to Washington. (Before 1833 the president personally signed every land patent.) The General Land Office became a central function of the new Department of the Interior created in 1849.

Office of Standard Weights and Measures, established 1832

With the importance of tariffs as a source of revenue, the accurate measurement of a wide variety of goods was of concern to both merchants and customs collectors. A congressionally mandated report on weights and measures in 1832 found wide disparity among the devices used in customs houses. The Office of Standard Weights and Measures was established in the Treasury Department the same year and in 1835 Ferdinand Hassler mass-produced sixteen standard sets of devices for each of the 100 custom houses. Eventually the office oversaw production of standard measuring devices for many federal agencies and each state. American national standards became international in 1843 when a complete set was given to the British government after its standards were lost in the fire that destroyed the Houses of Parliament. The Office for the Construction of Weights and Measures was established by Congress in 1890; in 1901 its name was changed to the National Bureau of Standards. The Bureau of Standards was transferred to the new Department of Commerce and Labor in 1903.

Life-Saving Service, established 1848

Early lifesaving efforts along the American coasts were organized by volunteer groups such as the Massachusetts Humane Society, which established networks of lifeboats and shelter huts to assist shipwreck victims. The Treasury Department's maritime functions were expanded with the establishment of the Life-Saving Service in 1848 to provide shore-to-sea lifesaving stations along a treacherous portion of the New Jersey coast. By 1853 Congress had funded additional lifesaving stations under the Revenue Marine Service on the coasts of New York, Rhode Island, Georgia, Florida, Texas, and the Great Lakes. Two tragic wrecks in 1854, costing more than 200 lives in each incident, led Congress to require the Treasury Department not just to equip the stations, but to hire and to supervise paid crews.

These lifesaving functions remained under the Treasury's Revenue Cutter Service until 1878, when it was established as a separate Treasury bureau called the Life-Saving Service. Sumner Kimball led the operation from 1871 until 1915 as the Service's only superintendent. In thirty-four years under his direction, the Treasury Department's lifesavers rescued nearly 175,000 people and saved almost $300 million in ships and cargo. When the Coast Guard was established in 1915, the Life-Saving Service was incorporated into that branch of the Treasury.

Steamboat Inspection Service, established 1852

The development of steam-powered ships brought a new hazard to America's waterways—boiler explosions. In 1832 alone more than a thousand lives were lost in explosions involving fully 14 percent of America's steamboats. Safety inspections of steamboats came under federal law in 1838, with enforcement by the Justice Department. Federal district judges appointed inspectors. The Steamboat Act of 1852 brought the program under Treasury Department oversight while also strengthening requirements for safety equipment, licensing of pilots and engineers, and routine inspections. New legislation in 1871 named the Steamboat Inspection Service and placed it under a supervisor. The Service was transferred to the new Department of Commerce and Labor in 1903. It was later moved back to the Coast Guard, now part of the Department of Homeland Security.

Supervising Architect of the Treasury Department, established 1852

From its beginning in 1789, the Treasury Department had the largest and most dispersed space needs among all the civil departments of the federal government. It fell to Treasury to house not only itself, but most of the other civil units. During the first half of the nineteenth century, the department often held architectural competitions for the designs of customs houses and federal courthouses. To coordinate its burgeoning building activities as the country expanded, the department created the Office of the Supervising Architect of the Treasury and the Bureau of Construction. Those units designed and coordinated construction of a wide range of federal buildings throughout the country, from massive multifunction ones in dozens of major cities to small assay offices on the western frontier. A succession of architects, including some of the most prominent of their time, were appointed supervising architect, while the bureau was headed by officers of the Corps of Engineers.

In 1893 the Tarnsey Act authorized the employment of private architects for the design of federal buildings but the supervising architect continued to oversee their construction. The act was repealed in 1912, returning the design of federal buildings exclusively to the Treasury's supervising architect. New Deal projects brought a huge amount of work, as approximately 1,300 federally funded buildings were constructed in more than 1,000 communities. The Office of the Supervising Architect and the Bureau of Construction became the Public Buildings Branch of the Treasury's Procurement Division in 1933. Artwork for buildings under the Treasury's jurisdiction was commissioned through the Treasury Section of Painting and Sculpture, beginning in 1934, and the Treasury Relief Art Project, started in 1935. Both programs ended in 1938. The next year Treasury's Procurement Division became part of the new Public Buildings Administration in the Federal Works Agency. The General Services Administration is now the lead agency for the design and construction of federal buildings.

Bureau of Internal Revenue, established 1862

From its beginnings until the Civil War, the federal government was financed almost entirely on "external" taxes—customs revenues—collected by the Treasury Department. The few "internal" taxes which were levied—on distilled spirits, snuff, sugar, and other goods and services—were also collected by the Treasury Department or under its supervision. The unpopular internal revenues were repealed in 1802. Internal taxes were again levied to finance the War of 1812, then promptly repealed until the huge costs of the Civil War demanded new and substantial revenue. The earlier post of Commissioner of the Revenue was revived to administer new internal taxes in 1861 and the next year personal income taxes led to the establishment of the Office of the Commissioner of Internal Revenue, with a network of local collectors known as the Bureau of Internal Revenue.

The wartime income tax was repealed in 1872 and most other internal taxes were removed in 1883. The Panic of 1893 and the economic depression that followed prompted Congress to restore an income tax, but it was found unconstitutional in 1895. The Sixteenth Amendment to the Constitution in 1913 allowed Congress to levy taxes on income, greatly assisting the country in meeting the general costs of the federal government and especially of World Wars I and II. The Bureau of Internal Revenue was reorganized as the Internal Revenue Service in 1953.

Bureau of Engraving and Printing, established 1862

Wartime Congresses, including the Continental Congress during the Revolution, often resorted to printing paper currency to defray war costs. Most paper currency in America was issued by private, state-chartered banks, with its value dependent on the security of the bank printing it. In response to the financial panic of 1857, as a temporary measure Congress authorized the Treasury Department to issue treasury notes printed by private contractors, their value backed by gold held in government coffers. In 1861 "demand notes" backed by gold coin were again authorized with green and black fronts and all-green backs—the famous "greenbacks." Private printers prepared sheets of notes which were shipped to the Treasury Building to be signed, separated, and trimmed. A dwindling gold reserve retired the demand notes in 1862 and replaced them with United States Notes, backed by the good faith of the government. Another act that same year moved the engraving and printing operation to the Treasury Building where it was generally known as the National Currency Bureau. In 1869 the Bureau of Engraving and Printing was formally established. In 1880 it moved to its own building where a wide array of federal documents, bonds, and certificates were also printed.

Office of the Comptroller of the Currency, established 1863

The National Currency Act of 1863 not only regulated the production and distribution of the nation's uniform currency, it also created the Office of the Comptroller of the Currency to establish a national banking system and regulate it by periodically examining the national banks to ensure their fiscal soundness. The creation in 1913 of the Federal Reserve System followed by the Federal Depositors Insurance Corporation (FDIC) in 1933 created some overlap in jurisdictions. In 1938 the three agencies reached an agreement on how to share examination of national banks. By the turn of the twenty-first century, the Office examined over 3,000 national banks annually through six district offices employing 2,400 examiners.

Secret Service, established 1865

President Lincoln created the Secret Service on April 14, 1865, as a specialized police force to combat counterfeiters of the national currency. (That evening he was mortally wounded by John Wilkes Booth.) The Secret Service's jurisdiction was expanded in 1867 to investigate federal crimes including mail theft, land fraud, subversion by groups such as the Ku Klux Klan, and other crimes. Throughout the nineteenth century, the operatives of the Secret Service were temporarily reassigned to many federal agencies to investigate wrongdoing from railroad scams to mining frauds. In 1908 nine Secret Service agents were permanently transferred to the Justice Department as special agents, forming the nucleus of the Bureau of Investigation, renamed the Federal Bureau of Investigation in 1935.

The Secret Service's most prominent assignment began in 1902, when two agents were assigned full-time to protect new President Theodore Roosevelt after President McKinley's assassination in 1901. In 1906 presidential protection was made a permanent responsibility of the Secret Service. This protective role has expanded steadily to include the president-elect (beginning in 1908), the president's immediate family (1917), former presidents (1951), and the vice-president and vice-president-elect (1961), among others. The White House Police were brought under the Secret Service's jurisdiction in 1930, becoming known as the Secret Service

Uniformed Division. The Division also protects foreign embassies and diplomatic missions in Washington and around the country. In 2003 the Secret Service became part of the new Department of Homeland Security.

Bureau of Statistics, established 1866

From the Treasury Department's establishment in 1789, Congress frequently requested reports concerning the state of American commerce. The Customs Service records providing systematic and accurate data on the import and export of goods were the basis of these reports. In 1844 Congress directed the department to gather statistical information and report annually on American agriculture and domestic trade as well. These and additional functions, such as publishing an annual registry of all American merchant vessels, were formally assigned to a new Bureau of Statistics in 1866. The Bureau was transferred to the new Department of Commerce and Labor in 1903.

Bureau of Navigation, established 1884

Among the many duties of the Customs Service when it became part of the Treasury Department in 1789 was the registration and certification of vessels entering and leaving American harbors. In 1884 Congress created a specialized Bureau of Navigation within the Treasury Department to register vessels and enforce a wide range of navigation laws. Like many nineteenth-century units of the Treasury Department, the Bureau of Navigation was made part of the Department of Commerce and Labor in 1903, but in this case Treasury's involvement did not cease. Customs officers—Treasury employees—continued to be the field staff of the Navigation Bureau which in 1932 was combined with another former Treasury

bureau to create the Bureau of Navigation and Steamboat Inspection, renamed the Bureau of Marine Inspection and Navigation in 1936.

During World War II, that bureau's functions were shared by the Treasury's Bureau of Customs and the Coast Guard. Customs resumed its responsibilities for vessel registration and retained that assignment when the Bureau of Marine Inspection and Navigation was abolished in 1946. Customs became part of the Department of Homeland Security in 2003.

Office of the Superintendent of Immigration, established 1891

The regulation of immigration into the United States was a Treasury Department responsibility for only two decades, but they were busy decades. The Immigration Act of 1882 authorized the Secretary of the Treasury to work with states to enforce federal immigration law. In 1891 the Office of the Superintendent of Immigration was established within the Treasury Department to process all prospective immigrants into the country. The next year Ellis Island in New York Harbor opened and became the centerpiece of Treasury's immigration responsibilities. The Office of Immigration was transferred to the Department of Commerce and Labor in 1903. Currently, the regulation of immigration is a responsibility of the Department of Homeland Security.

Office of the Supervising Tea Examiner, established 1897

Customs responsibilities of the Treasury Department were extended in 1897 with the passage of the Tea Importation Act. Inspectors touched, sniffed, and tasted samples of all imported teas to ascertain their "purity, quality, and fitness," guarding against the adulteration of tea with used leaves or other extenders. A federal Board of Tea Experts assisted the customs inspectors. The task passed to the Department of Agriculture in 1920.

Bureau of War Risk Insurance, established 1914

The gathering storm of the First World War brought new duties to the Treasury Department ahead of America's formal entrance into the military conflict. In 1914 the Bureau of War Risk Insurance was established within the Department to offer marine insurance to merchant vessels. Attacks by German U-boats on merchant shipping in the North Atlantic made private insurance unavailable or not affordable. Congress stepped in and customs collectors added "insurance agent" to their roster of responsibilities.

The program was significantly expanded in 1917 to insure the personnel on American merchant vessels and to extend death and disability benefits to members of the American military and their families. The program included rehabilitation and vocational training for wounded veterans. In 1918 most of these assignments were transferred to a new agency, the Federal Board of Vocational Rehabilitation, but Treasury's Bureau of War Risk Insurance retained oversight until the creation of the independent Veterans Bureau in 1921. The Department of Veterans Affairs now provides benefits and services to America's veterans.

Narcotics Division, established 1914

For over half a century, the Treasury Department was one of the front-line agencies regulating addictive drugs in America. This assignment arose from Treasury's involvement in taxation. The Harrison Narcotics Act of 1914 required registration, record keeping, and payment of a tax by dispensers of opium, coca leaves, and their derivatives. Treasury's Bureau of Internal Revenue established a Narcotics Division to handle these tasks. With the adoption of Prohibition in 1919, Treasury's Prohibition Unit was formed to enforce the regulations on "intoxicating liquor" as well as on narcotics. This unit became the Bureau of Prohibition in 1927, then the Federal Bureau of Narcotics in 1930. The list of regulated substances was expanded to include marijuana in 1937. Several federal departments were involved in various aspects of enforcement of drug laws by 1968, when President Lyndon B. Johnson consolidated the enforcement responsibilities into the Bureau of Narcotics and Dangerous Drugs under the Justice Department. In 1973 the Drug Enforcement Administration was created to consolidate federal anti-drug efforts.

Federal Farm Loan Bureau, established 1916

The Federal Farm Loan Bureau was established within the Treasury Department in 1916 to provide credit to farmers through a system of twelve federal land banks, financed with a combination of federal funds and private capital raised through the sale of tax-exempt bonds. The farmer-borrowers owned the banks. Twelve intermediate credit banks were added in 1923 in response to a deteriorating farm economy, which preceded the widespread onset of the Great Depression in 1929. President Franklin D. Roosevelt reorganized the federal agricultural credit programs into the independent Farm Credit Administration in 1933.

Office of the Commissioner of the Public Debt, established 1919

Since 1789 the Treasury Department has borrowed money on behalf of the federal government and repaid those public debts. From 1790 until the Revolutionary War-era debt was retired by 1836, the Commissioners of the Sinking Fund supervised the repayment. The Civil War increased the federal debt forty-fold to $2.7 billion. Divisions of the Treasury remained at the center of tracking and redeeming the public debt securities. The First World War again reversed the gradual progress in paying the Civil War debt and by 1920 the national debt had reached nearly $30 billion. In 1919 the various Treasury units involved in public debt were consolidated into the Office of the Commissioner of the Public Debt, renamed the Public Debt Service in 1921.

The Great Depression and the election of President Roosevelt brought new debt and new thinking to the federal role in the national economy. Roosevelt and his advisors believed that deficit spending could be beneficial to stimulate a depressed economy, and that reduced federal spending could be used to curb an overheated economy. His administration reorganized the Public Debt Service and other units in 1940 as the Bureau of the Public Debt. In 1986 the bureau was authorized to promote the sale of savings bonds along with administering the federal government's securities program.

Prohibition Unit, established 1919

The ratification of the Eighteenth Amendment to the Constitution in 1919 and the implementation of Prohibition under the Volstead Act in 1920 gave the Treasury Department a challenging enforcement assignment. A Prohibition Unit was organized in 1919 and a state-by-state network was developed of Prohibition Offices and enforcement agents—"revenuers" or "T-men." The Prohibition Unit, the Customs Service, and the Coast Guard achieved mixed results battling smugglers, illegal brewers and distillers, and the diversion of legitimately manufactured spirits. In 1927 the Prohibition Unit was christened the Bureau of Prohibition amidst charges of misconduct and outright criminality by some of its members. The enforcement responsibilities were reassigned to the Department of Justice in 1930, while tax-related assignments stayed with Treasury under a new Bureau of Industrial Alcohol. The Twenty-First Amendment repealed Prohibition in 1933 and the remaining regulatory duties returned to the Treasury Department, under the new Alcohol Tax Unit in 1934.

Office of the Commissioner of Accounts and Deposits, established 1920

Receipt and disbursement of the government's money is the Treasury Department's central function. The Register administered Treasury's central accounting activities until the Dockery Act of 1894 reorganized the department's fiscal management. The new Division of Bookkeeping and Warrants was created under the Register at that time. In 1920 the Register's various account and dispersing divisions were consolidated under the Office of the Commissioner of Accounts and Deposits. The Bureau of Accounts took over these functions in 1940 as part of the department's new Fiscal Service. That bureau became the Bureau of Government Financial Operations in 1974 and the Financial Management Service in 1984.

Bureau of the Budget, established 1921

For more than a century, the federal government operated without a comprehensive annual budget. Congress passed numerous revenue and tax bills to garner the resources and approved over a dozen separate appropriation bills to fund the various departments. Although a commission appointed by President Taft in 1910 recommended that the executive branch prepare an annual budget for the entire government, that was not required by law until 1921. The Bureau of the Budget was established within the Treasury Department to assist the president in preparing the budget. At the same time, the General Accounting Office was created to audit the federal budget for Congress. President Roosevelt transferred the Bureau of the Budget to the Executive Office of the President in 1939.

Alcohol Tax Unit, established 1934

Following the repeal of Prohibition in 1933, legitimate wineries, breweries, and distilleries quickly became an economic engine, employing more than 500,000 people within a year. President Roosevelt established an interim Federal Alcohol Control Administration in 1933 to regulate the industry, jointly administered by the Departments of Agriculture and the Treasury. The next year the Alcohol Tax Unit was formed in Treasury to monitor revenue from alcohol sales. In 1935 a separate Federal Alcohol Administration was established in the department that assumed the duties of the Federal Alcohol Control Administration. Five years later its functions were folded into the Alcohol Tax Unit and in 1942 the responsibilities of that unit were expanded to enforce taxation mandated by federal firearms laws. Tobacco taxes were added to the unit's jurisdiction in 1951 and it was renamed the Alcohol and Tobacco Tax Division. The assassinations of Dr. Martin Luther King Jr. and Robert F. Kennedy in 1968 spurred the adoption of the Gun Control Act that increased existing enforcement responsibilities for the Treasury Department in the area of federal firearms law. The division was then renamed the Alcohol, Tobacco and Firearms Division. The "ATF" was given bureau status in 1972. The reorganization of most of the federal security functions following the terrorist attacks of September 11, 2001, prompted the transfer of the ATF's inspection and enforce-

ment duties to the Justice Department in 2003. The Treasury Department retained the tasks of collecting and enforcing taxes on alcohol and tobacco, under a new Alcohol and Tobacco Tax and Trade Bureau.

Foreign Funds Control Office, established 1940

The Foreign Funds Control Office of the Treasury Department was instituted in 1940 to protect foreign assets under the federal government's control, especially of countries conquered by Nazi Germany or the Soviet Union. When America entered World War II, the office's role was expanded to restrict further the assets of enemy powers and to prohibit trade with belligerents. With these increased responsibilities, the office became a separate bureau within Treasury in 1942. The unit was abolished in 1947, its remaining functions assigned to the new Office of Internal Finance. In 1948 any remaining accounting for foreign wartime assets in America became a responsibility of the Justice Department.

The Korean War revived the need in 1950 for addressing the assets of belligerents, which Treasury met with the Division of Foreign Assets Control. President Truman authorized the office to block Chinese and Korean assets in American jurisdiction, and eventually the restrictions were extended to Vietnam and Cambodia. By 1953 the Division oversaw restrictions on offshore trading with any Soviet bloc country. The Division was reclassified as an office in 1962 in response to added assignments relating to Cuba, and in 1963 President Kennedy ordered Foreign Assets Control to block all Cuban assets in this country. The Office of Foreign Assets Control continues to exercise its roles in America's foreign policy, as well as maintaining the Specially Designated Nationals list—the "blacklist" of people, organizations, and countries under U. S. trade sanctions.

Savings Bonds Division, established 1950

The American government has sold bonds to finance its functions, especially in wartime, since the Revolution. Often these were issued in small denominations—so-called "baby bonds"—to make them accessible to a wide range of citizen investors. Called Liberty Bonds in the First World War and United States Savings Bonds during the New Deal, they were titled Defense Bonds in 1941 and War Savings Bonds after Pearl Harbor. The office of the Treasury that handled Savings Bonds after World War II was made a bureau with the outbreak of the Korean War in 1950. That division was abolished in 1993 and its functions were transferred to the Bureau of the Public Debt.

Federal Law Enforcement Training Center, established 1970

The Treasury Department was chosen in 1970 as the departmental home of the new Federal Law Enforcement Training Center, serving the departments of the Treasury, State, Justice, and the Interior as well as most of the agencies involved in federal law enforcement. The center operated temporarily in Washington before being relocated to the former Glynco Naval Air Station near Brunswick, Georgia. The school grew to serve 50,000 students annually from more than eighty federal agencies, as well as local, state, and international law enforcement organizations. In 2003 the Center became part of the Department of Homeland Security.

Office of Revenue Sharing, established 1973

The State and Local Fiscal Assistance Act of 1972 mandated the distribution of $30 billion in federal revenue to 40,000 state and local governments. Early in 1973 the Office of Revenue Sharing was established in the Treasury Department to administer the program. Extended in 1977, the program and the office were abolished in 1986.

Office of Thrift Supervision, established 1989

The Federal Home Loan Bank Board was established in 1932 in response to bank failures during the Great Depression. A policy of deregulation in the early 1980s was followed by 435 failures of thrift institutions between 1981 and 1983. The Office of Thrift Supervision was established in 1989 to replace the old Bank Board. The new office was placed within the Treasury Department to regulate federal and state-chartered savings institutions.

Financial Crimes Enforcement Network, established 1990

Twenty different federal agencies collaborate with the Treasury Department in the Financial Crimes Enforcement Network (FinCEN), established in 1990 to combat money laundering and other complex financial crimes. The Patriot Act of 2001 raised FinCEN to bureau status in the Treasury Department with added responsibilities in combating the financing of terrorist operations.

Illustration Credits

Athenaeum of Philadelphia: cover (bottom), 73, 213 (bottom)

author: 25, 39, 41, 45, 65, 75, 76, 104, 109 (bottom), 138, 188, 216, 260, 267 (top left), 276 (bottom), 277

Commission of Fine Arts: 281

Department of the Treasury: cover (top), 1, 3, 22, 63, 86, 90 (top), 94, 95, opp 103, 107, 125, 142, 155, 157 (top left), 157 (top right), 159, 162, 164, 186-187, 190, 200, 205, 207, 210, 211, 214, 219, 220 (top & bottom), 221 (xerox of unlocated National Archives original), opp 237, 265 (top), 267 (bottom & right), 270, 273

Gelman Library, George Washington University: 113

Mary Jane Glavis: 164 (inset)

Historical Society of Washington, D.C.: 240

The Huntington Library, Art Collections, and Botanical Gardens, opp 1, 16, 21

I.N. Phelps Stokes Collection, Miriam and Ira D. Wallach Division of Arts, Prints and Photographs, The New York Public Library, Astor, Lenox and Tilden Foundations: 37, 38

International Society, Daughters of Utah Pioneers: 170, 197

Library of Congress: 5, 6, 7, 9, 12, 18, 24, 27 (top & bottom), 29, 35, 40, 59, 60, 62, 68, 69, 71, 77 (top & bottom), 79, 81, 90 (bottom), 106, 108, 122 (bottom), 129, 132, 144, 166, 172, opp 179, 182, 184, 217, 238, 263, 274, 279 (top) 282

Maine Granite Industry Historical Society Museum: 128

Maine Historical Commission: 194

Maine Historical Society: 56

Maryland Historical Society: 31

Massachusetts Historical Society: 15

Metropolitan Museum of Art, Harris Brisbane Dick Fund: 1924 (24.66.1407 (41)), 58

National Archives and Records Administration: 48 (top & bottom), 49, 91, 105, 109 (top), 110, 111, 118, 120, 121, 122 (top), 124, 131, 134 (top & bottom), 136, 137, 141, 147, 149, 150, 152 (top & bottom), 153, 154, 157 (bottom), 158 (top & bottom), 160, 167, 169, 171, 180, 181, 191 (top & bottom),198, 201, 203, 213 (top), 215, 224, 227, 229 (top & bottom), 242, 243, 245 (top & bottom), 246, 247, 248, 249, 251, 256, 262, 269 (top & bottom), 276 (top), 279 (bottom)

Michael J. Osborne Books LLC: 185

© Peter Easton: 265 (bottom)

Smithsonian Institution, Department of Photographic History: opp 55

West Point Museum Art Collection, United States Military Academy, West Point, New York, 115

United States Patent Office: 209

Vermont Historical Society, 116

Washington Post: 13, 87, 97, 253, 259

Edward Zimmer: 89, 98

Bibliography

Government Printed Documents

American State Papers, Miscellaneous I:248–9.

Annals of Congress, 11th Cong., 2d sess., 1427–8, 1704, 1771–2.

Congressional Globe, 25th Cong., 1st sess., 1837, 331-7.

Congressional Globe, 25th Cong., 2d sess., 1838, 274-5.

Congressional Globe, 26th Cong., 1st sess., April 30 and May 1, 1840, 370-1.

Congressional Globe, 33rd Cong., 1st sess., February 21, 1854, 202.

Congressional Record, Emanuel Celler to Editor, May 25, 1928, 69 (pt. 9):9963.

Commissioner of Public Buildings, *Letter from the Commissioner of Public Buildings,* 27th Cong., 2d sess., 1842, H. Rep. 195, 1–7.

Commissioner of Public Buildings, *Workmen on the Public Buildings,* 26th Cong., 1st sess., 1840, H. Doc. 250, 1-5.

House Committee on Expenditures on Public Buildings, *Expenditures on Public Buildings,* 37th Cong., 2d sess., 1862, H. Rep. 137, 1-133.

House Committee on Public Buildings and Grounds, *National Edifices at Washington,* 28th Cong., 2d sess., 1845, H. Rep. 185, 1-24.

House Committee on Public Buildings, *New Executive Buildings,* 23d Cong., 2d sess., 1835, H. Rep. 90, 1-3.

House Committee on Public Buildings, *New Treasury and Post Office Buildings,* 25th Cong., 2d sess., 1838, H. Rep. 737, 1-38.

House Committee on Public Expenditures, *Treasury Building,* 27th Cong., 2d sess., 1842, H. Rep. 549, 1-5.

House Journal, 25th Cong., 2d sess., May 19, 1838, 905.

House Journal, 25th Cong., 2d sess., January 14, 1838, 901.

House Journal, 25th Cong., 2d sess., June 8-9, 1838, 1052-4; 1058.

House Select Committee, *Treasury Department,* 38th Cong., 1st sess., 1864, H. Rep. 140, 1-418.

President of the United States, *Burning of the Treasury Building,* 23rd Cong., 2d sess., 1841, H. Doc. 22, 1-61.

President of the United States, *Message of the President of the United States,* 24th Cong. 2d sess., 1836, H. Ex. Doc. 10, 1-4.

President of the United States, *Message of the President of the United States,* 27th Cong. 1st sess., 1841, S. Doc. 123, 1-47.

President of the United States, *Punishment of Incendiaries,* 24th Cong., 2d sess., 1837, H. Ex. Doc. 85, 1-9.

President of the United States, *Treasury Building,* 25th Cong., 2d sess., 1837, H. Ex. Doc. 38, 2-3.

Secretaries of War and Navy, *Additional Buildings for War and Navy Departments,* 27th Cong., 3d sess., 1843, H. doc. 85, 1-17.

Secretary of the Treasury, *Granite for the South Wing of the Treasury,* 35th Cong., 2d sess., 1859, S. Ex. Doc. 41, 1-11.

Secretary of the Treasury, *Letter of the Secretary of Treasury, Wrought Iron Beams,* 33rd Cong., 2d sess., 1855, S. Ex. Doc. 54, 1–10

Secretary of the Treasury, *Report in Answer to a Resolution of the Senate,* 35th Cong., 2d sess., 1859, S. Ex. Doc. 41, 1–10.

Secretary of the Treasury, *Report on the State of the Finances,* 40th Cong., 2d sess., 1868, H. Ex. Doc. 2, 1-502.

Secretary of the Treasury, *Report on the State of the Finances,* 42nd Cong., 2d sess., 1871, H. Ex. Doc. 2, 1-581.

Secretary of the Treasury, *Report on the State of the Finances,* 38th Cong., 1st sess., 1863, H. Ex. Doc., 3. 1-683.

Secretary of the Treasury, *Report on the State of the Finances,* 35th Cong., 1st sess., 1857, S. Doc. 1, 1-379.

Secretary of the Treasury, *Report on the State of the Finances,* 35th Cong., 2d sess., 1857, S. Ex. Doc. 2, 1-493.

Secretary of the Treasury, *Report on the State of the Finances,* 34th Cong., 1st sess., 1856, S. Ex. Doc. 2, 1-683.

Secretary of the Treasury, *Report on the State of the Finances,* 34th Cong., 3d sess., 1856, H. Ex. Doc. 2, 1-672.

Secretary of the Treasury, *Report on the State of the Finances,* 39th Cong., 1st sess., 1865, H. Ex. Doc. 3, 1-342.

Secretary of the Treasury, *Report on the State of the Finances,* 39th Cong., 2d sess., 1867, H. Ex. Doc. 4, 1-394.

Secretary of the Treasury, *Report on the State of the Finances,* 36th Cong., 1st sess., 1860, S. Ex. Doc.3, 1-374.

Secretary of the Treasury, *Report on the State of the Finances,* 33rd Cong., 1st sess., 1853, S. Ex. Doc. 2, 1-384.

Secretary of the Treasury, *Report on the State of the Finances,* 23rd Cong., 1st sess., 1833, H. Doc. 15, 1-60.

Secretary of the Treasury, *Treasury Extension—Contracts for Materials,* 34th Cong., 1st sess., 1856, H. Ex. Doc. 96, 1–97.

Senate Committee on Public Buildings and Grounds, *In the Senate of the United States,* 25th Cong., 2d sess., 1838, S. Rep. 435, 1-36.

Manuscript Sources

Athenaeum of Philadelphia
Papers of Thomas U. Walter.

Department of the Treasury
[Irving Atkins.] "Description of the National Archives Building," typescript.
A.C. Lieber Memorandum.

Historical Society of Washington, D.C.
J. Goldsborough Bruff Papers

Library of Congress, Manuscript Division
Papers of Robert Mills.
Papers of Salmon P. Chase.
Papers of Thomas Jefferson.

Massachusetts Historical Society
Timothy Pickering Papers.
Oliver Wolcott, Jr. Papers.

National Archives and Records Administration
R.G. 42, Records of the Office of Public Buildings and Public Parks of the National Capital.
    Entry 1. Letters Received.
    Entry 6. Letters Sent.
    Entry 14. Ledgers.
    Entry 15. Journals.
    Entry 16. Contracts.
    Entry 17. Estimates and Proposals.
    Entry 18. Receipted Accounts.
    Entry 21. Proceedings and Letters Sent, 1791-1802.
    Entry 23. Letters Sent.
R.G. 46, Records of the U.S. Senate
R.G. 53, Records of the Bureau of the Public Debt
    Entry 28. Estimates and Statements by the Register of the Treasury, 1791-1858.
R.G. 56, Records of the Department of the Treasury
    Entry 3, Letters Sent to Presidents, "A" Series, 1833-1878
    Entry 27, Miscellaneous Letters Sent, "K" Series, 1789-1878
    Entry 31, Letters Sent Relating to Appointments, Removals, and Other Personnel Matters.

    Entry 103, Miscellaneous Letters Received, "K" Series.
    Entry 213, Personnel Folders of Notable Treasury Employees, 1822-1940.
R.G. 121, Records of the Public Buildings Service
    Entry 7, Letters Sent Chiefly by the Supervising Architect, 1855-1930.
    Entry 13, Letters Sent Concerning Construction of the Treasury Extension.
    Entry 15, Letters Sent Concerning Purchase of Materials for the Treasury Extension.
    Entry 26, Letters Received, 1843-1910.
R.G. 200, Gift Collection, Correspondence of Robert Mills, 1830-31, Acc. NN. 369-46.
R.G. 217, Records of the General Accounting Office
    Entry 347, Records of the Accounting Officers of the Department of the Treasury
R.G. 233, Records of the U. S. House of Representatives.
    Entry 8, Reports of Committees Relating to Claims.
    Entry 13, Reports of the Government Operations Committee and Its Predecessors.

New York Public Library, Manuscript Division
A.J. Davis Diary, 1828-53.

South Carolina Historical Society
Papers of Robert Mills

Newspapers and Magazines

American Masonic Register and Literary Companion
Charleston Courier
Federal Gazette & Baltimore Daily Advertiser
The Huntress
Inland Architect
National Intelligencer
National Republican
New York Times
Washington Federalist
Washington Post
Washington Star
Washington Union
Workingmen's Advocate

Printed Sources

Adams, Charles Francis. *Memoirs of John Quincy Adams.* Philadelphia: Lippincott Bros., 1876.
Adams, Francis Colburn. *Siege of Washington, D.C.* New York: Dick & Fitzgerald, Publishers, 1867.

"Alexander Hamilton Bowman," *National Cyclopedia.* New York: James T. White & Co., 1907.

Ames, Mary Clemmer, *Ten Years in Washington, Life and Scenes in the National Capital.* Hartford: A.D. Worthington & Co., 1874.

"An Hour Among the Greenbacks," *Scribner's Monthly* 6 (April 1873): 657-669.

Arnebeck, Bob. *Through A Fiery Trial. Building Washington, 1790-1800.* Lanham, Maryland: Madison Books, 1991.

Benjamin, Marcus. *Washington During War Time.* Washington: National Tribune Co., 1902.

Billings, Elden E. "Social and Economic Conditions in Washington during the Civil War," *Records of the Columbia Historical Society* 63-65 (1965): 191-209.

Biographical Dictionary of the American Congress, 1774-1949. Washington: Government Printing Office, 1950.

Boatner III, Mark M. *The Civil War Dictionary.* New York: David McKay Company, 1988.

Briggs, Emily Edson. *The Olivia Letters.* New York: Neale Publishing Company, 1906.

Bryan, W.B. "The Sessford Annals,: *Records of the Columbia Historical Society* 11 (1908): 271-388.

_____ et al, comps. "The Writings of George Washington Relating to the National Capital," *Records of the Columbia Historical Society* 17 (1914): 3-232.

Burke, Lee H. *Homes of the State Department, 1774-1976.* Washington: Department of State, 1976.

Carroll, Anna Ella. *A Review of Pierce's Administration.* Boston: J. French & Co., 1856.

Carter, Edward C. II, ed. *The Papers of Benjamin Henry Latrobe.* Clifton, New Jersey: James T. White & Company for the Maryland Historical Society, 1976.

The Case of Beals & Dixon. Washington: McGill & Witherow, 1868.

Chittenden, L.E. *Recollections of President Lincoln and His Administration.* New York: Harper & Brothers, 1891.

Clark, S.M. *First Division, National Currency Bureau.* Washington: Government Printing Office, 1864.

Cohen, Jeffrey A. and Charles E. Brownell. *The Architectural Drawings of Benjamin Henry Latrobe.* New Haven: Yale University Press, 1994.

Colvin, Howard. *A Biographical Dictionary of British Architects, 1600-1840.* New Haven: Yale University Press, 1995.

Commission of Fine Arts, *Eighth Report.* Washington: Government Printing Office, 1908.

Cooke, Jacob Ernest. *Alexander Hamilton.* New York: Charles Scribner's Sons, 1982.

Cunningham, Noble. *The Jeffersonian Republicans. The Formation of Party Organization, 1789-1801.* Chapel Hill: University of North Carolina Press, 1957.

De Laitre, Margaret Nash. "Ammi Burnham Young and the Construction of the Boston Custom House," M.A. thesis, University of Virginia, 1979.

Dennett, Tyler, ed. *Lincoln and the Civil War and the Diaries and Letters of John Hay.* New York: Dodd, Mead & Company, 1939.

Dixon, Joan M. *National Intelligencer, Newspaper Abstracts, 1836-1837.* Bowie, Maryland: Heritage Books, 2001.

Doolittle, Laura M. "Uncle Sam's Strong Box," *Appleton's Journal* 5 (February 25, 1871): 232-233.

Dowd, Mary Jane, comp. *Records of the Office of Public Buildings and Public Parks of the National Capital, Record Group 42.* Washington: National Archives and Records Administration, 1992.

Drinkwater Jr., Norman. "The Stone Age of Dix Island," *Downeast Magazine* 10 (September 1963) 43-47.

Evelyn, Douglas Everett, "A Public Building for a New Democracy: The Patent Office Building in the Nineteenth Century," PhD diss., The George Washington University, 1997.

"Extract from the Report of the Committee [for the Government's Removal to Washington]," *Records of the Columbia Historical Society* 9 (1906): 226-241.

Fazio, Michael W. "Benjamin Latrobe's Designs for a Lighthouse at the Mouth of the Mississippi River," *Journal of the Society of Architectural Historians* 48:3 (Sept. 1989): 232-246.

_____and Patrick A. Snadon, *The Domestic Architecture of Benjamin Henry Latrobe.* Baltimore: John Hopkins University Press, 2006.

Field, Maunsell B. *Personal Recollections, Memories of Many Men and Some Women.* New York: Harper & Brothers, 1874.

Furgurson, Ernest B. *Freedom Rising, Washington in the Civil War.* New York: Alfred B. Knopf, 2004.

Gallagher, H.M. Pierce. *Robert Mills, Architect of the Washington Monument, 1781-1855.* New York: Columbia University Press, 1935.

Garraty, John A., and Mark C. Carnes, eds. *American National Biography,* New York: Oxford University Press, 1999.

Gilbert, Abby L. "Department of the Treasury," in George T. Kurian, *A Historical Guide to the U.S. Government.* New York: Oxford University Press, 1998.

Greenough, Horatio. *Aesthetics at Washington.* Washington: John T. Towers, 1851.

Griffin, Martin I.J. "James Hoban. The Architect and Builder of the White House and the Superintendent of the Building of the Capitol at Washington," *American Catholic Historical Researches* n.s. 3 (1907): 35-52.

Harris, C.M., ed. *Papers of William Thornton. Volume One, 1781-1802.* Charlottesville: University Press of Virginia, 1992.

_____"The Politics of Public Building: William Thornton and President's Square," *Washington History* 3 (1998): 174-187.

Hines, Christian. *Early Recollections of Washington City.* Washington: Chronicle Books, 1866.

Hooper, William. "The Treasury Cash Room," *Appleton's Journal of Literature, Science and Art* 7 (May 18, 1872): 551-552.

Hunt, Gaillard, ed. *The Writings of James Madison.* New York: G.P. Putnam's Sons, 1906.

Jackson, Donald, et al, eds. *Diaries of George Washington.* Charlottesville: University Press of Virginia, 1976-1979.

Kapsch, Robert James. "The Labor History of the Construction and Reconstruction of the White House, 1793-1817," PhD diss., University of Maryland, 1993.

Knox, John Jay. *United States Notes.* New York: Charles Scribner's Sons, 1884.

Lee, Antoinette J. *Architects to the Nation. The Rise and Decline of the Supervising Architects Office.* New York: Oxford University Press, 2000.

Lowrie, Walter and Walter S. Franklin. "Documents Legislative and Executive of the Congress of the United States." *American State* Papers. Washington: Gales and Seaton, 1834.

McKee, James L., and Arthur Duerschner. *Lincoln, A Photographic History.* Lincoln, Nebraska: Bicentennial Commission, 1976.

Micali, Giuseppe. "Storia degli Antichi Popoli Italiani," *North American Review* 48 (January 1839): 1-63.

Moore, Joseph West. *Picturesque Washington.* Providence: J.A. & R.A. Reid, 188.

Nicholay, Helen. *Our Capital on the Potomac.* New York: Century Company, 1924.

Osborne, John Ball. "Removal of the Government to Washington," *Records of the Columbia Historical Society* 3 (1900)" 136-160.

Ossman, Jennifer Laurie. "Reconstructing a National Image: The State, War and Navy Building and the Politics of Federal Design, 1866-90," PhD diss., University of Virginia, 1996.

Patent Centennial Celebration. *United States Bicentennial Edition of Proceedings and Addresses of the American Patent System.* Washington: Press of Gedney & Roberts Co., 1892.

Peters, Richard, ed. *The Public Statues at Large of the United States of America,* Boston: Charles C. Little and James Brown, 1846.

Pevsner, Nicholas. *A History of Building Types.* Princeton: Princeton University Press, 1979.

Pitch, Anthony S. *The Burning of Washington. The British Invasion of 1814.* Annapolis: Naval Institute Press, 1998.

Poore, Ben Perley, "Waifs from Washington," *Gleason's Pictorial Drawing Room Companion* 4 (February 5, 1853): 87.

Read, Georgia Willis, and Ruth Gaines, eds. *Gold Rush.* New York: Columbia University Press, 1944.

Robbins, Daniel, *The Vermont State House.* Burlington, Vermont: Vermont Council on the Arts, 1980.

Roose's *Companion and Guide to Washington and Vicinity.* Washington: Gibson Brothers, 1876.

Royall, Anne Newport. *Sketches of History, Life, and Manners in the United States.* New Haven: Privately printed, 1826.

Sandburg, Carl. *Abraham Lincoln, The War Years.* Boston: Charles Scribner's Sons, 1950.

Scott, James. *Recollections of a Naval Life.* vol. 3. London: Richard Bentley, 1834.

Scott, Pamela. *Capital Engineers, The U.S. Army Corps of Engineers in the Development of Washington, D.C., 1970-2004.* Alexandria, Virginia: U.S. Army Corps of Engineers, 2005.

_____"Power, Civic Virtue, Wisdom, Liberty, and the Constitution: Early American Symbols and the United States Capitol," in Donald R. Kennon, *A Republic for the Ages.* Charlottesville: University Press of Virginia, 1999.

_____ and Antoinette J. Lee. *Buildings of the District of Columbia.* New York: Oxford University Press, 1993.

Seale, William. *The President's House.* Washington: White House Historical Association, 1986.

Smith, Daisy Mullett. *A.B. Mullett Diaries, Etc.* Washington: Mullett-Smith Press, 1985.

_____*A.B. Mullett: His Relevance in American Architecture and Historic Preservation.* Washington: Mullett-Smith Press, 1990.

Stiller, Jesse. "Bureau of Engraving and Printing," in George Kurian. *A Historical Guide to the United States Government.* New York: Oxford University Press, 1995.

Stone, Charles P. "Washington in March and April, 1861," *Magazine of American History* 14 (July-December 1885): 1-24.

Syrett, Harold C., ed. *The Papers of Alexander Hamilton.* New York: Columbia University Press, 1966.

Topham, Washington. "The Winder Building," *Records of the Columbia Historical Society* 37-38 (1937): 169-172.

Townsend, George Alfred. *The New World Compared with the Old.* Hartford: S.M. Betts & Co., 1870.

_____*Washington Inside and Outside.* Hartford: James Betts & Co., 1874.

Treasury Department. *History of the Bureau of Engraving and Printing, 1862-1962.* Washington: Government Printing Office, 1962.

"United States Treasury Department," *Harper's New Monthly Magazine,* 262 (March 1872): 481-498.

U.S. Treasury Department, *The United States Treasury Register.* Washington: Government Printing Office, 1883.

Van Horne, John C., et al, eds. *The Correspondence and Miscellaneous Papers of Benjamin Henry Latrobe.* II, New Haven: Yale University Press, 1986.

Viator," [Joseph B. Varnum, Jr.], *Washington Sketch Book.* New York: Mohun, Ebbs & Hough, 1864.

Varnum, Jr., Joseph B. *The Seat of Government of the United States.* Washington: R. Farnam, 1854.

"Washington in 1859," *Harper's New Monthly Magazine* 65 (December 1859): 1-17.

Wolanin, Barbara. *Constantino Brumidi, Artist of the Capitol.* Washington: Government Printing Office, 1998.

Wolff, Wendy. *Capitol Builder: The Shorthand Journals of Montgomery C. Meigs, 1853-1859, 1861.* Washington: Government Printing Office, 2001.

Index